Insect Poetics

Insect Poetics

Eric C. Brown, *Editor*

UNIVERSITY OF MINNESOTA PRESS

MINNEAPOLIS • LONDON

Published by the University of Minnesota Press
111 Third Avenue South, Suite 290
Minneapolis, MN 55401-2520
http://www.upress.umn.edu

Library of Congress Cataloging-in-Publication Data

Insect poetics / Eric C. Brown, editor.
     p. cm.
   Includes bibliographical references and index.
   ISBN-13: 978-0-8166-4695-1 (alk. paper)
   ISBN-10: 0-8166-4695-3 (alk. paper)
   ISBN-13: 978-0-8166-4696-8 (pbk. : alk. paper)
   ISBN-10: 0-8166-4696-1 (pbk. : alk. paper)
   1. Insects in literature. 2. Insects. I. Brown, Eric C., 1971–
PN56.163157 2006
809´.9336257—dc22

                                    2006017386

Printed in the United States of America on acid-free paper

The University of Minnesota is an equal-opportunity educator and
employer.

12 11 10 09 08 07 06   10 9 8 7 6 5 4 3 2 1

Contents

INTRODUCTION

Reading the Insect

ERIC C. BROWN

In "The Various Kinds of Insects," book 11 of Pliny the Elder's influential *Natural History,* a work of "20,000 subjects . . . all worthy of attention," the author takes some pains to justify so much attention paid to so small a thing as an insect. His provocative rationale is that "nusquam alibi spectatiore naturae rerum artificio"—that, in other words, nowhere else does the *craft* of nature so prevail as in the miniature world of the insect.[1] Any dilettante can sculpt an elephant or a lion, he supposes, so sizable is the scale, but the detail required to shape the intricacies of the insect demands an artist. Such a statement, which has been variously but consistently refashioned by nearly every insect encyclopedist since, betrays a number of anxieties about the relationship between humans and insects. Foremost, perhaps, is the need felt by Pliny and those who have come after to begin by justifying the study itself. In this way, the insect has become a kind of Other not only for human beings but for animals and animal studies as well, best left underfoot or in footnotes. Second is the attention to insect form and materiality—that it is categorically the shape, the workmanship, the "artificio" of the insect that mark its singularity. Moreover, this artful world of the insect draws on our own imaginative faculties: we understand it first poetically, as a fantastic realm overlaying but not representing our own. The insect world must be mediated—by art, artifice, technology—as an (almost) impossibly *different* creation. Similarly, Pliny positions humans as the spectators to a kind of insect theater—we observe, detached, this other world unfolding before us, but we ourselves are kept somehow beyond (a paradigm obtaining even in childhood "ant farms," an entrancing plastic theater that, most former owners would attest, generally stages tragedies).

Part of the intent of the present volume is to "read" insects in texts and contexts, as subjects and objects, that demonstrate particular and exclusive discursive practices—especially those representations that engage with Pliny's seminal notion of insects and the artist. Indeed, insects have repeatedly been fusion points for the worlds of science and letters: a number of entomologists have been celebrated for their literature (Jean-Henri Fabre, Howard Ensign Evans, Edward O. Wilson), while a number of writers (Maurice Maeterlinck, Franz Kafka, Virginia Woolf, A. S. Byatt) have cross-pollinated the entomological and literary fields. Vladimir Nabokov may have most successfully merged these careers—he revised an entire butterfly genus while scattering abstruse lepidoptera throughout his novels, assimilations traced in *Nabokov's Blues*.[2] But the collection also aims to reintegrate the insect into animal studies more generally, for while insects often elicit superlatives—the grossest, the smallest, the most innumerable animals on the planet—few studies focus solely (if at all) on them, and many such studies are of the appreciative rather than critical variety.[3] Similarly, many recent excellent works on animal studies have largely omitted insects.[4] This gap reveals, perhaps, some of the same resistance apparent in the popular imagination, where insects preponderate as vectors for disease and psychosis (not to mention straightforward pestiferousness). In fact, on a daily basis insects probably produce more distress than disease: cockroaches routinely outrank other animals as the most repulsive species, and reality television shows like *Survivor* and *Fear Factor* exploit disgust at protein-laden arthropods to draw ratings. To further understand this gap is to recuperate the language we create about and collect from them, as well as to elucidate "the many ways that insect lives, real or imagined, have enriched the human condition" (to borrow a phrase from May Berenbaum).

For the idea of the "insect," we are indebted to Aristotle, who first categorized these creatures as "entoma" (whence "entomology"), stressing their existence "in sections," any one of which segments, he believed, would naturally persist on its own if severed from the whole.[5] That this should be the primary identifier of insects makes a convenient model for reading them as formulations for disintegration, incoherence, and even babble—not as the "creeping things" of the Old Testament but as "things in pieces." This interpretive position is already embedded in our language: white noise, mild intoxication, and collective but disembodied social momentum are all termed a "buzz." And it is partly this innate distortion, derangement, and fragmentation—their world ever fractured from our own—that marks insects as humanity's Other, even as their swarming, hiving, and colonizing behaviors reproduce various self-identifications in human beings.[6] It may be part of this individual sovereignty, under the guise of vast multiplicity, that begins to unsettle the stable containment of insects as spectacle. And in effect it seems often the form, rather than the material, of the insect that first repels humans. Insects are popularly termed "creepy" and "crawly"—both derived from their locomotions and six-leggedness—as opposed to the idioms for snakes, toads, frogs, that figure them as abhorrent texturally: slimy, slippery, greasy, or scaly. Rather, it is repeatedly their "insectability" in a variety of expressions that configures them as other.

Stephen R. Kellert has proposed five "motivational factors in the human tendency to dislike and fear arthropods":

First, many humans are alienated by the vastly different ecological survival strategies, spatially and temporally, of most invertebrates in comparison to humans. Second, the extraordinary "multiplicity" of the invertebrate world seems to threaten the human concern for individual identity and selfhood. Third, invertebrate shapes and forms appear "monstrous" to many people. Fourth, invertebrates are often associated with notions of mindlessness and an absence of feeling—the link between insects, spiders, and madness has been a common metaphor in human discourse and imagination. Fifth, many people appear challenged by the radical "autonomy" of invertebrates from human will and control.[7]

I would argue that each of these revulsions is informed by the categorizations of Pliny and Aristotle: that insects are imaginatively as well as apparently (spatially, temporally) different. Kellert's first motivation, for example, implies a kind of fictional exchange between the human and the insect: life strategies so "vastly different" as metamorphosis can seem an alchemical transmutation, the secrets of which remain enclosed, chrysalized, a blank page. The butterfly and moth, the "psyches" of the Greeks, have long been seen as representations of the soul freed from its mortal casing, but the transformations they embody are reminders of mystery rather than revelation, sublimation rather than illumination. The metamorphic for the human is always already metaphoric; the real monstrosity of the insect, as Pound recognized, is its reperforming of the functions of classical myths and fables: "The ant's a centaur in his dragon world," he wrote, a narrative fantasy we spin to make sense of ourselves.[8] Likewise Kellert's "multiplicity," a by-product of Aristotelian (in)divisibility, is coded here as sexual fecundity—the hyper-reproductivity that threatens human sovereignty. Few animals have longer lifespans than *Homo sapiens,* but the rapid reproduction that compensates for insects' ephemerality can make them evolve before our eyes, as if they are outstripping the advances of our prolonged lives. This multiplicity suggests, too, an overwrought abundance, a rhetoric of excessive, swarming, teeming congestion latent in even the simple divisions of the insect into head, thorax, abdomen. Their corporeality, inasmuch as it unfolds a fecundity of form, also presents a clear indivisibility—as if insects, like the travelers in some paradox of Zeno, represent some division prior to themselves. They are positioned, as forms, at the very edges of physicality, as the "atom" (with the same root as "entomology") once denoted something so small as to no longer be subsected. This formidable integrity—to be so small as to be indestructible—becomes popularly reimagined not only by virtue of their small(est) size, but by their armored exoskeletons, their relatively superheroic strength, their incessant seasonal reappearances, seemingly out of nowhere, and especially their tendency to become virtually two-dimensional when slipping through wall cracks or cabinet seams. Finally, the segmented form is a constant reminder of insects as adversaries. With one-third of their form devoted to eating, insects such as locusts, aphids, and beetles feed on our food, while mosquitoes, fleas, flies, and lice feed on us. No other animal makes humans so customary a source of sustenance. But of all Kellert's propositions, the most significant is the idea of "radical autonomy," a severing from "human will" that pushes Pliny's conceptualization of insects as spectacle. I take the fullest realization of this radical autonomy as integral to the poetics of the insect, for nowhere is the anxiety over multiplicity more manifest than in the insects' radical *autonymy:* they exist beyond our capacity for language, specifically unnameable by anyone but themselves.

The act of naming insects—that is, the taxonomy of the insect—creates a problematic disjunction between language and materiality. One entomologist puts it this way: "Terry Erwin has taken extensive examples of ants, beetles and other life in the tropical rain forest canopy and demolished the old estimate that there are 1.5 million species on earth. He figures that there are actually more like 30 million, almost all of them insects in need of names."[9] Because of a nearly unfathomable number of species, the plethora of insects "in need of names" beggars description (Shakespeare, for instance, with a vocabulary of some thirty thousand words, might barely have had enough to cover the bees). Linnaeus, since 1758 the father of binomial nomenclature, "commended the use of generic names taken from poetry or mythology," but even after using all sixty-eight Argonauts and the fifty daughters of Danaus to name his butterflies, he still fell infinitely short.[10] And yet this very anxiety over our inability to organize and categorize motivates a recuperation of the potency of language. Indeed, it is rarely pointed out that the process of scientific naming is a decidedly poetic one: the *International Code of Zoological Nomenclature* recommends that all new scientific names not only "should be short" but, more importantly, also "euphonious in Latin."[11] That is, the naming should be pleasing and even artful, a remarkable directive considering that the *ICZN* also directs that "a zoologist should not propose a name that, when spoken, suggests a bizarre, comical, or otherwise objectionable meaning."[12] The scientific names of insects, which demonstrate both an abundance and an abundant lack in the world of taxonomy, are often dazzling to the eye (witness *Parastratiosphecomyia stratiosphecomyioides*), but the expressive euphony is also evident: *Ephemerella subvaria* or *Libellula pulchella, Euborellia annulipes* or *Nannothemis bella.*[13] Such expressiveness underscores the ways in which poetry and the natural world collapse into each other, a pattern evident as well in species that take the poetry of their names from some of those most proficient at the art: Girault named a series of wasp genera after literati, including Dante, Keats, Carlyle, even the amalgamated *Goethaeana shakespearei.*

The extra-aesthetic value of insect names, including their common names, can be further seen in the insects' ties to national and local culture. Many American states have adopted an "official state insect," several preferring indigenous and eponymous species such as the California dogface butterfly (a poodle profile appears on its wing) and the Colorado hairstreak butterfly to the more generic honeybees and ladybugs.[14] In 2002, for the first time in nearly a century, an entirely new insect *order* was discovered (the equivalent in mammalian terms of finding out for the first time about the existence of rodents, or of a singular creature with an order all its own—another aardvark, pangolin, or manatee). Inhabiting Botswana and South Africa, the chimerical "Mantophasmatodea"—covered in spines and described as a cross between a cricket, mantid, and stick insect—was first baptized with the common name of "Gladiator," a sobriquet borrowed consciously from the popular film *Gladiator*, itself an insectarian film in which Romans dine on "honeyed butterflies, their wings still moving slightly."[15] The opting for such a truculent common name ended up also presaging combative politics. Credit for the African discovery went to a team of German scientists, an attribution resented by African citizens who saw the find as a national treasure; the creature now appears textualized on a postage stamp in Botswana in an effort to repoliticize the creature.[16] Yet the parameters of taxonomics are never without a political component: do the euphonies of Latin still resound to an ear accustomed to Setswana, or German, or English? In this case, the "Gladiator" common name redoubles the linguistic selectivity and affirms the irony of a voracious south African creature being named, however mellifluously, after a Roman warrior (and a distinctly fictive one). The process of naming replays one of the most visible ways in which humans and insects have been compared: insect "colonies" take their names from the Latin verb *colere*, meaning "to cultivate," especially agriculturally. Bee and ant colonies have over the centuries been imagined as ideal commonwealths—models, indeed, for human colonization, especially in the New World.[17] (The self-reflexivity of such processes is evident in the early writings attributed to Cortes, who was unable to find gold in Cozumel on his premier voyage and so, like a valiant worker bee, instead sent back to Charles V a shipment of honey.)[18] So too did the processes of species translocation mirror the human colonizing process: mosquitoes were unwittingly brought aboard Spanish ships into the otherwise inaccessible islands of Micronesia, even as the same creatures helped shape the direction of conquest in the Americas. More recently, invasive species of all sorts have made similar colonizations: cockroaches, fire ants, Japanese beetles, and even the European honeybee have flourished at the expense of native denizens. These corollary events—the colonizing by and as insects, the poetic Latinization of the zoological world—are perhaps the last but not least excursions of the bygone Roman Empire.

LITERAL ENTOMOLOGIES

The cultural poetics of insects form a backdrop for the rich metaphoric field they have long inhabited, and to which countless writers have added. I highlight here three significant variations—insects as poetry, insects as poets, and finally insects as poems. Petrarch saw in insects the fabrications of poetry itself: "It may all be summed up by saying with Seneca, and with Flaccus before him, that we must write just as the bees make honey, not keeping the flowers but turning them into a sweetness of our own, blending many very different flavours into one, which shall be unlike them all, and better."[19] The language of the natural world, recombined and organized, becomes the blended language of poetry. For Petrarch, these colonizing, cultivating, creative insects—bees, ants, wasps, termites—shape the natural nectars and refine, alter, and control them to produce a new material entirely. These are the mechanisms of language and poetry, a ceaseless process of coevolution and refinement, the kind performed by the sympathetic ants in the myth of Psyche, who sort bad seeds from good. In this vein of transformation through language, it was Shakespeare's Cassius who hectored Mark Antony: "But for your words, they rob the Hybla bees, / And leave them honeyless," and Brutus who added, "O yes, and soundless too; / For you have stol'n their buzzing."[20] Twentieth-century experiments demonstrated that such looting of honeyed words (not to mention such droning on) has been redeemed by the bees. Documented first by Karl von Frisch, the "buzzing" of bees belies a sophisticated communication system, in which bees "dance" in waggling struts and pirouetting circles to relay information about nearby food sources—including their distance from the hive, direction relative to the sun, and even their quality. The bees' linguistic proficiency has been called "the most complicated language of signs and symbols in the animal kingdom," and cognitive ethologist Donald R. Griffin terms it "the most significant example of versatile communication known in any animals other than our own species."[21] The signs deployed by the bees in their abstraction of spatial relationships are every bit as transformative as their sublimation of flower nectar into honey, realizing centuries after Petrarch the more-than-metaphoric poetry of the bee.

Lewis Carroll's hookah-smoking caterpillar in *Alice's Adventures in Wonderland,* as well as Tenniel's oft-reproduced illustration, may be the most famous of versifying insects: the caterpillar not only requests that Alice recite "You Are Old, Father William" but critiques her recitation. The more extravagantly poetic of insects, however, is the Gnat in Carroll's *Through the Looking Glass*, who like Petrarch's bees transforms Alice's standard horse-flies, butterflies, and dragonflies into "Looking Glass" forms: a "Rocking-horse-fly," a "Bread-and-butter-fly," and a "Snap-dragon-fly," whose "body is made of plum-pudding, its wings of holly-leaves, and its head is a raisin burning in brandy."[22] It does not seem coincidental that such figures would appear in books ostensibly for children, as the fabulous improbabilities of the insect world first appear to most of us during childhood. Inevitably, insects are the first nonhuman, nondomestic animals most humans encounter. The classic children's book *The Very Hungry Caterpillar* paints the progressive digestions of a caterpillar as the building blocks to resplendent adulthood (even as the caterpillar bores "holes" through the fabric of the book itself).[23] But most children at some point—under stones and logs or behind refrigerators—will come upon insects extratextually, in their "natural habitat" (yet another unsettling aspect of insects is their seeming lack of territory or decorum over personal space in general). The results of these encounters have produced a clichéd parade of insects squashed or dismembered, frozen in ice cubes or scorched by magnifying glasses.[24] But it is significant that insects are most apparent at the beginning and at the end of our lives (from ants on the sidewalk to carrion fauna), when the imagination of what's to come may be most potent. Roald Dahl reasonably thought magnified insects fit companions for his boyhood traveler in *James and the Giant Peach*, even while locusts the size of war horses are equally appropriate visions in the book of Revelation.[25]

For all their prominence, insects also burrow into the substrata of language, often remaining etymologically unnoticed: in colors like "vermilion," from the Latin word for a worm or grub; "crimson," from the kermes beetle, a source of red dye; "puce," the deep purplish tint that takes its name from a flea (*pulex*) and suggests the flea's imbruing wound; and "cochineal," the reddish pigment derived from crushed scale insects (*Dactylopius coccus*). (The latter substance remains a regular additive of some brand-name foods.) They are routinely commodified (honey, silk), even as they vanish behind their own materiality—into the "lac" of shellac, for instance, the resin excreted by *Laccifer lacca*. And for centuries written language itself depended on the technologies of insects: ink was produced by an admixture including the tannic acid of plant galls, especially those on oak, caused by the infestation of various insect species. On the other hand, book-worms—typically silverfish—lurk at the other end of production to devour the paste adhering texts themselves. Finally, blending the written and the chitinous, Calligrapha beetles are etched with inky flourishes on their parchment-colored elytra.

Insects and poetry merge most frequently in the figures of crickets and other orthopterans, long celebrated for their own songs in a number of countries, particularly China and Japan. Lovelace, Suckling, Carew, and other royalist poets in the seventeenth century adopted the grasshopper and its dewdrop-drinking song as their emblem for poetry, but e. e. cummings may have been the first to reproduce this sort of insect not *in* a poem but *as* a poem. His seemingly disjointed poem "r-p-o-p-h-e-s-s-a-g-r" depicts the jump of a grasshopper as interflowing lines and letters that "gather into a leap" only to "become rearrang[ed]":[26]

r-p-o-p-h-e-s-s-a-g-r
    who
a)s w(e loo)k
upnowgath
    PPEGORHRASS
        eringint(o-
aThe):l
    eA
        !p:
S   a
    (r
rIvInG .gRrEaPsPhOs)
        to
rea(be)rran(com)gi(e)ngly
,grasshopper;

Walter Ong helps parse the scatterings of this rhapsody: "At last letters come together in the final word 'grasshopper'—all this to suggest the erratic and optically dizzying flight of a grasshopper until he finally reassembles him-self straightforwardly on the blade of grass before us."[27] The play between syllable and sentence, punctuation and poem, re-creates rather than rep-resents the fragmented movements of the creature—the capitalization of the tensing prelude, the reader's eye fluttering to follow the leap that is a *leAp*, parentheses becoming still points along the body as the tumultuous wings settle and are folded in. One can playfully read, with cummings, the rhythm of an iamb as the salient leap of a grasshopper, or imagine a new insect subject entirely: the black and orange symmetry of a monarch butterfly as a royal couplet, or the paronomasia of "I fed David, an avid aphid, an affidavit" as the insidious cluster feedings of the plant pest. But cummings's poem is not only a statement of the materiality of the insect, with its camouflaged coloration, vibrating wings, and life of punctuated equilibrium, but a testament to the ways in which insect poetics and the natural world are cognate—neither ever resolved before us in their entirety, both chaotic and controlled at once.

THE COLLECTION

The anxieties over insects supposed by Kellert have spawned diverse counterreactions, beginning with Rachel Carson's accounts of the devastating effects of DDT and other insecticides in *Silent Spring* and continuing with a host of eco-friendly farming and gardening practices—ladybugs, praying mantises, and parasitic wasps all serve a kind of domesticated role in current agribusiness.[28] Insects have been put to positive use in criminal investigations, as well: forensic entomology uses the life stages of carrion insects to read the decomposition time of corpses.[29] And in one of the more gleeful appropriations, the release of butterflies (rather than rice or confetti) at weddings has come into vogue, with one business claiming, "You will depart under a veil of fluttering beauties who will remain for just the right amount of time before they gently and majestically fly away!"[30] Much of this still suggests an attempt at containing or distancing (note how the butterflies won't overstay their welcome at the wedding), retaining the view of spectacle like the paying audience at a vaudeville flea circus or, in a more contemporary setting, the interactive and ostensibly more environmentally conscientious butterfly gardens and petting zoos. A burgeoning trade in insects as pets (Madagascar hissing cockroaches, stag beetles, crickets, and stick insects, to name a few) rounds out some of the increasingly intimate associations insects have forged with humans.[31]

The essays that follow, grouped into three parts, are all further explorations of similar intimacies: of writing about insects, reading about insects, working with insects, playing with insects, even eating insects. Because most of the essays begin with inherently interdisciplinary theses, and because all are informed by a common theoretical inquiry—insects and issues of textuality or cultural poetics—there are some shared methodologies between parts. The essays in part I, however, are unified by their foregrounding of a central text or texts that help situate not only insects as a literary device but literature as itself an "insective" enterprise. "Literary Entomologies" begins with May Berenbaum's survey of insects in poetry. Berenbaum's selections are wide-ranging, and she establishes a number of insect tropes developed in subsequent essays. Following is Andre Stipanovic's close reading of classic insect similes in Vergil's *Aeneid,* a text he shows to be concerned with different forms of nation building as well as sociobiological behavior. My own chapter looks at insects in and as performance during the late sixteenth century and the early seventeenth, reading *Coriolanus* as Shakespeare's most sustained inquiry into insects and humans. Tony McGowan then assesses insects in the work of Thoreau and Melville in the context of one of the landmark works of Victorian natural history, Kirby and Spence's *Introduction to Entomology,* and Rachel Sarsfield reviews the lepidopterism of Virginia Woolf, beginning with her impassioned interest in moth hunts. Roy Rosenstein's essay on Kobo Abé traces the natural history of existentialism in the figure of the "underground" insect, and Heather Johnson finds gothic materiality above ground in the swarming poetry of Sylvia Plath and in Alice Maher's objective art (including a dress made of dead bees). Part I ends with Marion Copeland's lively analysis of a recurrent postmodern bug, the cockroach, in several contemporary American novels.

Parts II and III move increasingly away from literary readings. Part II, "Rhetorics and Aesthetics," hybridizes more than the others textual practices and the ontology of the insect by offering five ways of "reading" insects, each interrogating disparate textual and rhetorical strategies. It begins with Bertrand Gervais's meditation on reading itself as a kind of entomology, and each of the subsequent authors makes similar interrogations of conflated human and insect activity. Yves Cambefort returns to early visualizations of beetles in emblematic literature, and Erika Olbricht and Marc Olivier are both concerned with the role of gender in various insect discourses. Beginning with labor manuals in the seventeenth century, Olbricht explores the economics of English bees and silkworms and the ways in which they supported and subverted notions of labor. Olivier's study of the revolutions in aesthetics prompted by the microscope, or "flea-glass," moves to a consideration of insects in class and gender relations. Cristopher Hollingsworth discusses the appropriation of insects in political rhetoric, from Bosnia and Nazi Germany to Rwanda and present-day America, and offers an especially insightful analysis of the tropes of oppressive systems.

Part III takes on many of the popular conceptions and misconceptions of bugdom, almost all of which revolve around insects' "unsettling" effects. Charlotte Sleigh historicizes the exploration of insects and the psychology of creepiness, with close attention to the evolution of entomologists themselves. In an essay informed by both insect creation myths and anthropomorphized "alien" insect forms, Nicky Coutts continues the exploration of the grotesque by contemporary visual artists. Richard Leskosky offers a dazzling survey of monstrous "big bugs" on film, arguing that their horrors are directly proportional to reversals in physical scale. Finally Sarah Gordon offers an encompassing theorization of "entomophagy," or insect ingestion. Her essay is a fitting one with which to end, as it treats explicitly both how we see insects and how, through them, we see ourselves.

NOTES

I would like to thank Lisette Bordes, Christy Noel, and Shawn Brown for their suggestions on earlier drafts of this essay.

1. Pliny, *The Natural History*, trans. John Bostock et al. (London, 1855); *Naturalis Historia*, ed. Karl Mayhoff (Leipzig: Teubner, 1906).

2. Kurt Johnson and Steven Coates, *Nabokov's Blues: The Scientific Odyssey of a Literary Genius* (New York: McGraw-Hill, 2001).

3. See, for instance, Thomas Eisner, *For Love of Insects* (Cambridge: Harvard University Press, 2003); Erich Hoyt and Ted Schultz, eds., *Insect Lives: Stories of Mystery and Romance from a Hidden World* (Cambridge: Harvard University Press, 2001); Arthur V. Evans and Charles L. Bellamy, *An Inordinate Fondness for Beetles* (Berkeley: University of California Press, 2000); Gene Kritsky and Ron Cherry, eds., *Insect Mythology* (San Jose, Calif.: Writer's Club, 2000); Maraleen Manos-Jones, *The Spirit of Butterflies: Myth, Magic and Art* (New York: Harry Abrams, 2000); and James K. Wangberg and Marjorie C. Leggitt, *Six Legged Sex: The Erotic Lives of Bugs* (Golden, Colo.: Fulcrum, 2001). Closer to the tenor of the present collection are Joanne Elizabeth Lauck, *The Voice of the Infinite in the Small: Re-visioning the Insect-Human Connection* (Mill Spring, N.C.: Swan Raven, 1998); May Berenbaum, *Bugs in the System: Insects and Their Impact on Human Affairs* (Reading, Mass.: Addison-Wesley, 1995); and André Siganos, *Les mythologies de l'insecte: Histoire d'une fascination* (Paris: Librairie des Méridiens, 1985).

4. A number of books have been reconsidering the cultural construction of the "animal." See, for instance, Erica Fudge, *Perceiving Animals: Humans and Beasts in Early Modern English Culture* (Urbana: University of Illinois Press, 2002); Randy Malamud, *Poetic Animals and Animal Souls* (New York: Palgrave, 2003); Jonathan Burt, *Animals in Film* (London: Reaktion, 2003); Steve Baker, *The Postmodern Animal* (London: Reaktion, 2000); and Cary Wolfe, *Animal Rites: American Culture, the Discourse of Species, and Posthumanist Theory* (Chicago: University of Chicago Press, 2003); as well as the collected essays in *Zoontologies: The Question of the Animal*, ed. Cary Wolfe (Minneapolis: University of Minnesota Press, 2003); and *Representing Animals*, ed. Nigel Rothfels (Bloomington: Indiana University Press, 2002). Reaktion Press describes its Animal series, edited by Jonathan Burt, as "the first substantial collection of books to examine the cultural histories of members of the animal kingdom." The series includes Charlotte Sleigh's *Ant* (2003) and Marion Copeland's *Cockroach* (2004). The Johns Hopkins University Press also has a new series on animals under way, edited by Harriet Ritvo, that includes at least one work on ants, also by Charlotte Sleigh: *Six Legs Better: A Cultural History of Myrmecology, 1874–1975* (forthcoming). See too the quondam online journal *Cultural Entomology Digest* (vols. 1–4, 1993–97), http://www.insects.org/ced/index.html.

5. Aristotle, *Parts of Animals*, trans. A. L. Peck (Cambridge: Harvard University Press, 1945), 343–45.

6. In a 2005 ad campaign for Nextel Communications ("Nextel Helps Groups Get Things Done"), humans are digitally rendered as if ants on a worksite ("The Build"), and again as if bees in an office-hive ("The Deal"); but the visuals, in addition to showing humans crawling against gravity, lifting fifty times their weight, and bombinating about a metropolis, are primarily concerned with remote communication: as if Nextel mobile technologies have finally put us on an instrumental and organizational par with the insect.

7. Kellert, "The Biological Basis for Human Values of Nature," in *The Biophilia Hypothesis*, ed. Stephen R. Kellert and Edward O. Wilson (Washington, D.C.: Island Press, 1993), 57–58. See also Stephen R. Kellert, "Values and Perceptions of Invertebrates," *Conservation Biology 7*, no. 4 (1991): 845–55.

8. From Canto LXXXI, in *Ezra Pound: Selected Cantos* (New York: New Directions, 1970).

9. See Richard Conniff, "The *Verae peculya* Business of Naming New Species," *Smithsonian*, December 1996, 67. For more on this issue, see David Grimaldi and Michael S. Engel's magisterial *Evolution of the Insect* (Cambridge: Cambridge University Press, 2005), 36.

10. See John L. Heller, "Classical Mythology in the *Systema Naturae* of Linnaeus," *Transactions and Proceedings of the American Philological Association* 76 (1945): 333–57, 335; and Heller, "Classical Poetry in the *Systema naturae* of Linnaeus," *Transactions and Proceedings of the American Philological Association* 102 (1971): 183–216.

11. International Commission on Zoological Nomenclature, *International Code of Zoological Nomenclature,* 3rd ed. (London : International Trust for Zoological

Nomenclature, in association with the British Museum [Natural History]; Berkeley: University of California Press, 1985), 193.

12. Ibid., 93. On exceptions to this conservatism, see Conniff, *Verae peculya,* 66–70.

13. Respectively the stratiomyid fly, midboreal mayfly, twelve-spot skimmer, ring-legged earwig, and bluebell dragonfly.

14. The drive toward a perfect insect community has been treated variously: see the animated film *Antz* (dir. Eric Darnell and Tim Johnson, 1998), in which ants search for Insectopia, and, in extremis, Will Self's short story "Flytopia," in *Tough, Tough Toys for Tough, Tough Boys* (New York: Grove Press, 1998), 23–42.

15. *Gladiator,* dir. Ridley Scott (2000); script by David Franzoni accessed January 23, 2005, at http://www.hundland.com/scripts/Gladiator_SecondDraft.txt.

16. The bounded stamping of the mantophasmids marks a further means of containment, a common discursive mode in human-insect relations; as Malamud perceptively observes, "If we are going to expend our attention on any creatures so small and trivial and ubiquitous, we feel compelled to inscribe the enterprise in the adventuring tropes of safaris or other quests for the *rara avis,* and to collect insects the way we collect coins and stamps" (*Poetic Animals,* 36).

17. See Eric C. Brown, "Insects, Colonies, and Idealization in the Early Americas," *Utopian Studies* 13, no. 2 (2002): 20–37.

18. *The Letters of Cortes to Charles V,* trans. Francis A. MacNutt, vol. 1 (Cleveland: Clark, 1908), 145.

19. *Petrarch: The First Modern Scholar and Man of Letters,* ed. James Harvey Robinson (New York: Greenwood, 1969), 291.

20. *Julius Caesar,* 5.1.34–35, 36–37, in *The Riverside Shakespeare,* ed. G. Blakemore Evans, 2nd ed. (Boston: Houghton Mifflin, 1997).

21. John Sparks, *The Discovery of Animal Behavior* (Boston: Little, Brown, 1982), 188; Griffin, *Animal Minds: Beyond Cognition to Consciousness* (Chicago: University of Chicago Press, 2001), 190. See also Elizabeth Atwood Lawrence, "The Sacred Bee, the Filthy Pig, and the Bat Out of Hell: Animal Symbolism as Cognitive Biophilia," in *The Biophilia Hypothesis,* ed. Stephen R. Kellert and Edward O. Wilson (Washington, D.C.: Island Press, 1993), 301–41.

22. See Martin Gardner, ed., *The Annotated Alice: Alice's Adventures in Wonderland and Through the Looking Glass* (New York: Meridian, 1960), 222–23. The Gnat's conglomeration is inspired by a Christmas diversion popular with Victorian children in which flaming raisins were snatched and eaten.

23. Eric Carle's *The Very Hungry Caterpillar* (New York: Philomel, 1969) is only one of numerous children's books with insects at the core. Douglas Florian has versified a collection of arthropods in *Insectlopedia: Poems and Paintings* (New York: Harcourt Children's Books, 1998), containing paeans even to ticks and "evil" weevils.

24. Lynne Truss borrows from the language of childhood insect-torture, tacitly transforming insects into the building blocks of syntax, in *Eats, Shoots & Leaves*

(New York: Gotham, 2003): "Now there are no laws against imprisoning apostrophes and making them look daft. Cruelty to punctuation is quite unlegislated: you can get away with pulling the legs off semicolons; shrivelling question marks on the garden path under a powerful magnifying glass; you name it" (36).

25. Dahl, *James and the Giant Peach* (New York: Knopf, 1961); Revelation 9.7–9. For background on insects and finality, see Eric C. Brown, "The Allegory of Small Things: Insect Eschatology in Spenser's *Muiopotmos*," *Studies in Philology* 99, no. 3 (Summer 2002): 247–67.

26. From E. E. Cummings, *Complete Poems: 1904–1962*, ed. George J. Firmage (New York: Liveright, 1963).

27. Ong, *Orality and Literacy: The Technologizing of the Word* (New York: Routledge, 1988), 129. See also Norman Friedman, *E. E. Cummings: The Art of His Poetry* (Baltimore: Johns Hopkins University Press, 1960), 123–24; Richard D. Cureton, "Visual Form in E. E. Cummings' *No Thanks*," *Word and Image* 2 (1986): 245–77; and Stephen Cushman, *William Carlos Williams and the Meanings of Measure* (New Haven: Yale University Press, 1985), who adds that "the grasshopper may be camouflaged in the grass as the word 'grasshopper' is camouflaged in the first line."

28. Carson, *Silent Spring* (Boston: Houghton Mifflin, 1962).

29. For a full account, see M. Lee Goff, *A Fly for the Prosecution: How Insect Evidence Helps Solve Crimes* (Cambridge: Harvard University Press, 2000).

30. Http://www.themonarchy.com/butterfly_wedding_planning.html, January 10, 2005.

31. Extending the domestication are a flurry of digitized and other electronic insects, such as those in *SimAnt: The Electronic Ant Colony* (Maxis Software, 1991) or *A.I. Wars: The Insect Mind* (Tactical Neuronics, 2001), as well as battery-operated katydids in Japan. On artificial animal life, see Ursula Heise, "From Extinction to Electronics: Dead Frogs, Live Dinosaurs, and Electric Sheep," in *Zoontologies*, 59–81.

PART I

Literary Entomologies

1

On the Lives of Insects in Literature

MAY BERENBAUM

Insect scientists and literary figures would seem, on the surface, to have little in common other than the fact that the terms "entomology" and "etymology" bear a fortuitous resemblance. As the entomologist W. R. Walton remarked over eighty years ago, the "entomology of poetry . . . seems a contradiction in terms. What natural relation possibly can exist between poetry and 'bugs'? As well mention music and sauerkraut or lilies of the valley and garlic."[1] And for his part, the poet Ogden Nash (1902–71), Walton's contemporary, mused (most appropriately) in rhyme, "I find among the poems of Schiller / No mention of the caterpillar, / Nor can I find one anywhere / In Petrarch or in Baudelaire."[2] In point of fact, though, Walton and Nash both knew that insects and the written word are long-time companions. Insect references abound in prose and poetry irrespective of class or status—writers of all descriptions, from the greatest literary geniuses to the most obscure hacks, have relied on the insect world to make a point, elicit an emotion, or evoke a memory. This odd partnership is hardly a passing fancy—writers who call upon six-legged muses include some of the earliest poets as well as some of the most contemporary lyricists and span the continuum from Petronius to Pearl Jam. It's unlikely that any other class of organisms creeps so relentlessly into the written pantheon.

Why, it can legitimately be asked, do insects, a group usually if not outright detested then at least studiously avoided, show up with such remarkable frequency in world literature? One possible explanation for the embarrassment of entomological riches is that successful writers often draw their inspiration from their own lives, and it is exceedingly difficult on this planet to live a life free of insects, given their staggering abundance, ubiquity, and close association with humans. Even a poet who never ventures beyond his dank garret runs the risk of encountering, at the very least, cockroaches, flies, and, depending on personal hygiene habits, body lice. As far as most people are concerned, insects are as different from humans as an organism can be and still be of this planet, with an embarrassment of appendages, a basic body plan that's inside out and upside down from a human perspective, and lifestyles and abilities that often defy the imagination. Nash, for example, in contemplating the extraordinary light-producing capabilities of fireflies, was moved to remark, "I can think of nothing eerier / Than flying around with an unidentified glow on a person's posterior."[3] In reality, however, insects and humans share remarkable similarities. In some cases these similarities give rise to the perceived hostilities (as when insects choose to share the food we are trying to grow for ourselves), and in other contexts they give rise to interdependencies (as when we enjoy honey, silk, wax, and the many fruits of pollination). Insects are the only organisms that have colonized the planet to the extent that we humans have; they live wherever we live, even hitching a ride on our bodies on occasion to do so.

Although, proportionately speaking, relatively few poems, novels, or plays are exclusively about insects, these inspiring creatures appear in a variety of guises to suit a variety of literary purposes. Perhaps the most frequent use of insect imagery is for metaphorical or figurative purposes—particular insects embody or epitomize some trait or characteristic so well that an author can take advantage of the inextricable association to express an idea or make a point. A metaphor works only so long as people understand the connection, and since the majority of potential readers, willingly or not, share their lives with a diversity of insects, there is plenty of metaphorical material to work with. Moreover, as far as a poet is concerned, precise life history details or species descriptions are irrelevant; what matters is the popular conception of the insect or entomological phenomenon.

Perhaps the most metaphorically evocative aspect of insect life is the process of metamorphosis, whereby, in a quiescent state called the pupa, larval tissues are broken down and reassembled to constitute the radically different adult stage. Thus the nineteenth-century poet Christina (Georgina) Rossetti (1830–94) captures the transformative nature of life:

Brown and furry
Caterpillar in a hurry
Take your walk
To the shady leaf or stalk
Or what not
Which may be the chosen spot
No toad spy you
Hovering birds of prey pass by you
Spin and die
To live again a butterfly.[4]

That caterpillars destined to be butterflies rarely spin more than a silken girdle or anchor before metamorphosis (caterpillars destined to be moths are the ones who spin a cocoon) is immaterial; people instantly appreciate the enormity of the transition to adulthood. This theme spans centuries and genres and even appears, virtually unchanged, in twentieth-century pop music (as in Donovan's "First There Is a Mountain," with the lyric "caterpillar sheds his skin to find the butterfly within."[5]

Literature is about language and sound, and many insects are unusual among living creatures, particularly among invertebrates, in that they share the human capacity for acoustic communication. Certainly, birds can sing, and birdsong figures prominently in poetry, but the eight thousand species of birds in the world are easily outchorused by the tens of thousands of species of noisemaking insects; these include the familiar grasshoppers, crickets, and cicadas, as well as the less-renowned deathwatch beetle, bess beetle, and hissing cockroach. There are even singing caterpillars known to science, if not to poets.[6] Thus pastoral and rural scenes in poems and stories resonate with the singing, squeaking, or slurring of insects. In "Elegy Written in a Country Churchyard," by Thomas Gray (1716–71), "Now fades the glimm'ring landscape on the sight / And all the air a solemn stillness holds, / Save where the beetle wheels his droning flight, / And drowsy tinklings lull the distant folds."[7] And Alfred Lord Tennyson (1809–92) writes in "Claribel," "At eve the beetle boometh / Athwart the thickest lone / At noon the wild bee hummeth / about the moss'd headstone." Although John Keats (1795–1821) dedicated his famous ode to a nightingale, he evoked the "murmurous haunt of flies on summer eve" in doing so.[8]

As things that go bump in the night, insects can also evoke frightening, dark, weird, and creepy sensations. Their association with decay and putrefaction (since biblical times) contributes to the power of insect images in eliciting dark feelings of mortality. More than seven centuries ago, Geoffrey Chaucer (c. 1343–1400) described in "The Monk's Tale" how "The wreche of God hym smoot so cruelly / That thurgh his body wikked wormes crepte"; and Percy Bysshe Shelley (1792–1822), over two hundred years ago, wrote in "Queen Mab" of "Hell, a red gulf of everlasting fire, / Where poisonous and undying worms prolong / Eternal misery to those hapless slaves / Whose life has been a penance for its crimes."[9]

Such diversity exists within the class Insecta that there are even species whose activities bring to mind love, romance, and even occasionally raw passion or naked lust. It may be their fabled procreative powers, or the frequency with which they can be observed in flagrante delicto, relative to more reclusive vertebrates, that elicits these thoughts. The role that insects play in pollination has inspired romance, perhaps in subconscious recognition of their function as *entremetteurs* in the sex lives of plants. In "The Green Linnet," William Wordsworth (1770–1850) described how "bird, and butterflies, and flowers / make all one band of paramours"; and in a poem titled "Two Worlds," Emily Dickinson (1830–86) relates how

Auto-da-fe and judgment
Are nothing to the bee;
His separation from his rose
To him seems misery.[10]

Insects appear to appreciate the beauty of flowers as we do because we share their ability to see the spectacular display of colors and shapes. We, however, are the eavesdroppers on this conversation; the colors and shapes are signals from the plant to the insect partner.

Again, the diversity of lifestyles among insects provides endless fodder for fables and morality tales. Aesop, master of the fable, a short story with a moral, knew more than 2,500 years ago that the lives of the insects of his day could illustrate useful life lessons; the story of the diligent ant and wastrel grasshopper has been told and retold for thousands of years. So did Isaac Watts (1674–1748), known as the father of children's "hymnology," who penned, in his "Divine Songs for Children," the immortal lines:

How doth the little busy bee
Improve each shining hour,
And gather honey all the day
From every opening flower!

How skillfully she builds her cell!
How neat she spreads the wax!
And labours hard to store it well
With the sweet food she makes.

In works of labour or of skill
I would be busy too:
For Satan finds some mischief still
For idle hands to do.[11]

In the nineteenth century, the French poet Wilhelm Apollinaris de Kostro-witsky, writing under the name Guillaume Apollinaire (1880–1918), expressed much the same theme, albeit with a different insect inspiration—*la chenille* (the caterpillar):

Le travail mène à la richesse,
Pauvres poètes, travaillons!
Le chenille en peinant sans cesse
Devient le riche papillon.
[Work leads to wealth.
Poor poets, work on!
The caterpillar, by struggling ceaselessly,
Becomes the rich butterfly.][12]

And in the twentieth century, Don Marquis (1878–1937) wrote of ambition and desire from the perspective of a cockroach in the poem "the lesson of the moth":

i was talking to a moth
the other evening
he was trying to break into
an electric light bulb
and fry himself on the wires

why do you fellows
pull this stunt I asked him
because it is the conventional
thing for moths or why
if that had been an uncovered
candle instead of an electric
light bulb you would
now be a small unsightly cinder
have you no sense

plenty of it he answered
but at times we get tired
of using it
we get bored with the routine
and crave beauty
and excitement
fire is beautiful
and we know that if we get
too close it will kill us
but what does that matter
it is better to be happy
for a moment
and burned up with beauty
than to live a long time
and be bored all the while
so we wad all our life up
into one little roll
and then we shoot the roll
that is what life is for
it is better to be a part of beauty
for one instant and then cease to
exist than to exist forever
and never be a part of beauty
our attitude toward life
is come easy go easy
we are like human beings
used to be before they became
too civilized to enjoy themselves

and before i could argue him
out of his philosophy
he went and immolated himself
on a patent cigar lighter
i do not agree with him
myself i would rather have
half the happiness and twice
the longevity
but at the same time I wish
there was something I wanted
as badly as he wanted to fry himself.[13]

Insects, in the grand scheme of things, are small creatures; their small size and often reclusive habits mean that they can easily be overlooked (with few adverse consequences). Thus "insect" has come in many contexts to signify minuteness or insignificance. In the "Prologue" and "Tale of the Nun's Priest" in his *Canterbury Tales*, Chaucer derides a distasteful story with the ultimate put-down—"Youre tale anoyeth al this compaignye. / Swich talkyng is nat worth a boterflye" (lines 2789–90). Small size also makes insects vulnerable to the vicissitudes of life, a point not lost on poets looking to describe human frailties and corporeal evanescence. William Blake (1757–1827) captured the essence of the thought in his poem "The Fly" (1794):

Little Fly
Thy summer's play
My thoughtless hand
Has brush'd away.

Am not I
A fly like thee?
Or art not thou
A man like me?

For I dance
And drink & sing,
Till some blind hand
Shall brush my wing.

If thought is life
And strength & breath,
And the want
Of thought is death;

Then am I
A happy fly,
If I live,
Or if I die.[14]

The thought in twentieth-century garb is well expressed in the song "Fly on a Windshield," by Genesis:

The wind is blowing harder now,
Blowing dust into my eyes.
The dust settles on my skin,
Making a crust I cannot move in
And I'm hovering like a fly, waiting for the windshield on the freeway.[15]

So—does it matter that when Emily Dickinson wrote, "The pedigree of honey / Does not concern the bee; / A clover, any time, to him / Is aristocracy," she got her genders wrong? Male bees never forage for nectar; rather, they sit in the colony and are fed by the female workers until winter arrives and food supplies grow short, at which point they're unceremoniously driven out of the hive and, incapable of feeding themselves, left to starve.[16] William Shakespeare (1564–1616) made the same mistake, describing honey bee society in *Henry V*:

They have a king, and officers of sorts,
Where some, like magistrates, correct at home;
Others, like merchants, venter trade abroad;
Others, like soldiers, armed in their stings,
Make boot upon the summer's velvet buds,
Which pillage they with merry march bring home
To the tent-royal of their emperor,
Who busied in his majesty surveys
The singing masons building roofs of gold.[17]

Honey bee colonies have a queen, not a king. Even today, people make the same mistake. The contemporary blues classic by Slim Harpo (James Moore) "I'm a king bee, buzzin' 'round your hive" is eerily reminiscent of Shakespeare in its male chauvinism.[18]

While it is undoubtedly true that poets have for centuries taken liberties with insect biology to make a metaphorical point, entomologists would be missing the point to raise technical objections to such poetic license. Indeed, it's better for entomologists to celebrate the many ways that insect lives, real or imagined, have enriched the human condition. Insects have inspired and enthralled the human spirit for centuries and will almost certainly continue to do so. Scientist and sonnet writer alike should appreciate these remarkable creatures both for what they share with us and for what they uniquely possess. We are destined to cohabit this planet with insects; we may as well appreciate them, even if that appreciation is unlikely to be reciprocated. This was a fact that Ogden Nash, a writer who appreciated insects more than most, made abundantly clear in his poem "The Louse": "Robert Burns, that gifted souse, / Kindly immortalized the louse, / Who probably won't when he is master, / Immortalize this poetaster."[19] And despite the fact that Nash decried the absence of caterpillars from the writings of Baudelaire, there is at least one reference to *les chenilles*, in a poem called "L'irréparable":

Pouvons-nous étouffer le vieux, le long Remords,
Qui vit, s'agite et se tortille,
Et se nourrit de nous comme le ver des morts,
Comme du chêne la chenille?
[Can we choke the old, the lingering remorse,
Which lives, turns, and twists itself,
And feeds on us like the worm on the dead
Like the caterpillar on the oak?][20]

Regrettably, the work of Petrarch does appear to be entirely free of larval lepidoptera.

NOTES

1. Walton, "The Entomology of English Poetry," *Proceedings of the Entomological Society of Washington* 24 (1922): 159–203. Cf. P. Faulkner, "Insects in English Poetry," *Science Monthly* 33 (1931): 53–73, and E. Phipson, "Insects," in *The Animal Lore of Shakespeare's Time* (London: Kegan Paul Trench, 1883), 389–433.

2. Nash, *The Private Dining Room and Other New Verses* (Boston: Little Brown, 1952).

3. Nash, *Good Intentions* (Boston: Little Brown, 1942).

4. J. Marsh, ed., *Christina Rossetti: Poems and Prose* (New York: Everyman, 1994).

5. See "First There Is a Mountain," http://www.hmg.hu/rock/folk/donovan_lyrics.htm.

6. P. J. DeVries, "Singing Caterpillars, Ants and Symbiosis," *Scientific American* 267 (October 1992): 76–82.

7. Arthur Thomas Quiller-Couch, *The Oxford Book of English Verse* (Oxford: Clarendon, 1919).

8. Keats, *The Poetical Works of John Keats* (London: Macmillan, 1884).

9. Chaucer, in *The Riverside Chaucer,* ed. Larry D. Benson, 3rd ed. (Boston: Houghton Mifflin, 1987), lines 2615–16; Shelley, *The Complete Poems of Percy Bysshe Shelley,* Modern Library Edition, vol. 4 (New York: Random House, 1994), lines 214–17.

10. T. H. Johnson, ed., *The Complete Poems of Emily Dickinson* (Cambridge: Belknap Press of Harvard University Press, 1983).

11. L. Untermeyer, ed., *The Golden Treasury of Poetry* (New York: Golden Press, 1959).

12. Apollinaire, *Bestiary, or The Parade of Orpheus* (Boston: David R. Gardiner, 1980).

13. Marquis, *archy and mehitabel* (New York: Doubleday, 1927).

14. *The Complete Poetry and Prose of William Blake,* ed. David V. Erdman, commentary by Harold Bloom (New York: Anchor-Doubleday, 1988), 23–24.

15. http://www.apluslyrics.com/lyrics/37086/Genesis/Fly_on_a_Windshield.

16. On bee social structures, see May R. Berenbaum, *Bugs in the System: Insects and Their Impact on Human Affairs* (Salem, Mass.: Addison Wesley, 1995), 63–72.

17. In *The Riverside Shakespeare,* ed. G. Blakemore Evans et al., 2nd ed. (Boston: Houghton Mifflin, 1997), 1.2.186–98.

18. http://www.bsnpubs.com/excello.html.

19. Nash, *Good Intentions.*

20. Charles Baudelaire, French version of *Les fleurs du mal* from *The Flowers of Evil,* ed. Marthiel Matthews and Jackson Matthews (New York: New Directions, 1989), 292. English version from William Aggeler, *The Flowers of Evil* (Fresno, Calif.: Academy Library Guild, 1954).

2

Bees and Ants

Perceptions of Imperialism in Vergil's *Aeneid* and *Georgics*

ANDRE STIPANOVIC

Now, that man is more of a political animal than bees . . . is evident.

—ARISTOTLE, *Politics*

Insect poetics help to make a significant political statement in Vergil's *Georgics* and *Aeneid*. How common was this use of insect metaphors in ancient Greco-Roman literature? Before I begin to unravel Vergil's poetry, let me first answer this question by discussing some of Vergil's predecessors. To begin with, Homer's epics undoubtedly display complex insect metaphors in support of his narrative, and this must have influenced Vergil to some extent. But how far these similes and metaphors are able to comment on their contemporary political context is rather difficult to ascertain. Cris Hollingsworth presents an in-depth literary analysis of bees in Homer, but even here Homer's treatment of the hive cannot reveal the same layering that in Vergil bridges the gap between nature and the Roman Senate.[1] The extended metaphor of bee and ant poetics after Homer and before Vergil seems to be little more than a passing mention here and there in poetry, especially for ants.[2] Although other Roman poets like Lucretius mention bees, these treatments remain mostly within the realm of nature. One of the most poetic examples serves as praise for Epicurus's own words: "You [Epicurus] are our father, the discoverer of truths, you supply us with a father's precepts, from your pages, illustrious man, as bees in the flowery glades sip all the sweets, so we likewise feed on all your golden words."[3] Lucretius's examples of bees are used primarily in this poetic manner or as support of Epicurus's science.[4] Vergil differs by raising the status of the hive to the political and national. Another Roman writer, Varro, presents the agricultural or scientific side of bees in *De re rustica*,[5] the content of which is mirrored in many instances in the *Georgics*. However, Varro's style, apart from the quasi-Platonic dialogue of characters expostulating on farming, is mostly a straightforward prose that makes little poetic reference to anything like a political commentary. Should Varro then be considered within this Vergilian realm of insect poetics and politics? Again, compared to Vergil, I should think not. One possible exception is a quote that comes the closest to what Vergil will poetically and subtly develop in more depth. In describing the beehive community, Varro uses a simile: "Their commonwealth is like the states of men, for here are king, government, and fellowship."[6] Earlier Greek writers like Plato and Aristotle extend this comparison in actual discussion of politics and the state. For this reason, I would also like to consider their contribution to insect poetics alongside Vergil.

Plato's didactic dialogues are often considered "poetic," but in terms of my argument, Plato's most notable contribution is in first conjoining the notion of the "harmonious beehive" with a long, serious discussion of government in his *Republic*.[7] For example, in speaking of the irresponsible citizen, Plato writes: "Shall we, then, say of him that as the drone springs up in the cell, a pest of the hive, so such a man grows up in his home, a pest of the state?"[8] This famous quote poetically echoes Hesiod and other authors.[9] Plato mentions drones in the context of the state many times as not fulfilling their role in the hive, just as a lazy citizen threatens the state with his lack of commitment. All the while, Plato extends the bee metaphor over the course of books 7 and 8, in which he describes various forms of government and their shortcomings. Aristotle, though not as poetic, lays out his *Politics* in similar fashion. As is his custom, he details the composition of various governmental constitutions without overextending the hive metaphor in Plato's fashion. While Plato's hive metaphor forecasts what Vergil does in both the *Georgics* and the *Aeneid,* Aristotle's lack of metaphor is more than made up for in his research on bees.[10] My essay will shed some light on how Vergil the poet succeeds in balancing these scientific, artistic, and philosophical inspirations together in his poetry and how he sets the Western standard in insect poetics for, as Hollingsworth puts it, a "poetics of the hive," as well as, I would say, a "politics of the hive."

THE EMERGENCE OF A CULTURAL POLARITY IN THE *AENEID*

The power of similes in Vergil to express depth of feeling has long been acknowledged as part of the pleasure in reading his work. Whereas nature is often invoked in a simile to help illustrate a culminating event in the story, Vergil's reference to insects (bees in particular) is extensive in both the *Aeneid* and the *Georgics.* While reading these references closely in their immediate context, the context of Vergil's work as a whole, and the historical context of Vergil's time, I began noting a distinction between Vergil the narrator and Vergil the author. As I read the poetry of Vergil the narrator, I found Vergil the author using bees and ants to comment on Roman society, culture, and the early stages of the imperial regime. Gordon Williams supports this view of narrative and authorial intention through Vergil's general use of the epic simile. Williams brings up an important issue concerning the distance between Vergil the "author" and Vergil's authorial persona as the "narrator" of the epic.[11] For now, I would like simply to designate Vergil the author as the "voice of the poet speaking in the authentic tones of a man of the Augustan age" so as to explore the two similes more closely. Both the bee and ant similes add much more than decoration and detail to the Aeneas legend. These similes not only help to shed light on the story's development but also reveal judgments made by the author on Roman imperialism during the Augustan Age. This observation has also been noted with Vergil's other similes in David West's "Multiple-Correspondence Similes."[12] Further analysis of the details of the bee and ant similes will reveal an interesting perspective of Rome's own image of itself.

After Aeneas's meeting with his mother Venus, book 1 of the *Aeneid* shows the Trojan hero approaching Carthage in the process of being built. Aeneas gains a vantage point on a high hill in order to look down on the city and share with us, the readers, his view of the construction:[13]

> Meanwhile, they took up the way where the path shows. And already they were ascending a hill, which very much juts out onto the city and looks at the opposing fortifications from up on high. Aeneas admires the enormity [of the city], [which was] previously huts; he wonders at the gates and the noise and the paved streets. The eager Tyrians press on [with their work]: some extend the walls and build up the citadel and roll up rocks with their hands, some to choose a site for a building and to enclose it with a ditch;

they select laws and magistrates and the sacred senate. Over here some are excavating harbors; there some set the deep foundations for theaters, and carve huge columns out of cliffs, high decorations for future stages. (*Aeneid* 1.418–29)

Aeneas sees this activity, which is likened by Vergil to that of a beehive:

Just as when labor occupies bees in the early summer through the floral countryside when they [the bees] raise the grown offspring of their race, or when they cram liquid honey and they swell their honeycombs with sweet nectar, or they receive the freight of those arriving or, with a battle-line formed, they ward off the drones, a lazy herd, from the hives; the operation bustles and fragrant honey is redolent with thyme. (*Aeneid* 1.430–36)

Just as Carthage itself is described in lines 418–29 with images of humans constructing a city, so here too the bees are described within an overall picture of industry and hard work. For both bees and humans, the details as a collage of images and the sudden shifts from one image to another could signify Aeneas's excitement over what he is seeing. John Grant, in his article "Dido Melissa," makes key observations between the description in lines 418–29 and the bee simile in 430–36. Grant mentions that "often a simile (or landscape description) reflects in its tone and atmosphere the mood and feelings of a character, who sees what is being described. But sometimes even the comparison itself appears to be a projection of the person's thoughts."[14] The simile is Vergil's extension of Aeneas's visual experience. The shifting of images through Aeneas's eyes (lines 418–29) implies his inner feelings of watching the city being built. Grant asserts that this passage's "tone and atmosphere reflect Aeneas's emotional reaction to what he sees: it reflects in part the uplifting wonderment which he experiences as he sees others already busily establishing their city."[15] We, the audience, recognize that the human action and effect described through Aeneas's eyes are part of his ongoing narrative and personal journey. However, at another level, through the use of simile (lines 430–36), Vergil subtly intercedes and calls our attention to certain details relating to the character of the Carthaginians and what they symbolize in relation to Aeneas and the Trojans.

In comparison, the ant simile in book 4 reverses the viewer and viewed, where "Queen Bee" Dido is now watching Aeneas, the "King Ant." Vergil's decision to use insects for both similes helps the reader recollect the previously mentioned simile in book 1. However, through Dido's perspective, Vergil successfully portrays the inner emotions of Dido while completing the dialectic begun with the bee simile.

After the climactic dialogue in book 4 in which Aeneas is not convinced to remain with Dido, the Carthaginian queen retreats to her bedchamber high in a tower overlooking the shores of her great city. From this vantage point, Dido is able to look down on the assembling Trojans and share with us, the readers, her view of Aeneas's men preparing for departure by sea. As with the bee simile, the vantage point of the observing character is from above, additionally allowing for both the reader's and narrator's perspective on events. Again, the activity of the characters is coupled with a simile even more obviously initiated by the narrator:

> You might see them [the Trojans] migrating and rushing from out of the whole city just as ants when mindful of winter ravage a huge pile of spelt-grain and store it in their shelter, a dark battle-line goes on the plains and they carry off their booty through the grass on a narrow path: some having set to with their shoulders push the huge grains, some drive on the ranks and punish the lingerers, the whole lane glows with activity. (4.401–7)

Grant carefully reads Vergil's words as a characterization of Dido's thoughts: "Poeschl is certainly correct when he adduces it as an example of those similes where there is 'inner accompaniment' and says that it symbolizes 'the darkness and heaviness of Dido's soul.'"[16] However, in comparison with the bee simile's presentation, Vergil's own authorial presence here is shown to be even stronger. Significantly, Dido herself is not describing the Trojans as ants. Vergil is not even saying outright that Dido is thinking, "The Trojans look like ants." Indeed, even more forcefully than with the bee simile, Vergil is asserting his authorial presence and almost engaging in conversation with the reader: for example, in line 401, *cernas*, "*you* (the reader) might see."

In addition to the uses of similes involving insects, deliberate narrative intervention, and character point of view from a high vista, imagery and word choice show a deeper correspondence between the two similes. Both similes also employ a collage effect by shifting from one image to another. This brevity of focus is likewise set in the slower tempo of meter for both similes. The narrator thus combines the collage of images with a slow, un-emotional "camera pan" (i.e., the calm narrator's intervention might be seen here to be at odds with both characters' emotional states). Word choice coincidentally includes a common verb, *fervet* (to boil, glow, swarm), that emphasizes the industrious activity of both bees and ants. The key word *fervet* is also included in the last line of each simile.[17] Similarities such as this one are enough to remind a watchful reader of the general correspondence between the two similes.

On the other hand, through significant differences of the bee and ant similes, a subtle polarity emerges that sets "Roman" in contrast to "non-Roman." This polarity is only openly declared and defined later in book 6:

> Some will softly beat out breathing bronze (indeed I believe), they will lead forth living faces from marble, they will plead cases better, and they will measure the dimensions of the sky with the rod and proclaim the rising [of the] stars: you, Roman, remember to rule peoples with sovereignty (these will be your arts), to impose the custom of peace, to spare the humbled and to war down the proud. (6.847–53)

Here the spirit of Anchises (Aeneas's deceased father) takes care to explain to Aeneas that there will be those who will demonstrate great skill in the arts and crafts. The Romans' great skill, however, will be in supervising others. Aeneas must first wrestle with the problem of reaching a land unknown to him. The term "Roman" is ironically as foreign to him as it is familiar to the audience of the *Aeneid*. Likewise, the polarity emerging between Roman and non-Roman in the text is just as enigmatic to Aeneas at this moment as it is revealing to the reader familiar with Vergil's *Aeneid* and Augustan Rome. The insect similes foreshadow a cultural polarity in books 1 and 4 well before the appropriate moment comes in book 6 for a clearer contrast of the two. Anchises' advice to Aeneas in book 6 certifies for the reader what has already been implied by Vergil in the contrast of these two earlier insect similes. Interestingly, this cultural polarity proves to be a dilemma common to both Aeneas and the Augustan audience of Vergil's text.

The main differences between the similes may be seen initially in their content. The backdrop for the bees' activity is during the summer and in the countryside. The brightness of sunshine illuminates the main crop of the bees' production, honey. The overall impression is one of splendor and brightness. This "golden aura" that seems to pervade is recalled subsequently in the many instances when the adjectives "bronze" and "golden" describe various aspects of Dido and her city (e.g., 1.448, 449, 492, and here and there in book 4). In contrast to these key words and phrases for the bees, the ants are mindful of "winter," and Vergil introduces his ant simile with how "you might see those migrating out of a city." Since ants are assumed to reside underground in their colony, the darkness of winter, as well as the complex of the city, is appropriate to their description. This backdrop is defined even more by the "dark" line of their procession, which is in the process of ravaging a huge pile of spelt grain. While the bees are busy producing golden honey, the ants are associated with a less-than-brilliant grain.

The contrast of bee and ant activity is significant. We have seen both bees and ants laboring hard, but the *type* of labor for each differs. In the bee simile, Vergil uses verbs concerned with the raising of their young and with storing honey. Besides possessing in abundance, the bees are also shown producing their own sustenance. Vergil describes the ants with a similar triad of verbs like "ravage," which quite contrarily corresponds to the more peaceful and domestic raising of the bees' young. (The Latin verb *populant* also seems to imply simple "breeding" or "populating" as opposed to more formal and deliberate "educating.") The ants' "storing" and "carrying off" grain both contrast with the bees' "cramming" and "swelling" their honeycombs in that the ants are shown to be merely "carrying" their looted plunder back to their colony for storage, rather than "stocking and inventorying" it. The ants' labor is primarily in the plundering of others' products, that is, the "spelt grain" (which had already been planted, harvested, and stored by others). A kind of parallelism continues in the Latin original. While the bees are "receiving" their own product for storage, the ants are using their energy to "push" others to continue carrying a plundered product back for their own storage. Likewise, the bees "ward off" lazy drones, while the ants "coerce" subordinates to continue the work.[18]

These contrasts emphasize a larger passive-aggressive contrast between the bees and ants respectively. For the bees, leadership is not emphasized except in raising their young (*educunt*); for the ants, division of labor and delegation of authority are emphasized. For both insects, hard work is present, but the bees' (i.e., the Carthaginians) main activity is production, while the ants (Trojans) help themselves to others' produce, which will eventually be taken to Italy. If value judgments were to be made concerning the

conduct of Carthaginians and Trojans, Vergil's portrayal of the ants emphasizes the consumptive side to an otherwise industrious insect. *Georgics*
1.185–86 also supports an image of consumption rather than production:
"both the weevil ravages a huge pile of grain, and the ant fearing for a
destitute old age." Richard Thomas makes a telling observation: "The ant's
usual role of frugality and industry is here reversed."[19] The deliberate contrast between ants and bees seems to segregate the two species in their similes; this is not so in the Roman Empire. The "bees" and "ants" were forced
to coexist under the emperor, with the result that Rome as a whole would
prosper for some time to come, but at what cost, culturally speaking?

From Civil Wars to Pax Romana in the *Georgics*

In book 6, lines 847–53, we have seen how Anchises reveals the destiny of the
future Roman people to his son Aeneas. Vergil's contrast of cultural distinctions defines Roman societal contributions in relation to other cultures. The
emphasis on Roman administrative skills distinguishes their culture from
others as one that feeds on and regulates others' production. Skills specific
to the Roman are not described except for a future destiny to rule. The
specific mission of the future Rome includes an ambiguity surrounding
Rome's primary art or skill. This ambiguity adds suspense to Aeneas's clear
knowledge of what his ultimate destiny will be. From the author's point of
view, however, a clearer statement of Roman values is made to his audience
through poetic license in an age when direct judgment of the regime was
not safe.

Through the use of similes, Vergil is able to develop a Roman/non-Roman
polarity within a narrative concerned with Roman prehistory. On the surface, the bee and ant similes can stand as metaphors for Carthaginians
and Trojans (Romans) respectively. These metaphors are closely tied to the
story of Aeneas. Grant himself states, "The Carthaginians are seen as creators, the departing Trojans are likened to plunderers."[20] However, Vergil's
own point of view and his modification of history through the Aeneas legend allow for deeper meaning to emerge and a more telling commentary
on Augustan Rome. In this way, both artistic expression and political obligation to Augustus are effectively preserved.

In the first simile, we might conclude that Aeneas's observation of a
bustling, thriving Carthage reveals the aspects he most admires in his own

quest to establish a settlement. Vergil, however, also reminds the reader of his own historical moment in the lines preceding the bee simile. We take a last look at lines 418–29:

> Meanwhile, they took up the way where the path shows. And already they were ascending a hill, which very much juts out onto the city and looks at the opposing fortifications from up on high. Aeneas admires the enormity [of the city], [which was] previously huts; he wonders at the gates and the noise and the paved streets. The eager Tyrians press on [with their work]: some extend the walls and build up the citadel and roll up rocks with their hands, some to choose a site for a building and to enclose it with a ditch; they select laws and magistrates and the sacred senate. Over here some are excavating harbors; there some set the deep foundations for theaters, and carve huge columns out of cliffs, high decorations for future stages.

Augustus's renovation of Rome may be recognized in the present "enormity" that was once a collection of archaic "huts." Gates, noise, and paved streets accompany the construction work going on in verbs like *extend, build up, roll up, choose a site, enclose*. Laws are established, officials are selected, ports are excavated, theaters are built, and columns are erected, adorned for "future" staged productions. The familiarity of these scenes to contemporary urban Romans must have been obvious while Augustus was transforming Rome from a city of brick to one of marble.

But just as Vergil superimposes contemporary Rome on a burgeoning Carthage, he then abruptly reminds the reader of the historical distance of his narrative by digressing with a simile comparing the activity of the Carthaginians with those of bees, as we have already seen in lines 1.430–36. As much as this simile might reveal about the actual life of bees, it reveals much about Aeneas's perception of another culture. His fascination with, and admiration of, Carthage's construction in line 437 could be said to have found its fulfillment in Augustan Rome: "O fortunate ones, whose city walls now rise!" Adam Parry says in reference to this particular line: "His [Aeneas's] every utterance perforce contains a note of history, rather than of individuality," and, speaking more generally, "The sonorous lines tend to come out as perfect epigrams, ready to be lifted out of their context and applied to an indefinite number of parallel situations."[21] Are Aeneas's famous words in praise of Carthage? Rome? Civilization in general? While the Carthaginians' empirical achievements are symbolic of Rome's future renovations and opulence in this particular simile, their cultural achievements are shown to differ when the ant simile is brought into contrast. What is Aeneas seeing? More importantly, what is the audience of the *Aeneid* being shown by its narrator? Its author?

Some possible answers to these questions may begin with Vergil's handling of the bees in book 4 of the *Georgics*. John Grant's article eventually moves to a discussion of allusions between the *Georgics* and the *Aeneid:* "The vocabulary in general of the ant simile is reminiscent of *Georgics* 4."[22] Grant's explorations eventually lead to the conclusion that Carthage's destiny is compromised by *amor* and Dido's misjudgment. The glory, splendor, and immortality of the bees will pass to the Trojans, as evidenced in *Aeneid* 7.68–70 with the portended "swarm of bees which settle on the sacred laurel in the palace of Latinus."[23] I would argue that there is a more complex argument to be made here. I believe that in a closer comparison with *Georgics* 4, Vergil's authorial voice with respect to Augustan Rome will subtly shift to a more critical one when the *Aeneid* is seen to follow Vergil's expression in the *Georgics*.

If the bee and ant similes in the *Aeneid* point to a difference in non-Roman and Roman values within an imperial new order, then Vergil's earlier description of beekeeping in *Georgics* 4 might help to verify or disallow such a statement. The *Georgics* as a whole is a dense and difficult poem to interpret. Book 4 is and has been the source of many different interpretations by many critics. However, I have found that Vergil's tone and development of the material do reveal enough for us to see an important shift between his work in the *Georgics* and in the *Aeneid*.

Like the *Aeneid*, *Georgics* 4 also presents the bees in a favorable light, as evidenced in lines 1–250. Their society is a productive one with enough surplus to feed others, including the human beekeeper and external predators. The beehive is constructed with soft materials close to the ground. It is open and vulnerable, with only the community's intense labor and efficiency to make up for its vulnerability to external threats. In lines 251–80, the bees' vulnerability to a plague is at times even too much for the beekeeper himself to make up for. Thus the unfortunate demise of the bee society leads to the history and description of the *bougonia* process and the creation of a new hive in lines 281–558. The second half of book 4 is concerned mainly with the finality of death and the possibility of resurrection through art, which is reinforced by the Orpheus tale told to Aristaeus by Proteus. In the *Aeneid*, the beehive (Carthage) is vulnerable to, and threatened by, external forces (Trojans and neighboring African tribes). The hive loses its queen (Dido) and begins to suffer. In *Georgics* 4, a new hive is created through the process of *bougonia*, which involves the sacrifice of a bull. The result is a swarm that forms like a "hanging cluster of grapes" (4.558). As Grant has pointed out in *Aeneid* 7.64–67, the Trojans' arrival in Italy coincides with the portent of a swarm of bees hanging from the topmost part of the sacred laurel tree. Yet at this point, literary tradition and context reveal some shocking distinctions.

The *Georgics* reveals a pattern of dark and light in the order of its four books. Especially in the last two books, the earthiness and mortality of live-stock contrast with the bees as a portent of the ideal human society. In book 3, according to Parry, "The transition at the end from animals to men makes explicit the symbolic purpose of the whole book. All existence, including human, is doomed, despite even our best labours, to annihila-tion," and the general forecast for humanity is pessimistic.[24] Of book 4, how-ever, Parry states, "It is left to the fourth book to find a resolution of the tension of the first three between the joy and beauty of nature and its ulti-mately destructive power."[25] The historical context of the *Georgics* comes at the heels of the Roman civil wars. Vergil's aim at the time of the *Georgics* may have been to show some realistic optimism before concluding his masterpiece: "They [the bees] are a faultless social organization, offering in this sense a corrective model to the chaos of human society."[26] In response to the limits of animals and men presented in book 3, Vergil seems to pre-sent a utopian answer in book 4 with the society of bees. This Platonic ideal stands in contrast to the reality of life on the ground, represented promi-nently by cattle in book 3. The *bougonia* process in 4.281–314 seems to com-bine the suffering of a bovine with the renaissance of the bee. Even with regard to the Aristaeus epyllion, Vergil surrounds the tragedy of Orpheus with the birth of the bee society.[27] In his years writing the *Georgics*, Vergil was very aware of, and concerned with, the violence of the civil wars. Yet the sense that some good can prevail for mankind seems itself to "rise above the herd" like a swarm of bees.

The *Aeneid* shows a similar "yin and yang," but with an overriding pes-simism rather than optimism. If *bougonia* eventually leads to new birth, the process itself is not without pain and suffering. Aeneas damages the beehive of Carthage, and Dido is symbolically sacrificed like the bull. Are the bees that settle on top of the laurel tree in book 7 of the *Aeneid* the result of *bougonia*? If so, then a personal price has been paid by Dido and Aeneas. If not, then what does this swarm symbolize if not what the *vates* (prophet) proclaims? Bees are used in various ways in the *Aeneid* as well as in other ancient literature: "Bees are, very occasionally, mentioned as symbols of rebirth, as Norden recalled in connection with *Aeneid* 6. 706ff, where the souls waiting to be reborn are likened to bees, though we must bear in mind that bees were symbolic of many other things also in antiquity."[28] As one of two portents that will bring unbridled civil war to Italy, the bee swarm may still be a symbol of rebirth (for Rome), but at what incredible cost? Perhaps the bee portent in book 7 is an allusion to Homer's *Iliad* 2.87–93, where the gathering Achaian armies are compared to an amorphous swarm of bees:

> Like the swarms of clustering bees that issue forever
> in fresh bursts from the hollow stone, and hang like
> bunched grapes as they hover beneath the flowers in springtime
> fluttering in swarms together this way and that way,
> so the many nations of men from the ships and the shelters
> along the front of the deep sea beach marched in order
> by companies to the assembly.[29]

This allusion would make much more sense at this moment of book 7 in the *Aeneid*. Instead of a peaceful and productive image of the hive as was portrayed earlier in book 4, the swarm may connote something else. As Hollingsworth notes:

> While the swarm may indeed hold within it a potential city, since it is less civilized than the hive, the swarm's action tends to be direct. Impatient and peripatetic, if it must labor, it does so in order that it may sustain or resume travel. To live, the swarm must gather what it needs but cannot produce. It may build, but what it makes cannot be permanent. It has been known to enslave or kill any who would interfere.[30]

This sort of allusion seems to recall the devastation of the ants rather than the production of the beehive. Furthermore, by the end of book 12, the

Aeneid does not portray the rebirth of an orderly society, which was only hinted at in book 8 with Aeneas's visit to Evander. The *Aeneid* instead ends with the final sacrifice of Turnus, which shows Vergil's focus to be on the pain and suffering associated with the *bougonia* at this point of his artistry, rather than the ultimate renaissance itself. Shouldn't Augustus's Pax Romana have brought about peace by the time of the *Aeneid's* composition? Why is Vergil potentially regressing to the violence of the civil wars? When will the *bougonia* result in the society represented by the bees for Rome? Has Vergil indeed become more pessimistic? Ultimately how will the Trojans settle with the Latins? We know from book 12 that Jupiter and Juno's pact sets the terms for peace. The Trojans will no longer be called Trojans but will be incorporated with the Ausonians (native Italians), who will also keep their language and way of life. The only contribution from the onetime Trojans is possibly their reverence for the gods (12.836–37). Is this any real victory for the Trojans? Will the *bougonia* result in a new swarm of bees? An eventual beehive? Or just another anthill? Vergil does not seem to wish to go that far in the *Aeneid*. In the *Georgics* 4.67–108, Vergil depicts two hives of bees at war with each other. One must fall to the other, but either way a race of bees prevails. In the *Aeneid*, bees are contrasted with ants as the ants are shown to prevail over the bees for the moment. If Carthage's beehive is really Augustan Rome, then yes, the *bougonia* will produce a new society of bees. If Carthage's beehive is instead interpreted as Carthaginian and non-Roman, then perhaps Rome's fate is ironically always to be on the outside looking in.

NOTES

1. Searching for the intersection of "insect" and "literature" in the classical world has been an ongoing struggle of mine since I began this project seven years ago, especially when I further limit "insect" to "bee and ant." The idea for this article originated in a high school AP Latin class that I had taught, but the roots of this idea must be traced farther back to my graduate school days. When Cris Hollingsworth and I attended Rutgers in the early 1990s, we must have fed from the same trough at some point. Recently, his *Poetics of the Hive: The Insect Metaphor in Literature* (Iowa City: University of Iowa Press, 2001) established a comprehensive and groundbreaking argument that stretches back to the Greco-Roman tradition. Some of my basic argument has already been addressed in his book, but my treatment here is much more selective and humble in its mission. Nevertheless, I owe a great deal to him for his encouragement and collegiality. I would also like to

recognize my colleague Ayaz Pirani's help and encouragement in proofreading my work, and many thanks to Eric Brown for his help and patience.

2. R. D. Williams writes that "apart from one example in Apollonius (4.1452f., where ants are mentioned briefly along with flies) this is the only simile in Greek or Latin epic concerned with ants." *The Aeneid of Virgil: Books 1–6* (Surrey, U.K.: St. Martin's, 1992), 369.

3. W. H. D. Rouse, trans., and Martin F. Smith, rev. trans., *De Rerum Natura* (Cambridge: Harvard University Press, 1975), book 3.9–12, p. 189.

4. Ibid., 4.678–80, pp. 328–29.

5. Section 3.16, to be exact. L. P. Wilkinson, *The Georgics of Virgil: A Critical Survey* (Norman: University of Oklahoma Press, 1997), 260–61n.

6. W. D. Hooper and H. B. Ash, trans., *Cato and Varro: On Agriculture* (Cambridge: Harvard University Press, 1935), 501. The "king" bee was not yet recognized as female at this time.

7. Dave Robinson and Judy Groves, *Introducing Plato* (Cambridge, U.K.: Totem Books, 2000), 100.

8. Paul Shorey, trans., *Republic*, vol. 2 (Cambridge: Harvard University Press, 1969), 267–69.

9. Ibid., 268. Shorey refers the reader in a footnote to a variety of authors: Plato's *Laws* 901a, Hesiod's *Works and Days* 300f., Aristophanes' *Wasps* 1071 ff., Euripides' *Suppl.* 242, Xenophon's *Oecon.* 17.15, and Virgil's *Georgics* 4.168.

10. Wilkinson, *The Georgics of Virgil*, 260.

11. "First the simile measures the gap between two aspects of the poetic text: on the one hand, the narrative in which the poet imagines himself engaged (along with his reader) in events of the twelfth century as they actually take place; on the other hand, the persona—by no means to be regarded as identical with the poet's personal identity as an individual—in which he is a poet occupied with poetic problems in the age of Augustus. Second, in virtue of the textual establishment of that gap, the simile represents the voice of the poet speaking in the authentic tones of a man of the Augustan age, redressing the events of the twelfth century B.C. by appeal to a timeless world which includes the age contemporary with the poet." Gordon Williams, *Techniques and Ideas in the Aeneid* (New Haven, Conn.: Yale University Press, 1983), 166.

12. "So Virgil repeatedly places the Rome of his own day in the long perspective of the legendary past, supplying here an historical justification for her contemporary hegemony." See D. A. West, "Multiple-Correspondence Similes," in *Oxford Readings in Vergil's "Aeneid,"* ed. S. J. Harrison (New York: Oxford University Press, 1990), 439.

13. The anachronism of "Carthage's" foundation coupled with Aeneas's admiration and Vergil's elaborate description of public works suggest something other than Carthage, that is, Vergil's own Rome. All English translations of Vergil are mine unless otherwise noted.

14. John Grant, "Dido Melissa," *Phoenix* 23, no. 4 (1969): 383.

15. Ibid., 384.

16. Ibid., 386.

17. The original Latin in the bee simile, "*fervet* opus redolentque thymo fragrantia mella" (1.436), compares with that of the ant simile, "opere omnis semita *fervet*" (4.407). I would also mention the word *semita* (path, lane), which can be found in book 1, albeit some lines before the bee simile: "Corripuere viam interea, qua semita monstrat" (1.418).

18. The specific correlations of English and Latin terms are numerous: the bees (*apes*) sequence has Dido looking down from a great height, while the ants (*formicae*) sequence has Dido looking down from a great height; the bees "*fervet* opus redolentque thymo fragrantia mella" (1.436), while the ants "opere omnis semita *fervet*" (4.407); spondees generally predominate in the quantitative meter of each of the sequences. The contrasts likewise reveal design: the bees are active in summer (*aestate*), in the countryside (*rura*), under the sun (*sole*), surrounded in a golden or bronze aura of light (*liquentia mella, aereus, aeneus, aureus*), while the ants are associated with winter (*hiems*), the city (*urbe*), and the dark (*nigrum*) line of their procession. The bees produce their own honey (*mella*), while the ants plunder others' grain (*farris*). A triad of verbs characterizes the activity of each: the bees raise and instruct their young (*educunt*) and pack and fill (*stipant, distendunt*) their cells, while the ants ravage (*populant*), store away (*reponunt*), and carry off (*convectant*) another's stock. Whereas Vergil pictures the bees receiving (*accipiunt*) each other's load in a cooperative assembly line process, the ants are shown using their energy to strenuously push (*trudunt*) their plunder along. As for efficiency and division of labor, the bees ward off (*arcent*) lazy drones, while the ants coerce (*cogunt*) subordinates to continue the work. Last, Vergil even juxtaposes the olfactory and visual senses by contrasting a fragrant image of bee honey "redolentque thymo fragrantia mella" (1.436) with the somewhat hasty, if not panic-stricken, sight of mass exodus: "migrantis cernas totaque ex urbe ruentis" (4.401).

19. Richard F. Thomas, ed., *Virgil: "Georgics,"* vol. 1 (New York: Cambridge University Press, 1990), 100. Indeed, the typical modern assessment of ants seems to follow this tradition. For example, according to Wilhelm Goetsch, "Most ant societies are organized for total warfare. . . . Fighting goes on constantly in nearly all ant colonies, mostly in single combats. Battles are continuously in progress on the borders of the colonies, which include not only the nest but the nearby hunting grounds." See Goetsch, *The Ants* (Ann Arbor: University of Michigan Press, 1957), 41. In fact, a specific species of ants is particularly ruthless: "The workers of the blood-red ant are as fierce as the queen. Large troops of them invade the nests of other ants and kidnap the pupae, which they either eat immediately or store away for food. If the pupae belong to certain closely related species, however, the invaders carry them off to their own nest to add to the number of helpers [also called 'slaves' elsewhere in the text]" (ibid., 33).

Likewise, O. W. Richards, in *The Social Insects* (New York: Harper and Brothers, 1961), portrays the bees in a more favorable light: "[The honey bee has] been domesticated by man from at least the time of the early Egyptians, and an immense body of tradition and literature has grown up around them" (103); and again, "The honey bee is thus committed to a completely social life, since the queen cannot found a colony alone like a queen humble bee, while the workers cannot normally reproduce themselves" (105). Like Dido, the queen's and her subjects' fates are intertwined.

20. Grant, "Dido Melissa," 385.

21. Adam Parry, "The Two Voices of Virgil's *Aeneid*," in *Virgil: A Collection of Critical Essays*, ed. Steele Commager (Englewood Cliffs, N.J.: Prentice Hall, 1966), 118.

22. Grant, "Dido Melissa," 385.

23. Ibid., 391.

24. Adam Parry, "The Idea of Art in Virgil's *Georgics*," in *Modern Critical Views: Virgil*, ed. Harold Bloom (New York: Chelsea House, 1986), 92.

25. Ibid., 93.

26. Ibid.

27. Gordon Williams, in *Techniques and Ideas*, refers to Brooks Otis in this quotation: "The Aristaeus framework is in an objective Homeric style and the Orpheus-Eurydice insert is subjective and highly emotional; its moral impact (as Otis points out) is that Aristaeus learns to do the correct thing and is successful while Orpheus' visit to the underworld ends in disaster because of his failure to observe the conditions required" (212).

28. Wilkinson, *The Georgics of Virgil*, 118.

29. Richmond Lattimore, *The Iliad of Homer* (Chicago: University of Chicago Press, 1967), 78.

30. Hollingsworth, *Poetics of the Hive*, 18.

3

Performing Insects in Shakespeare's *Coriolanus*

ERIC C. BROWN

Not once does Shakespeare ever use the term "insect," and almost all his "bugs" are shorthand for "bugbears": nagging, disturbing, even terrifying creatures akin, as Reginald Scot made clear, to "spirits, witches, urchens, elves, hags, fairies . . . and such other bugs."[1] So Hamlet, "such bugs and goblins in my life" (5.2.22), and Petruchio, "Tush, tush, fear boys with bugs" (1.2.210), are alternately disturbed by, and dismissive of, creatures from folklore rather than the "creeping things" of Genesis.[2] Nonetheless, the idea of the insect proves a stimulant for a number of Shakespeare's plays (Robert Patterson first detailed the swarm of Shakespeare's allusions "not to eulogise the writings of Shakespeare, but to bring before you the habits of such insects as he has named"), not least because of the relationship of insects to drama itself.[3] The relationship is partly embedded in the etymology: the Greek root "en-toma," whence "insect," was applied by Aristotle to capture the most important identifying characteristic of these creatures: segmentation. These segmented forms bear the residue of performativity: "entoma" denotes something "cut into pieces," and was most often used by other classical authors to convey the hewn fragments involved in ritual sacrifice. The transferral of this religious enterprise into a theatrical one can be read in the *sparagmos* of classical drama—or the sort of sacred cutting that the sons of Shakespeare's Titus Andronicus make of the captive Alarbus when his "limbs are lopped" (1.1.143).[4] Theatrically, the ritual of sparagmos further suggests a violent rendering of the multiplicity of personae, comically restabilized or tragically disarrayed. But in what moment or place or physicality is the human

29

being ever whole unto itself? Augustine extended this question to collective divinity: "Do single things contain single parts, greater things containing greater parts and smaller things smaller parts? . . . Or are you [God] entire in all places?"[5] For Shakespeare, the divisibility of the human becomes reimagined as a question not of form but of performance.

The taxonomy of divisibility had, for Aristotle, more to do with insect survival than their sacrificial value, since he considered each individual section of the insect an independently controlled part that could express the whole even when separated from it. Indeed, this is the foremost of three reasons Aristotle adduces for the "insected" bodies: first, "these creatures have several sources of control; and on that account they have the 'insections' in their bodies"; second, "so that they may curl up and thus escape injury and remain safe. . . . Those that do not roll up increase their hardness by closing up the insections"; and third, because they possess an additional survival mechanism: "Plants can live when they are cut up; so can insects."[6] Thus in addition to their processional life cycle, a tripartite progress of larva, chrysalis, and adult, insects are always already self-differentiated, synecdochical, embodying the expression of the whole by the part.[7] It is to these shifting forms, the slippage of one identity into another, that Shakespeare was repeatedly drawn.[8] He might have been prompted, as well, by the increasing materialization of insects onstage in the early modern period, a development yet to be fully noticed by current criticism of animals and the Renaissance theater. Finally, it is in *Coriolanus* that Shakespeare's insect poetics are most fully realized. This tragedy of a Roman warrior embraced, elevated, and ultimately erased is partly predicated not only on Aristotelian ideas of entomology, on the repercussions of the part's complicated relation to the whole, but on the natural history of insects burgeoning around the time of the play's composition.

PERFORMING INSECTS

The paradoxes of insect metamorphosis are summed up succinctly in *Coriolanus* when Menenius observes, "There is a difference between a grub and a butterfly, yet your butterfly was a grub" (5.4.11–12). These transmutations, for many early modern writers, came to suggest performance itself: the costuming that allows a butterfly to seem a grub, and vice versa, and finally the maturation of an individual over time, in which multiple anthropomorphic parts are played. (Jacques's division of "the ages of man" in *As You Like It* imparts to human beings these same discrete sections.) Robert Greene, in his sartorial satire *A Quippe for an Upstart Courtier* (1592), concludes a long list of professionals and their attire with three figures who must perform for their livelihood: a Poet, who thinks gentlemen "beholding to him if he do but bestowe a fair looke," a Player, who "trot[s] to the stage," and finally a Musician, "a leader into all misrule."[9] Accompanying the Player, more-over, are "two boies in cloakes like butterflies: carrying one of them his cutting sword of choller, the other his daucing rapier of delight."[10] That the Player's boys should inhabit butterfly cloaks, indeed that the Player should have such valets at all, suggests on the one hand the ostentation of the actor, whose apparel is later described as like that of "peacockes and painted asses."[11] Shakespeare uses a similar trope in *King Lear* when Lear tells Cordelia, "So we'll live, / And pray, and sing, and tell old tales, and laugh / At gilded butterflies, and hear poor rogues / Talk of court news" (5.3.11–14), where the "gilded butterflies" double for the giddy vicissitudes of courtly life, both superficial and, with an eye to the proverbial "gilded lily," superfluous.[12] But the cloaks also convey a sense of the shifting iden-tities inherent in play: the butterfly-boys signify with their "choler" and "delight" the masks of tragedy and comedy; and the Player must be ver-satile enough for both the "cutting sword" and the "dancing." These various personae, Greene suggests, are kaleidoscopic covers, and the wings of but-terflies emblematize not only Greene's criticism of gaudy performers living beyond their means but also the metamorphic instability of acting itself.[13] Moreover, Greene helpfully underscores two traditional readings of butter-flies: one as ornament of delight—fragile, prettified, sometimes resplen-dent—and one as threatening, mortal, even choleric.[14] In short, the cloaks of the Player's boys form themselves a winged diptych, and the poetics of these contrasting representations can be see operating even more com-pletely in Shakespeare's *Coriolanus,* which draws on the lore of butterflies as signifiers of both fragility and martial destructiveness.

Equally important for Shakespeare's conception of an insect poetics were the actual performances of insects themselves, on the stages and in the streets of London. Thomas Moffet borrows from the dramatic tradition for the title of his compendium *The Theater of Insects,* first licensed in 1590, in which he conceives of insects as even more spectacular than other animals being paraded on the English scene:

It is common to the English and to all mankinde, who that they may see
those large beasts that carry towers, the African lion, the huge Whale, the
Rhinocerous, the Bear and Bull, take sometimes a long journey to London,
and pay money for their places on the scaffold, to behold them brought upon
the stage: yet where is nature more to be seen than in the smallest matters,
where she is entirely all? for in great bodies the workmanship is easie, the
matter being ductile; but in these that are so small and despicable, and almost
nothing, what care? how great is the effect of it? how unspeakable is the
perfection?[15]

The tradition of performing animals can be traced back to the medieval
court, where, as E. K. Chambers notes, minstrels often "came in masked
as animals, and played the dog, the ass or the bird with appropriate noises
and behaviour"; this in turn led to the presentation of "real animals: generally bears or apes, occasionally also horses, cocks, hares, dogs, camels and
even lions. Sometimes these beasts did tricks; too often they were baited,
and from time to time a man, lineal descendant of the imperial gladia-
tors, would step forward to fight with them."[16] By the seventeenth century,
these displays increasingly reflected the colonial impulse to collect and
parade exotica. Henry Farley, in *St. Paules-Church Her Bill for the Parlia-
ment* (1621), offers a critique of the traveling menageries, which at once
comprised a popular aspect of public spectacle and shared space and attention with touring players: "To see a strange out-landish Fowle, / a quaint
Baboon, an Ape, an Owle, / A dancing Beare, a Gyants bone, / . . . / Or Players acting on a Stage, / There goes the bounty of our Age."[17] And Henry
Herbert, as master of revels, records such creatures as camels, an elk, a lion,
an elephant, a "*strange fish*," "a live Beavr & a Racoon," and "an outland-
ish creature called a *Possum*" among the seventeenth-century attractions
licensed for presentation.[18] Even native English species could find stardom:
in 1623, William Reece and Thomas Gittins were allowed to "make shewe of
a strange Ratt for a yeare."[19] Yet the attraction for extraordinary fauna more
often took center stage, and this could extend to the insect world: Aphra
Behn reports in *Oroonoko, or The Royal Slave* (1688) how she contributed
to the king's collection of curiosities, "his Majesty's Antiquary," by offering
"some rare Flies, of amazing Forms and Colours, presented to 'em by my
self; some as big as my Fist, some less; and all of various Excellencies, such as
art cannot imitate."[20] Behn underscores the recurrent difference attributed

to insects by Moffet and others: their small size defies artistic represen-tation in a way not evident in other animals. This proves especially the case when analyzing their appearance in the shared human/animal space of the stage.

Perhaps the most famous example of staged insects is the flea circus. Though its amalgam of vaudeville patter, tiny costumes, trapeze, and can-non is widely thought of as a Victorian fashion, various literati composed numerous celebrations of fleas and other insects as performers during the late sixteenth century and early seventeenth.[21] The enthused Moffet, for instance, writes of the flea, "They have . . . a very short neck, to which one *Mark* an *Englishman* (most skilfull in all curious work) fastned a Chain of Gold as long as a man's finger, with a lock and key so rarely and cunningly, that the Flea could easily go and draw them, yet the Flea, the Chain, lock and key were not all above a grain weight: I have also heard from men of credit, that this Flea so tied with a Chain, did draw a Coach of Gold that was every way perfect, and that very lightly; which much sets forth the Artists skill, and the Fleas strength" (1101).[22] A more renowned performing flea was not, as "Mark the Englishman's," a flea of flesh, blood, and neck, but a mechanical contrivance. Moffet's 1599 treatise on the silkworm offers one manifestation: "Nay, for to speake of things more late and rife, / Who will not more admire those famous Fleas, / Mad so by art, that art imparted life, / Making them skippe, and on mens hands to seaze, / And let out bloud with taper-poynted knife, / Which from a secret sheathe ranne out with ease: / The those great coches which themselves did drive, / With bended scrues, like things that were alive?"[23] The competing representations of these fleas, both natural and artificial, point to an important theatrical split between "real" fleas and their illusory cousins: those "flea circuses" that use no actual insects but rather play on the willing belief (or myopia) of the spectator. The movements of the circus are mechanical, the flea an imag-ined adjunct.[24] The display, if not the training, of fleas for the modern nat-ural flea circus seems to have changed little in four hundred years:

Typically, flea performers are *Pulex irritans*, the human flea—females are preferred at least partly because, being larger, they're more visible. Tradition-ally, would-be flea circus operators . . . begin their training by enclosing them in bottles underneath a light. Sensitive to both light and heat, the enclosed fleas tend to remain in the bottom of the bottle. After a while, the cork in the bottle is replaced by a glass cover; fleas that jump and hit the glass cover gradually habituate to jumping only a particular height. . . . After about a two-week training period, the fleas are ready for the stage. They can be hooked up with fine tiny wires to wagons or coaches, dressed up as historical personalities, or equipped with tiny swords for mock battles. Some audiences were invited to view the performances under a magnifying glass. . . . The end of the performance is traditionally marked by the owner offering the performers a hearty meal—on his arm—in full view of the audience.[25]

In particular, the appearance of the "wagons and coaches," the "mock battles," and the final reversion to "natural" flea behavior—the consumption of human blood—maintain patterns of performance evident in those presented by Moffet. Peter Stallybrass and Allon White's perspicacious reading of the performing animals brought to London fairs applies equally to the early modern flea. Speaking of creatures such as a "little Marmoset" who "dances with 2 Naked Sowrds," they remark, "when we look closely at the acts and the little performances which these creatures are taught to do, we can see that they play with the thresholds of culture in an interesting fashion. . . . In each case the manners taught imitate European forms of culture or politeness and amusingly transgress, as well as reaffirm, the boundaries between high and low, human and animal, domestic and savage, polite and vulgar."[26] Insects add to these "transgressive affirmations" the boundary between real and imagined, the very embodiment of the theater.

The popularity of insects as Renaissance *jongleurs* is attested to in Jonson's *The Alchemist* (1616).[27] When Lovewit, the play's "master of the house," who has temporarily vacated to escape the plague, returns to his home, left meanwhile in the hands of his servant and lately transformed into a well-visited den of various iniquities, he wonders at the crowd gathered before it:

What should my knave advance,
To draw this companie? He hung out no banners
Of a strange Calfe, with five legs, to be seene?
Or a huge Lobster, with six clawes?

Nor heard a drum strooke, for Babiouns, or Puppets?

Sure he has got
Some bawdy pictures, to call all this ging;
The Frier, and the Nun; or the new Motion
Of the Knights courser, covering the Parsons mare;
The Boy of six yeere old, with the great thing:
Or 't may be, he has the Fleas that runne at tilt,
Upon a table, or some Dog to daunce? (5.1.6–9, 14, 20–26)

Most of this inventory of low-class entertainments involves some form of prodigious bestiality—the display of exotic or marvelous animals, from the grotesque calf and lobster to the baboons and dancing dogs, the "new" puppetry of two horses copulating. Two additionally parody plays and courtly entertainment: the priapic "Boy of sixe" likely alludes to *The Knight of the Burning Pestle*, while the "Fleas that runne at tilt upon a table" reduce the proportions of chivalry even further. The knights are now minuscule fleas, their "great things" the miniature lances for a tiny joust. The sequence of marvels and spectacles here includes most of what Jonson disliked, including the preponderance of puppet shows. But the popularity of insect entertainments such as flea shows was not limited to the lower classes (despite the fact that in England today, a "fleapit" still refers to "a cheap or squalid theater").[28] As with many of the items in Lovewit's accounting, insects as performers often shared space with plays and drew attention from literate and popular audiences. As Erica Fudge and Bruce Boehrer have detailed, such shared accommodations at once erase and reinforce the line between human and nonhuman.[29] At a basic level, anthropomorphic insects often informed dramatic characterization: Jonson's Mosca, the "fly," in *Volpone*, or even more readily "Fly" in *The New Inn*.[30] (In pronunciation, "flea" and "fly" were commonly homonymic.) Shakespeare's Moth in *Love's Labor's Lost* seems an analogue to Jonson's parasites, even if "moth" is taken to indicate a tiny "mote" rather than the insect itself. But a number of Shakespeare's plays involve the staging of insects outright, a device that draws on the energies of the performing fleas even as the plays make bolder connections between the insect and the theater.[31]

Though neither Fudge nor Boehrer discusses the staging of insects, both underscore the conflation of animals and humans in performance space and in anthropomorphic persona. Fudge's insightful reading of the theatricality of bear gardens, which included not only bears and dogs but apes costumed as men, provokes some comparisons with the flea circus, which also relies on an anthropomorphism such that "the spectator was invited to perform two acts of recognition: to recognise the anthropoid nature of the animal, but also to recognise that anthropoid only ever means human-like, it can never mean human."[32] So Jonson, in his critique of fleas that run at tilts, relies on the distancing of this image from reality to assert its ridiculousness. Boehrer too argues that the lines between human and animal are blurred; he asks, for instance, "If even so unsophisticated an organism as a bee can communicate information to other bees . . . to what extent can language be viewed as an exclusively human property?"[33] The staging of insects introduces a number of hermeneutic tangles, however, including their presence in the first place. What, for instance, of the fly-killing episode in *Titus Andronicus?* Ought a performance to maintain a stable of expendable *Drosophila* understudies? Or should such representations be emptily mimed, time after time, with the buzz of *Musca domestica* artificially contrived or imagined, an absence comparable to the flea circus without fleas? Similarly, among the "properties" in *The Merry Wives of Windsor* for the final deceit of Falstaff, the fairy masque, how literally can one take the directive of Hugh Evans, "And twenty glow-worms shall our lanthorns be" (5.3.78)? After purchasing the silk and vizards, should the masquers try for fairy verisimilitude with real insects lighting their way, certainly an eerier luminescence for the "tricking" of Falstaff than straightforward lantern light? The latter instance, in fact, works to bridge the worlds of insect and theater: Chambers describes the "cressets" that illuminated the Elizabethan stage as "baskets of tarred and flaring rope," homologous versions of Hugh Evans's glowworm lanterns.[34] These "flaring ropes" are also suggested by Shakespeare's other reference to the glowworm, in *A Midsummer Night's Dream:* Titania charges her fairies, "The honey-bags steal from the humble-bees, / And for night-tapers crop their waxen thighs, / And light them at the fiery glow-worm's eyes" (3.1.168–70). Either of these sinuous sources of fire—ropes and worms—complicates the metadramatic finale in *The Merry Wives of Windsor,* collapsing the difference between theater and play and inscribing the theater, too, as an analogously insective space.[35]

The appearance of insects within the theater may also be self-reflexive. In the spaces that doubled as bear pits, which Jonson in his induction to *Bartholomew Fair* described as "being as durty as Smithfield, and as stinking every whit" (ind. 159–60), flies were at least as available as the bears themselves. Are insects, then, animals that are always onstage? Does Crab in *The Two Gentlemen of Verona,* or even Petruchio's horse in *The Taming of the Shrew* (with an infestation "so begnawn with the bots" [3.2.54–55]), presuppose a host of assorted parasites?[36] Certainly they were part of the material construction of the plays themselves: as Fudge notes, the vellum on which works were written is an animal product; the ink itself, moreover, derives from the insect and the excrescent gall it produces on trees like the oak. Shakespeare recites the ingredients twice, in *Twelfth Night* 3.2.52 ("gall enough in thy ink") and in *Cymbeline* 1.1.101 ("though ink be made of gall"). The material role of the insect in the written word, however, belies its most insidious effect on the theater: the shutting of its doors. It is difficult for a modern reading to escape the sinister subtext of Mistress Ford in *The Merry Wives of Windsor,* for instance, who could defend her home by proclaiming, "If you find a man there, he shall die a flea's death" (4.2.150–51), without knowing how many were dying "a flea's death" as the result of their spreading plague and contagion. Shakespeare's dramatization in *1 Henry IV* of "the most villainous house in all London road for fleas" (2.1.14–15) further registers the very conditions that had led to the flea-carried plague closing the theaters themselves only a few years earlier.[37] Though of course unaware of the part insects played in the plague, Shakespeare nevertheless draws frequently on insects for the anxieties they produce. The sanguine attacks of fleas work as an interpretive model for reading other anxieties over insects that reach a height in *Coriolanus*: the one outnumbered by the many, the organic collective threatened by invasion and disruption, aggression and evacuation, and finally the anagogical associations of insects as signifiers of apocalyptic ends.

Butterflies and Dragons in *Coriolanus*

As a number of critics have pointed out, the opening of *Coriolanus* and its politicization of desperate hunger is significantly informed by both the Midlands Revolt of 1607 and insufferable dearth in England the following year. The initial uprisings were sparked by the meteoric price of grain as well as enclosure acts that truncated arable land for pasture, and the threat of rebellion extended well into 1608.[38] A paucity of available corn is also part of the classical Coriolanus narrative, but two possible sources have been overlooked in explicating the famine with which the play begins. The

first, a plague of insects vividly described in the Old Testament, parallels
in its prophesied attack the destructive power not only of widespread starvation but of Coriolanus himself, who threatens the massacre of Roman
and barbarian alike. The second, Edward Topsell's *The History of Serpents*,
first appeared in 1608 (a year after his *History of Four-Footed Beasts*) and
seems to have shaped Shakespeare's treatment of insects in the play. Taken
together, these texts establish a discourse in which insects are no longer
valued for their small size, or their popular appeal, but rather feared for
their fierce martiality, their consuming appetite, and their mobbing numbers. When Menenius paints Coriolanus late in the play as a metamorphic
creature, one whose transformation mimics but also supersedes the lepidopteran cycle, it is this discourse he evokes: "There is a differency between
a grub and a butterfly, yet your butterfly was a grub. This Martius is grown
from man to dragon: he has wings, he's more than a creeping thing" (5.4.11–
14). The sense here is quite close to that of Topsell's *History of Serpents:* "For
although a worm afterwards be not that thing which before it was, (so far
as is apparent to outward sense), yet for any thing we can gather or perceive, it is that which it was, and this *That,* is more by a great deal now
then before it was" (668). Part of the tragedy of *Coriolanus* is crediting this
"*That*" with difference while failing to account for its similitude to what
was. As Janet Adleman and others have pointed out, Coriolanus's complicated maternal anxieties generate a flux in his character, oscillating between
undeveloped boy and overdetermined man.[39] The insectivity of Coriolanus,
similarly, is deployed both in his self-destructivity (his Aristotelian ideas of
self-sufficiency even when fragmented, parted) and in his drive to destroy
or devour others.[40]

The book of Joel provides a narrative that Shakespeare may be evoking
to underscore this devouring drive, as well as the problematic deification,
of Coriolanus. One of the plagues in Exodus, of course, is a swarm of all-
consuming grasshoppers, those that "eat all your trees that bud in the field"
and "all the herbes of the land" (Exod. 10.5, 12). In Joel, the plague, by which
"the field is wasted: the land mourneth: for the corne is destroyed" (Joel
1.10), is comprised of manifold insects: "That which is left of the palmer
worme, hathe the grashopper eaten, and the residue of the grashopper hathe
the canker worme eaten, and the residue of the canker worme hathe the
caterpiller eaten" (Joel 1.4). They are harbingers of final judgment and are
repulsed only at the entreaty of the penitent: "Gather the people: sanctifie

the congregacion, gather the Elders: assemble the children, and those that sucke the breasts: let the bridegrome go forthe of his chambre, and the bride out of her bride chambre. Let the Priests, the ministers of the Lord wepe betwene the porche and the altar, and let them say, Spare thy people, o Lord, and given not thine heritage into reproche that the heathen shulde rule over them" (Joel 2.16–17). In consequence of this salvation from the heathen army, figured as hordes of worms and caterpillars, the people of Judah celebrate the "remove farreof" of the "Northren armie" and are later ready to answer Joel's exhortation: "Breake your plowshares into swordes, and your sieths into speares: let the weake saie, I am strong" (Joel 3.10). While much of this rhetoric is fairly common in the biblical narratives of threat, repentance, and salvation, the structure parallels the progress of Coriolanus as a deified instrument of condemnation, famine, and destruction. At the start of the play, the citizens conceptualize the patricians as a devouring force, such that "If the wars eat us not up, they will" (1.1.85), while Menenius revisits the biblical analogue of divine force: "For the dearth, / The gods, not the patricians, make it, and / Your knees to them (not arms) must help" (1.1.72–74). And Shakespeare's peasants borrow from Joel's compelling transformation of plowshares into swords, scythes to spears, for their own instruction: "Let us revenge this with our pikes, ere we become rakes" (1.1.22–23).

As Shakespeare could have learned from Topsell, these voracious plagues were the provenance not solely of locusts and grasshoppers but of butterflies as well.[41] Moffet makes clear that a number of butterfly "wars" were carried out in the sixteenth century:[42]

Wert thou as strong as *Milo* or *Hercules,* and wert fenced or guarded about with an host of Giants for force and valour; remember that such an Army was put to the worst by an army of Butterflies flying in Troops in the air, in the year 1104. and they hid the light of the sun like a cloud. *Licosthenes* relates, that on the third day of *August,* 1543. that no hearb was left by reason of their multitudes, and they had devoured all the sweet dew and natural moisture, and they had burn'd up the very grasse that was consumed with their dry dung. Also in the year 1553. as *Sleidanus* reports, a little before the death of *Mauritius,* the Duke of *Saxony,* an infinite Army of Butterflies flew through great part of *Germany,* and did infect the grasse, herbs, trees, houses and garments of men with bloudy drops, as though it had rained bloud.[43]

Yet another hemorrhaging recurred in Aix-la-Chapelle, France, in 1608, deduced by the naturalist Nicholas-Claude Fabri de Peiresc to have come from the excrescence of butterflies. The desiccating effects of these swarms, "devouring all the sweet dew," replicate anxieties over dearth and hunger common in the discourse of insect armies, while the gory, blood-spattered invasions add to this an appalling materiality, one intermingled with even the "houses and garments of men." The penetrating blood challenges the inherent separability of human and insect, so that it is not only devastation that is feared but loss of a distinct corporeality. Topsell's *History of Serpents*, however, provides the closest analogue for the swarm effect in *Coriolanus*: "In the year of our Lord GOD 1570. there were two great and sudden swarms of Caterpillers that came rushing into *Italy* in the space of one Summer, which put the *Romans* into an exceeding great fear, for there was nothing left green in all their fields that could be preserved from their ravine, and from their gluttonous and pilling maw."[44] Such a passage may have drawn Shakespeare's attention for its conjoining in the city of Rome an attack, famine, and a ravenous opponent. As with Coriolanus's march into Rome, which prompts Aufidius to plot, "When, Caius, Rome is thine, / Thou art poor'st of all; then shortly art thou mine" (4.7.56–57), the caterpillars provoke an admonition from Topsell: "We may be warned by other mens punishments, lest that poor creature, which we imagine to be the silliest and least able to do us harm, we finde the most heavy" (671). Shakespeare writes on numerous occasions of such voracity (e.g., *2 Henry VI*: "Thus are my blossoms blasted in the bud, / And caterpillars eat my leaves away" [3.1]), but it is Coriolanus, in his circulation of grub and butterfly, who embodies the energies contained in Joel and Topsell.

While Menenius's "Fable of the Belly" has drawn a full helping of commentary, both for its seemingly ill-chosen metaphor of the stomach as a means to quell the rumblings of the hungry Roman citizens and for its failure to accommodate the complex politics of either the ancient or Jacobean worlds, less has been made of Coriolanus's tacit role in the fable's failure.[45] The fable's concern for the part's relation to the whole clearly encompasses a number of other thematics—division, apportionment—applicable to Coriolanus and the rest of his Roman society. Martius's condemnation of the mutinous masses, however, makes mention early on of another device that will inscribe his own position as supernumerary: "Trust ye? / With every minute you do change a mind, / And call him noble, that was now your hate; / Him vild, that was your garland" (1.1.181–84). The reference to the garland is a self-reference, since a few scenes later he is "crown'd with an oaken garland" (2.1.162 s.d.).[46] The oak he bears further intensifies the conspicuous display of consumption by the patricians. For while, as Plutarch notes, the oak was given to one "that had saved a cittizens life," for which heroism in battle Shakespeare's Coriolanus "prov'd best man i' th' field, and for his meed / Was brow-bound with the oak" (2.3.97–98), it also signifies abundance and nourishment.[47] In fact, Plutarch offers several possible reasons for the oak as a fitting reward, the last that oak was "thought amongst other wilde trees to bring forth a profitable fruite, and of plantes to be the strongest" (145–46). Volumnia embraces this latter aspect when early in the play she recalls how her son returned from "a cruel war" with "his brows bound with oak" (1.2.13–15), a suggestion of fortitude as much as honor. But Plutarch augments the oak as a signifier perhaps foremost of provision: "Moreover, men at the first beginning dyd use akornes for their bread, and honie for their drincke: and further, the oke dyd feede their beastes, and geve them birdes, by taking glue from the okes, with which they made birdlime" (146). Thus the adornment of Coriolanus with the oak gestures beyond his martial prowess: his appearance is a constant and ironic reminder to the citizens that Coriolanus has the power to provide for them. In its association with honey, in particular, the oak for Coriolanus is yet another mark of his insectivity, in this case as a kind of presiding king of the hive, under whom, as in *Henry V,* the ideal commonwealth serves. The wreath is thus a tantalizing display of plenty in a time of dearth, and even its material promise of acorns flaunts the people's lack of corn. The absence of both acorns and corn, indeed, may be the most materially significant lack in the play. In Plutarch, the oaken cornucopia immediately gives way to Coriolanus's own unsated desires, even as it feeds the image: "It is daylie seene, that honour and reputation lighting on young men before their time, and before they have no great corage by nature: the desire to winne more, dieth straight in them, which easely happeneth, the same having no deepe roote in them before. Where contrariwise, the first honour that valliant mindes do come unto, doth quicken up their appetite" (146). The valiant Coriolanus, then, whose appetite is quickened by the honors he receives, and whose courage and desire are both "rooted," represents competing energies. To the citizens, his very brow is a reminder that they, by the sweat of theirs, toil fruitlessly, while Coriolanus withdraws and isolates the very nourishment they seek. To himself, his garland is only a reminder of a greater lack, a limitless desire for reward that in its unquenchability contributes to his bellicose devouring of the surrounding lands.[48] All this becomes explicit in Plutarch's narrative when Coriolanus later leaves Rome to invade the Antiates and takes by force "great plenty of corne, and had a marvelous great spoyle" (157–58), with which he and his men return laden to Rome to the offense of those "hometarriers and housedoves" still without (158). But Shakespeare submerges this episode in other conspicuous displays of consumption.

Later in act 1, young Martius is driven to destroy a "gilded butterfly" (1.3.60–61), though his motivations are unclear. Valeria confesses, "Whether his fall enrag'd him, or how 'twas, he did so set his teeth and tear it. O, I warrant, how he mammock'd it!" (1.3.63–64). The boy's aggressions are further likened to those of his father, since "he had rather see the swords and hear a drum than look upon his schoolmaster" (1.3.55–56). These various drives are replicated in his father, or as Gail Kern Paster put it, "it is possible to see the young Martius in this context tearing apart the butterfly with his teeth as a training exercise for the heartier fare and bloodier appetite of the grown fighter."[49] The vulnerability of the flies is later exploited in a speech by Cominius that collapses the difference between the old and young Martius: "He is their god; he leads them like a thing / Made by some other deity than Nature, / That shapes man better; and they follow him / Against us brats with no less confidence / Than boys pursuing summer butterflies, / Or butchers killing flies" (4.6.90–95). The two scenes develop each other further, since young Martius is really the grub of his winged father, and his obliteration of the ostentatious fly, who rises, falls, escapes, and is caught over and over again, can also be seen as an ominous sign of the Coriolanus butterfly's eventual destruction, even as it is prompted by his own bloodline in the figure of Volumnia.[50] The other side of Menenius's analogy works here: every grub is also a butterfly, and where Cominius sees the Romans as butterflies pursued by a band of boys intent on mammocking them, Menenius elevates the fly to conqueror; the Romans are debased further, both as the grubs to Coriolanus's butterfly and as men subject to the wings of a "dragon." The passage parallels Gloucester's simile in *King Lear*, "As flies are to wanton boys are we to th' gods, / They kill us for their sport" (4.1.36–37), and there is an element of whimsy to the killing in Gloucester's rhetoric that inheres for the young Martius as well.

The mammocking of the butterfly invites a number of interpretive angles: appetite, destruction, solitariness. Indeed, Valeria has served as spectator to his butterfly play, and yet she can tell nothing of his motivations: does he destroy the creature out of anger, embarrassment, or simply curiosity?[51] The exact nature of this "mammocking" adds a further dimension. The *OED* cites *Coriolanus* as the first use of the word as a verb, deriving from "mammock," originally "a scrap, shred, broken or torn piece." The word, moreover, seems especially to connote the kind of table scraps one finds as remains after a meal: the first cited use, for instance, is John Skelton's in *Colin Cloute* (1529): "When mammockes was your meate, with moldy bread to eat" (654).[52] That Martius should "set his teeth" to the creature is highly suggestive of entomophagy, or the eating of insects. The precedent for such behavior is partly biblical: the Mosaic laws allow that "of everie foule that crepeth, and goeth upon all foure which have their fete and leggs all of one to leape withall upon the earth, Of them ye shal eat these, the grashoper after his kinde, and the solean after his kinde, the hargol after his kinde, and the hagab after his kinde."[53] The grasshoppers and their kin—various species of locusts—were the sole insect exceptions, however, as "everie creping thing therefore that crepeth upon the earth shalbe an abomination, and not be eaten" (Lev. 11.41). The proscribed menu is echoed in the New Testament, when John the Baptist is detailed: "And this John had his garment of camels heere, and a girdle of skin about his loynes: his meat was also locustes & wilde honie" (Matt. 3.4). The Geneva Bible glosses this passage as an extension of Leviticus 11 and 22, with John feeding on "such meates as nature broght forthe without mans labour or diligence."[54] Should the skittish butterfly be cataloged as "more than a creeping thing," or is Martius's act additionally transgressive, flouting biblical dispensations about what he puts in his mouth? The destruction and possible devouring of the butterfly, one of a number of gustatory references in the play, resonate further with the fable of the belly. While peasants starve for grain, young Martius eats the refined and the beautiful. The consumption becomes a transgressive act against the city-state, even as Martius consumes out of anger rather than need, and perhaps too against performance. When the first citizen laments, "We are accounted poor citizens, the patricians good. What authority surfeits on would relieve us. If they would yield us but the superfluity while it were wholesome, we might guess they relieved us humanely" (1.1.15–19), his words foreshadow young Martius's violatory act, feeding on the utterly superfluous—the gilded wings of the butterflies that for Shakespeare, as for Greene's player boys, are almost always sallied forth for their excess.

The movements of the butterfly, traced vividly in the young Martius's pursuit—"and after it, and over and over he comes, and up again," until an apparent fall—are recast in Valeria's visualization of Virgilia. "You would be another Penelope" (1.3.82), she tells her, evoking the spinning and un-spinning of Penelope's threads, the unceasing rhythm of ascent and descent captured in Valeria's earlier account of Martius. The raveling and unravel-ing explicitly recalls those lines when Valeria further notes: "Yet they say, all the yarn she spun in Ulysses' absence did but fill Ithaca full of moths" (13.82–84). By turning Penelope's industrious fidelity into a kind of Tartar-ean punishment, eternally recycled and naively unproductive, eliciting only moths that consume her very work—Valeria's play on Penelope's suitors, who are themselves eventually massacred—she recollects that gilded but-terfly whose graceful movements lead ultimately to a fall and violent un-doing. Valeria here also plays with the idea of moths as emblems for the dangers of attraction and unbridled desire. A common aphorism for men drawn to superficial beauty uses moths and candles: Moffet advises, "O fool! remember the fate of the *Phalena* butterfly, which being invited by the light of the candle, as by a fair beauty, is consumed by the flame it fell in love withall" (975). In *Shakespeare and the Emblem Writers* (London, 1870), Henry Green supplies from Corrozet's *Hecatomgraphie* (Paris, 1540) another motto more befitting the action of *Coriolanus*: "The Butterflies themselves are about to burn / In the candle which still shines on and warms; / Such foolish, wish to battle fields to turn, / Who know not of the war, how much it harms." Here the butterfly soldiers of Moffet and Topsell have become further anthropomorphized: now they are not mere extensions of divine or natural will, sent to strike the hubristic, but (un)conscientious partici-pants in the moral and political order. However, it is not only the flame of the battlefield itself, death for death's sake, that mesmerizes Coriolanus, but also the instinctual monomania exhibited by those emblematic butterflies and moths flitting to their candle. No matter how many burn before them or around them, each thinks itself the one that will survive.

The solitariness critics have detected in the play, then, is partly one of strident unaffectedness. Coriolanus does not so much seek to "be every man himself" (3.1.265) as to be a man whose diverse personae are able to persist and survive independently of the others. Absence is preferred to presence, a condition Volumnia celebrates in 1.3: for her son to have honor alone "was no better than picture-like to hang by th' wall, if renown made it not stir" (1.3.11–12). Even if her son had died in action, "his good report should have been my son; I therein would have found issue" (1.3.20–21). Neither the tongues nor eyes nor ears of Fame are invoked here; for Volumnia, life is always processed in a vacuum of unbridgeable gulfs. If she is a suffocating mother, it is less by engulfing Coriolanus than by thinning the air around him. Their relationship is diffuse, a series of scattered dispersals. She produces fittingly a son whose tragedy is always to be asymptotic. G. W. Knight observed something like this when he wrote with different purpose, "We can no more blame Coriolanus for his ruthless valour than we blame the hurtling spear for finding its mark. And yet Coriolanus has no mark: that is his tragedy."[55] The relationships in the play, like the spear and its mark, are devoid of fruition; perhaps more importantly, they are also devoid of nourishment. Breast milk is displaced by blood or absent entirely (as when Coriolanus is figured as male tiger). Young Martius's pursuit of a butterfly is suggestive of similar infinite regress—"and when he caught it, he let it go again, and after it again, and over and over he comes, and up again; catch'd it again" (1.3.61–63). The brutal rending is the boy's and the play's only answer to the gulf between two beings, where the "differency" between grub and butterfly is also the gap between one character and another. Bonds are defined by their severing rather than their cementing.

When Coriolanus leaves Rome "Like to a lonely dragon, that his fen / Makes fear'd and talk'd of more than seen" (4.1.30–31), it is the serpent's solitary nature at the fore and not its wrath, as in *King Lear*. Shortly thereafter, when Aufidius remarks how Coriolanus "Fights dragon-like" (4.7.23), the metaphor is somewhat surprisingly *still* not to do with fury: he "Fights dragon-like, and does achieve as soon / As draw his sword" (4.7.23–24). Which is to say, Coriolanus succeeds by *not* interacting: "All places yield to him ere he sits down" (4.7.28), says Aufidius, and he'll be to Rome "As is the aspray to the fish, who takes it / By sovereignty of nature" (4.7.33–35). Such actions of Coriolanus are always before him, never in him. As Cominius relates, "He was a kind of nothing, titleless, / Till he had forg'd himself a name a' th' fire / Of burning Rome" (5.1.13–15). One can trace similar patterns in Coriolanus's movement through his performative parts: though he first advises Volumnia of a rigid antitheatricality—"Would you have me /

False to my nature? Rather say, I play / The man I am" (3.2.14–16)—he concludes that he has behaved "Like a dull actor now" and "forgot my part, and am out, / Even to a full disgrace" (5.3.40–42). Yet to be man and dragon is to be subject to the metamorphics of acting, whether one resists the part or forgets it. Coriolanus is never more a performer than when scouring himself of dramatic trappings.

The draconian characterization is doubly significant since it completes Coriolanus's butterfly metamorphosis. By pronouncing Coriolanus "a grub and a butterfly," "grown from man to dragon" (5.4.12, 13), Menenius charts how far above other mortals Coriolanus has risen, but also reconfigures this supremacy as isolation. He continues this characterization throughout the scene, calling him an immovable "cornerstone," an "engine" of war, a very "god" who lacks only "eternity and a heaven to throne in," and finally "a male tiger," drained of the "milk" of mercy (5.4.2, 19, 24, 28). The hierarchy of fabulous forms, a construction of which Menenius is especially fond, identifies men with grubs—the same base association he casts on the "musty chaff" (5.1.31) for which the "one poor grain or two" (5.1.27) in Rome must burn. The grubs and the chaff have a further, ouroboric relation in the discourse of insect predation. While the former consumes the latter, the latter spawns the former. In Menenius's conception, it is a cycle of futility from which Coriolanus has broken free. He has become the psychic butterfly, the soul risen from the dross of the body. Menenius's description also answers Sicinius's query, "Is't possible that so short a time can alter the condition of a man?" (5.4.9–10). Menenius paradoxically suggests that Coriolanus is both impossible to change—no more than "yond coign a' th' Capitol" might be displaced with a "little finger" (5.4.4–5)—and the very embodiment of change. He is as much butterfly and grub together as the difference between them. Like Hamlet's cycle of ouroboric worms who eat and are eaten, the butterfly as psyche suggests both the rebirth of the soul and the killing of its own larval prefiguration. It is death and life together, a self-contained cycle reinscribed by the analogy made to Coriolanus as both man and dragon, slayer and slain. The final marker for this apotheosis, the dragon lording over men, is, however, not defined by the typical claw, jaw, or sting, or again a dragon's wrath, but instead those very instruments that, when analogized with the butterfly, seem most delicate: the wings.

Topsell's *History of Serpents* provides an extended treatment of "winged dragons" that Shakespeare could have used to enlarge the discourse of dangerous insects. In fact, *Coriolanus* has more mentions of the dragon than any other play, perhaps because "the ancient Romans . . . carried in all their Bands the Escutchion of a Dragon, to signifie their fortitude and vigilancy" (702). Though some of the language of the entries is echoed in Menenius's conceit (Topsell quotes an observation of Lucan, "You shining Dragons creeping on the earth, / . . . / Mounted with wings in th' air we do behold" [705]), there are two details that help illuminate Coriolanus. The first is that according to Topsell, "except a Serpent eat a Serpent, he shall never be a Dragon: for . . . they grow so great by devouring others of their kinde" (703). As Aufidius proposes, he will have Coriolanus by following a similar principle: "One fire drives out one fire; one nail, one nail" (4.7.55). Aufidius first conceives of Coriolanus as a kind of snake—"We hate alike," he tells him, "Not Afric owns a serpent I abhor / More than thy fame and envy" (1.8.2–4)—and later the "entwining" of Aufidius's "arms about that body" imitates their serpentine movement (4.5.106–7). By "hating alike," Aufidius hopes to overcome, but in effect the bond of their initial hatred, like so many bonds in the drama formed through antagonism, creates nearly indissoluble attachments. Difference, in other words, creates cohesion, while sameness repels. Both follow the pattern of the serpents who become dragons—devouring others of their kind.

The second detail from Topsell blends the dragon with the insect and moves the creature from a purely fantastic discourse into a political one. Topsell concludes his discussion of winged dragons:

> [The] Emperor Tiberius Caesar, had a Dragon which he daily fed with his own hands, and nourished like good fortune, at the last it happened that this Dragon was defaced with the biting of Emmets, and the former beauty of his body much obscured: Wherefore the Emperor grew greatly amazed thereat, and demanding a reason thereof of the Wisemen, he was by them admonished to beware the insurrection of the common people. (716)

Coriolanus's final manifestation is as a dragon in Menenius's eyes, but in nearly everyone else's he is nothing more than a scarred shell of the heroic, a fallen king (the merry Messenger announcing Coriolanus's departure from Rome relates it to "th' expulsion of the Tarquins" [5.4.43]. Or in Topsell's terms, he has been a dragon nourished on good fortune whose death by the masses—here figured as pincer ants—has "obscured" the body. The "insurrection of the common people" spells Coriolanus's final tragedy. At times the devouring insect, at others the object of their devouring, Coriolanus is finally a figure whose identity is in flux, whose name is "nothing," until at last he hits the mark he has been aiming for all along: death itself.[56]

Shakespeare's last insect conceit returns to the meandering flight of the butterfly pursued by young Martius, and by extension to the textile ravelings of Valeria. Coriolanus explodes to Aufidius, upon being called a "boy of tears" (5.6.100), "Cut me to pieces, Volsces, men and lads, / Stain all your edges on me. 'Boy,' false hound! / If you have writ your annals true, 'tis there / That, like an eagle in a dove-cote, I / Flutter'd your Volscians in Corioles. / Alone I did it. 'Boy'!" (5.6.111–16). In Coriolanus's invitation to cut him into pieces, to re-create him as an insect, he fashions himself as an entity entire only in sections. North's translation of Plutarch describes the attack simply as "they all fell upon him, and killed him in the market place" (189). So the disintegration into sections, repeated later with the citizens' cry "Tear him to pieces!" (5.6.120), is specific to Shakespeare's treatment, as well as a kind of grotesque return to the fable of the belly.[57] The body is not a single homogeneous structure but a collection of parts: the belly and the members, the "eyes and ears" that Aufiduis addresses in his final exhortation to kill Coriolanus. But what Coriolanus feels at the name "boy" may be the same humiliation experienced by his own son in pursuit of his butterfly. The "fluttering" motions of wings in flight, for Coriolanus the analogous doves rather than butterflies, also recasts him as his own boy, destroying what he cannot preserve. By fashioning himself as an eagle among doves, he unwittingly corroborates Aufidius's charge: he remains puerile to the end, a more intense but no better adapted figure than his insect-eating son. If Menenius conceived of Coriolanus as a winged dragon among grubs, a soaring creature among "creeping things," now in the trappings of an eagle among doves, Coriolanus finds his own metaphors to instantiate a distance from those who surround him. In death, and more importantly in this last distancing, Coriolanus nevertheless achieves a "noble memory" (5.6.153)—absent to the end, fulfilled by emptiness, divided now into chapter and act by "annals true."[58]

NOTES

My thanks to Daniel P. Gunn for reviewing an earlier draft of this essay.

1. Scot, *The Discoverie of Witchcraft* (1584; reprint, New York: Dover, 1972), 86. The *OED* has the noun "insect" entering English with Philemon Holland's translation of Pliny's *Natural History* (1601).

2. All references to Shakespeare's works are from *The Riverside Shakespeare*, ed. G. Blakemore Evans et al., 2nd ed. (Boston: Houghton Mifflin, 1997).

3. Patterson, *Natural History of the Insects Mentioned in Shakespeare's Plays* (London, 1841), 113.

4. The currency of this etymology can be seen in Shakespeare's "team of little atomies" (*Romeo and Juliet* 1.4.57), beings who are literally indivisible (or "a-tomic"): their small size precludes further fissions.

5. Augustine, *Confessions*, trans. John K. Ryan (Garden City, N.Y.: Image, 1960), 44.

6. See *Parts of Animals*, trans. A. L. Peck (Cambridge: Harvard University Press, 1945), 343–45.

7. Carla Mazzio and David Hillman, editors of *The Body in Parts: Fantasies of Corporeality in Early Modern Europe* (New York: Routledge, 1997), have comprehensively described the early modern period as an age defined by its conception of the part's relation to the whole: cultural fragmentation, whether by "punitive dismemberment, pictorial isolation, poetic emblazoning, mythic *sparagmos,* satirical biting, scientific categorizing, or medical anatomizing" (xi), created a network of "the body in parts," which is, however, "not always the body in pieces" (xi).

8. Andre Siganos notes briefly this aspect of Shakespeare's work: "Toutefois, l'insecte, ou ses divers stades de maturation peuvent ne pas être mis en scène avec autant d'évidence, tout en jouant un rôle finalement plus important que celui d'une simple métaphore: le théâtre shakespearien en est une preuve tangible." See "L'insecte tragique chez Shakespeare et Sartre," *Arquipelago* 5 (1983): 7–23, 10.

9. Greene, *The Life and Complete Works in Prose and Verse of Robert Greene,* ed. Alexander B. Grosart, vol. 11 (New York: Russell and Russell, 1881–86), 291, 292.

10. Ibid., 290. Similarly, Spenser in his mock-heroic *Muiopotmos* (1591, a year before *Upstart Courtier*) outfits his butterfly prince, Clarion, with "two sharpe speares," the antennae stemming from his helmet, where "outstretch his fearefull hornes." See *Edmund Spenser's Poetry*, ed. Hugh Maclean, 2nd ed. (New York: Norton, 1982), 474–75. Spenser also makes much of the multicolored wings, comparing them as well to "Junoes Bird," the peacock. Though Spenser creates a swirl of pride and envy around their appearance, he has the natural splendor of the butterfly "passing farre / All Painters skill." However, Clarion must, as with Greene's boys, costume himself in these wings—they are attachments like his helm, horns, and breastplate—suggesting that Spenser too sees the potential for artifice in their display. Later, in fact, his own poem celebrates the unsurpassed ekphrastic possibilities of the butterfly, as if such creatures were emblematically, unnaturally

wrought. Greene's Players—imitative butterflies imitating heroes—are at least one step removed from Spenser's actual butterfly, who, though he imitates heroes like Hercules and Achilles, is nevertheless an insect at heart.

11. Greene, *Life and Complete Works*, 292.

12. Achilles disparages the performative abilities of butterflies in *Troilus and Cressida* when he remarks, "For men, like butterflies, / Show not their mealy wings but to the summer" (3.3.78–79), which is to say that men's "true colors" are never displayed openly but are always instead subject to the whims of seasonal fortune. It is perhaps ironic given that his warrior Myrmidons trace their legendary ancestry to transformed troops of ants.

13. Greene's device augments an earlier work by Stephen Gosson, *The Schoole of Abuse, Containing a pleasaunt invective against Poets, Pipers, Plaiers, Iesters, and such like Caterpillers of a Commonwealth* (London, 1579). Critical of, among other abuses, the "sutes of silke" worn by even "the very hyerlings of some of our players," Gosson's "caterpillers of a commonwealth" are both overwrought silkworms and lowly, underdeveloped, yet consumptive parasites. See E. K. Chambers, *The Elizabethan Stage*, vol. 4 (Oxford: Clarendon, 1923), 203–5. Shakespeare returns to Gosson's phrasing in *Richard II*, when Bullingbrook promises to exterminate "Bushy, Bagot, and their complices, / The caterpillars of the commonwealth, / Which I have sworn to weed and pluck away" (2.3.165–67).

14. The Greek "psyche," it is often noted, means both "soul" and "butterfly," concretizing in the insect some idea of rebirth and release into a spiritual world from the material cocoon of this world. The butterfly becomes a primary Elizabethan memento mori, both for its short-lived beauty and its sublimation of forms. Moffet writes, "Learn therefore O mortal man, who ever thou art, that God that is best and greatest of all, made the butterfly to pull down thy pride, and by the shortness of their life (which is of no great continuance) be thou mindful of thy own failing condition" (3.974). The Pythagorean account of butterflies in Ovid also makes a grim association with last things; not only is the butterfly the culmination of its own life cycle, but caterpillars "ferali mutant cum papilione figuram"—they are changed into the form of "funereal" butterflies, or death's-head moths. See the *Metamorphoses*, ed. Hugo Magnus (New York: Arno, 1979), 15.372–74.

15. Moffet, preface to *The Theater of Insects*, vol. 3 of Edward Topsell's *The History of Four-Footed Beasts and Serpents and Insects* (London, 1658; reprint, New York: Da Capo, 1967).

16. Chambers, *The Mediaeval Stage*, vol. 1 (Oxford: Oxford University Press, 1903), 71–72.

17. Quoted in Erica Fudge, *Perceiving Animals: Humans and Beasts in Early Modern English Culture* (New York: St. Martin's, 2000), 25.

18. See N. W. Bawcutt, *The Control and Censorship of Caroline Drama: The Records of Sir Henry Herbert, Master of the Revels, 1623–73* (Oxford: Clarendon, 1996), 175, 204.

19. Ibid., 144.

20. Behn, *Oroonoko, or The Royal Slave* (New York: Norton, 1973), 2. On this passage and Behn's place in colonial discourse generally, see Margaret W. Ferguson, "Feathers and Flies: Aphra Behn and the Seventeenth-Century Trade in Exotica," in *Subject and Object in Renaissance Culture,* ed. Margreta de Grazia, Maureen Quilligan, and Peter Stallybrass (Cambridge: Cambridge University Press, 1996), 235–59. Ferguson insightfully links Behn's butterflies to "displaying, *as* objects and for profit, the exotically garbed and painted and tattooed bodies of non-Europeans who were brought to the stages of European cities, and European courts" (247).

21. The standard nineteenth-century insect dissertation, William Kirby and William Spence's *An Introduction to Entomology,* 4 vols. (London, 1815–26), contains an anecdote affirming the appeal of the circuses: "'Dear Miss,' said a lively old Lady to a friend of mine, (who had the misfortune to be confined to her bed by a broken limb, and was complaining that the fleas tormented her,) 'don't you like *fleas?* Well, I think they are the prettiest little merry things in the world.—I never saw a dull flea in all my life'" (1:105).

22. Geoffrey Whitney's *A Choice of Emblemes* (Leyden, 1586) offers several on the widespread fable of industrious ants, readying food for winter, and the grasshoppers who to their detriment only play and sing all summer. One depicts a team of ants pulling a chariot containing both weeping "Idlenes" and triumphant "Labour," with the motto "*Otiose semper egentes,* the idle ever destitute." See *A Choice of Emblemes,* ed. Henry Green (New York: Benjamin Blom, 1967), 175. Equivalent energies seem at work in the flea circus: the impossibility of the action adds to the impact.

23. Moffet, *The Silkewormes and Their Flies: A Facsimile (1599),* ed. Victoria Houliston (Binghamton, N.Y.: Renaissance English Text Society, 1989), 35.

24. Scot, *The Discoverie of Witchcraft,* notes that Pharaoh's magicians could not create lice, and that some have reasoned their inability to be the result of a special property of insects: "The divell (saie they) can make no creature under the quantitie of a barlie corn, and lice being so little cannot therefore be created by them" (178). The Geneva Bible offers only that "God confounded their wisdome & autoritie in a thing moste vile" (sign. g.iii.v). Moffet refers to the episode as well: "Yet when the Egyptian Magicians deceived Pharaoh by producing the greater creatures, in the forming of this so contemptible a creature, they yeelded the garland to Moses" (preface, n.p.). Like the imaginary flea circus, perhaps the spectacles of lice are already illusions, already irreproducible because they are not in fact there.

25. May R. Berenbaum, *Bugs in the System: Insects and Their Impact on Human Affairs* (Reading, Mass.: Addison-Wesley, 1995), 339.

26. Stallybrass and White, *The Politics and Poetics of Transgression* (Ithaca: Cornell University Press, 1986), 41.

27. All references to the works of Jonson are from *Ben Jonson,* ed. C. H. Herford, Percy Simpson, and Evelyn Simpson, 11 vols. (Oxford: Clarendon, 1925–52).

28. *The American Heritage Dictionary of the English Language,* 3rd ed. The *OED* similarly defines "fleapit" as "an allegedly verminous place of public assembly, e.g., a cinema." Meanwhile the *OED* defines "flea-circus" as "a show of performing

fleas," the term originating in the United States as early as 1928. Jonson, however, writes in *The Devil Is an Ass* (1616) of "keep[ing] fleas within a circle" (5.2.11). The character of Pug offers a litany of impossible tasks, reminiscent of John Donne's "Go and Catch a Falling Star," including "milking of Hee-goates," "Catching the windes together in a net," "Mustring of ants, and numbering atomes," and lastly "a thought more: I would sooner / Keepe fleas within a circle, and be accomptant / A thousand yeere, which of 'hem and how far / Out-leap'd the other, then endure a minute / Such as I have within" (5.2.2, 7, 8, 10–14). Pug, then, in his position as trainer of insects—one who "musters ants"—and as sentinel over this dramatic "flea circle," becomes both director and ringmaster. In Pug's hypothetical flea circus, however, his failure to contain the dramatic action is not only consistent with his tribulations in Jonson's play; it also suggests an opposing discourse for the hypercontrol exerted over other performing insects, real and mechanical, that precede it, stressing that for Jonson such endeavors were always antithetical to the aims of true drama. Ironically, Pug's flea watching is an Aristophanic holdover: in *The Clouds,* Socrates is lambasted for such fruitless pursuits as "questioning Chairephon about the number of fleafeet a flea could broadjump." See Aristophanes, *The Clouds,* trans. William Arrowsmith (Ann Arbor: University of Michigan Press, 1962), 19. This play also marks an early instance of implied insects on stage, as several scenes feature Strepsiades on his mattress, tormented by bedbugs.

29. Fudge, *Perceiving Animals;* Boehrer, *Shakespeare among the Animals: Nature and Society in the Drama of Early Modern England* (New York: Palgrave, 2002); see also Stephen Dickey, "Shakespeare's Mastiff Comedy," *Shakespeare Quarterly* 42, no. 3 (1991): 255–76.

30. *The New Inn* begins with the Host criticizing the scientific experiments of two guests, Ferret and Lovel:

> Here, your master,
> And you ha' beene this for[t]night, drawing fleas
> Out of my mattes, and pounding 'hem in cages;
> Cut out of cards, & those rop'd round with pack-thred,
> Drawne throw birdlime! a fine subtilty!,
> or poring through a multiplying glasse,
> Upon a captiv'd crab-louse, or a cheese mite.
> To be dissected, as the sports of nature,
> With a neat Spanish needle! Speculations—
> That doe become the age, I doe confesse!
> As measuring an Ants egges, with the Silke-wormes,
> By a phantastique instrument of thred,
> Shall give you their just difference, to a haire!
> Or else recovering o' dead flyes, with crums! (1.2.24–37)

Given the notorious failure of this late play, the Host's disturbance at these melancholic explorations—capturing fleas, dissecting mites, measuring ant eggs, and resurrecting dead flies—seems a futile effort to stem the displacement of plays not only by low-class diversions, whether bearbaiting or flea shows, but by the increasing empirical attention to the microscopic world over the world of brusque sensuality the Host hopes his tavern, and Jonson his play, will represent: "*Be merry, and drinke Sherry;* that's my poesie! / For I shall never joy i'my light heart / So long as I conceive a sullen ghest, / Or any thing that's earthy!" (1.2.29–31).

31. Later instances of performing insects include Thomas Randolph's *Pastoral of Amyntas, or the impossible dowry* (London, 1640), with its "antimasque of fleas; jig of pismires."

32. Fudge, *Perceiving Animals*, 12.

33. Boehrer, *Shakespeare among the Animals*, 14. On the history of communication between bees and human beekeepers, see Keith Thomas, *Man and the Natural World: Changing Attitudes in England, 1500–1800* (Oxford: Oxford University Press, 1983), 96 (citing Pliny 11.20).

34. Chambers, 2:543. He further cites Cotgrave's *French-English Dictionary* (1611): "a cresset light (such as they use in playhouses) made of ropes wreathed, pitched and put into small and open cages of iron" (2:543), and Shakespeare refers to them in *1 Henry IV,* when Glendower elevates them into the sky: "At my nativity / The front of heaven was full of fiery shapes / Of burning cressets" (3.1.13–15).

35. For an extended account of glowworms and other insects in early modern literature, see Kitty W. Scoular, *Natural Magic: Studies in the Presentation of Nature in English Poetry from Spenser to Marvell* (Oxford: Clarendon, 1965), 81–117. She observes "an English proverb which ran 'You will make me believe that glowworms are lanterns'" and that "the Greek name 'Lampyrides' might easily suggest 'Lamps'" (106).

36. E. K. Chambers notes numerous instances of horses and other quadrupeds being ridden onstage, though he sees in some cases "some kind of 'hobby' more likely than a trained animal." See Chambers, *The Elizabethan Stage*, 3:75.

37. For later effects, see J. Leeds Barroll, *Politics, Plague, and Shakespeare's Theater* (Ithaca: Cornell University Press, 1991).

38. See, for instance, E. C. Pettet, "Coriolanus and the Midlands Insurrection of 1607," *Shakespeare Survey* 3 (1950); Annabel Patterson, *Shakespeare and the Popular Voice* (Cambridge: Basil Blackwell, 1989); and David George, "Plutarch, Insurrection, and Dearth in *Coriolanus,*" *Shakespeare Survey* 53 (2000): 60–72.

39. See Adelman, "Anger's My Meat: Feeding, Dependency, and Aggression in *Coriolanus,*" in *Representing Shakespeare: New Psychoanalytical Essays,* ed. Murray Schwartz and Coppelia Kahn (Baltimore: Johns Hopkins University Press, 1980), 129–49; and further discussion in *Suffocating Mothers: Fantasies of Maternal Origin in Shakespeare's Plays, "Hamlet" to "The Tempest"* (New York: Routledge, 1992).

40. A number of recent critics have explored similar issues of fragmentation in *Coriolanus* as well as early modern culture generally. In addition to the works assembled in Mazzio and Hillman's *The Body in Parts,* see especially Zvi Jagendorf, "*Coriolanus:* Body Politic and Private Parts," *Shakespeare Quarterly* 41 (1990):

455–69; Lee Bliss, introduction to *Coriolanus* (Cambridge: Cambridge University Press, 2000); Stanley Fish, who writes of Coriolanus's "rejection of the community and his intention to stand alone, as a society of one, as a state complete in himself," in "How to Do Things with Austin and Searle: Speech Act Theory and Literary Criticism," in *Is There a Text in This Class* (Cambridge: Harvard University Press, 1982), 197–245; Stanley Cavell, "*Coriolanus* and the Interpretation of Politics ('Who Does the Wolf Love?')," in *Disowning Knowledge in Six Plays of Shakespeare* (Cambridge: Cambridge University Press, 1987); Janette Dillon, "'Solitariness': Shakespeare and Plutarch," *Journal of English and German Philology* 78 (1979): 325–44; W. Hutchings on Aristotelian solitude in "Beast or God: The Coriolanus Controversy," *Critical Quarterly* 24 (1982): 35–50; and Leonard Barkan, *Nature's Work of Art: The Human Body as Image of the World* (New Haven: Yale University Press, 1975), 100–108.

41. Charles Darwin observed that "although butterflies are weak and fragile creatures, they are pugnacious, and an emperor butterfly has been captured with the tips of its wings broken from a conflict with another male. Mr. Collingwood, in speaking of the frequent battles between the butterflies of Borneo, says, 'They whirl round each other with the greatest rapidity, and appear to be incited by the greatest ferocity.'" See *The Descent of Man,* chapter 11, in *The Origin of Species by Means of Natural Selection and The Descent of Man and Selection in Relation to Sex* (Chicago: Encyclopedia Britannica, 1952), 422.

42. Shakespeare could have gleaned warlike insect metaphors from Pliny's *Natural History,* where swarms of locusts "of exceptional size . . . fly with such a noise of wings that they are believed to be birds, and they obscure the sun . . . scorching up many things with their touch and gnawing away everything with their bite, even the doors of the houses as well." See *Natural History,* trans. H. Rackham, vol. 3 (Cambridge: Harvard University Press, 1940), 497. Consequently, in "the district of Cyrene there is actually a law to make war upon them three times a year . . . with the penalty of a deserter for the man who shrinks" (495–99). Lucian's *True History* may have been the first work to enlist fleas in such affairs: a fantastic lunar war between Endymion and Phaeton includes "archers mounted on fleas . . . the fleas in question being approximately twelve times the size of elephants." See *Lucian: Satirical Sketches,* trans. Paul Turner (1961; reprint, Bloomington: Indiana University Press, 1990), 255. Kirby and Spence wryly note an updated but no less ridiculous battle between fleas and humans: "You may shoot at them with a cannon, as report says did Christina Queen of Sweden, whose piece of artillery, of Liliputian calibre, which was employed in this warfare, is still exhibited in the arsenal of Stockholm" (1:106, quoting Linneaus, *Lachesis Lapponica, or A Tour in Lapland,* vol. 2 [London, 1811] 32).

43. Moffet, *Theater of Insects,* 975.

44. *The Historie of Serpents* (London, 1608), 671. Hereafter cited in the text.

45. See, for instance, Michael Schoenfeldt, "Fables of the Belly in Early Modern England," in *The Body in Parts: Fantasies of Corporeality in Early Modern Europe,* ed.

Carla Mazzio and David Hillman (New York: Routledge, 1997), 243–62; Arthur Riss, "'The Belly Politic': *Coriolanus* and the Revolt of Language," *ELH* 59 (1992): 53–75. On the decline of the body politic metaphor, see also James Holstun, "Tragic Superfluity in *Coriolanus*," *ELH* 50 (1983): 485–507; Andrew Gurr, "*Coriolanus* and the Body Politic," *Shakespeare Survey* 28 (1975): 63–69; and David George Hale, "*Coriolanus*: The Death of a Political Metaphor," *Shakespeare Quarterly* 23 (1971): 197–202.

46. This reward is accompanied by his new appellation, from Martius Caius to Coriolanus, yet another instance of his identity slippage. On issues of naming, see Jonathan Goldberg, "The Anus in *Coriolanus*," in *Psychoanalysis, Historicism, and Early Modern Culture*, ed. Carla Mazzio and Doug Trevor (New York: Routledge, 2000); Burton Hatlen, "The 'Noble Thing' and the 'Boy of Tears': *Coriolanus* and the Embarrassments of Identity," *English Literary Renaissance* 27, no. 3 (Autumn 1997): 393–420.

47. See vol. 2 of *Plutarch's Lives of the Noble Grecians and Romans*, trans. Thomas North, 6 vols. (London, 1579; reprint, New York: AMS, 1967), 145. Subsequent citations in the text are to this edition.

48. On appetite in the play, see Gail Kern Paster, "'To Starve with Feeding': The City in Coriolanus," *Shakespeare Studies* 11 (1978): 123–44, who observes that "to see human beings rather primitively as component parts is a constant reminder of mortality and the physical vulnerability of the body" (135). Jonathan Goldberg, in *James I and the Politics of Literature* (Stanford: Stanford University Press, 1989), argues that "Coriolanus aims at devouring the world in order to become it" (187). But if Coriolanus seeks such absolute totality, it must be secondary to the part as whole unto itself, the particularity of the Aristotelian insect.

49. Paster, "To Starve with Feeding," 137.

50. Christopher Givan, "Shakespeare's *Coriolanus*: The Premature Epitaph and the Butterfly," *Shakespeare Studies* 12 (1979): 143–58, has also linked the "rhythm of loss and recovery" in the butterfly passage with the play's broader designs: "Marcius senior gets into trouble several times by losing his temper, becoming 'enraged' and destroying something quite fragile, such as his election to the consulship. . . . Marcus junior plays a game in which the sport consists of capturing the butterfly, releasing it, and catching it again. . . . Coriolanus is caught in a rhythm of winning and losing to which the only final release appears to be definitive destruction" (153).

51. Annabel Patterson shrewdly argues that the citizens' outcry against the patricians' wasting hoarded grain displays "the bottom line in the symbolic computing of personal net worth": "the patricians *need* the dearth as a physical demonstration of the reality of their own wealth, of economic difference." See *Shakespeare and the Popular Voice*, 133. I would extend this model to the butterfly episode: it is Valeria's very indifference to Martius's motivation that undercores Coriolanus's own insouciance. Why Martius mammocks the butterfly, for Valeria, is beside the point. Rather, it is important only that Martius has the leisure to pursue gamely

such endeavors. He does not have to worry about what he puts into his mouth, unlike the starving citizenry, and Coriolanus reconfigures this symbolically when he later declines to put what he deems excess words into his own mouth: "When blows have made me stay, I fled from words" (2.2.72).

52. The Variorum *Coriolanus,* ed. H. H. Furness (Philadelphia: Lippincott, 1928), notes W. A. Wright's citation of "Major Moor," who "in his *Suffolk Words and Phrases,* gives 'Mammock. To cut and hack victuals wastefully" (96n).

53. From Leviticus 11:21–22, in *The Geneva Bible: A Facsimile of the 1560 Edition* (Madison: University of Wisconsin Press, 1969). Subsequent biblical references are to this edition by chapter and verse.

54. *The Geneva Bible,* sig. AA.iii.r.

55. Knight, "An Essay on *Coriolanus*" (1930), 160. T. S. Eliot, in his *Coriolan* poems inspired by the play he deemed Shakespeare's greatest success in tragedy, seems virtually to gloss Knight's essay. Knight's emphasis on metallic and mechanical imagery becomes sublimated in Eliot's opening lines, "Stone, bronze, stone, steel, oakleaves, horses' heels / Over the paving," and his later litany of "rifles and carbines," "machine guns," and other engines of war. Eliot, in fact, provided the introduction to Knight's volume, while his own unfinished *Coriolan* poems were composed a year later (1931). Eliot picks up too on the pervasion of insects: "Difficulties of a Statesman" culminates with the lines "Come with the sweep of the little bat's wing, with the small flare of the firefly or lightning bug, / Rising and falling, crowned with dust, the small creatures, / The small creatures chirp thinly through the dust, through the night" (47–49). The thin, dusty enervations of these creatures capture something of the void supposed in Knight's spear-mark analysis. See Eliot, *Collected Poems, 1909–1962* (New York: Harcourt Brace, 1963).

56. That Coriolanus should be "eaten by insects" is a less-surprising image when taken with an earlier desire of his mother's, namely, that he be "humble as the ripest mulberry / That will not hold the handling" (3.2.79–80). Her choice of "mulberries"—the exclusive diet of the silkworms, whose industry James I was championing around the time of *Coriolanus*—positions her son early on as victim of a swarm. The juice stains of the overripe berries also recall Volumnia's gory conflation of fluid, that the "breasts of Hecuba, when she did suckle Hector, looked not lovelier / Than Hector's forehead when it spit forth blood" (1.3.41–43). The drawing in and spilling out replay a number of similar patterns in the life of Coriolanus. When Aufidius says that Coriolanus broke his oath to the Volscians "like / A twist of rotten silk" (5.6.94–95), the image completes this image cycle: the mulberry-devouring caterpillars have, like Coriolanus, moved from grubs to butterflies to death to putrefaction, and even the silk they left behind has rotted. The foreshadowing of Coriolanus's own imminent death, who has undergone the metamorphosis of man, is clearly evoked in this image, but so too is his memorialization in the end. The silk has rotted, "Yet he shall have a noble memory" (5.6.153).

57. On reading the "body cut to pieces" as either a religious or an "obstinately secular final image," see Jagendorf, "*Coriolanus:* Body Politic," 468–69.

58. Alongside the various commodifications of Shakespeare in modern Stratford-upon-Avon, one can now visit at Swan's Nest Lane the Stratford Butterfly Farm, claiming to be the "world's largest," where one can "enjoy the unique pleasure of watching hundreds of the world's most spectacular and colourful butterflies flying all around" (http://www.butterflyfarm.co.uk). The emphasis on color and spectacle resuscitates Greene's critique of the butterfly players, and the butterfly farm very much markets the visual. Also significant is the distancing of audience and spectacle: rather than projecting the "farm" as a participatory sort of ecotravel, where one might interact with creatures in their own environment, the marketing for exhibits such as the "Caterpillar Room" and "Insect City," where one may "observe the fascinating and strange," constructs the visitor as an audience distinct from the spectacle itself. The "Insect City," for instance, "boasts an exceptional range of Insects, safely behind glass and easy to see. The leaf-cutter ants walk above your head in their tireless mission to get leaves and our mini-beast section has giant millipedes, snails, and crabs." The metaphorical fourth wall of the theater, here reified as protective glass, establishes a clear distinction between performer and spectator. The insects are also "easy to see," as if their small size might be a deterrent to potential visitors, perhaps having witnessed too many flea circuses with their invisible charioteers. And so the farm in fact offers at least two "unique pleasures": watching a gallimaufry of lepidoptera "flying all around," and observing a miniature menagerie of insects, mollusks, and arthropods go about their daily business. The latter are almost subversive elements, attested to in their roles as "mini-beasts," with snails and crabs only marginally acceptable to even the least taxonomically inclined as being "insects." The ants are in constant dress rehearsal on their "tireless mission," still safely contained above the heads of visitors, while the butterflies are in some manner reduced to their gilded selves, to pure spectacle.

4

İmperfect States

Thoreau, Melville, and "Insectivorous Fate"

TONY MCGOWAN

Nations! What are they? Tartars! and Huns! and Chinamen!
Like insects they swarm.

—THOREAU, *Journals*

From its chrysalis state, the silkworm but becomes a moth, that
very quickly expires. Its longest existence is as a worm. All vanity. . .
to seek in nature for positive warranty to these aspirations of ours.
Through all her provinces, nature seems to promise immortality
to life, but destruction to beings. . . . If not against us, nature is
not for us.

—MELVILLE, *Mardi*

In what follows, I consider insect poetics in the writings of Henry David
Thoreau and Herman Melville. I find that their prose meditations
hatch complex anxiety over American, midcentury, domestic space. In
Thoreau, this anxiety emerged during the difficult period he spent after his
return from the pond, when he was once again "a sojourner in civilized life"
struggling to revise *Walden* for publication.[1] For Melville, "insectivorous"
anxiety appeared at Arrowhead, his farm in the Berkshires, where he strug-
gled to write enough to support his growing family. I first revisit the traditional way we read domestic space in Thoreau and Melville, and then go
on to explore what Thoreau actually "found" in the Kirby and Spence *Introduction to Entomology*—his main source for all things "insectivorous."[2] I
argue that this fascinating book is an important, underappreciated influence on Thoreau's imagination.[3] Then, in my concluding remarks, I read the
ending of *Walden* against Herman Melville's obscurantist tale "The Apple-
Tree Table." Both contain very different versions of the same remarkable
insect hatching.

"I Find it in Kirby and Spence"

In *Walden*'s "Higher Laws," which precedes and balances the chapter "Brute Neighbors," Thoreau directly invests in the contemporaneous midcentury fashion that civilization had turned its back on the good in human nature, that it had metamorphosed into a new savagery.[4] Like Melville, another reluctant reformer, Thoreau undercuts the popular sense in which to be civilized had come to mean the unquestioning embrace of various American gods—comfort, materialism, industrialization, and expansionism, among them. Instead, Thoreau considered it a critical mistake to equate these idols with "civilized life"; he thought the equation an emergency calling for personal action—perhaps an action like the writing of *Walden*. The book is Thoreau's new-style, free-form jeremiad, a wedding of transcendental thought and the simple, material husk of lived experience. It is Thoreau's attempt to "wake his neighbors up," to correct unexamined assumptions he believed destined to lead from individual sloth and greed directly to democracy's decay. The centerpiece of Thoreau's call, of course, is for a new independence, and a doubled one at that—one both *from* the baser instincts of the self, and then *of* that new "man," in a kind of defensive retreat, from society itself. So on July 4, 1845, like "a snake cast[ing] its slough," or so goes the fiction, Thoreau shed town for country and took up residence in his hut at Walden Pond (15). Thoreau certainly went to Walden to be in nature, but he did not do so entirely for nature's sake; that turn would come later.[5] Instead he left society in clear expectation of his return, because, as he wrote in his journal, "He approaches the study of mankind with great advantages who is accustomed to the study of nature" (63). If Melville's Harvard and Yale were a whale ship, Thoreau's self-schooling occurred at the pond. It is in this conservative sense, first, and before a real but post-*Walden* turn toward ecology as we know it today, that Thoreau should be recognized as a preservationist. Here is Thoreau from "Higher Laws":

> I believe that every man who has ever been earnest to preserve his higher or poetic faculties . . . has been particularly inclined to abstain from animal food, and from much food of any kind. It is a significant fact, stated by entomologists, I find it in Kirby and Spence, that "some insects in their perfect state, though furnished with organs of feeding, make no use of them"; and they lay it down as "a general rule, that almost all insects in this state eat

Perfect state insects from *An Introduction to Entomology: or, Elements of the natural history of insects; with plates,* by William Kirby and William Spence (1822–26).

much less than that of larvae. The voracious caterpillar when transformed into a butterfly . . . and the gluttonous maggot when become a fly," content themselves with a drop or two of honey or some other sweet liquid. The abdomen under the wings of the butterfly still represents the larva. This is the tidbit which tempts his insectivorous fate. The gross feeder is the man in the larva state; and there are whole nations in that state, nations without fancy or imagination, whose vast abdomens betray them. (461)

In this graphic appeal to "insectivorous" anatomies, Thoreau lashes out against the bloated appetite, or "abdomen," of his contemporaries. Clearly the human individual or "whole state" is the *ground* of this trope, and insect life the *tenor*. Thoreau seems to seek here an inner, ascetic, even "hindoo" hunger that might both transcend and mirror natural models. One of the deepest problems in Thoreau studies, and I explore it hereafter, is why he turns in awe and reverence *toward* examples from nature and yet distills from that turn not just a renewed love of nature but also an urgent call for our necessary divorce *from* nature. In short, Thoreau found himself both attracted to nature and repelled by it, not for what nature was in itself but for what it told him about humanity. This difficulty resides at the core of Thoreau's romantic (almost necromantic) rhetoric of obscurity in *Walden* and, I would argue, persists as a significant dilemma for a still-transforming contemporary sociobiology.[6]

Thoreau's voice is distinctly composite, reaching here toward Emerson or scripture, there toward the classics, and yet elsewhere toward the emergent natural sciences. His readers, however, unlike Melville's, have underreported the complex manner in which Thoreau inflects the concerns of social reform advocates. *Typee,* we should remember, appeared some eight years before *Walden* and had already launched a withering, controversial attack on missionary (and other) exploitations in the Pacific basin. The differences between *Walden* and *Typee* are, of course, as vast as that Pacific—one glaring example being that Melville traveled, really traveled, while Thoreau claimed to have found "a great deal" of meditative space at home, in and about Concord.[7] Oceanic difference aside, an important similarity inheres in how effectively each answered popular reform platforms through remarkable spatial tropes for the domestic realm.

Consider together Thoreau's hut and Melville's forecastle. They are both complex tropes for domestic space, both metaphors that seem to ponder

Emerson's central question in his second-series essay "Fate"—"How shall I live?" Emerson's conclusion, as it turns out, is up in the air, or in aporia, for the dual claimants of a predetermined (biological) fate and of a personal (rational) will equally lean on our being; nature and nurture, Emerson intimates, are indissolubly wedded, much like Melville's water and meditation. In at least this respect, the darker, second-series Emerson relapses to an earlier moment in American moral and ethical history, to the doctrine of a freedom of the will within constraint put forth by Jonathan Edwards. But in Thoreau, in an age negotiating the collapse of the old religion and the rise of a new scientific imagination, we find that biological necessity, or nature, has largely refigured Edward's Providential sort.[8] Indeed, Emerson casts the problem of how we are to live in very earthly terms. "Every spirit makes its house; but afterwards the house confines the spirit," he wrote, and more than one teacher has since then noticed that Thoreau seemed to take this metaphor as something like a literal command (332–33).

Consider Thoreau's hut first, and its hinged nature. At times it is where a hermetic avatar of a more social self, set aside but for a time, and for the sake of intellectual and spiritual metamorphoses, stubbornly preserves the silence of solitude. This hut is an impermanent, semipermeable monk's cell.[9] Or, more isolated still than some cell in a larger retreat, Thoreau's abode is a cocoon, a self-manufactured chrysalis, an entomological space altogether set apart from society. In this romance it hangs on the slope of Walden's bank like a monarch's cocoon on the underside of a milkweed leaf—something, by the way, that Thoreau often searched for but never found. At other times, in a brilliantly subtle turn against the long procession of frontier writings in which the stockade proffered protection from a lurking savagery *without,* Thoreau's selfish chrysalis not only shields him from savage, elemental force, while providing a perch from which he might view the same, but also insulates him from the village itself, from the lurking herd urge *within* each and all of us.

Now consider Melville's forecastle life; it comes with a hatch that barely opens to elemental force, and that refuses to set the self apart—as do more lofty, unenclosed Melvillean spaces, like Marquesan promontories, or *Pequod* mastheads. Instead Melville's forecastle corrupts the entomologists' imagining of the perfectly ordered hive. His forecastle is a space not of racial purity or martial order but of seamy, fluid organicism, a hybrid state; it is a space set apart from andocentric idealizations of nature. The self in

Melville, wherever directly figured (and this is true for Ishmael, Redburn, White-Jacket, Bartleby, Pierre, and Billy Budd, to name a few), generally inhabits a figurative belowdecks, an abstract space precommitted to raucous communality and suffering. Abstractly considered, this space can as easily be a law office (as it is in "Bartleby") as the lower depths of an urban tenement building (as it is in *Pierre*).

A carnivalesque mix of race, sex, and work animates Melville's forecastle. In this space the self encounters what Ishmael calls both "the universal thump" of subjection before indiscriminate power, as well as, and as often, the self-inflicted sufferings of one's own internal "Hyenas."[10] While it is true that the "milk and sperm of human kindness" can momentarily flood this space, it is also quite sure to wash away like a sea through scuppers. Indeed, communality and division enfold each other in Melville's forecastle, and in a kind of rhetorical wave action—a to and fro of pain and delight. A good example of this appears in *Moby-Dick*'s "The Spouter-Inn," where a comic tone renders the feeding frenzy of brute sailors simultaneously savage and collegial. Or consider how, in "The Counterpane," Ishmael and Queequeg's intimate love nest prefigures the cramped forecastle existence of the shipmates' imperfect floating society. In "The Counterpane," both the fear and the delight of one self's encounter with another are tucked in, side by side. We witness this affective to-and-fro in the fantastic emergence, or hatching, of Queequeg's tattooed skin from his Western garb—his humdrum chrysalis. A third example of this forecastle press of bodies, still hybridized, still racialized, but now stripped of the comic repose infusing the early *Moby-Dick*, appears belowdecks in *Benito Cereno*'s shaving scene, where Melville's anxieties about American race relations finally boil over into horror.

On November 11, 1852, some ninety-two months after beginning work on his hut, and while in the throes of finishing *Walden*, Thoreau walked into the Society of Natural History on Mason Street in Boston. He returned the first volume of a British book, one *Introduction to Entomology* by William Kirby and William Spence, and borrowed the second volume. He had held volume 1 for more than a month. He would keep volume 2 for more than five months. The *Introduction*, which comprised four volumes, had been the leading text of entomology for a generation.[11]

The text is significant to science, but to the student of rhetoric, it is fascinating. In an attempt to enliven the study of insects, the authors infuse their book with "fancy and imagination." The nineteenth century was a less-fixed, more-experimental time for writers of science than today, and for Kirby and Spence, the promise of an increased readership clearly trumped any potential erosion of their claim to scientific rigor. They made a couple of very surprising moves. First, they adapted the epistolary style from the English novel; each of their chapters is cast as a letter to an imaginary, generalized, young, male naturalist. Second, Kirby and Spence collapsed their separate voices into one, adopting the personal pronoun "I" for their speaker. They write, for example: "I hope this account has reconciled you in some degree to the destructive termites:—I shall next introduce you to social insects, concerning most of which you have probably conceived a more favorable opinion" (2:44). Direct address to the reader is, of course, a centerpiece in *Walden* as well, but the difference between these first persons is telling. *Walden* opens with the conservative assertion that "in most books, the I, or first person, is omitted; in this it will be retained" (1:1). Thoreau's buried pun, of course, concerns the conservation of the self; he points to how, when we *spend* ourselves, we risk joining with "the luxurious and dissipated who set the fashions which the herd so diligently follow" (24). Where Thoreau stands tall for the preservation, or retention, of the "I," we find Kirby and Spence ingeniously recognizing that this "I" is really always constructed. Indeed, the lesson Thoreau could not evade is that the first person must always first be constructed before it is preserved.

While each personalized letter in Kirby and Spence tackles a different subject in entomology, every letter worries over the specter of godlessness rising within science in general. Like Thoreau's *Walden*, then, the *Introduction* is no objective peep into the microlandscapes and doings of savage races. Rather, it is a foray into natural scripture—a courting and unmasking of "higher law" within the Book of Nature. In the introduction to volume 1 of Kirby and Spence, the editors both name the enemy and outline the authors' plan of attack:

And here it may be proper to observe, that one of their first and favorite objects has been to direct the attention of their readers "from nature up to God." For, when they reflected upon the fatal use which has too often been made of Natural History, and that from the very works and wonders of God, philosophists, by an unaccountable perversion of intellect, have attempted to derive arguments either against his being and providence, or against the

Religion revealed in the Holy Scriptures, they conceived they might render some service to the most important interests of mankind, by showing how every department of the science they recommend illustrates the great truth of Religion, and proves that the doctrine of the Word of God, instead of being contradicted, are triumphantly confirmed by his word.

"To see all things in God," has been accounted one of the peculiar privileges of the future state; and in his present life, "To see God in all things," in the mirror of the creation to behold and adore the reflected glory of the Creator, is no mean attainment; and it possesses the advantage, that thus we sanctify our pursuits, and, instead of loving the creatures for themselves, are led to the survey of them and their instincts to the love of Him who made and endowed them. (xi–xii)

Here insects will be loved not "for themselves" but insofar as they "sanctify" the "pursuit" of those ultimacies beyond natural appearance. Here the project of reading nature into a new revelation theology precludes a more objective ecology, and it is fair to say that Thoreau, in *Walden,* is still caught up in this project. But unlike Kirby and Spence, Thoreau was no doctrinal servant of the Church of England, or of any explicitly joinable faith, but rather one for whom the face of God remained a promissory fact, something as true and as obscure as his famous "hound . . . bay horse, and . . . turtle-dove."[12] Still, in both *Walden* and the *Introduction* there inheres, on every page, spiritual supplement to scientific inquiry, and both texts might be thought to promise a "natural theology."[13] But the texts part company here, for if Thoreau recognizes "Him" as the ultimate reference, it is of course not only God, as first cause, but also Emerson's transparent man— that famous "god in ruins." Nature, for Thoreau, functions as a text within which man can't quite be made to fit, a text where both the divinity and the ruination of his destiny is made manifest. And this destiny in Thoreau is as historical as it is theological; the writer's remove from the world may happen in the nick of time, but it is temporary, chrysalis-like, and therefore semipermeable to exterior force. It makes sense, therefore, that Thoreau invokes historical ground to his still-romantic study of nature, and of insects. Remarkably, he "finds" this as well in the *Introduction.* As far as I can discern, the following passage from Kirby and Spence has not yet been read as communicating with *Walden*'s famous battle of the ants in "Brute Neighbors":

Having, I apprehend, satiated you with the fury and carnage of myrmidon-
ian wars, I shall next bring forward a scene more astonishing, which at first,
perhaps, you will be disposed to regard as the mere illusion of a lively imagination. What will you say when I tell you that certain ants are affirmed to
sally forth from their nests on predatory expeditions, for the singular purpose of procuring slaves to employ in their domestic business; and that
these ants are usually a ruddy race, while their slaves themselves are black? I
think I see you here throw down my letter and exclaim—"What! Ants turned
slave-dealers!"

Unfortunately in this country we have not the means of satisfying ourselves by ocular demonstration, since none of the slave-dealing ants appear
to be natives of Britain. (74–75)

Kirby and Spence actually mean that their slave-taking race of ants inhabits Eurasia and not Great Britain, but the language speaks as well to the fact
that, in 1815, when they wrote, the active slave trade had ended in England,
if slavery would still be legal there for more than a decade. They mean as
well to point a metaphorical finger at America, where the natives still deal
in slaves. If this winking yet obfuscating moment in Kirby and Spence
seems familiar, that is because it is close cousin to Thoreau's rhetoric at the
end of his much-discussed "battle of the ants." After directly quoting the
catalog of ant wars in classic texts in Kirby and Spence, Thoreau concludes
his three-page anecdote with the following: "The battle I witnessed took
place in the Presidency of Polk, five years before the passage of Webster's
Fugitive Slave Bill" (154).

If mention of slavery in Kirby and Spence finds its way into Thoreau's
"battle of the ants" and emerges as historical foreboding, it starts quite
simply, with the borrowing of individual ideas, even words. Early in his
anecdote, for example, Thoreau directly lifts the nationality of his red and
black ants from Kirby and Spence; they are, in both texts, "Myrmidons"—
Achilles' troops in the Trojan War. Then, fleshing out the appropriation,
Thoreau casts farther afield, until his mock-heroic passage evolves into a
referential field barnacled all over with wars and warriors. The ants are cast
as Spartan youths, and one becomes "some Achilles" ready to "avenge or
rescue his Patroclus." Eventually, as Thoreau leans into the scene, he will
find Austerlitz, Dresden, and finally even the battle of Concord there, and
all writ small—comically contained. But upon rereading, the mock-heroic

tone seems a carefully intended pose, an archaism of form. Its purpose is to deliver us with a shock to the present, to "Webster's Fugitive Slave Bill." Thoreau performs, only to dismantle, the overwrought confidence, or "Faith," that Emily Dickinson will soon describe (and link to both class and gender), in her marvelous little condensation of religion and science:

"Faith" is a fine invention
When Gentlemen can see—
But Microscopes are prudent
in an Emergency.[14]

As in Dickinson's lines, Thoreau's ant battle aims at exposing a certain dislocation of a viewer's perspective, but in Thoreau there is a difference; recourse to the power of microscopic focus becomes the problem, instead of the solution. "It was the only battle which I have ever witnessed," he says, reinforcing the spatial and temporal divorce of viewer from subject, "the only battle field I ever trod while the battle was raging; internecine war; the red republicans on the one hand, and the black imperialists on the other." But the present moment in Thoreau's America is one of anxiety, of war; thirty years of peace have ended with the Mexican-American War, and the next war, fratricidal this time, is already looming. By this point Thoreau has spent his night in jail, has collapsed the War of Independence on his transcendentalist mission into American savagery. The mock-heroic tone, the wink toward historical backdrop he takes up from Kirby and Spence, far from being a simple borrowing, achieves a new urgency in the battle of the ants.

If the mock-heroic tone of the battle of the ants can be read as defensive, so can the choice of battle types. It is interesting that Thoreau chooses to linger over the Kirby and Spence passage concerning ant race war, or "internecine" war. There were many other choices in the *Introduction*—and one that would seem to perfectly fulfill Thoreau's standoffish desire to survey "numerous armies." "If you would see more numerous armies engaged," write Kirby and Spence, "and survey war in all its forms, you must witness the combats of ants of the same species, you must go into the woods where the hill-ants of Gould (F. *rufa*, L.) erect [their] habitations. There you will sometimes behold populous and rival cities, like Rome and Carthage, as if they had vowed each other's destruction, pouring forth their myriads by the various roads that, like rays, diverge on all sides from their respective metropolises, to decide by an appeal to arms the fate of their little world" (72). Two pages later, the discussion of ant civil war ends with graphic notice of body-strewn battlefields, and reports of survivors cannibalizing the corpses of fallen warriors. The brand of war that Thoreau chose to relate certainly lets him look back at the Revolutionary War, and it allows him to confront the race issue. Thoreau in the mid-1850s could of course not see around time's corners, but his avoidance of the fratricidal swarmings in Kirby and Spence seems a tellingly tame path.

As critics of Thoreau, we have overlooked other borrowings from Kirby and Spence. Some are simple, seemingly discrete, but actually lead to a more diffuse fashion in which the *Introduction* informs *Walden*. Take, for example, the wonderfully microscopic description that occurs after Thoreau removes a "chip" of the larger ant war to the security of his hut for observation. The moment itself is brilliant, because, in placing the *duellum* under glass, he physically becomes a deus ex machina, a more-than-rhetorical force able to intervene and recontain the swarming *bellum*. Here is what he sees:

> They struggled half an hour longer under the tumbler, and when I looked again the black soldier had severed the heads of his foes from their bodies, and the still living heads were hanging on either side of him like ghastly *trophies* at his saddle-bow, still apparently as firmly fastened as ever, and he was endeavoring with feeble struggles, being without feelers, and with only the remnants of a leg, and I know not how many other wounds, to divest himself of them. (153–54; italics mine)

Thoreau's primary source for "battle of the ants" is his journal, but the entry in question does not contain any notice of severed heads or "trophies." He found this in Kirby and Spence. When the authors press their argument that ants "exhibit a semblance" of right human "government and morals," they project that "if ants feel the force of love, they are equally susceptible to the emotions of anger. . . . Two strong mandibles arm their mouth, with which they sometimes fix themselves so obstinately to the object of their attack, that they will sooner be torn limb from limb than let go their hold;— a *trophy* of his valor, which, however troublesome, he will be compelled to carry about him to the day of his death" (29, 67; italics mine). This moment suggests that Thoreau did more than simply mine Kirby and Spence for the passages that make their way directly into *Walden*.

Indeed, Thoreau finds much more than details and anecdotes in the *Introduction;* he discovers his own class-bound anxiety about migrations between seemingly sovereign states. Upon opening the second volume of the *Introduction* and pushing into a casual reading of the letter on "imperfect societies of insects"—those societies defined as combining forces only in the face of some ecological necessity—Thoreau would have found an array of alarming anecdotes crafted to curry favor with the authors' young naturalist audience. Thoreau, of course, was no young naturalist. He was a social critic immersed in a rapidly changing America. For this man seeking to make sense of America's absorption of poor, hungry, uneducated immigrant masses from Ireland and points east, the forty-year-old anecdotes in Kirby and Spence must have had an unexpected impact. Here is the first story he encountered—one relating the amazing migrations of imperfect societies: "Meinecken tells us, that he once saw in a village of Anhalt, on a clear day, about four in the afternoon, such a cloud of dragonflies (*Libellulae,* L.) as almost concealed the sun, and not a little alarmed the villagers, under the idea that they were locusts" (10). Reference to locusts must have brought Thoreau, via the language of biblical typology, right to the brink of current American immigration anxiety. The next anecdote, with its water crossing and its inference of an invading "army," could only have brought a finer edge to the connection. Here a mythic "swarm" penetrates to the heartland: "Mr. Woolnough of Hollesley in Suffolk, a most attentive observer of nature, once witnessed such an army of the smaller dragon flies (*Agrion,* F) flying inward from the sea, as to cast a slight shadow over a field of four acres as they passed" (10). As the anecdotes in Kirby and Spence become more and more detailed, they begin to characterize the male witness of these marvels. He emerges as a gentlemen of keen synthetic vision, a man alone in his dwelling, and a naturalist: "Professor Walch states, that one night about eleven O'clock, sitting in his study, his attention was attracted by what seemed the pelting of hail against his window, which surprising him by its strong continuance, he opened the window, and found the noise was occasioned by the flight of the froth frog-hopper (*Cicada spumaria,* L.) which entered the room in such numbers as to cover the table" (11). Is this a writing table, such as Thoreau kept in his hut? This invasion is echoed in still another swarm anecdote, where a good British gentleman, "stationed in Bombay," survives a flight of bugs "going westward . . . [and] so numerous as to cover everything in the apartment in which he was sitting" (12). How is a gentlemen supposed to write with such a swarm on his desk?

In the pages that follow, Kirby and Spence cannot marshal science for an explanation of these "swarms," especially because they "are not wholly social insects." They are, instead, individual members of more chaotically designed societies, thrown together "merely for the purpose of emigration." By the time Kirby and Spence are through describing this imperfect social state, they seem to almost directly rehearse the generalized prejudice and pity that more native Americans then harbored toward immigrants aboard crowded boats daily unloading at Boston, New York, and other American ports:

> On the eastern coast, I have, at certain times, seen innumerable insects upon the beach, close to the shore, and apparently washed up by them. Though wetted, they were quite alive. . . . What invites them to this [emigration] is one of those mysteries of nature, which at present we can not penetrate. A scarcity of food urges the locusts to shift their quarters; and too confined a space to accommodate their numbers occasions the bees to swarm. . . . It is still more difficult to account for the impulses that urge these creatures, with their filmy wing and fragile form, to attempt to cross the ocean, and expose themselves, one would think, to inevitable destruction. (12)

Consider again the reference to the "abdomen" of an "insectivorous" humanity in the passage from "Higher Laws," with which we began. Mention of this "abdomen," of course, ties into Thoreau's "hindoo" ascetics, his deprivative code for the conduct of life. But to his horror, or through his design, Thoreau's simplified, perfect man remains distinctly out of reach, remains a "future state" of being, and his earthly semblance must carry around, in his shrunken abdomen, "tidbit" proof of his lowly origins. Thoreau wants to be rid of this tidbit, but what is it? It is at least a connection to the mass of men, trace evidence of relation, of the romantic's failure to entirely sacrifice relation. In this "tidbit" we see again the elitist Thoreau. The higher man, the more perfect man, achieves divorce from "John or Jonathan" only by shrinking his abdomen, by tucking from sight this gross, imperfect tidbit of his former larval state. If he does not, he risks becoming a drone in the larger colony. This "abdomen" seems terribly undemocratic, when it is considered in this way, as disavowed evidence of communality in struggle.

Yet we have not fully grasped the material, anxiety-ridden, and undemocratic nature of this "abdomen" until we discern that Thoreau crafted it in reaction to an astoundingly memorable passage he encountered in Kirby and Spence. The repetition of the term "abdomen" in the following passage, as well as the authors' use of the word "vast," helps me argue that this passage is an important and overlooked source for *Walden*. Thoreau simply must have noted it while revising his book:

> When the business of oviposition commences [the neuter workers] take the eggs from the female, and posit them in the nurseries. Her abdomen begins now to gradually extend, til in process of time it is enlarged to 1,500 or 2,000 times the size of the rest of her body, and her bulk equals that of 20,000 or 30,000 workers. This part, often more than three inches in length, is now a vast matrix of eggs, [and] is also remarkable for its peristaltic motion, . . . which, like the undulations of water, produces a perpetual and successive rise and fall over the whole surface of the abdomen, and occasions a constant extrusion of the eggs, amounting sometimes in old females to sixty in a minute, or eighty thousand and upwards in twenty-four hours. As these females live two years in their perfect state, how astonishing must be the number produced in that time. (2:36)

The subject here is reproduction in "white ant" (or termite) colonies. The abdomen of this perfect-stage insect is a model of industry; it is the source of the workers and warriors necessary for the expansion of the colony's empire. For Thoreau, yet not because its description must disgust certain readers, this "state" is a grotesque perfection, a perfect design for a horribly imperfect society. Kirby and Spence describe a mindless, hungry industrial system where "insectivorous" growth promises only incessant expansionism, a place with a bloated abdomen as its engine and core. No simplified, individual architecture for living can exist in this place. The monstrous queen (she has returned in recent science fiction films) is the locus of the society's existence; she is that perfect state of being (and making) for which millions of workers and soldiers would instantly die. Her vast abdomen, though perfect, is precisely what Thoreau cannot stomach. It spews out lowly larvae, enslaving both them to "the herd" and her to the means of

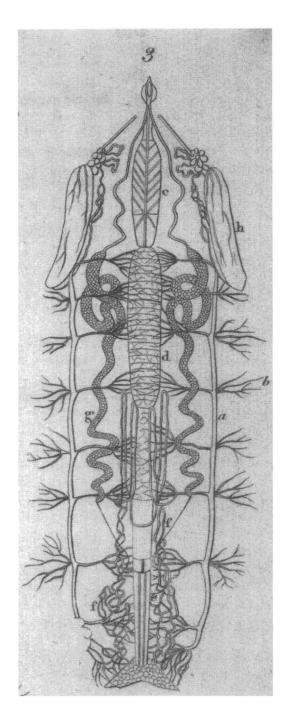

Diagram of a digestive
system taken from Kirby
and Spence.

their production, which is equivalent to the state's reproduction. That this model for society is an undemocratic, ponderous, gendered, "emasculating" thing would not have been lost on Thoreau. He saw it all around him, and he went to Walden to both escape it and think about it. Kirby and Spence make explicit the fact that this individual higher state being is a slave, for in a supporting passage we find that legions of blind, neuter workers have tended the queen during her rise to power. They have enclosed her in a royal prison chamber. They have again and again enlarged her royal chamber to accommodate her swelling abdomen, but always in such a way as to ensure she won't escape during the remodeling. She is perfect, but the state to which she gives birth is a trap for all and forever. The colony is a place as unmotivated by the "higher laws" of "imagination and fancy" as are the blind larvae she spawns into a self-perpetuating slavery.

This is what Thoreau finds in Kirby and Spence, and it frightens him. Close reading of Thoreau's reading suggests that an underreported, class-bound fear of society's grotesque abdomen, a fear of the "mass of men who lead lives of quiet desperation," resides side by side with bittersweet recognition of everyman's imperfect struggle for self-culture. A grotesque version of society underwrites Thoreau's optimism and reveals an undercurrent of dejection.[15] As in the example of Hawthorne, Occidental (and seemingly accidental) change in and around the year 1848 brings Thoreau, via an insect poetics, near to a conservative rhetoric. Sacvan Bercovitch has made a similar argument in *The Rites of Assent*. He argues that Hester Prynne's "decision" to stay in America, to further convert her Letter (from Adulterer to Angel, etc.) rather than to escape to the continent with Pearl, signals, at the level of plot, the author's practice of a conservative "thick propaganda"— a stealth-ideological position taken up in defense against the emergence of progressive ideas abroad and at home.[16] Remember that 1848 was a watershed year, notable for, among other things, the publication of *The Communist Manifesto* in Germany, the Seneca Falls Convention in America, and franchise expansion in England. In this light, Thoreau's squeamishness about appetites and abdomens, taken together with his refusal to do more than point to future hatchings (until his remarks on John Brown), signals, at the level of theme, a conservative tendency similar to Hawthorne's.

In a traditional reading of the radical Thoreau, it makes sense that he recoiled from the matriarchal, hierarchical, industrial, expansionist, and antidemocratic society of white ants. It makes sense that he opted for private, shrunken abdomens over gravid, partitioned, bloated ones. His heroism, after all, is gendered male; it is numbered singular.[17] His patriotism, wisely vague though it was, still rejected "overseers of the self," such as those inherent to hierarchies of bondage, or primogeniture. Therefore he would have us all shrink the source of such grotesque fertility, have us all individually and continuously revolt against such frighteningly, perfectly fixed states.

That said, and the half-life of this traditional reading beyond doubt, we must consider the competing possibility that this "abdomen" also signifies Thoreau's fear of revolutionary violence—the fear that the desperation of the mass of men will *not* remain quiet. Reconsider Thoreau's point that the tidbit abdomen of the perfect butterfly risks an "insectivorous fate." Whose fate, after all, is this? On the one hand, throughout the pages of Kirby and Spence, this fate is mass extinction, wholesale self-consumption by cannibal tribes, or more pitiable holocausts, like the prospect of American shores littered with "filmy wing and fragile form." But Thoreau implies not only that an alienated mass of men threatens to consume or extinguish itself but also that violence might cross the deadly space *between* states, between class-bound verities, between neuter workers and philosophically gravid queens. Read from this perspective, the higher being's vestigial, tidbit abdomen not only "betrays" a relation to the mass of men but tempts the voracious appetite of man as "gross feeder." On the one hand, Thoreau mourns the slumber of the great mass of men, mourns the "sleepers" (here blind worker and warrior ants) who toil to serve their colony, just as *Walden's* immigrants toil to lay down "sleepers" (cross-ties) for the railroad; he regrets and would redress the alienation of state from state, or even of man by the state. On the other hand, Thoreau knows that on the ground of his imaginary, future place, where "the best government . . . governs least," and where self-culture is our only hope, his privileged butterfly might find its way onto the menu. Hasn't he written into the passage that a vast, voracious sea of workers might revolt and consume the winged higher state? Reading is rereading: "The abdomen under the wings of the butterfly still represents the larva. This is the tidbit which tempts his insectivorous fate. The gross feeder is the man in the larva state; and there are whole nations in that state, nations without fancy or imagination, whose vast abdomens betray them."

The vast tragedy in *Walden* is its undertow of dejection. It forcefully reaches us only when we see that "the gross feeder" would eat even the "tidbit" of that land, or state, promised to him by self-reliance, that he would thereby seal his fate within the present communal chaos. Indeed, these alienated workers are the metonymic extension of the bloated queen that Thoreau must have recoiled from in Kirby and Spence. Recognition of this brings us back to what must have been a terrible thought for Thoreau; the corruption of the one is part and parcel of the corruption of the many.

The calm, self-possessed remove to Walden Pond, the deliberate anatomy of chrysalis construction, the sense of unruffled, partitioned meditation over the economies of experience—all this is not only what it seems. If the social anxiety that Thoreau likely projected on, and then discovered within, his entomological source has penetrated *Walden*, then the "I" of the text may be "retained," as Thoreau exults in his opening, but not simply to preserve a naturalness to expression, and not to cleverly foreground the fact that self-culture is the "present subject" of *Walden*, but also as a rhetorical strategy that might deploy a constructed, singular repose against reformist fury. We must remember that Thoreau's embrace of John Brown, and of a more radical politics (and naturalism), does not hatch until after the *Walden* meditations. Thoreau's book is at once a call for revolution and, in light of the grotesquerie he found in "insectivorous" social models, also a conservative attempt to downsize the nature of that revolution. In this nonconformist vision, revolution in *Walden* must start and end with the individual larva. Read from a certain naturalistic angle of vision, Thoreau's revolution ends in dejection and presents not even a single apotheosis.

Perfect Summer Life at Last

The ending of *Walden*, perhaps the most significant insectivorous moment in American literature, is also one of the most compressed and complex rhetorical flourishes in the high style of American romanticism. It is well worth remembering here in full:

> Every one has heard the story that has gone the rounds of New England, of a strong and beautiful bug which came out of a dry leaf of an old table of apple-tree wood, which had stood in a farmer's kitchen for sixty years, first in Connecticut, and afterwards in Massachusetts,—from an egg deposited in the living tree many years earlier still, as appeared by counting the annual layers beyond it; which was heard gnawing out for several weeks, hatched perchance by the heat of an urn. Who does not feel his faith in a resurrection

and immortality strengthened by hearing this? Who knows what beautiful and winged life, whose egg has been buried for ages under many concentric layers of woodenness in the dead dry life of society, deposited at first in the alburnum of the green and living tree, which has gradually been converted into the semblance of its well-seasoned tomb,—heard perchance gnawing out now for years by the astonished family of man, as they sat around the festive board,—may unexpectedly come forth from amidst society's most trivial and handselled furniture, to enjoy its perfect summer life at last!

I do not say that John or Jonathan will realize all this; but such is the character of that morrow which mere lapse of time can never make to dawn. The light which puts out our eyes is darkness to us. Only that day dawns to which we are awake. There is more day to dawn. The sun is but a morning star. (221)

Thoreau's attraction to insect metaphors like this one has directly to do with their imperfect ability to illuminate human society. Indeed, Thoreau turned to entomological images not only because he found them apt but because they retain disturbing supplement to their legible meanings.[18] This is a difficult idea, but one Thoreau learned well from Emerson. In "Circles," Emerson says, quite tragically, that "our moods do not know each other." He then turns immediately to the balm of literature, which, because the "field cannot be seen from within the field," as he says, might provide fixed marks to compensate for our swinging moods. At the end of *Walden*, then, and again taking Emerson literally, Thoreau turns to a text outside "the field," one from which he might turn back with borrowed perspective on humanity. Yet there is an obvious problem in this strategy, because, far from being objective, "the book of insects," as Thoreau found it, was itself informed by mood. I have shown this to be the case in Kirby and Spence. The *Introduction* harbors a fear that science will be perverted for atheistic ends. An awareness of race and class underwrites an odd, epistolary "science." In short, this British book is empirical also in the sense that it carries an awareness of its place in the empire of British letters. We have, then, both a source and a scholarly set susceptible to the inconstancy of mood; we have, in fact, redoubled our tendency to inconstancy. If there is no getting outside the "field," here, we need to be careful when, in *Walden*'s conclusion, we find one final, hidden appropriation of the *Introduction*'s insectivorous terminology.

In Thoreau's final flourish, we read of a "perfect summer" hatching. Kirby and Spence tell us that that "perfect societies . . . are associated in all their states, live in a common habitation, and unite their labors to promote a common object;—and [that] imperfect societies, [are] those that are associated during part of their existence only, or else do not dwell in a common habitation, nor unite their labors to promote a common object" (10). But we also know, after discovering Kirby and Spence, that Thoreau confronted imperfect swarms and perfectly horrible queens—that *perfection*, as a term, cannot be trusted. In its appearance at the end of *Walden*, and still in an entomological context, the term signifies not only transcendental salvation but also grotesque efficiency—the progress of a streamlined, mechanical greed and corruption. This embedded meaning is something Thoreau reasonably assumes "John or Jonathan," the British and the American everyman, will not "realize." In short, Thoreau's "sun is but a morning [and mourning] star." This play on words reveals intentionally hidden dejection, an affect in obscure yet irresolvable tension with the positive meaning of the passage. Thoreau certainly signals that he mourns his *unintended* unreadability—his inability to "wake [his] neighbors up" (57). He would not be an isolatoe, but for, as he writes earlier in *Walden*, "there [being] more secrets in my trade than in most men's, and yet not voluntarily kept, but inseparable from its very nature" (11). By the end of *Walden*, these secrets *are* voluntarily kept, and exposure to an entomological perspective on human society—with its window into elemental violence, its grotesque perfection—is part of the cause. Finally, Thoreau's breed of transcendentalism cannot evade the horrible materiality of nature. Thoreau "would gladly tell all" and would not "propose to write an ode to dejection," but as a naturalist building a distinctly unromantic appreciation for how amorality and necessity underwrite natural designs, he found the conditional voice thrust upon him.

One might achieve more confidence in this stark reading of *Walden*'s ending by looking at how Thoreau rehearsed it earlier in his book, for in the early meditation on clothing, he also considers the promise of American "resurrection," this time cast as an American "molting season" (15). Distant from Kirby and Spence, but still pondering bugs, Thoreau laments that the "maggot" of "fashion" persists in the "heads" of certain Americans; he expresses regret that we live for "fashion" and not in self-reliance (17). The problem, it seems, is that the "maggot of fashion hatche[s] . . . from an

egg deposited . . . nobody knows when, for not even fire kills these things"
(17). The maggot of fashion is from Paris, he says, it is a European muse, and
it persists in the woodlike heads of "emasculated" Americans. We should
kill these things, and do try, suggests Thoreau, but they persist, so much so
that burning them as we might wood, and did witches, accomplishes nothing. The persistence of that "worm," that buried promise of a resurrected
self, that we encounter in the conclusion is here the "maggot" of a lingering malaise, but the problem is not in the maggot of fashion itself but in
its habitat, for this fashion victim's woodlike head, if common, or "handselled," contains no "green and living" "alburnum." It is, and always was,
dead wood. But Thoreau stops here and pulls back from his indictment of
the common man. Indeed, he sounds almost fearful of having reached too
far. "Nevertheless," he writes, "we will not forget that some Egyptian wheat
is said to have been handed down to us by a mummy" (17). In this mummy
we return to the dead human wood and look forward to the "tomb" of the
"apple-tree wood" passage. In the mummy's legacy a gift lies dormant,
awaiting, like the hieroglyphic secret of the Egyptians, some latter-day
Champollion. Here is a telling difference between the two versions. The
entombed worm of the conclusion does not wait but, rather ominously, is
"heard by the astonished family of man gnawing out now for years as they
[sit] round the festive board" (221). This strange, winged messiah-life,
whatever it is, moves toward us, not we toward it. If not quite "slouching
toward Bethlehem to be born," as in Yeats's much later gothicism, Thoreau's
image—quickening, gnawing, overlooked—is equally dreadful. Because we
are not awake, says Thoreau, we risk being blinded (having our eyes "put
out," as he actually writes) by some violent, hungry, and perhaps revolutionary apotheosis. This particular insectivorous fate confounds the ending's talk
of morning and resurrection and stands as our best proof that Thoreau's
book is foremost a warning—the return of a molted Calvinist jeremiad.

Melville's comic tale is no such thing. "The Apple-Tree Table" appeared
in *Putnam's Magazine* two years after Thoreau published *Walden,* and to
date there seems to be no sure way to tell if it is a direct engagement with
Thoreau's use of the popular tale. [19] Melville seems to turn over the language and meaning of Thoreau's apple-tree table story, but there is every
chance that this occurs simply because each used the same popular source.
Melville, for example, not only gives us the "festive board" of "the family
of [a] man" but actually suspends his entire plot on their "astonish[ment]"

before the worm's "gnawing." The "urn" that in Thoreau warms the table and jump-starts the hatching also appears in "The Apple-Tree Table," that is, until Biddy, the maid, removes it. Instead of Thoreau's "alburnum of the green and living tree," we find Melville's "living greenness" of "trees" (1330). Instead of Thoreau's "well-seasoned tomb," we find Melville's bizarre meditation on "Democritus and the tombs of Abdera," where the point seems to be that isolation and democratic thinking, taken together, make a joke (1338–39).

The embattled patriarch of the tale, a figure more explicitly presented in "I and My Chimney," at first seems to share a great deal with Thoreau's conservationist of the self. Both, for example, explicitly defend against what Thoreau calls "emasculating" social force. In Thoreau, however, this force is abstracted and seems not necessarily gendered female. But in an odd way, Thoreau's unambiguous disdain for women survives the dispersing force of abstraction, and it is Thoreau who crosses the ages as a more thorough-going misogynist. He is even more unwilling than Melville to seriously take up a hybrid social space where men and women suffer together. Melville takes hybridity seriously and ironically he does so through the leveling power of humor. There is no such embrace of hybrid sexual space in Thoreau. Remember that Thoreau prefers the butterfly's sexless, ascetic perfection, the higher body that seems to live on ambrosia, yet he can't quite erase the tidbit abdomen, our trail back to the perfection of the gravid termite queen. In Melville, the narrator's social surround is gendered female and certainly threatens, yet the henpecked husband comes across as complexly alive—a being fully in the world. For all the attacks on his "chimney" and "writing table," he clearly loves his wife and daughters. Humorously, almost joy-ously, he inhabits the same space they do; he experiences the marvels they do; he even discovers his own subjectivity by honing it against two influential texts: modern spiritualism (advocated by Julia's Kirby-and-Spence-like reading of the book of nature) and Cotton Mather's *Magnalia* (rescued from the attic along with the apple-tree table). An author can deploy humor to raise anxiety, but in this tale it works differently. It softens the manifest anxieties of the patriarch; it renders Thoreau's urgent, philosophical, hier-archical thinking obsolete. More interesting still, in worrying along with and trying to correct the women in the tale, Melville's speaker exposes that his maleness is contingent on everyday sexual combat; his bluster and defense transform into a lovingly embedded communal sort of bickering communion in sexual difference. This is more true as the story reaches its conclusion. Why does the speaker appeal to "Professor Johnson, the [eminent] naturalist," to set the record straight (1348)? Is it because he needs to redouble his attack on the women? If so, it is interesting that the wife suggests an appeal to this lifeless character. We must wonder how she has come to usurp and "feminize" the patriarch's role. We might draw a straight line from the aggression of the wife in the tale to gendered threat in Thoreau—to the gravid termite queen. But to do so would be to overlook another option for reading. It is possible that Melville's speaker, in his appeal to "the prosy," lifeless figure of the naturalist, as much divorces himself from rationality as appeals to it.

This does not mean that Melville was a good husband, or that the author was somehow ahead of his time in respecting women; it was, after all, Frederick Douglass, not Herman Melville, who attended the convention at Seneca Falls. I want instead to suggest that Melville's speaker votes both *with* the people and *as* an embedded, untraumatized figure in this tale—a reasonable reading largely overlooked by critics. In the end, the patriarch seems quite open to the spiritual lesson in the bug's hatching. Consider that in Melville we find out who Thoreau says has "his faith in a resurrection and immortality strengthened" by the tale of the "beautiful bug." It turns out first to be a *she*, for the narrator's daughter, Julia, has her faith in more mystical hatchings only redoubled (even when confronted with the naturalist's recourse to naturalistic explanations):

> "Say what you will," said Julia, holding up, in the covered tumbler, the glorious, lustrous, flashing, live opal, "say what you will, if this beauteous creature be not a spirit, it yet teaches a spiritual lesson. For if, after one hundred and fifty years entombment, a mere insect comes forth at last into light, itself an effulgence, shall their be no glorified resurrection for the spirit of man?" (1349)

But Melville is our wizard of swinging moods and abandoned subject positions. Just when we are ready to claim the speaker's reluctant embrace of regendered, near-Thoreauvian "spiritual manifestations," we find that the resurrected worm "did not long enjoy its radiant life; it expired the next day" (1349). Nothing lovely lasts in Melville's tragic vision. Just as when Ishmael's stilt-walking, masthead Platonism is revealed as hovering over Cartesian vortices, so the only sure thing here is impermanency.

Matters of time also divorce Melville and Thoreau. Thoreau, of course, purports to be about improving the "nick of time." He puns that "the present was my next experiment" (57). But at crucial moments, like the last paragraphs in the book, he abstracts the domestic scene in space and time. "We have all heard" of this past hatching, he writes, and we are lulled by "mere lapse of time" into imagining a sort of higher second coming of this "winged life." The messianic thematics here are hardly veiled: it will come again; it will be born of the low; it will be missed. The urn, as well, is an appeal to Christian mythos; it is the heat that goes before and signals the fire; it is the harbinger, the poet prophet; it is the "I" retained to foretell the good news; egotistically considered, it is Thoreau himself, or *Walden* as sacred text. The transcendental tragedy is that in spite of what the poet says, we miss that this winged life already inhabits us—that we do not know our true selves, whether gnawing or hatching. Finally, Thoreau's messianic play pushes resurrection quite out of the present. He asserts that life was, and will be, but is not now. The Melville tale, on the other hand, not only brings the hatching into the present but does so, as in the original New England story, three times. Two bugs, of course, hatch from the table. The first, strangely like Thoreau's battling ants, gets "clapped" under a "tumbler" (1341). And like Thoreau, Melville's narrator turns away from the marvel. When he returns he finds that the maid has "put the bug in the fire" (1343). The second "expire[s] the next day" (1349). But the third hatching is the most interesting, and most easily missed, for it is the narrator himself looking to burst the confines of his home. This passage also is worth quoting at length:

On every hand, some strange insect was seen, flying, or running, or creeping, on rafter and floor. . . . Indeed, the whole stairs, and platform, and ladder, were festooned, and carpeted, and canopied with cobwebs. . . . In these cobwebs, swung, as in aerial catacombs, myriads of all tribes of mummied insects. . . . Climbing the stairs to the platform, and pausing there, to recover my breath, a curious scene was presented. The sun was about half-way up. Piercing the little sky-light, it slopingly bored a rainbowed tunnel clear across the darkness of the garret. Here, millions of butterfly moles were swarming. Against the sky-light itself, with a cymbal-like buzzing, thousands of insects clustered in a golden mob. . . . Only after long peering, did I discover a little padlock, imbedded, like an oyster at the bottom of the sea, amid matted

masses of weeds, chrysalides, and insectivorous eggs. . . . I tried to pick the
lock, when scores of small ants and flies, half-torpid, crawled forth from
the key-hole, and, feeling the warmth of the sun in the pane, began frisking
around me. . . . Presently, I was overrun by them. As if incensed at this invasion of their retreat, countless bands darted up from below, beating about
my head, like hornets. At last, with a sudden jerk, I burst open the scuttle. And
Ah! What a change. As from the gloom of the grave and the companion-
ship of worms, man shall at last rapturously rise into the living greenness
and glory immortal, so, from my cobwebbed old garret, I thrust forth my
head into the balmy air, and found myself hailed by the verdant tops of green
trees, growing in the little garden below—trees, whose leaves soared high
above my topmost slate.

What Melville accomplishes in this passage is nothing short of necro-
mancy. Mummies come to life. Air circulates, quickening "insectivorous
eggs" and the "handselled furniture" alike. It is a remarkable passage, one
of the most joyous in Melville's opus. Here, as in disputations that follow
in the forecastle space downstairs, under this garret, Melville's speaker
imagines himself as already in the mix. In the garret, a wildly hybrid swarm
surrounds the speaker. The mix of life and death surrounding him seems
to speak to what is at stake in our spiritual hatching, and it too enlivens
the speaker; it drives him upward, creating the strange social friction that
causes his emergence into "the perfect summer" of a living world. This is
Melville's version of "the heat of an urn," the poet immersed in life as it is—
communal. This fact in the passage is easily missed—that the frisking, invading, beating, surrounding millions are also trapped. Thousands cluster
in the skylight itself or dart upward to join in a golden orb of trapped life.
In a wonderful and dizzying inversion (one that recalls the Catskill eagle's
rhetorical flights from *Moby-Dick*'s "The Try-Works"), the patriarch finally
swims to "the bottom of the sea," "pick[s] the lock," and bursts topside,
"above [the] topmost slate." The swarm *must* emerge as well, though there
is no mention of this concomitant, bursting salvation. Melville's is a communal hatching, or none at all, and there is absolutely no fear of the swarm
at *this* moment. When the speaker descends from this old garret masthead,
it is only to enter the present mix again, and again.

When Thoreau places his ants under a tumbler, they are not quite the
self. He still wants them to be, but they are not. First, they are, well, ants

under a tumbler, and then mock-heroic figures in the past, in the promised future, or on some distant field of war—but they are never the self in the present. Like Emerson's ungraspable death in "Experience," the ants stay strange, stay "unhandsome," and signify a tragedy that Thoreau, like his John or Jonathan, will not "realize" in the present book. When Melville's speaker claps the beautiful bug under a tumbler, he tries, sardonically, but fails to "look at the strange object in a purely scientific way" (1341). Tragically, comically, lovingly, he cannot push the self away even with the help of an "eminent naturalist." In Melville, there is no avoiding the press of the world as it is. Indeed, Melville's glad message, once we see it, is that the garret hatching has already happened, that the bug is the self, and that it is no isolatoe. It may "expire," or descend, and even do so in repetition, but it does so in the social, hybrid, domestic realm where the narrator's "girls have preserved it" (1349).

NOTES

1. Henry David Thoreau, *Walden, or Life in the Woods* (New York: Library of America, 1985), 1.

2. William Kirby and William Spence, *An Introduction to Entomology: or, Elements of the natural history of insects; with plates,* 4 vols. (London: Longman, Hurst, Rees, Orme, and Brown, 1822–26). Hereafter cited in the text.

3. See David Spooner's recent book *Thoreau's Vision of Insects and the Origins of American Entomology* (Xlibris, 2002). Spooner briefly explores how Thoreau's appropriations from Kirby and Spence are "accurate only in a symbolic sense," but, as an entomologist, he angles away from my concern with American domestic space in order to unpack how *Walden* and the journals reveal a "full picture of animal and insect life [in New England], and of the ecological situation in the mid-nineteenth century" (45).

4. See T. Walker Herbert, *Marquesan Encounters: Melville and the Meaning of Civilization* (Cambridge: Harvard University Press, 1980), for a foundational work of new historicism, and perhaps the most thoughtful study of the centrality of the term "civilization" in nineteenth-century American literature. Thoreau's investment in this popular concern is direct and unambiguous in *Walden.* Consider these lines from the "Shelter" section of "Economy": "But how happens it that he who is said to enjoy [material wealth] is so commonly a *poor* civilized man, while the savage, who has them not, is rich as a savage? If it is asserted that civilization is a real advance in the condition of man,—and I think that it is, though only the wise improve their advantages,—it must be shown that it has produced better dwellings

without making them more costly; and the cost of a thing is the amount of what I will call life which is required to be exchanged for it, immediately or in the long run" (20–21).

5. See Lawrence Buell, *The Environmental Imagination: Thoreau, Nature Writing, and the Formation of American Culture* (Cambridge: Harvard University Press, 1995), for an in-depth meditation on the slow turn toward a less-romanticized, more properly ecological "green Thoreau"—both in Thoreau's own work and in the historical reception of his writings.

6. For an example of this dilemma, see E. O. Wilson's seminal text *Sociobiology: The New Synthesis* (Cambridge: Belknap, 1975). Wilson's remarkable introduction, now thirty years old, speaks hopefully of the humanities' incorporation within sociobiology—something that has yet to occur. Warming up, Wilson carefully attacks "sociology *sensu stricto*" as a hybrid science, lacking vigor, something like the humanities' halfway covenant with the emergent truth of sociobiology. To Wilson, sociology lags behind "because of its largely structuralist and non-genetic approach." It seems that thinkers not willing to admit the "modern" dictum that there is a "biological basis for all social behavior" (or, more correctly, thinkers unwilling to comply for fear of how far Wilson's *basis* might reach toward unmasking art as *superstructure*) risk being incorporated like some animalcule succumbing to an engulfing pseudopod. "It may not be too much to say," writes Wilson, "that sociology and the other social sciences, as well as the humanities, are the last branch of biology waiting to be included in the Modern Synthesis. One of the functions of sociobiology, then, is to reformulate the foundations of the social sciences in a way that draws these subjects into the Modern Synthesis. Whether the social sciences can be truly biologized in this fashion remains to be seen" (4). Thoreau's own seduction before the example of biology, especially the examples of social insects and their drives, brought him back both to his senses and to the limits of metaphor. In the end, the entomological analogies he offers attune him both to the benefits of obscurity and to the risk of losing one's self in the imperfect extension of metaphor.

7. Thoreau was not such a homebody as he declared, and neither man traveled from Emersonian "ruins to ruins" or lugged about untranscendable baggage. Still, much of Thoreau can be tracked back to figures in Emerson, and this, of course, is one example. See "Self-Reliance" for Emerson's consideration of travel as escapism. I note the famous discipleship of Thoreau under Emerson early on in this essay because the idea is too common, and resting with this sense of Thoreau is dangerous. Thoreau's detailed use of entomology marks one important aspect of his extreme divergence from Emerson. For more on this subject, see David Robinson's essay "Emerson's Natural Theology and the Paris Naturalists: Toward a Theory of Animated Nature," *Journal of the History of Ideas* 41, no. 1 (1980): 69–88. See Buell's *The Environmental Imagination* for an exhaustive consideration of Thoreau's difference from his greatest mentor, and for thoughtful consideration of Thoreau's increasing investment in an ecological, or "biotic," mode of thinking.

8. Emerson's "Fate" is rife with forays into what passed as science in his day. See, for example, his oddly racist dabbling with phrenology: "As in every barrel of cowries brought to New Bedford there shall be one *orangia,* so there will, in a dozen millions of Malays and Mahometans, be one or two astronomical skulls" (338). Samuel Otter's remarkable *Melville's Anatomies* (Berkeley: University of California Press, 1999) is probably the best extant work on the nexus of imaginative literature and several of the emergent "sciences" of the day.

9. See, for example, Max Lerner's 1939 piece "Thoreau, No Hermit," in *Twentieth Century Views: Thoreau, a Collection of Critical Essays,* ed. Sherman Paul (Englewood Cliffs, N.J.: Prentice Hall, 1962). It is one of many pieces to make the point that the author's monkish behaviors hardly severed him from the social concerns of his day.

10. Herman Melville, *Moby-Dick* (New York: Norton, 2002), 22, 188.

11. See James Rennie, *The Natural History of Insects* (New York, 1833). This is an American text that was quite popular in the era as well, and I can find no record of Thoreau's having read it. This slightly later book makes frequent and worshipful reference to Kirby and Spence. Indeed, Rennie's first pages are a patchwork of direct quotes from his English predecessors.

12. See Barbara Johnson's wonderful essay "A Hound, a Bay Horse, and a Turtle Dove: Obscurity in Walden," in *A World of Difference* (Baltimore: Johns Hopkins University Press, 1987).

13. See Robinson's "Emerson's Natural Theology and the Paris Naturalists." Robinson deftly locates the central problem for Emerson, which was only a more urgent concern for the more dedicated naturalist, Thoreau. "While arguments from the design of nature could easily establish the existence of God," he writes, "they could not so easily serve as a foundation for moral action. Nature clearly indicated a creator, but to derive an elaborate moral code from it, or even the moral principles necessary for the conduct of life, was much more problematic" (74).

14. Emily Dickinson, *Final Harvest* (Boston: Little Brown, 1961), 20.

15. See Philip Fisher's now classic "Democratic Social Space: Whitman, Melville, and the Promise of American Transparency," in *The New American Studies: Essays from Representations,* ed. Philip Fisher (Berkeley: University of California Press, 1991). Fisher considers immigration pressure, among other ideological pressures, as yielding both the practical American fantasy of assimilation, as well as literary notice of "damaged social space"—textual space that undermines the cartographical imagining of American society as something like a perfect hive, "cellular and unlimited" (76). Thoreau's consideration of (im)perfect insect societies seems unconsciously to erase the complexities and disappointments he must have found in his entomological models.

16. Sacvan Bercovitch, *The Rites of Assent* (New York: Routledge, 1993), 194.

17. Thoreau wrote the following in his journal on January 31, 1851: "In the East, women religiously conceal that they have faces; in the West, that they have legs. In both cases they make it evident that they have but little brains."

18. See Pamela Schirmeister, *Less Legible Meanings: Between Poetry and Philosophy in the Work of Emerson* (Stanford: Stanford University Press, 1999), for an eloquent discussion of the transferential uses of obscurity in Emerson.

19. Herman Melville, "The Apple-Tree Table," in *Herman Melville: Pierre, Israel Potter, The Confidence-Man, Tales,* ed. Harrison Hayford (Library of America, 1984), 1328–50. In January 1954 Frank Davidson published "Melville, Thoreau, and 'The Apple-Tree Table'" in *American Literature* 25, no. 4 (1954): 479–88. More than fifty years have passed, and critical inquiry has transformed. Davidson's is a strong essay, focusing quite brilliantly on Melville's personal and spiritual hatchings, but because he sidesteps Thoreau, as well as the fact that both Thoreau's book and Melville's response are as much about America's political rebirth as about any personal, authorial growth, the essay is now far out of date.

In the spring of 1971, Carolyn Karcher updated Davidson in *American Quarterly* 23, no. 1 (1971): 101–9. Her essay "The 'Spiritual Lesson' of Melville's 'The Apple-Tree Table'" corrects Davidson's failure to regard Melville's satire of spiritualist cults of the 1850s—his satire of cult figures like the Fox sisters. Karcher is right to assert that the tale "shed[s] new light . . . on [Melville's] judgment of the religious preoccupations of his contemporaries." Yet in her reconstruction of one relevant historical setting, we lose sight of the argument with Thoreau's final paragraphs in *Walden*, and of the general argument between self-culture and communal culture so central to Melville's stealth critique of anxiety in *Walden*.

5

From the Chrysalis to the Display Case

The Butterfly's "Voyage Out" in Virginia Woolf

RACHEL SARSFIELD

Watching him [the moth], it seemed as if a fibre, very thin but pure, of the enormous energy of the world had been thrust into his frail and diminutive body. As often as he crossed the pane, I could fancy that a thread of vital light became visible. He was little or nothing but life.

Yet, because he was so small, and so simple a form of the energy that was rolling in at the open window and driving its way through so many narrow and intricate corridors in my own brain and in those of other human beings, there was something marvellous as well as pathetic about him. It was as if someone had taken a tiny bead of pure life and decking it as lightly as possible with down and feathers, had set it dancing and zig-zagging to show us the true nature of life.[1]

This glowing tribute to an insect from Virginia Woolf's essay "The Death of the Moth" (1942) provides the perfect starting point for discussing her use of lepidoptera (butterfly and moth) imagery, which serves several key metaphorical functions in her writing.[2] In this short piece, the narrator is first fascinated by the eponymous insect's fluttering and then oddly moved by the sudden onset of its death throes. And while this composition is as diminutive and easily overlooked as the moth itself, it can nevertheless be seen as the ultimate expression of Woolf's "butterfly manifesto," where the narrator's view of the moth as "a tiny bead of pure life," which indeed is central to his or her interest in it, is wholly typical of the author's constant obsession with capturing "life" in her writing, as well as of her belief that lepidoptera, at once animated and elusive, ideally represent it. Thus a thorough analysis of Woolf's lepidoptera imagery, a key trope in her work, is crucial to a complete understanding of her artistic philosophy and objectives, something that prior criticism has yet to undertake.[3] Accordingly, I intend to trace the butterfly's or moth's "voyage out" in her writing (although this phrase is wholly metaphorical: her first novel, *The Voyage Out* [1915], will not play a major part in my discussion). Rather, my concern is with the lepidoptera trope's figurative journey across Woolf's oeuvre, from the chrysalis of undeveloped potential to the display case of the text, as mapping this voyage provides an entirely new insight into her unique authorial perspective.

THE SOURCE: "BUG-HUNTING"

Having stated that lepidoptera are of primary importance to Woolf's thinking and writing, my first task, before examining this imagery in detail, is to question why these insects might hold special significance for her: why she should have written about the death of a *moth*, rather than any other creature. Of course, as a modernist, Woolf was in good company in finding entomological metaphors valuable, as modernist literature practically swarms with insects: from perhaps the best-known literary bug of the age, the man-turned-beetle Gregor Samsa in Franz Kafka's "The Metamorphosis" (1912), which Steven Connor has called "the canonical insect text of modernism," or Jean Rhys's nightmare vision of commuters morphing into giant fleas in her story "The Insect World" (1944), to Ezra Pound's assertion that the technologizing of modern life is making society increasingly insectile: "In his growing subservience to, and adoration of, and entanglement in machines, in utility, man rounds the circle almost into insect life."[4]

Woolf is thus typically modernist (albeit in a less paranoiac vein than some of her peers) in turning to insect metaphors, and indeed, lepidoptera imagery so pervades her writing that numerous readers have noted its presence, often relating it to the family hobby of "bug-hunting," or butterfly and moth collecting, that she enjoyed in her youth. Nevertheless, no prior discussion has recognized the full extent of the lepidoptera trope's proliferation throughout her work, or how closely connected it is with the author's (concept of her) writing. For example, while Harvena Richter's influential essay "Hunting the Moth: Virginia Woolf and the Creative Imagination" (which has greatly shaped thinking on Woolf's lepidoptera metaphors) argues for the moth's importance as a creative symbol, Richter nevertheless achieves only a partial reading.[5] First, Richter states that only the moth—and not its close relative the butterfly—has metaphorical significance for Woolf, whereas in fact she does not distinguish between the two, using both interchangeably. Second, Richter asserts that the author's early mental breakdowns (the first occurring at thirteen, following her mother's death), together with the traumatic impact of her brother Thoby's death from typhoid when she was twenty-four, led Woolf to choose the nocturnal, mysterious moth as a suitably ominous emblem of her creative consciousness.[6] However, since Richter's article first appeared, the publication of previously unseen Woolf material—specifically her early journals (published in 1990) and an expanded edition of her memoirs *Moments of Being* (1985)—throws new light on her lepidoptera imagery.

This new material reveals not only that Woolf had attached figurative meaning to lepidoptera long before Thoby's death but also that the bereavements triggering her adolescent breakdowns colored her artistic development more than the breakdowns themselves. Bug hunting, just one of many hobbies she and her siblings shared, might never have become important to Woolf had it not straddled the two most significant periods of her childhood: the idyllic summers spent at the family's holiday home in Saint Ives, Cornwall (a routine discontinued after her mother's death in 1895), and the unhappier epoch following this loss. The trauma of losing her mother was compounded two years later by the death of her half sister Stella Duckworth, who had assumed the vacant maternal role. In this context, an 1899 diary entry describing a typical moth hunt gains an additional, darker resonance:

The leader [i.e., Thoby], should one of his guests strike his fancy, uncorks his poison pot, gently taps the specimen on the nose—the cork is shut—& the moth, his brain dazed with the delicious fumes of liquor, sinks into an all-embracing arm. Death might come more painfully. The other night, as the light cautiously advanced, it was abruptly told to halt by the leader, a Red underwing was on the tree. . . . We gazed one moment on his splendour, & then uncorked the bottle. I think the whole procession felt some unprofessional regret when, with a last gleam of scarlet eye & scarlet wing, the grand old moth vanished.[7]

This entry shows a keen interest in lepidoptera and a faintly morbid fascination with the moth's demise, making this probably the earliest record of Woolf's later obsession with netting "life" in print. In addition, the recent loss of her mother and sister, alluded to in the comment that "death might come more painfully," is a likely source of this obsession. Of course, Virginia had firsthand knowledge of the truth of this statement, particularly in the case of Stella, who died after months of illness and pain.[8] Thus the painfully close link Woolf was to draw in her work between lepidoptera and (ephemeral) life was evidently already forming when she wrote this journal entry; and when, seven years later, Thoby died suddenly at age twenty-six, the loss of her brother, the keenest family bug hunter, reinforced rather than created the association between life and lepidoptera. So from the outset of her career, Woolf's writing demonstrated an interest in pursuing "life," as one would a moth or butterfly; however, she was to find catching this prey far harder than it was for Thoby to trap the drowsy red underwing on that night in 1899.

THE EMERGING IMAGE:
FEMALE CATERPILLARS IN THE PATRIARCHAL "COCOON"

Understandably perhaps, the highly emotive associations that Woolf could (and did) attach to lepidoptera led her to identify with this imagery both personally and artistically. The personal aspect is apparent in the following extract from her memoir "A Sketch of the Past" (1939–40). Woolf's recollection of her emotional state at fifteen offers two important clues to her development as a writer: first, that the deaths of her mother and Stella were the defining events of her formative years, and second, that these losses may well have sparked the connection she was later to draw between lepidoptera and life:

> I was thinking; feeling; living; those two lives that the two halves [of her bedroom] symbolized with the intensity, the muffled intensity, which a butterfly or moth feels when with its sticky tremulous legs and antennae it pushes out of the chrysalis and emerges and sits quivering beside the broken case for a moment; its wings still creased; its eyes dazzled, incapable of flight.
>
> Anyone, whether fifteen or not, whether sensitive or not, must have felt something very acute, merely from what had happened. My mother's death

had been a latent sorrow—at thirteen one could not master it, envisage it, deal with it. But Stella's death two years later fell on a different substance. . . . I remember saying to myself after she died: "But this is impossible; things aren't, can't be like this"—the blow, the second blow of death, struck on me; tremulous, filmy eyed as I was, with my wings still creased, sitting there on the edge of my broken chrysalis.[9]

Woolf's explicit comparison between her psyche and a butterfly or moth emerging from its chrysalis indicates in just how personal a fashion she relates to lepidoptera imagery, as well as how closely she connects it with the pain of her family losses.[10] Particularly striking is her accurate reference to the butterfly or moth as having "its wings still creased; its eyes dazzled, incapable of flight." As she correctly notes, the butterfly's or moth's wings are limp, wet, and tightly folded when it leaves the chrysalis, and it must remain motionless (and susceptible to attack) while its wings gradually dry and expand, unable to fly until they are both fully expanded *and* completely dry, an hour or more after it emerges.[11] Woolf powerfully equates her adolescent vulnerability with this limbo between emergence and flight, particularly when asserting that the second "blow" of Stella's death "struck on me; tremulous, filmy eyed as I was, with my wings still creased, sitting there on the edge of my broken chrysalis," which implies that the emotions underlying this identification were deeply traumatized ones. The strength of this association between lepidoptera and (her own) life, particularly her overt connection between the newly emerged butterfly or moth and her personal development, prompts an examination of the extent to which one can relate the cycle of caterpillar, chrysalis, and adult insect to Woolf's *artistic* development, and of what we can learn about her aims by considering how this cycle, with which she was clearly familiar, operates figuratively in her work.

If the chrysalis corresponds to adolescence, then logically the previous stage of the cycle, the caterpillar, correlates to childhood. In Woolf's writing, childhood is often an emotive subject, repeatedly linked with frustration and suppression. Perhaps unsurprisingly, then, she consistently associates caterpillar imagery with arrested or repressed emotions, and, by extension, with narrow-mindedness, even bigotry. For example, her account of meeting George Bernard Shaw's wife Charlotte caustically states that she is "very stupid, and has rolled herself up in Indian mysticism, like a caterpillar in a cocoon, in self defence. When she got me alone she tried to convert me."[12] Blinkered religious sentiment is even more directly—and negatively—connected with caterpillars in Woolf's angry response to her composer friend Ethel Smyth's worries about Woolf's spiritual well-being: "How you religious caterpillars (quotation from [John] Webster) make my gorge rise! 'We' that is Ethel and Elizabeth [Ethel's great-niece], having saved our souls, and purged our grossness, faintly and vaguely perceived in you, Virginia, signs of grace—or are they only spots on the sun? . . . Swollen with egotism, thats [sic] what you are—gout d'you call it? . . . Lord! How I detest these savers up of merit, these gorged caterpillars" (Letters, August 8, 1934, 5:321).[13]

Indeed, Woolf is equally alert to cultural "caterpillardom," of what she sees as insular or bigoted thinking, whether occurring on an individual or on a wider, even global, level. One character in her fiction whose inward-looking mind-set is strikingly related to caterpillar imagery is Susan in The Waves (1931), the only woman among the novel's six narrators who is a wife and mother. As these roles wholly define Susan's adult identity, it seems apt that one of the first things she reports seeing as a child is "a caterpillar . . . curled in a green ring."[14] This caterpillar prefigures the way in which Susan's emotional development will later turn in on itself, permanently confined within the circle of an obsessive and self-righteous maternity (just as her ability to achieve her full life potential, and hence figuratively to emerge as a "moth," is contained within, and seemingly circumscribed by, her chosen label of "moth-er"). When imagining this future role, Susan declares, "I shall lie like a field bearing crops in rotation; in the summer heat will dance over me; in the winter I shall be cracked with the cold. . . . My children will carry me on: their teething, their crying, their going to school and coming back will be like the waves of the sea under me" (The Waves, 99). This state-ment reveals her as a maternal "caterpillar," with all the sanctimoniousness Woolf associates with "religious caterpillars" in her letter to Ethel Smyth, just as her description of these "caterpillars" as "swollen with egotism" would be equally applicable to the smugness Susan displays as a mother. Thus the caterpillar in a ring that she saw as a child represents both the unending cycle of generation and her blind loyalty to this cycle: hence she sees motherhood in terms of cyclical rhythms, whether of seasonal change or of her children's successive passage through the life stages of teething, going to school, and returning again.

The Waves's image of a caterpillar curled in a ring is closely mirrored some years later in Woolf's radical political essay *Three Guineas* (1938). However, by now the caterpillar's meaning has shifted from Susan's maternal zeal to something far more sinister:

> Are we not all agreed that the dictator when we meet him abroad is a very dangerous as well as a very ugly animal? And he is here among us, raising his ugly head, spitting his poison, small still, curled up like a caterpillar on a leaf, but in the heart of England. Is it not from this egg, to quote Mr Wells again, that "the practical obliteration of [our] freedom by Fascists or Nazis" will spring? And is not the woman who has to breathe that poison and to fight that insect, secretly and without arms, in her office, fighting the Fascist or the Nazi as surely as those who fight him with arms in the limelight of publicity?[15]

The smug bug has now reached monstrous, international proportions as the embodiment of women's oppression spitting a sexist poison just as damaging to personal and political freedom as the acknowledged dictators of 1930s Europe (indeed, the more dangerous for being unacknowledged). Equally arresting is her conflation of the political and the domestic dictator, hinting that the external and internal tyranny of a patriarchal society conspires to encircle and oppress women. This caterpillar image reappears later in the essay, again to support Woolf's view that the closed circle of a male-dominated civilization is unlikely to embrace change willingly. To emphasize this, she alludes to the game in which children join hands and pace in a ring, chanting a refrain that constantly repeats the line "Here we go round the mulberry bush, the mulberry bush, the mulberry bush."[16] Woolf twice refers to this song (altering "bush" to "tree"), using its repetitive refrain to denote male opposition to admitting women into universities and the workplace: "Almost the same gentlemen intone almost the same refusals for almost the same reasons. It seems as if there were no progress in the human race, but only repetition. We can almost hear them, if we listen, singing the same old song, 'Here we go round the mulberry tree, the mulberry tree, the mulberry tree'" (*Three Guineas*, 190). Here the joined hands of the circling children stand for men's "childish" refusal to let women in, while the endless loop of both song and dance underlines the monotonous predictability of their response. The second reference to the game unites the "mulberry bush/tree" refrain with the caterpillar, already established as an emblem of society's vicious circle, the implication being that the existing system of gender relations constitutes a "game" no longer worth playing:

> We, daughters of educated men, are between the devil and the deep blue sea. Behind us lies the patriarchal system; the private house, with its nullity, its immorality, its hypocrisy, its servility. Before us lies the public world, the professional system, with its possessiveness, its jealousy, its pugnacity, its greed. The one shuts us up like slaves in a harem; the other forces us to circle, like caterpillars head to tail, round the mulberry tree, the sacred tree, of property. It is a choice of evils. Each is bad. Had we not better plunge off the bridge into the river; *give up the game;* declare that the whole of human life is a mistake and so end it? (*Three Guineas,* 199; italics mine)

Woolf powerfully stresses the need for women to escape the endless, maddening circling "like caterpillars head to tail, round the mulberry tree" of social convention, which, in lepidoptera terms, means leaving the caterpillar stage behind, in order to emerge from the chrysalis in a new form. Indeed, while her references to the "mulberry *tree*" apparently misquote the "mulberry bush" song, they are, in fact, an allusion to the lepidopteran life cycle, as the mulberry tree's leaves are the sole food plant of silkworms (i.e., silk moth caterpillars). This suggests a certain overlap between caterpillar and chrysalis imagery, as silk is harvested when these caterpillars are at the *chrysalis* stage.

Figuratively speaking, then, the chrysalis represents someone who has not yet "emerged" into independence or maturity, and hence in Woolf's writing, chrysalises carry similar connotations to caterpillars, being associated with repression, stagnation, and (female) constraint within prescribed social roles. This overlap is typified in *The Waves* by the maternal "caterpillar" Susan, who also relates chrysalis imagery to her motherhood: "I am no longer January, May or any other season, but am all spun to a fine thread round the cradle, wrapping in a cocoon made of my own blood the delicate limbs of my baby" (*The Waves,* 130). Likewise, Woolf commonly uses the chrysalis as shorthand for personal or artistic arrest, as when she comments that "the Bloomsbury group was stunted in the chrysalis" compared to the lively intelligence of young people she is meeting in the north of England

(*Letters*, August 12, [1914], 2:51), or notes in her diary that when she is ill, "something happens in my mind. It refuses to go on registering impressions. It shuts itself up. It becomes chrysalis."[17]

But undoubtedly Woolf's most intriguing use of the chrysalis to signify personal repression occurs in her second novel, *Night and Day* (1919), where the silkworms bred by the heroine Katharine's cousin Cassandra Otway offer a metaphorical bridge between the author's (creative) past and her future work. Cassandra's silkworms anticipate the figurative connections in *Three Guineas* between caterpillars, mulberry trees, and female oppression, as is evident from the appearance of her bedroom, which is full of mulberry leaves, while the view from her window is tellingly "blocked with cages" of caterpillars.[18] These silkworms reflect her "cocooned," dependent state as one expected to achieve marriage and nothing else: for as silk moths must be killed before they emerge, in order to harvest the silk (as the chrysalis is spun from a single thread),[19] the fact that she is consistently linked with these cocoons destined never to hatch hints that, like them, she will never be allowed to reach maturity and "fly" independently.[20] However, Cassandra's silkworms also potentially embody the chrysalis's other, more liberating connotation of emergence and breaking free from (patriarchal) bonds: while her mother Lady Otway, a dutiful and wholly passive wife, vegetates in the drawing room in a silk dress that is, of course, the end product of these silkworms, Cassandra's bedroom upstairs also contains "home-made machines for the manufacture of silk dresses" (*Night and Day*, 175). This signals the potential for her to support herself through independent labor, as well as figuratively to "manufacture" her own role in life. Such self-sufficiency would be the antithesis of the ornamental, compliant femininity epitomized by Lady Otway, and so, perhaps unsurprisingly, Cassandra's mother strongly opposes her keeping silkworms or "taking to these nasty insects," as she terms it (175).

Evidently, the silkworm's implicit threat lies in the fact that, unless killed promptly upon forming its chrysalis, there is an imminent risk of it hatching (as silkworms remain at the cocoon stage for only two weeks), which would be equally disastrous for silk production and for the status quo. For if the silk moth does emerge as an adult insect, the single thread of silk from which the chrysalis was spun will be shredded, making it impossible to gather or use it. Hence becoming a moth or independent (writing?) woman means breaking the thread of cultural continuity that, for generations, has kept and keeps women circling the mulberry tree. While Cassandra fails to achieve this, the newly emerged butterfly that later appears in close proximity to her cousin Katharine highlights the possibility of gaining such autonomy, something that has intriguing implications for Woolf's own emergence as a writer.

"The Unseizable Force":
Letting the Cat(erpillar) Out of the Bag

While Woolf's writing unfailingly associates both caterpillars and chrysalises with repression and stagnation, when the butterfly or moth emerges from the chrysalis, by contrast, this symbolically denotes an emergence into maturity and independence. Thus, while she gives space and attention to lepidoptera even in her earliest writing, as in her teenage diary account of moth hunting, or the butterflies and moths that occasionally flit into view in her first novel, *The Voyage Out*, it is telling that the image of an emerging butterfly repeatedly appears in her work at just that period (approximately 1919 to 1922) that sees her "emerging" as an author, finding confidence in her voice and unique method. Moreover, this theme of emergence is mirrored by a growing focus on the connection between lepidoptera and "life," a connection assuming an increasingly prominent—and figuratively loaded—role in her writing.[21]

In *Night and Day*, Cassandra's spiritual link with the chrysalis contrasts with the heroine Katharine, who, while visiting the zoo with her future husband Ralph Denham, observes a "lately emerged and semiconscious butterfly" that offers a subtle comment on her own situation (312). In direct opposition to Cassandra's silkworms, fated never to emerge from their chrysalises, this butterfly reflects both Katharine's burgeoning, hence "semiconscious," love for Ralph and the "lately emerged" option of achieving personal freedom by marrying him (as he is her soul mate). Likewise, Woolf's short story "Kew Gardens," contemporary with *Night and Day*, similarly associates the emerging butterfly with those just reaching adulthood. This story focuses on the various people passing a Kew flowerbed on a summer's day, who wander past "with a curiously irregular movement not unlike that of the white and blue butterflies who crossed the turf in zigzag flights."[22] Recalling Katharine and Ralph's visit to Kew in *Night and Day* (and mutually undeclared love), these people include a couple, tongue-tied with unprofessed feelings, who are "both in the prime of youth, or even in that season which precedes the prime of youth, the season before the smooth pink folds of the flower have burst their gummy case, when the wings of the butterfly, though fully grown, are motionless" (*Shorter Fiction*, 94).

The emerging butterflies in these two texts are presently succeeded by the significant appearance of a mature insect in Woolf's story "An Unwritten Novel" (1920), which she regarded as a breakthrough, inspiring the formal experimentation of her next novel *Jacob's Room* (1922) and all that followed it. It is also a "breakthrough" as the first Woolf text overtly to connect lepidoptera with the writer's compulsion to access the life within another person. The story centers on a train journey, during which the narrator scrutinizes a stranger, guessing at the hidden inner life of "Minnie Marsh," as he or she names her. As would so often be the case in *Jacob's Room* and Woolf's subsequent work, the narrator's belief that the task is probably impossible is central to this fascination:

> Have I read you right? But the human face—the human face at the top of the fullest sheet of paper holds more, withholds more. Now, eyes open, she looks out; and in the human eye—how d'you define it?—there's a break— a division—so that when you've grasped the stem the butterfly's off—the moth that hangs in the evening over the yellow flower—move, raise your hand, off, high, away. I won't raise my hand. Hang still, then, quiver, life, soul, spirit, whatever you are of Minnie Marsh—I, too, on my flower—the hawk over the down—alone, or what were the worth of life? (*Shorter Fiction*, 117)

Here the speaker not only pictures Minnie's "life, soul, spirit" as a butterfly or moth but also pictures himself or herself in lepidopteran form when pursuing it ("I, too, on my flower"). This labeling of both artist and subject as insects recurs in *Jacob's Room*, which obliquely suggests a parallel between the hero Jacob Flanders, whose life is tragically curtailed fighting in World War I, and the short-lived butterflies and moths he collects in his teens. Likewise, the passage's fluttering fluidity of syntax and sense—where the subject's identity rapidly slips from butterfly or moth to "the hawk over the down"—points ahead to the narrator's identification with the hawk moth in *Jacob's Room*: in a key statement about the compulsion to capture Jacob in writing (and the difficulty of this), he or she insists that "something is always impelling one to hum vibrating, like the hawk moth, at the mouth

of the cavern of mystery."[23] The narrator later reinforces the connection
between lepidoptera and life when complaining about the latter's butterfly-
or mothlike elusiveness, which writers vainly pursue, like so many bug
hunters: "It is thus that we live, they say, driven by an unseizable force. They
say that the novelists never catch it; that it goes hurtling through their nets
and leaves them torn to ribbons" (*Jacob's Room*, 137).

There is a certain irony in the narrator's use of a hawk moth metaphor to
describe his or her inability to "capture" Jacob, considering that Jacob himself successfully adds a hawk moth to his collection: "Rebecca [the nanny]
had caught the death's-head moth in the kitchen" (*Jacob's Room*, 17). Once
again, Woolf draws on her childhood memories of hunting species including the death's-head hawk moth—named for the distinctive skull-shaped
marking on its thorax—which she always identified using Francis Orpen
Morris's illustrated guides *A History of British Butterflies* (1853) and *A History of British Moths* (1859–70).[24] Indeed, in a nicely intertextual touch, Jacob
follows his creator in consulting Morris to identify his catches: "Morris
called it 'an extremely local insect found in damp or marshy places.' But
Morris is sometimes wrong" (17).

Tellingly, the emerging butterfly motif found in earlier texts continues
into *Jacob's Room:* when Jacob approaches the Cornish coast by boat, a peacock butterfly appears on a nearby cliff top, "fresh and newly emerged, as
the blue and chocolate down on his wings testified" (44). This butterfly
may be emblematic of the hero's youthful potential (particularly as it is also
a species he collects), but it is equally representative of the text's newfound
experimental form, which is similarly "fresh and newly emerged." Thus the
lepidoptera trope, now fully emerged into prominence, reflects the fact that
the correlation Woolf draws between this imagery and her pursuit of life,
of what *Jacob's Room* calls the "unseizable force," is likewise fully developed.
Both here and elsewhere, moreover, the emphasis is on the unseizable: as
signaled by her consistent use of lepidoptera, those elusive insects, to represent "life," Woolf's eagerness to snare this life in her writing, bug-hunter-
like, is matched by her conviction that life is as essentially intangible as a
flitting butterfly. A key instance of this occurs in her essay "Modern Fiction" (1925), an expanded version of the earlier "Modern Novels" (1919),
commonly viewed as her manifesto on style and technique. These essays
are an analysis of contemporary fiction criticizing authors such as H. G.
Wells and Arnold Bennett for being "materialists," that is, for focusing on

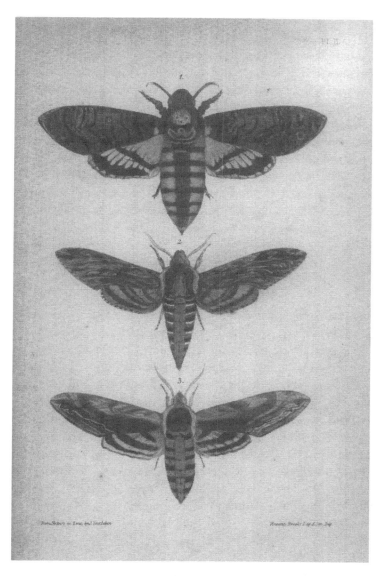

Death's-head hawk moth (*Acherontia atropos*), from F. O. Morris, *A History of British Moths* (London: Knox, 1871), 1:4, plate 2. Traditionally believed to bring bad luck (due to its sinister skull marking), the death's-head moth conceivably acts as a harbinger of death within *Jacob's Room*, its tiny memento mori prefiguring Jacob's untimely death at age twenty-six fighting in World War I. Courtesy of the Edmund S. Muskie Archives and Special Collections Library, Bates College.

the material world to the exclusion of character and life. She finds Bennett the worst offender in this respect, and in censuring his failure to capture "life" in his writing, "Modern Fiction" imagines him as a keen but unsuccessful butterfly hunter:

> Can it be that, owing to one of those little deviations which the human spirit seems to make from time to time, Mr. Bennett has come down with his magnificent apparatus for catching life just an inch or two on the wrong side? Life escapes; and perhaps without life nothing else is worth while. . . . Admitting the vagueness which afflicts all criticism of novels, let us hazard the opinion that for us at this moment the form of fiction most in vogue more often misses than secures the thing we seek. Whether we call it life or spirit, truth or reality, this, the essential thing, has moved off, or on, and refuses to be contained any longer in such ill-fitting vestments as we provide. (*Essays*, 4:159–60)

Here Bennett is envisaged wielding his outdated fictional technique as if it were a deluxe butterfly net (a "magnificent apparatus for catching life") that always slightly misses its target, coming down "just an inch or two on the wrong side," like a child chasing butterflies with more enthusiasm than accuracy, earnestly swiping downward with a net that never quite traps its prey. Woolf intimates that Bennett's method, in being thus "wide of the mark," allows "life," like a deftly dodging butterfly, to "escape" (and, as she stresses, "without life nothing else is worth while"). The lepidopteran connotations given to life here are strengthened by her insistence that the writer's chief task is that of catching "the thing we seek," whether this is called "life or spirit, truth or reality," a phrase recalling "An Unwritten Novel," which imagined Minnie Marsh's unreachable "life, soul, spirit" as a butterfly or moth (*Shorter Fiction*, 117). And this recurring notion of the butterfly-like qualities of the "life" that writers pursue, together with Woolf's identification both with the bug hunter and with the butterfly or moth subject, find their logical conclusion in a series of artist figures in her fiction on whom these ideas are projected: a group I term the "insect artists."

Insect Artists: Painting "the Light of a Butterfly's Wing"

In drawing inspiration from lepidoptera and closely associating them with the writing process, Woolf's viewpoint echoes that of the novelist Olive

Schreiner, who saw the creative process as analogous to the butterfly's life cycle, equating the caterpillar with the initial "receptive state" of absorbing information, the chrysalis with the static phase of processing ideas, when the insect or writer "seems to be dead, it doesn't move, it doesn't grow, it takes in nothing from the outside," and writing itself with the insect's emergence ("at last out comes the butterfly").[25] Likewise, as we have seen, "An Unwritten Novel" and *Jacob's Room* both clearly demonstrate Woolf's readiness not only to characterize the life she pursues artistically as butterfly-like, but also to envisage herself, as an author, in lepidopteran form. Thus the conviction expressed in "An Unwritten Novel" that accessing Minnie's inner self (the "moth that hangs in the evening over the yellow flower") means mentally assuming the same shape ("I, too, on my flower" [*Shorter Fiction,* 117]) is matched by the narrator of *Jacob's Room,* who maintains that attempting to capture Jacob as a subject means "hum[ming] vibrating, like the hawk moth" over his inscrutable figure (61).

As a natural development from these instances of lepidopteran fusion between subject and artist come the "insect artists," characters present in the majority of Woolf's novels who not only are authorial avatars—sharing her compulsion to portray life in their work—but also embody her preoccupation with lepidoptera both in themselves and in their art. Consequently, insect artists share two main characteristics: first, their receptiveness to that essence of life that Woolf so closely associates with lepidoptera makes them prone to see insect qualities in everything around them, as well as frequently seeing actual butterflies or moths; and second, this sensitivity to their surroundings manifests itself through their possessing telltale insect attributes (such as figurative antennae) themselves. Accordingly, as insect artists both internalize and externalize the lepidoptera trope, they potently express Woolf's ideas: standing at once for the artist, the creative act, and the energy of life itself, which characters and author alike are eager to convey, lepidoptera imagery is thus intimately entwined with (the representation of) the creative process.

The first insect artist in Woolf's oeuvre is Charles Steele in *Jacob's Room,* a painter who briefly appears in the opening scene, painting the beach where we first meet the young Jacob and his family. When Jacob's mother, Betty, stands up, unwittingly spoiling Steele's composition, his paintbrush quivers impatiently: "Like the antennae of some irritable insect it positively trembled. Here was that woman moving—actually going to get up—confound her!" (4). The presence, at the start of this text, of an artist figure whose "tool of the trade" is compared with the insect's interpretative tool, its antennae, foreshadows the way in which the narrator will subsequently "paint" events and characters with an "insect" brush, consistently describing them using entomological imagery. This character is mirrored by Woolf's next insect artist, Lily Briscoe in *To the Lighthouse* (1927), another painter who reads like a revised version of Charles Steele. Just as Steele's brush "trembled" like "the antennae of some irritable insect" when he was disturbed, so too on Lily's first appearance (like Steele, busy at her easel), her brush similarly "quiver[s]" with annoyance at being interrupted. Furthermore, Steele's antennae-like brush has metamorphosed into Lily's display of her own "antennae": when she paints, we learn that she "kept a feeler on her surroundings lest someone should creep up, and suddenly she should find her picture looked at."[26] Lily's insect artist identity is further underlined by her frequently quoted description of the scene she is painting: "She saw the colour burning on a framework of steel; the light of a butterfly's wing burning on the arches of a cathedral" (*To the Lighthouse*, 54); this image, evoking the name of her insect artist predecessor, Charles *Steele*, is later repeated in similar terms as "one colour melting into another like the colours on a butterfly's wing; but beneath the fabric must be clamped together with bolts of iron" (186). Such an oxymoronic marriage of elements aptly represents the impossibility of depicting life that Woolf so often stresses (and associates with lepidoptera), and indeed, Lily finds the vista before her infuriatingly "unseizable," as it invariably escapes her "in that moment's flight between the picture and her canvas" (23).[27]

Woolf's fantastical mock biography *Orlando* (1928), the story of a nobleman who lives from the sixteenth century to the present without aging (but with an unexpected, spontaneous male-to-female sex change en route), contains perhaps the most important insect artist in her oeuvre, in the eponymous hero(ine), who also understands the frustration of that "moment's flight" between the subject and the canvas (or page). Orlando's insect artist status is first signaled during the opening description of the boy Orlando: in a close echo of Lily's wish for her painting to have the "light" or "colours" of "a butterfly's wing," the reader's attention is drawn to Orlando's hand, "coloured red, blue and yellow like a butterfly's wing" by the sun shining through a stained-glass window.[28] As well as creating a striking continuity with Woolf's previous novel *To the Lighthouse*, this detail seems to point to

Orlando's future writing vocation, almost like an identifying mark. Indeed, even as a boy, Orlando readily uses lepidoptera as an artistic prop, visiting the family chapel at night to reflect on mortality "with a bat or death's head moth for company" (*Orlando*, 50). After being both connected with lepidoptera imagery and drawing inspiration from it in adolescence, it seems only natural that, as an adult (female) author, Orlando should be simultaneously both an artist and the subject of the text-as-biography. As the only insect artist to hold this dual role, it is fitting that Orlando later becomes the focus of a notably metafictional discussion about the frustratingly intangible, butterfly-like nature of life. As a subject, the ageless, transgender Orlando is inherently "unseizable" on several levels, refusing to be confined within even those biological and chronological parameters that most real and fictional individuals must obey. This intractability often frustrates the narrator, who complains at one point, when Orlando does nothing for a year but sit and write, that this gives him or her nothing to write about: "Orlando sat so still that you could have heard a pin drop. Would, indeed, that a pin had dropped! That would have been life of a kind. Or if a butterfly had fluttered through the window and settled on her chair, one could write about that" (184–87). While this choice of items that could provide interest—a pin and a butterfly—may seem random, it in fact wittily alludes to the writer's twin tools, the pin/pen and the butterfly, the author's favored emblem of life. Significantly, however, the butterfly does *not* obligingly flutter through the window, while the wished-for pin, instead of securing it, is pictured "dropp[ing]" uselessly to the floor; Woolf's imagery thus stresses the narrator's (and hence her own) inability to "pin down" Orlando as a subject. This points us to the final destination of Woolf's "butterfly" subject: "life," more generally, which faces being pinned in the display case of the text, just as the real butterfly is pinned and displayed by the collector once caught.

THE DISPLAY CASE: "WHEN WORDS ARE PINNED DOWN THEY FOLD THEIR WINGS AND DIE"

As both an (insect) artist and the subject of the text's "biography," Orlando shows a quietly knowing refusal to be pinned—by conforming to the narrator's expectations—which implies that, in her dual capacity as both writer and writer's muse, she knows the true significance of such pinning. This knowledge becomes apparent when Orlando takes tea with Alexander Pope: when she absentmindedly drops sugar into the poet's cup with "a great plop," he promptly rebukes her "with the rough draft of a certain famous line in the 'Characters of Women'" (*Orlando*, 149). This line, probably the poem's infamous opening assertion, "Nothing so true as what you once let fall, / 'Most women have no characters at all,'"[29] confirms her previous suspicions about what many men truly think of women:

> A woman knows very well that, though a wit sends her his poems, praises her judgement, solicits her criticism, and drinks her tea, this by no means signifies that he respects her opinions, admires her understanding, *or will refuse, though the rapier is denied him, to run her through the body with his pen.* (*Orlando*, 148–49; italics mine)

The narrator's wish to "pin down" Orlando, subliminally expressed through the imagined marrying of pin and butterfly, takes a far more threatening shape here: as Orlando is only too aware, she risks being "stabbed in the back" by a sly pen, pinned into a prescribed female stereotype by (written) male opinion. This alarming conflation of the stabbing pin and pen, evidently both mightier *and* deadlier than the sword, recurs in *A Room of One's Own* (1929), which began as lectures given in the month of *Orlando*'s publication and considers why, historically, women's writing has not equaled that of men. When the narrator's research on "women and fiction" takes her to the library of the British Museum, her anger at encountering a mountain of misogynist writing is revealingly expressed when she draws a doodle in her notes of the imaginary "Professor von X.," who stands for all the authors she has been reading, just as his "monumental work entitled *The Mental, Moral and Physical Inferiority of the Female Sex*" represents all these texts.[30] Studying her sketch, she reflects that the professor's expression "suggested that he laboured under some emotion that made him jab his pen on the paper as if he were killing some noxious insect as he wrote. . . . Could it be his wife, I asked, looking at my picture? Was she in love with a cavalry officer?" (*A Room of One's Own*, 28). While the means of killing and pinning lepidoptera are not identical (as they are killed before pinning occurs), nevertheless the act of penetration or fixation remains analogous, just as Pope and Professor von X. are equally keen to pin that attractive specimen, woman, within rigid bounds of acceptable female behavior or qualities ("*The Mental, Moral and Physical Inferiority of the Female Sex*"). In thus powerfully juxtaposing pinioned insect and stabbing, phallic pen(is), Woolf's imagery reveals just how vulnerable she feels women are to the power of the patriarchal establishment.

These examples bring me to the last stage of my argument, also the last stage of the butterfly's journey, whether textual or actual: pinning and death. As Woolf links her artistic pursuit of life with bug hunting, thus consistently associating life with lepidoptera, logically the lepidoptera trope's ultimate destination is the display case of the text. However, this inevitable outcome creates a serious artistic conflict—indeed, a seemingly insoluble paradox—for her as a writer. This paradox lies in Woolf's repeatedly expressed view that, much as the butterfly or moth, when caught, must be killed before it can be secured to the display board, so likewise attempts to pin down life in words will leave one with only a stiff, lifeless shell of the original item remaining to be preserved in the display case of the text. That is, she feels that to "pin" or narrowly define reality is so antithetical to the unconstrained nature of life's "unseizable force" that no author can actually succeed in fixing life to the page. By this logic, not only does Woolf believe that it is, by definition, impossible for writing to capture the life with which she associates lepidoptera, but also (and far more importantly) the very attempt to do so, the act of pinning, is an inherently destructive and ultimately futile undertaking. A typical instance of this viewpoint is expressed by *Orlando*'s biographer, who asserts that to pin reality in words will invariably mean destroying it:

> Something . . . is always absent from the present—whence its terror, its nondescript character—something one trembles to pin through the body with a name and call beauty, for it has no body, is as a shadow without substance or quality of its own, yet has the power to change whatever it adds itself to. (*Orlando,* 223)

This "something . . . always absent from the present" is another depiction of life as an "unseizable force," the eloquence of which only highlights the speaker's inability—and indeed unwillingness—to describe it, to "pin [it] through the body with a name and call [it] beauty." Furthermore, this claim that trying to define life through language is the aggressive equivalent of a "pin through the body" anticipates the conclusion that Woolf increasingly draws toward the end of her (writing) life: that *all* language aiming to represent reality signifies the destructive pin that can affix the butterfly of life, but only at the expense of the very vitality that led the author to pursue it in the first place. Especially in her later work, she articulates this view with increasing frequency and vehemence: for whether the "pinning" metaphor appears in a figurative or an artistic context, its connotations are both restrictive and destructive. For example, in her late essay "Thoughts on Peace in an Air Raid" (1940), written at the height of wartime aerial attacks on Britain, she reports that when a German bomber plane was directly overhead, "All feeling, save one dull dread, ceased. A nail fixed the whole being to one hard board. The emotion of fear and of hate is therefore sterile, unfertile. Directly that fear passes, the mind reaches out and instinctively revives itself by trying to create" (*Death,* 157). Characteristically, Woolf immediately incorporates her sensation of fear (vividly realized through this image of the self as a pinned insect) into the essay's central argument that people's failure to communicate with themselves or each other causes all conflict, great or small. Moreover, by directly relating this "nail[ing]" or "fix[ing]" of the self to the "sterile" emotions of fear and hatred, which she immediately combats "by trying to create," she intimates that the personal is not so much political—as the wartime context might suggest—as artistic, and hence that personal and artistic "pinning" or constraint are synonymous.

This notion is more directly correlated with linguistic "pinning" in a piece such as "Craftsmanship" (1937), a rumination on the meaning of language that imagines words themselves as butterfly-like, arguing that the current age has no great writers because "we refuse words their liberty. We pin them down to one meaning, . . . and when words are pinned down they fold their wings and die" (*Death,* 132). Similarly, in a sketch titled "Evening over Sussex: Reflections in a Motor Car" (1927), she describes her appreciation of the countryside outside the vehicle as "one's perceptions blow[ing] out rapidly like air balls [balloons] expanded by some rush of air," yet soon makes the panicky discovery that

> when all seems blown to its fullest and tautest, with beauty and beauty and beauty, a pin pricks; it collapses. But what is the pin? So far as I could tell, the pin had something to do with one's own impotency. I cannot hold this—I cannot express this—I am overcome by it—I am mastered. Somewhere in that region discontent lay; and it was allied with the idea that one's nature

demands mastery over all that it receives; and mastery here meant the power to convey what one saw now over Sussex so that another person could share it. And further, there was another prick of the pin: one was wasting one's chance; for beauty spread at one's right hand, at one's left; at one's back too; it was escaping all the time; one could only offer a thimble to a torrent that could fill baths, lakes. (*Death*, 12)

The paradoxical, contradictory notions pile endlessly on top of each other: the conviction that life is too multitudinous a subject to portray, and yet at the same time *can* be pinned; that to attempt to pin it down is invariably to destroy it, yet feeling ceaselessly compelled to try, while still feeling that the task is impossible. This belief that the life that writers pursue will disintegrate the moment one tries to capture it suggests a poetics of lepidoptera, as the continual overlapping and repeating of these mutually exclusive ideas in Woolf's writing call to mind the overlapping, repeating layers of scales on the butterfly's wing: scales that, although intricately structured and patterned, nevertheless dissolve into dust at the slightest touch, as anyone who has ever tried to pick up a trapped butterfly—leaving their fingertips coated with a layer of colorful scales—will know. However, despite this, it seems that Woolf does regard the butterfly's wing as a valuable creative or formal model, if we remember the dreamy eloquence with which she connected the artist's aims with this image in *To the Lighthouse:* Lily Briscoe's memorable desire for her painting to have "one colour melting into another like the colours on a butterfly's wing" implies that, in spite of the butterfly's problematic, "unseizable" intangibility, the author nevertheless cannot resist its fragile, jewellike glamour.

In conclusion, it seems that Woolf's consistent artistic identification with lepidoptera meant that she set herself an impossible task as a writer, that of pinning the metaphorical butterfly or moth of life without, paradoxically, extinguishing its vital spark through the very act of defining it. However, although she ultimately felt that this task was beyond her powers, nevertheless in the process she created new ways of seeing life that themselves defy the pinning of categorization. Hence the unending dance of the pin and the butterfly forms an essential part of Woolf's work and meaning, one that itself has not been nailed by prior readers. Needless to say, my exposition may not have definitively pinned her meaning either, but perhaps, all things considered, it is best that this should be so.

NOTES

1. Woolf, *The Death of the Moth and Other Essays* (London: Hogarth Press, 1945), 9–10. Hereafter cited in the text as *Death*. An early version of some of the thoughts developed in my essay appeared as "Cassandra's Worms: Unravelling the Threads of Virginia Woolf's Lepidoptera Imagery" *Hungarian Journal of English and American Studies* 9, no. 1 (2003): 101–17.

2. It should be noted that Woolf did not always use a particular image consciously, as the recurrence of (for example) chrysalis imagery in her work owes more to subconscious associations she makes between such imagery and a particular meaning than to any deliberate attempt to create a symbology. Accordingly, I will be investigating the consistent trend of lepidoptera metaphors throughout Woolf's oeuvre rather than claiming that she had an intentional figurative framework relating to these insects.

3. Woolf's aesthetics and artistic philosophy have of course been subject to many (and varied) readings: for example, Sue Roe states that Woolf's writing reveals her "attempt, not to make a particular shape or to tell a particular story, but rather to forge a language which could both reflect and enable the construction of gendered identity within a work of art" (Sue Roe, *Writing and Gender: Virginia Woolf's Writing Practice* [New York: St. Martin's Press, 1990], 10); Jane Goldman has explored "the feminist implications of Woolf's aesthetics," as discernible from her "manipulation of an imagery of light, dark and colour" (Jane Goldman, *The Feminist Aesthetics of Virginia Woolf: Modernism, Post-impressionism and the Politics of the Visual* [Cambridge: Cambridge University Press, 1998], 2–3); and Andrew McNeillie has asserted that Woolf's "aesthetic values" were influenced both by the ideas of Walter Pater and G. E. Moore and by her "extensive, independent reading in Plato" and "fascination with 'Greek,'" which shaped "the Socratic roots to many of her most deeply held humane beliefs" (Andrew McNeillie, "Bloomsbury," in *The Cambridge Companion to Virginia Woolf*, ed. Sue Roe and Susan Sellers [Cambridge: Cambridge University Press, 2000], 2). Joining this debate on Woolf's aesthetics and philosophy, I argue that no previous reading has acknowledged the equal importance of the lepidoptera trope in her writing or realized how it is used to articulate her artistic philosophy and aims.

4. Connor, "As Entomate as Intimate Could Pinchably Be," http://www.bbk.ac.uk/eh/sk/insects, December 6, 2003; Rhys, *Sleep It Off Lady: Stories by Jean Rhys* (London: Andre Deutsch, 1976), 125–36; and Pound, postscript to translation of Remy de Gourmont's *The Natural Philosophy of Love* (1922), cited in Jessica Burstein, "Waspish Segments: Lewis, Prosthesis, Fascism," *Modernism/Modernity* 4, no. 2 (1997): 158.

5. Richter, "Hunting the Moth: Virginia Woolf and the Creative Imagination," in *Virginia Woolf: Revaluation and Continuity*, ed. Ralph Freedman (Berkeley: University of California Press, 1980), 13–28.

6. Several other readers have addressed Woolf's butterfly and moth imagery since Richter, often referring back to her discussion. For instance, Christine Froula's analysis of lepidoptera metaphors in *The Voyage Out* follows Richter in connecting

them with Woolf's authorial identity (Christine Froula, "Out of the Chrysalis: Female Initiation and Female Authority in Virginia Woolf's *The Voyage Out*," in *Virginia Woolf: A Collection of Critical Essays*, ed. Margaret Homans [Englewood Cliffs, N.J.: Prentice-Hall, 1993], 136–61); and the most recent discussion of the topic, in an unpublished doctoral dissertation by Judy Larrick Robinson, catalogs the incidence of lepidoptera in Woolf's novels and some short stories and essays, relating this imagery to women's oppression by, and entrapment within, patriarchal society (Judy Larrick Robinson, "Netting Moths and Butterflies in Virginia Woolf: Her Lepidopteran Lexicon for Scenes of Power and Paralysis" [Ph.D. diss., University of Toledo, 2000; abstract in *Dissertation Abstracts International*, sec. A, 61:3 (2000), 1002]). However, neither these nor any previous readings of Woolf's lepidoptera metaphors do the topic full justice, as none has identified the additional layer of significance that I am exploring here: the connection between this imagery and her artistic conception—and pursuit—of "life."

7. Woolf, *A Passionate Apprentice: The Early Journals, 1897–1909*, ed. Mitchell A. Leaska (San Diego: Harcourt Brace Jovanovich, 1990), 145.

8. Quentin Bell, *Virginia Woolf: A Biography*, vol. 2 (London: Hogarth Press, 1972), 54–57.

9. Woolf, *Moments of Being*, ed. Jeanne Schulkind, 2nd rev. ed. (London: Grafton Books, 1989), 136–37.

10. There is, of course, a further possible source for the connection that Woolf consistently makes between lepidoptera and "life": the Psyche myth. As Marina Warner has noted, lepidoptera were widely associated with the soul in the ancient world: "Butterflies figured soul in ancient Egypt, and Plato spoke of the winged soul, in a famous passage of the *Phaedrus*; Greco-Roman antique cameo portraits of the deceased and memorials on sarcophagi frequently show the deceased with a butterfly." Similarly, Warner argues that in Apuleius's second-century satire *The Metamorphoses of Lucius, or The Golden Ass*, in which the Cupid and Psyche myth originated, Psyche's name was consciously chosen to evoke the Greek term's dual connotations of the soul and of lepidoptera (the Greek *psukhē* signifies "breath, soul," as well as the butterfly or moth), thus pointing up the story's metamorphosis theme. Marina Warner, *Fantastic Metamorphoses, Other Worlds: Ways of Telling the Self* (Oxford: Oxford University Press, 2002), 90. This association was later reinforced in art, as Pompeian paintings depicted Psyche as "a little winged girl, like a butterfly," playing with winged Cupids. Pierre Grimal, *The Dictionary of Classical Mythology*, trans. A. R. Maxwell-Hyslop (Oxford: Blackwell, 1986), 397. As Woolf studied Greek and Latin in her teens, the classical precedents for identifying lepidoptera with the life or soul within people are likely to have influenced the similar association she makes in her own writing; however, the link may have been purely subliminal, as nowhere in her writing does Woolf refer either to the Psyche myth—although she would have been aware of it—or to the term "psyche."

11. Helga Hofmann and Thomas Marktanner, *Butterflies and Moths of Britain and Europe* (London: HarperCollins, 1995), 153.

12. *The Letters of Virginia Woolf*, ed. Nigel Nicolson and Joanne Trautmann, 6 vols. (London: Hogarth Press, 1975–80), 2:103, June 25 [1916]. Hereafter cited in the text as *Letters*.

13. The quotation Woolf is groping for is probably Marlowe's *The Jew of Malta*, 4.1.22, where the arrival of two friars is announced with the words "Look, look, master; here come two religious caterpillars." *Christopher Marlowe: The Complete Plays*, ed. J. B. Steane (Harmondsworth: Penguin, 1980), 399.

14. Woolf, *The Waves*, ed. Kate Flint (London: Penguin, 1992), 5. Hereafter cited in the text.

15. Woolf, *Three Guineas* [with *A Room of One's Own*], ed. Michèle Barrett (London: Penguin, 1993), 175–76. Hereafter cited in the text.

16. Ivor H. Evans, ed., *Brewer's Dictionary of Phrase and Fable*, 14th ed. (London: Cassell, 1990), 754.

17. *The Diary of Virginia Woolf*, ed. Anne Olivier Bell and Andrew McNeillie, vol. 3 (London: Hogarth Press, 1977–84), 287, February 16, 1930.

18. Woolf, *Night and Day*, ed. Julia Briggs (London: Penguin, 1992), 175. Hereafter cited in the text.

19. R. L. E. Ford, *Practical Entomology* (London: Frederick Warne, 1963), 74–78.

20. Sonya Rudikoff has proposed that Cassandra's characterization draws on the life of nineteenth-century society hostess Lady Dorothy Nevill, whose *Life and Letters* Woolf reviewed in 1919, later reworking this review into a biographical outline for her 1925 essay collection *The Common Reader*. Sonya Rudikoff, "A Possible Source for *Night and Day*'s Cassandra Otway," *Virginia Woolf Miscellany* 28 (1987), 4–5. In *The Common Reader*'s sketch of Lady Dorothy's life, Woolf compares her refined but restricted existence with "a cage . . . full of charming diversions," one of which was her hobby of keeping silkworms: "She took up the cause of silkworms, almost threatened Australia with a plague of them, and 'actually succeeded in obtaining enough silk to make a dress.'" *The Essays of Virginia Woolf*, ed. Andrew McNeillie, to be completed in 6 vols. (London: Hogarth Press, 1986), 4:203. Hereafter cited in the text as *Essays*.

21. This is not to say that lepidoptera imagery is equally prominent (or significant) in all of Woolf's novels: for example, *Mrs. Dalloway* (1925) is almost totally devoid of lepidoptera, barring two unimportant passing references. This absence might be related to the fact that many of the novel's characters (including its heroine, Clarissa Dalloway) consistently conceal or deny their true inner selves and feelings, and hence lepidoptera—which Woolf so unerringly associates with the inner essence of life and people—would accordingly have little place in the text.

22. Woolf, *The Complete Shorter Fiction*, ed. Susan Dick (London: Triad Grafton Books, 1991), 90. Hereafter cited in the text as *Shorter Fiction*.

23. Woolf, *Jacob's Room*, ed. Sue Roe (London: Penguin, 1992), 61. Hereafter cited in the text.

24. F. O. Morris, *A History of British Butterflies*, 5th ed. (London: George Bell and Sons, 1870); *A History of British Moths*, 6th ed., 4 vols. (London: John C. Nimmo,

1903). The death's-head hawk moth has the unusual ability to produce a "strikingly loud squeaking sound" as a defense when disturbed, by forcing air through its proboscis (Hofmann and Marktanner, *Butterflies and Moths,* 118), a skill that has contributed to the traditional fear of this species. This robust use of expressivity as a defense mechanism stands in marked contrast to Jacob's characteristic reticence and silence, and considering this, his habitually tongue-tied, passive inability to express or assert himself through language seems figuratively linked to his inability to resist his looming fate (death on the battlefield), as toward the end of the narrative, Jacob silently disappears, without even a mothlike "squeak" of protest.

25. *Olive Schreiner Letters: Volume I, 1871–99,* ed. Richard Rive (Oxford: Oxford University Press, 1988), 97.

26. Woolf, *To the Lighthouse,* ed. Stella McNichol (London: Penguin, 2000), 22. Hereafter cited in the text. Lily's artistic "antennae" are later matched by those displayed by her host, Mrs. Ramsay, as she oversees a dinner party (indicative in her case of social rather than artistic talent): "It was as if she had antennae trembling out from her, which, intercepting certain sentences, forced them upon her attention" (116).

27. Lily's frustration anticipates that of the playwright Miss La Trobe in Woolf's final novel, *Between the Acts* (1941), whose belief, during the performance of her pageant, that she has failed to capture "life" in her writing is similarly connected with lepidoptera: "Another play always lay behind the play she had just written. Shading her eyes, she looked. The butterflies circling; the light changing; the children leaping; the mothers laughing—'No, I don't get it,' she muttered." Woolf, *Between the Acts* (London: Vintage, 1990), 39.

28. Woolf, *Orlando,* ed. Brenda Lyons (London: Penguin, 2000), 12. Hereafter cited in the text.

29. Pope, "An Epistle to a Lady: Of the Characters of Women," in *Alexander Pope: The Oxford Authors,* ed. Pat Rogers (Oxford: Oxford University Press, 1993), 350.

30. Woolf, *A Room of One's Own* [with *Three Guineas*], ed. Michèle Barrett (London: Penguin, 1993), 28. Hereafter cited in the text.

6

The End of Insect Imagery
From Dostoyevsky to Kobo Abé via Kafka

ROY ROSENSTEIN

Of Flies and Fleas and Literature

The locus classicus for insect imagery in the Western literary tradition may
well be found in Plato's *Apology* with Socrates' characterization of himself
as a stinging fly. This dismissive portrait is at once self-disparaging but also
self-important because Socrates has settled on the back of that lazy thor-
oughbred which is Athens.

The fly is here represented as petty and annoying, to be sure, but not
without a function within the larger scheme of events as political agita-
tor, everywhere "rousing, persuading, reproving."[1] Much later, Renaissance
lovers would dreamily imagine themselves to be a fly or more often a flea,
whose good fortune they so flatteringly portrayed and claimed to envy
because of the intimacies the little creature enjoyed on their lady's person.[2]
But this momentary popularity was to be short-lived, like a fly itself. In
most centuries before our times, the utilitarian perspective on the lowly
creature that is the common housefly was lost. Independently Augustine
and Luther each denounced God's little insect. Augustine was mystified
by the fly: if there was any purpose to it in creation, he confessed ignorance
of it. "More boldly," continues Bertrand Russell, Luther said that the fly was
the devil's work, created by him solely to distract Luther from writing good
books. This judgment Russell himself claimed to have found "plausible."[3]
In sum, and in defiance of biology, the church fathers thought they had laid
the matter of the fly to rest in dismissing any significance to it. Only again
much later with the preromantic William Blake's "The Fly" would man and

insect be associated as they had been in Plato: "Am not I / A fly like thee? / Or art not thou / A man like me?"[4] Finally came Dostoyevsky, who would change human-insect relations forever, beginning with the fly.

In Dostoyevsky's *Notes from Undergound* (1864), the nameless, mouse-like narrator recalls Socrates' positive role as gadfly: "I had been treated like a fly!" he adds, "before that whole world, a foul, obscene fly—more intelligent, more developed, more noble than everyone else—that went without saying—but a fly."[5] But as the Underground Man acknowledges, he is unable to become anything at all, a hero or an insect, even a little beetle.[6] For so he labels his classmates Zverkov and Ferfichkin, while he himself inhabits "the mousehole" under the floorboards. Many subsequent authors would write about undergound men in the wake of Dostoyevsky's antihero and in most cases as his disciple. These writers in turn all kept in mind the frequent insect imagery of *Notes from Underground*. Thus Gorky refers to cockroaches and maggots in *The Lower Depths,* Kafka presents a famously big brown beetle in "The Metamorphosis," and Wright evokes an unspecified insect with antennae in "The Man Who Lived Underground."[7] Finally Kobo Abé is attentive to a certain light-colored beetle, as we shall see. All allude at least in passing to the implicit ties between underground men and their opposite numbers from the insect world, whether in a subterranean doss-house in tsarist Russia at the turn of the century, in a family flat in Prague in 1912, in the sewers of Philadelphia circa 1940, or in a Japanese outpost lost in the sand dunes in 1955.[8] That is to say that as many works crawl out from under Dostoyevsky's floorboards as supposedly Dostoyevsky himself said come out from behind Gogol's cloak.[9] The most recent renewal of the metamorphosis from human to insect (and back) in the Russian tradition is Victor Pelevin's *The Life of Insects,* in which geographic and political borders are blurred and humans and insects become virtually interchangeable.[10]

One century to the year after the publication of *Notes from Underground* there appeared what is certainly the most entomologically explicit of those and other fictions of the underground man. In it an individual insect plays not just a cameo role but the most central and telling part, following the model of Kafka. This audaciously modern work was Kobo Abé's *The Woman in the Dunes* (English translation, 1964), probably more familiar to Western eyes as Hiroshi Teshigahara's film of the same year and name.[11] Its female lead will always be known only as the woman in the dunes, because in the novel, as in the eponymous film, she also bears no name. But she is no underground woman, contrary to other works resembling Dostoyevsky's novel in which the subterranean protagonists remain anonymous, such as Ralph Ellison's *Invisible Man* or Samuel Beckett's *Play*.[12] In Abé instead it is the named male protagonist who is revealed to be the undergrounder, as he himself will discover only in the course of the novel. By accepting shelter from the woman in the dunes for one night, he first unwittingly, then unwillingly, joins the village in its endless battle against the shifting sands. Much later, when the opportunity to leave arises, he will decline to act on it. *The Woman in the Dunes* is the story of how he as her captive and pupil will develop willy-nilly from an insect into a man, reversing the development of his most immediate predecessor, Kafka's Gregor Samsa, who from a man had become an insect.

Kobo Abé, Entomologist and Existentialist

Born in Mukden in Japanese-occupied Manchuria in the year of Kafka's death, the Japanese novelist and playwright Kobo Abé (1924–93) grew up under Western eyes, as it were. His preferred readings seem from the first to have been in European literature and philosophy.[13] Perhaps he read Conrad, but we know for certain he was fascinated by Poe, presumably including "The Gold Bug." In any case, the American writer was a first love who inspired the boy Abé to write while growing up in Manchu-Kuo, where his father was teaching medicine. As a young man, Abé grew seriously interested in insect collecting, becoming an amateur entomologist. Although his university degree was in medicine, Abé would never practice. It is sometimes suggested that his degree was awarded on the condition precisely that he not practice on humans. His lifelong fascination with entomology was evidently more abiding than any inherited interest in medical science.

Abé's fascination with insects and insect imagery is attested to throughout his writings, not only in *The Woman in the Dunes* but equally conspicuously in *The Ark Sakura,* published five years before Abé's death in 1993. In this late, penultimate novel, the entomological presence is strong. Its protagonist is a man, nicknamed Pig or Mole, who lives in a vast subterranean quarry. At a mazelike rooftop bazaar in the city, he meets a stall keeper who specializes in insect specimens, particularly in a variety of Coleoptera called *Eupcaccia,* that is, the Japanese *tokeimushi* or English clockbug. This creature with atrophied legs eats its excrement, rotating counterclockwise with its antennae just enough to ingest its own waste from dawn to sunset, when it goes to sleep. Because its head is always facing toward the sun, it doubles as a timepiece, rather like a living sundial. Mole at once recognizes himself in the sedentary, self-sufficient creature, buys a specimen, and bonds with the insect dealer. The balance of the novel recounts his adventures in his arklike cave with the insect salesman and his shill or *sakura.* Beyond this insect presence in *The Ark Sakura,* only in *The Woman in the Dunes* is the overlap between human and insect more patent, as we will see. If in *The Ark Sakura* the two species cohabit, in *The Woman in the Dunes* they share and exchange identities.

After Poe and insects, Kafka was the next revelation, but only after Abé had already decided to become a writer. With both Poe and Kafka he later declared he had felt a closeness, a relationship, a shared emptiness. As a young existentialist, he sought inspiration in Nietzsche, Jaspers, Husserl, and Heidegger while developing his private, if Westernized, worldview. But he found the spiritual and intellectual suppport he was seeking in Dostoyevsky's *Notes from Underground.* At first Abé did not care for the theme of isolation in Camus. And he claimed never to have learned to adopt Sartre's brand of existentialism. But Beckett interested him at once for their common interest in the stagnation of human relationships, which is addressed in *The Woman in the Dunes,* no doubt with broad parallels to Camus's *Outsider* and Sartre's *No Exit* as well.[14]

Given such reading tastes as these, it is not surprising that all of Abé's protagonists are lost souls, isolated and lonely. Resembling the author himself in less negative ways, Niki Jumpei, the man in *The Woman in the Dunes,* was also born in 1924. And like his creator, Jumpei is an amateur entomologist. A descendant of earlier undergrounders beginning with the unnamed persona of Dostoyevsky's *Notes,* Jumpei is identified by name only once in the text (81), then again in the announcement of his disappearance at the end of the novel (240–41), when he has shed his meaningless name, sloughed off like so much dead, molted skin, like an empty carapace left behind on earth. He becomes simply an anonymous man in the dunes, but one who finds himself there in developing a new, more substantial identity.

From Mo(ts)chulsky to Jumpei

The novel begins in the most universal terms: "a man" has disappeared. It continues in the same, flat, deadpan tone, as if to dwell on his commonness, his mediocrity, his insectlike anonymity. This man of no importance has been spending his weekends far from the unnamed city, among the dunes, collecting insects, chasing a rare species of Coleoptera, to him highly important. In his town garden, he had once failed to capture a smallish, light-pink insect resembling a double-winged garden beetle, labeled by Jumpei in the novel as *Cicindela japonica* Motschulsky. But no such creature exists in the textbooks. In name it might seem to be closest to the beetle known as *Cicindela japana* Motschulsky, discovered by Victor Ivanovitch Motschulsky (1810–71) in 1857. Yet here it is also linked by Abé to a different variety, discovered in 1781 by another entomologist: *Cicindela japonica* Thunberg, whose physical description matches that of Jumpei's beetle. The beetle as represented by Jumpei is indeed remarkable: its legs are not black, slender, and agile, as the entomology textbooks would lead us to expect, but "round, almost chubby, cream-colored" (12), and evidently pollen-smeared, as if they had some growth or hair on them. That is tantamount to saying that this astonishing beetle has stout, pinkish, hairy legs! Jumpei is thus pursuing a peculiar variety of insect, humanoid in coloring with anthropomorphic flesh.

By this point a parallel revelation should have struck any reader conversant not only with entomology but, like Abé again, with Dostoyevsky too. Another Motschulsky is equally relevant here, perhaps more so, for Konstantin Mochulsky, as the same surname may alternatively be transliterated, is the distinguished Soviet biographer of Dostoyevsky.[15] It cannot be by chance that the two varieties of Japanese beetles, *Cicindela japana* Motschulsky and *Cicindela japonica* Thunberg, are here crossed to breed the new *Cicindela japonica* Motschulsky. According to the description given, the colorful beetle that Jumpei is pursuing is Thunberg, yet the collector calls him Motschulsky instead. Either the amateur entomologist has unconsciously confused the two Japanese beetles, or the Westernized novelist consciously preferred the one bearing the name of Dostoyevsky's biographer. In any event, whether intentionally or not, Motschulsky and Mochulsky, the discoverer of the beetle known to Abé and the biographer of the author so admired by him, are not associated fortuitously. Given

Abé's knowledge of entomology and devotion to the novelist, it is likely that the Dostoyevsky researcher and the beetle researcher are here provocatively conflated. If the indeed unattested type of beetle at the genesis of Jumpei's quest is ambiguously named, the name of the author of *Notes from Undergound* is unmistakably a reference to be reckoned with in Abé's novel.

The presumed identity and name of this special beetle are revealing of the research Jumpei has long undertaken in his free moments: "I wanted to find a new species on this vacation" (58). A dedicated if amateurish entomologist increasingly resembling his creator, then, Jumpei has set out to make a name for himself, indeed to give his own name to the new variety of bug he is seeking. His discovery is perhaps playfully intended to rival or supplant in importance the creatures studied by Dostoyevsky and Kafka, even the one studied by Dostoyevsky's biographer Mochulsky:

> The true entomologist's pleasure is much simpler, more direct [because un-interested in the gaudier examples, like dragonflies or Nabokov's butterflies]: that of discovering a new type. When this happens, the discoverer's name appears in the illustrated encyclopedias of entomology appended to the technical Latin name of the newly found insect; and there, perhaps, it is preserved for something less than eternity. His efforts are crowned with success if his name is perpetuated in the memory of his fellow men by being associated with an insect. (10)

Again, at this point in the novel, the protagonist does not yet have a name. *The Woman in the Dunes* thus chronicles this one man's search for an insect that resembles him, in order to give it, but also himself, a name and an identity: that is, the insect sought is no other creature than the man himself. At the end of the novel, the insignificant creature that he was will indeed have taken his name on the death certificate, bringing a bureaucratic end to his life as an insect in the world beyond the dunes. But he will first have to recognize that he is the dune beetle "with yellowish front legs" (12) that had captivated him in the city and he had so earnestly wanted to identify. When he at last becomes a man, he will no longer have need of that insect name he carried and can allow the insect that he no longer is to bear it for him.

From Dung Beetle to Dune Beetle

The man named Jumpei is thus seeking a variety of dune beetle, not a dung beetle or *Mistkafer,* as Gregor Samsa's housekeeper generously, if extravagantly, calls Kafka's antihero, according to another literary entomologist, Vladimir Nabokov.[16] The habits of dung beetles have long been known and are much described, but the less familiar dune beetles are Jumpei's target. When he first sighted his beetle near his city home—where else would a beetle bearing his name be found but in close proximity to its and his native habitat?—its flight pattern had been peculiar, as if inviting him to follow it in leaving their home: "It flew away, and then as if to say 'Catch me!' it turned and waited. When he approached it cautiously it flew away again, turned around, and waited" (12). In short, it seemed "mercilessly tantalizing" to him: the very term in English anticipates the coming underground context. Once in the dunes, this man will similarly be enticed to her dwelling by a villager but then snared by the woman herself, "exactly like a mouse or an insect" (51). In sum, "he had been lured by the beetle into a desert from which there was no escape—like some famished mouse" (50). The commonalities in the destinies of mouse and insect reinforce their close association in Dostoyevsky's rhetoric, where they are the two subhuman creatures with whom the Undergound Man is associated. Here the woman could have accomplished her deception only with the complicity of the neighbors: they are suggestively assimilated to fellow insect collectors much as the woman in the dunes is perhaps a variety of black widow. Having already lost her husband and child in the drifting sands, "she looked like some kind of insect" hungrily fixated on its male prey (63). The villagers sound him out at first to identify him, but they are mistaken to suppose him to be someone, anyone, much as all the dead characters in Sartre's *No Exit* are initially mistaken for someone else, for someone perhaps even still alive. On the contrary, this man has always been no one, a nobody, a nonperson like Kafka's K., who in *The Castle* will have to invent a fraudulent identity for himself.[17] In Jumpei's case, the villagers who find the man in the dunes provide him instead with an identity by forcing on him his new role as homemaker and family man. These unfamiliar roles he adopts first reluctantly, then warmly. He himself will be the last to understand that he has been trapped. But once he accepts his fate, he will ultimately embrace his new life in the dunes. Free to choose, he will in the long term again choose indecision and thereby renounce freedom. When his escape ladder again becomes available and reclaiming his freedom is an option, he opts to stay in the dunes. In this he resembles Garcin, who, having banged on the door to escape Sartre's *No Exit* remains there once the previously locked door springs open. But for the moment for Jumpei there is no ladder, no escape, no exit. He therefore is desperate to find one, no doubt precisely because the door is closed to him.

"Certain types of insects and spiders, when unexpectedly attacked, fall into a paralytic state, a kind of epileptic seizure" (54). So did Dostoyevsky's Underground Man, incapable of acting, and indeed so perhaps did Dostoyevsky. His lifelong epilepsy has been the subject of speculation since the nineteenth century. Not at all similar is the case of our man in the dunes, who is not broken in spirit, as he had been previously on the face of the earth. Quite the contrary: he is dynamized, revitalized, initially only in his determination to escape. He feels like a caged animal, "a big black fly that thought it had taken flight when it was only bumping its head against the windowpane in its efforts to get out. [The scientific name is *Muscina stabulans*]" (116). This variety of fly is particularly associated with human cadavers, but Jumpei is more quick than dead. The shock of his entrapment, his lost liberty, provokes in him a drive to escape confinement. When he tries to do so by climbing the dunes around the woman's house, however, he impotently falls back down into his own specimen box. That box, destined to collect other insects, has now collected him: he perhaps dimly grasps that he has become one of his insects, precisely the one named Jumpei that he was seeking. The box, full of dead specimens, was until now empty of its rich implications for him. As he takes his rightful place in it, the anagnorisis is symbolically accomplished: the collector and the collected are one. And we hear no more of his box after this scene because he has broken it, broken out, in a manner of speaking. Thereafter it ceases to play any role in his development: he abandons the role of collector to focus on his insecthood, later on his humanity. Only once caught in his own trap can he break free of it, as collector and as specimen. The overflowing box that can no longer contain him serves as an emblem of his until-now vacuous existence. It resembles nothing so much as the briefcase full of worthless testimonials that Ellison's Invisible Man carries around with him as useless baggage until his end. Jumpei's insect box too tells a life story that is at an end along with those of the insects he has known. Thus Jumpei becomes his own prime specimen: "He made a backward somersault and was thrown out on the sand. Under him his insect box gave out an unpleasant sound" (107).

In effect, he must choose between remaining an overgrown insect worthy of his collection box or becoming the mature man of the house in the dunes. The villagers toss down water, food, and occasionally other items to the couple alongside their matchbox dwelling until the two are equally acclimatized to a shared existence as a team among the dunes. Their nightly digging in the dunes, "quite like the behavior of the beetle, he thought" (38), proves not to be purposeless: the villagers and now he along with them "exist only for the purpose of clearing away the sand." But to participate in this activity is touted as a collective responsibility without which the village would be doomed to be swallowed up by the sands. Even Jumpei is obliged to acknowledge that his life among insects in the dunes constitutes a successful means of escape for him, both from his so-called obligations in the world and in reality from the unrecognized "inactivity of his life" (40). That new burden of commitment or engagement has been accepted. As Garcin concludes in Sartre's underground hell, "Eh bien, continuons," that is, "Let's get on with it."[18] Here, perhaps for the first time in his life, Jumpei drops from healthy exhaustion after a night's intense physical labor, as he probably never did after a day's work at the job he fell into, watching generations of students pass him by. Now "work seemed something fundamental for man, something which allowed him to endure the aimless flight of time" (158). Suddenly made conscious of the living, shifting hourglass of the dunes all around him, Jumpei has finally taken his head out of the sand. No longer will it slip through his fingers.

The man and the woman together assume their tasks, which unite them in a common existential cause, keeping themselves alive and the sands of time at bay, thus halting the inexorable advance but also giving their own lives some purpose and therefore meaning. If time stops momentarily when the damp sands eat into Jumpei's self-importance and ruin his watch at the end of part 1, he will in good time by part 3 be forced to learn how to survive by culling the moisture in his new habitat and building a life-giving well. Eternal symbol of life, water is the natural antidote to the aridity of his world: it will restore and renew him from his dehydrating alcoholic binge on sake and deliver him from dependence on the villagers. What had been a trap in the dunes becomes an escape route through them, for Jumpei now dominates his brave new world. Earlier, when broken by thirst, he had been tormented by the firewater provided by the villagers; the same lack of water among the dunes had almost broken his will when he could not wash, could not drink, could not refresh himself after his exertions. From the sand that had represented his weakness and fragility he has extracted a new sign of his strength and independence. *The Woman in the Dunes* in this way becomes a success story, however improbable that might have seemed at the outset of his captivity, to protagonist and reader alike.

A more pragmatic, less existential reader response might counter this positive view of the prisoner of the sands: with nothing to return to, there is nothing to escape from. "Bachi ga nakereba nigeru tanoshimi mo nai," reads the epigraph, translated by Saunders as "Without the threat of punishment there is no joy in flight." Yet, significantly, Jumpei did indeed attempt to flee, falling back into his collection box once, as we have seen, then another time sliding back down the dunes to where he had started. But when he succeeds in escaping on a third attempt, after forty-six days in the pit, it is only to grow disoriented aboveground, then slowed in his flight, and finally trapped more dangerously in quicksand: fearing to be swallowed up by the sands at home, he comes close to being liquidated outside it. The quicksands are a new manifestation of the old quagmire he left behind on earth. Reeking of Sartrean viscosity, neither here nor there, not liquid or solid but in suspension between empty freedom and definitive petrification, the slushy quicksand constitutes a no-man's-land between the daily, unceasing existence of his life among the dunes and his previous, stultifying-because-lifeless essence in town. Better to choose any satisfying form of existence underground before his aimless essence in the world runs out. And happily for him, the villagers will rescue him from this near-fatal, insoluble dilemma, but only when he finally breaks down and cries out to their society for help. They come to his rescue as a group and save him from the quicksand, as in effect they have saved him before, despite himself, from his dead life in the city. When on this final occasion he tries to run away from the dunes, much as he has been in flight all his life, he is not abandoned and forgotten at all as he had been in town by his close acquaintances and fellow city dwellers.

Jumpei is pursued and saved by villagers whom he barely knows. In the quicksand he has suffered a liberating ordeal by water that doubles as a ritual baptism, itself preceded by the trial by fire that he had endured on arriving in the dunes. Those in the village whom he had accused of seeking to lose him, to bury him, have rather disinterred and preserved him from the shadow of certain death awaiting him beyond the woman's thermal sandpit. Instead he is safely taken back to his new home, cleansed not only of the accumulated filth of the world but also of his desire to run, and restored willy-nilly to his woman in the dunes: "His dreams, desperation, shame, concern with appearances—all were buried under the sand" (203). When he had learned earlier that the husband and child of his hostess had been submerged by the sands, he had felt trapped. And indeed he was all but swallowed up in a choking sand slide when he tried to scale the walls of his canyon. Now this final encounter with the quicksand is instead liberating. His will, or what little he had until now, may be broken, but he is saved from the Underground Man's indecisiveness and his own: "He was still in the hole, but it seemed as if he were already outside" (235). No longer is he trapped like an insect. As if suspended over the trap he has made, supremely in control of his life for the first time, he can look down on an earlier image of himself.

Only gradually does the reader recognize the extent of Jumpei's new freedom. Jumpei is himself even slower to fathom how he has ultimately undertaken to build the family that he had never begun earlier with his occasional visiting girlfriend in the boardinghouse aboveground. Their protected, distant sex always guaranteed there would be no issue. He never did take off his rubber hat to this woman, whom he did not love, and who as a result accused him of a psychological venereal disease. Now he calls her the other woman, "the other one," despite her prior claim: in the nameless world of Beckett's *Play,* she would be W1, the first woman, not W2, the Other Woman. In the dunes, on the other hand, he can "spread his wings" in "a voracious passion," opting for passionate love over "commutation sex" (140, 141, 143). With the woman in the dunes, his lovemaking will be spontaneous and uninhibited, indeed "hatless," that is to say, unprotected, leaving the woman, his woman, with child. That this should be an extrauterine pregnancy cheekily suggests only the future child's current outsider status. Now, with a family in the making, Jumpei sees at last that he has definitively escaped his previous life—for he no longer feels lost or trapped in the sand. And he slowly begins to understand how, on his vacations spent chasing after the elusive magic beetle, he had instead been running away from the meaningless rat race of his own life in town, a flight fully achieved now by chance, despite his resistance. Only in fleeing himself has he come to find himself. In following the mysterious pattern and message of his so-called letter-bearer beetle's flight from the city, he has been beguiled into discovering his identity (12). Such was the beetle's invitation, to chase it but also to capture himself in the dunes.

In the course of his *descensus Averno*, Jumpei's alienation and outsiderhood are made abundantly clear through flashbacks to his previous life aboveground before the novel's beginning, a technique also employed by Dostoyevsky and Wright in presenting an undergrounder from the first pages buried in his mouse hole or his sewer. But no less evident is the integration that the woman in the dunes has brought to his private world by allowing him to climb slowly to the surface, as Liza might have done for the Underground Man in *Notes from Underground,* and as Hermine did for Harry Haller in *Steppenwolf.*[19] These women too, not undergrounders any more than the woman in the dunes, have recovered men from a premature burial in the underground. But both Liza, who is driven away, and Hermine, who is killed, are rejected by those whom they would save. The woman in the dunes is not expelled, for it is her home that welcomes Jumpei. She alone conquers her man's resistance by bringing small joys, some satisfaction, and above all a sense of usefulness and community to one who was chronically dissociated. She integrates him through her work ethic, her positive spirit, her practical-minded ambitions, and by her love as an earth mother. Despite the vulnerability of their house of sand, set against a backdrop of frustration and despair, their new home stands sturdier than the aboveground dwellings and relationships he has left behind on the face of the earth. The worst hell is shown to have been that world above, which he has abandoned once and for all for his refuge in the dunes. Abé's vision of the underground thus marks a reversal with respect to the unending death sentence passed on their own characters by Sartre in 1944 and Beckett in 1964, the same year that saw publication in English of *The Woman in the Dunes.* In an unmistakably infernal setting, Jumpei has discovered, to his surprise and ours, the unexpected breath of life.

In Jumpei's former life as a schoolteacher, neither neighbors nor colleagues had cared for or about him. He defiantly announced to the villagers that the teachers' union, the Board of Education, and the Parent-Teacher Association would all come looking for him, as if to bring him back to the unhappy world everyone else assumed he had justifiably fled. Yet much to his surprise, when he disappeared into the dunes there was hardly anyone to notice his absence or report his disappearance, not even his so-called life partner. Only his mother misses him and files a missing-person report. For as Dostoyevsky would have remembered from the moralizing poet whom he quotes in *Notes from Underground* and elsewhere, Nekrasov said of mothers: "Im ne zabit' svoikh det'ey," that is, they alone will never forget their lost children. When after seven years Jumpei does not return, the court rules that neither his existence (!) nor his death (therefore?) can be established. He is then considered to be definitively "missing": "absent," to use the euphemism for "dead" that Estelle proposes in *No Exit*. We know otherwise, of course: his failure to return means not simply that he has disappeared quite literally from the face of the earth but that in addition he has discovered a new dwelling among the dunes. There he has found the identity denied to him in traditional society, where his boardinghouse room, "smelly and close," he remembered significantly as "a hole," not a home (80). He had never known a Home Sweet Home until now, in a sixty-foot hole. Now this hole in the sand becomes his home in the dunes. The LOVE YOUR HOME plaque he spotted on the wall of the community offices is no joke, as he had first suspected, but a testimony to the elemental yet fulfilling natural stronghold against the world that the dunes come to constitute for him (22, 37). In the isolation of the dunes, he has rejoined the mainstream of life. Rather than carry his underground with him, Jumpei has left it behind, for the underground, rather than a place, is a state of mind.

The End of Insect Imagery

In this sometimes artificial, always elemental allegory of the dunes, the defining imagery in the novel—and not surprisingly, even more so in the film—is the product of a narrow field of vision. The camera's perspective is deliberately myopic, much like its protagonist, who cannot see or does not look beyond his feet and remains generally taciturn. "Beetles are not especially gregarious," that is to say, essentially antisocial. Like some small insect, Jumpei does not aspire to peer beyond the quotidian commonplaceness of his dronelike life aboveground. Around these scurrying insects, the other two defining images are Bachelardian archetypes that overdetermine the insect habitat.[20] The contraries that are sand and water ensure the novel's relentless, mechanical, but always-evolving insistence on the basic elements among which the insect-man *Cicindela japonica* Jumpei, promoted to the status of a Sisyphus and a Tantalus, must adapt and evolve to survive. He is a Sisyphus figure, recalling the servant in Kafka's *The Castle* with his subterranean wheelbarrow or more generally Camus's *Myth of Sisyphus*.[21] The Sisyphus dung beetle, as it is called, struggles with the perpetual burden of his house, which he pushes ahead of him everywhere he goes. For the man in the dunes, the burden is immensely heavy. Yet somehow when Jumpei reaches out, his life slips through his fingers like the sand of which it is made. He is a Tantalus too, reaching out for water that, until his chance invention of the well, was ever retreating beyond his grasp—tantalizingly, as noted earlier. In this natural world, insect and man, sand and water, the constituent elements of a bleak landscape, are initially at odds, like the man and the woman themselves. But again like man and woman, these extremes are soon revealed to be complementary, overlapping, embedded. Jumpei mocks the uneducated woman when she insists (naively, in his learned opinion) that sand, contrary to reason, is wet: he is confident that "the sand of course was not damp" (28). His cut-and-dry conception of sand, like the dunes themselves, will shift as he finds that sand and water, dryness and moisture, man and woman, are not poles apart when opposites meet, as they do here. If sand is equated with the perpetual movement of time and therefore life, it is because it is itself not dead matter, as Jumpei believes, but alive and moist with the liquidity, the fluidity, of Sartrean existence that precedes essence. To his own desiccated worldview he learns to add a measure of water, a liquor more precious than sake. Jumpei is by nature viscous, indecisive, inconclusive, unbalanced by impossible choices between polar opposites. He nevertheless has now made those decisions, if not by engagement and commission, then ultimately by default or omission through his failure to choose. When he announces he will count to ten before acting, he is still hesitating at thirteen (101). Happily or unhappily, those choices are made for him when in bad faith he abdicates, vanquished but saved.

Jumpei's triumph is no doubt modest. But positive it surely is, given the existential hell—Sartrean or Beckettian, as Abé would likely have acknowledged—in which he finds himself. His final status is most impressive when juxtaposed with that of other underground men, and particularly Dostoyevsky's. Unlike those earlier undergrounders, Jumpei has successfully escaped the flawed temptations of the aboveground world, which in retrospect seemed alternately unreachable and undesirable to his predecessors: the nameless narrator in Dostoyevsky's *Notes from Underground*, Pepel and company in Gorky's *The Lower Depths*, K. in Kafka's *The Castle*, Harry Haller in Hesse's *Steppenwolf*, Fred Daniels in Richard Wright's *The Man Who Lived Underground*, and the anonymous narrator in Ellison's *Invisible Man*. Jumpei has found relative fulfillment in his lunar underground, which Abé represents as a viable world by expanding it beyond individual isolation to embrace a nuclear family at home.

Alone in this long tradition of undergrounders, Jumpei comes out on top, not in escaping the underground of the dunes but in adopting them and adapting to them. Like Fred Daniels before him, Jumpei discovers that "perhaps the world has been turned upside down" (235). And now as never before he is on top of that world. The former teacher has learned his underground lesson well: there is no need to fly from the dunes, because he has made his nest among them. Having succeeded in his escape from conventional society at the invitation of a beetle named Motschulsky and a biographer named Mochulsky, Jumpei has established his own elemental value system among the dunes, like Fred Daniels and Invisible Man in their basement spider holes. But those two African American figures enjoyed there only an empty freedom from societal constraints. Both have their many watches or clocks set to different hours under blinding, unblinking lights. Unfortunately for them and us, such lucidity without enactment is still flight from reality. The two men are effectively cut off from any sense of time and identity, having not so much created a new world as retreated from an old one. They are not Robinson Crusoes who have colonized the underworld but two isolated figures who have lost themselves in it. Unlike them, Niki Jumpei—called a castaway by Abé (124)—was initially a slave, playing Friday to the villagers whose bidding he was compelled to execute. But he then learns to bond with his fellows and to build a sense of community and family that he had never felt before among men or with a woman. When he thinks back to his colleagues in the aboveground underground that he has forsaken, in the end he perceives them all as "tiny and insect-like" (236). Here at last is the sole descendant of the Russian Underground Man who has triumphed, not in approximating an insect as do characters in Dostoyevsky or Gorky or Wright, but in exemplifying the one insect who has at last become Man.

NOTES

1. Plato, "The Apology of Socrates," in *The Last Days of Socrates*, trans. Hugh Tredennick (London: Penguin, 1974), 63. There is a less-remembered precedent in the stubborn "daring of a fly" in Homer, *The Iliad*, trans. E. V. Rieu (London: Penguin, 1950), 331.

2. See Marcel Françon, "Un motif de la poésie amoureuse au XVIe siècle," *PMLA* 56 (1941): 307–36; and an iconography in chapter 2 of John Grand-Carteret's *Le Décolleté et le Retroussé* (Paris: Bernard, 1897).

3. Russell, *Religion and Science* (New York: Oxford University Press, 1961), 65n.

4. Blake, *The Portable Blake*, ed. Alfred Kazin (New York: Viking, 1946), 109.

5. Fyodor M. Dostoyevsky, *Notes from Underground*, trans. Richard Pevear and Larissa Volokhonsky (New York: Vintage, 1993), 49, 52.

6. "Kozyavka," in Dostoyevsky's *Zapiski iz podpol'e/Notes d'un souterrain*, ed. Tzvetan Todorov, trans. Lily Denis (Paris: Aubier, 1972), 138, 150. Variously translated as "insect" or "beetle" but equally accurately and disparagingly as "little snot" by Pevear and Volokhonsky (62, 69).

7. See Maxim Gorky, *Na Dne/The Lower Depths*, ed. Kurt Klein and Ira Goetz (Letchworth: Bradda, 1966), as well as *The Lower Depths*, trans. Kitty Hunter-Blair and Jeremy Brooks (London: Methuen, 1973); Franz Kafka, *Die Verwandlung/La Métamorphose*, trans. Brigitte Vergne-Cain and Gérard Rudent (Paris: Livre de Poche, 1988); Richard Wright, *The Man Who Lived Underground*, ed. Michel Fabre, trans. Claude-Edmonde Magny (Paris: Aubier, 1971).

8. On this theme generally, see Edward F. Abood, *Underground Man* (San Francisco: Chandler and Sharp, 1977).

9. On this inaccurate but oft-cited dictum from De Vogüé, see Robin Millner-Guland, "Gogol's 'Overcoat,'" *Times Literary Supplement*, February 28, 1997.

10. Pelevin, *The Life of Insects*, trans. Andrew Bromfield (New York: Farrar, Straus and Giroux, 1998).

11. *The Woman in the Dunes*, trans. E. Dale Saunders, with drawings by Machi Abé (New York: Knopf, 1964; Random, 1972). The Random Vintage edition is cited parenthetically throughout this essay. Other editions include *La femme des sables*, trans. George Bonneau (Paris: Stock, 1968), and *Suna no onna* (Tokyo: Orion, 1964). For the film script, see Hiroshi Teshigahara, *Woman in the Dunes* (New York: Phaedra, 1971).

12. Ellison, *Invisible Man* (London: Penguin, 1976); Beckett, *Play*, in *Words and Music, Play, Eh Joe*, trans. Samuel Beckett (Paris: Aubier, 1972), 181–231.

13. See Nancy S. Hardin, "An Interview with Abé Kobo," *Contemporary Literature* 15 (1974): 439–56; and Armando Martins Janeira, *Japanese and Western Literature: A Comparative Study* (Rutland, Vt.: Tuttle, 1970), 208.

14. Cf. *No Exit*, in *No Exit and Three Other Plays*, trans. Stuart Gilbert (New York: Vintage, 1955), 1–47.

15. See Mochulsky, *Dostoevsky, His Life and Work,* trans. Michael Minihan (Princeton: Princeton University Press, 1967).

16. Nabokov, "Franz Kafka: 'The Metamorphosis,'" in *Lectures on Literature,* ed. Fredson Bowers (New York: Harcourt, 1980), 260.

17. Kafka, *The Castle,* trans. Willa Muir and Edwin Muir (London: Penguin, 1975).

18. Sartre, *Huis clos,* ed. Jacques Hardré and George B. Daniel (London: Methuen, 1964).

19. Hermann Hesse, *Steppenwolf,* trans. Basil Creighton (New York: Bantam, 1977).

20. See Gaston Bachelard, *L'eau et les reves: Essai sur l'imagination de la matière* (Paris: Corti, 1942).

21. Kafka, *The Castle,* 261; Albert Camus, *Le mythe de Sisyphe: Essai sur l'absurde* (Paris: Gallimard, 1962). For Kafka's models generally, including Dostoyevsky, see my contributions in *Dictionary of Literary Influences: The Twentieth Century,* ed. John Powell (Westport, Conn.: Greenwood, 2004), 279–80.

7

Dangerous Skin

Bees and Female Figuration in
Maher and Plath

HEATHER JOHNSON

"A black intractable mind," Sylvia Plath's telling description of the amass-
ing insects in her poem "Swarm" (line 58), encapsulates the potency
of the image of bees for Plath: it gestures to both the embodiment
of the swarm and the intentionality of its attendant "mind." In her choice
of an insect as poetic image, Plath could count among her precursors the
poet Emily Dickinson and her well-known poem "I heard a Fly buzz—
when I died" (1896), a poem in which the insect represents the speaker's
failing sense of consciousness. By inference, the speaker's body is motionless, immanent and yet purportedly escapable ("What portion of me be /
Assignable," lines 10–11), while the fly gives expression to an imagined mind
or consciousness, which, separate from its corporeal form, circles restlessly
with "uncertain stumbling buzz" (line 13) overhead in the room. We will
see how this implied division of the self, between the material and immaterial, recurs in Plath's poetry, as does the uncertain position of Dickinson's
speaker, who seemingly speaks from a place "after" death. In a number of
Plath's poems, meanwhile, it is the bee that operates as the central image,
and not the more ordinary domestic fly, an insect popularly associated with
persistent irritation: "Shoo fly, don't bother me." And the bee is entirely
more threatening and exotic. Exciting a more visceral response than that
caused by the lone fly circling aimlessly, the bee has been used by other
writers to explore identity and to intimate a sense of the gothic. In Virginia
Woolf's novel *The Waves,* for example, the buzzing of bees expresses a new
version of subjectivity,[1] while the Scottish novelist Emma Tennant describes
the "Gothic atmosphere" of her childhood home, where she read in the attic

amid a "floor covering of dead bees."[2] Such detail lends this writer's memory of a formative scene the romantic thrill of muted danger emitted by the dead insects along with the gothic's sense of precarious identity. Even when dead, bees continue to reverberate with a certain energy or force.

It is this same promise of danger, with its gothic tenor and contingent sense of identity, on which the Irish visual artist Alice Maher draws in her work entitled *Bee Dress* (1994). Viewing this small dress with its covering of dead bees, its feminine figuration, and its gothic undertones, a reader of Plath unavoidably attends to the resonance of her poetic imagery in Maher's sculptural work. A consideration of the artist's use of bees as her material returns us to the poems, while a rereading of Plath's "bee cycle" will in turn affect our perception of Maher's work. As in Dickinson's vision, where corporeal immanence is contrasted with the incessant, apparently limitless motion of consciousness figured by the insect, a similar relation can be discovered in the works of Plath and Maher. Both are clearly attracted to this dual nature within the bee image itself, and their choice of the bee leads us

Alice Maher, *Bee Dress* (1994). Honey bees, cotton, wire. 13 × 26 × 27 cm. Collection of Arts Council of Northern Ireland. Courtesy of the artist.

to consider how the insect operates as an expression of a female "self." The implications of this female figuration will be explored here, as will the ways in which this figuration is informed by a contemporary gothic aesthetic. While Plath's poetry and Maher's art form each carry their own biographical or mythological context, both tap into the cultural significance of bees, and considering their work together opens up further readings around the representation of female identity.

Before introducing the specific contexts of Maher's and Plath's work, it is worth remarking that my interdisciplinary comparison generally subscribes to what Mieke Bal has called "a double, differential reading" of images and texts, whereby "the iconographic and the visual-narrative modes of reading need to be acknowledged, exploited, and maintained concurrently."[3] So it is practical to speak of "reading" and its descriptive qualities while remaining attentive to the significance of "viewing" and the "appeal to visuality."[4] As a mental picture, an "image" in a poem bears the mark of the visual already, and though belonging to different disciplines, the poetry and artwork under discussion here reveal surprising points of commonality across the iconography of the central bee image. In discussing the context of each artist's choice of the image of the bee, it is possible to look at the shared "language" around this trope and its conceptual or spatial composition. A self-consciousness in the use of their very materials prompts a focus on language in the poems and artwork. A sense of gothic danger arises in both cases: in Maher's work, the material of clustered dead bees in the shape of a dress alludes to pain and danger; in Plath's poems, the words themselves seem to be threatening and full of noise: Ted Hughes's perception of her writing in such terms—"Your page a dark swarm," "a cloud of gutturals"—follows Plath's own association of the bee imagery with language in her phrase "unintelligible syllables."[5]

Both material and metaphor, then, the bee image here can be read comparatively within a series of interpretive frames: cultural, biographical, and generic. The gothic in particular yields points of similarity in this study. Attending to gothic undertones initially reveals a figuration of the female self conceived as both embodied and disembodied. To understand the bee image in terms of this figuration both facilitates and then limits a reading of its effect in Plath's and Maher's work. Ultimately this essay argues that a reading that avoids such limitations is a reading that has regard not only for representational practices alone but for a Deleuzian "logic of

sensation." For figuration grounded exclusively in this dualism of embodiment and disembodiment is increasingly being challenged by feminist
theorists, and this challenge, as we shall see, urges us to read women's literature and art in newly attentive ways.

In her recent work *Portraits*, Alice Maher presents a series of photographic
self-portraits in which objects collected from the natural world interact
with the artist's body. In *Helmet* a woman's face disappears into a cluster
of mollusks; *Limb* reflects surprise at the apparent eruption of yew leaves
along the length of her arm; and in *Flock* Maher's open mouth receives a
"flight" of large black feathers. These stylized tableaux continue Maher's
exploration of themes of transformation and myth, originating in earlier
works such as *Nettle Coat, Berry Dress,* and, our main focus here, *Bee Dress.*
As in the self-portraits, these small-scale clothing pieces have been fashioned from vernacular materials. Maher's act of collecting natural objects
is regarded by one critic as fetishistic,[6] and certainly in her search for found
objects such as shells, feathers, and bees, Maher's practice imbues the collected items with talismanic meaning, an ostensibly "magical" power.

Critics have commonly read the meaning thus generated by these natural objects in terms of Irish mythology and fairy tale.[7] While she should
not be regarded primarily as a folk artist, Maher's engagement with folk
tradition does belong to a feminist practice of the revisions of fairy tales,
specifically the reinstatement of their more violent and sexually explicit
aspects.[8] One example of this is her *House of Thorns*—a small house completely covered in chocolate-brown rose thorns—which bears echoes of the
frightening gingerbread house in *Hansel and Gretel.* Rather than the simu-
lation of a cozy Irish cottage, however, this object speaks to the simultaneous beauty and danger of the natural world. At once diminutive and fierce,
and without windows or doors, *House of Thorns* also counts as part of
Maher's world of uncanny objects. Responding to this world of miniatures
and the unexpected, critics have failed to balance interpretations of her
work based on fairy tale with other readings.[9] Dissatisfied with readings
that posit a simple "cuteness" in her art, Maher herself has said in reference
to *The Thicket* that she prefers to think of its girl protagonists as "subversive rather than sweet."[10]

Yet this subversive drive, and indeed her creation of "fetishized" objects,
can be more usefully related to the genres of surrealism and the gothic.

Created from ordinary objects, often found or collected, and thought to be charged with "latent content," a surrealist work such as Meret Oppenheim's fur-lined teacup (*Object*, 1936) offers an unmistakable antecedent.[11] Oppenheim's teacup is seen as an example of surrealism's "love of alchemical transformation," a preoccupation comparable to Maher's self-professed focus on metamorphosis.[12] In creating objects that often startle and unnerve the viewer, and in fashioning clothes out of natural materials such as leaves, berries, and bees, Maher undoubtedly follows Oppenheim's juxtaposition of artifacts from the cultural realm with elements of nature, suggesting a reappraisal of each, but at the same time forging something unique. Maher clearly plays with the surrealist effect thereby created: "Objects fetched indoors from a wild, self-sufficient existence become uncanny."[13]

Her recent *Necklace*, with its bloody lambs' tongues worn against the artist's bare skin, epitomizes the way in which Maher's pieces both fascinate and unnerve the viewer. Such effects equally belong to a gothic sensibility. Maher's *Berry Dress*, a small dress covered in deep red rosehips, reveals

Alice Maher, *Berry Dress* (1994). Cotton, rosehips, pins. 16 × 26 × 30 cm. Collection of Irish Museum of Modern Art. Courtesy of the artist.

an engagement with the gothic's twinned concerns of violence and girl-hood.[14] The fabric forming the shoulders and puff sleeves has apparently been stained by the bloody buds, and looking beneath the skirts, one sees the enormous (because not scaled) sewing pins stuck through each rosehip holding it in place. Maher's "nature" clothes seem haunted by virginal fig-ures of gothic as well as fairy tale. *Berry Dress* speaks to the innocence, vio-lence, and debauchery that feature in both.[15]

While one may readily bring these generic concerns to bear in a read-ing of *Bee Dress*, Maher's treatment of her materials is also personal and, in a sense, organic: "I build up very strong relationships with materials as I work with them, their history, their associations." The act of collecting itself remains for the artist an inextricable component of those works that are fashioned out of the collected materials.[16] There is an evident awareness, too, of the overall effect of constructing a piece out of a large number of miniature objects—an effect in the spirit of Plath's line "Small, taken one by one, but my god, together!" ("The Arrival of the Bee Box," line 20).

Maher's choice of the bee as "fabric" in *Bee Dress*, along with its gothic undercurrents and apparent engagement with female figuration, can evoke the image of the bee in Sylvia Plath's "bee cycle" poems. In these poems it is clear that the bee held similarly powerful associations for Plath—in this case, biographical, psychological, and mythic (both personal and epic)[17]—associations that inform a reading of the poems that seeks to explore their iconography (rather than principally testing for biographical verisimili-tude). The breakdown of her marriage with the poet Ted Hughes and an actual meeting with a beekeeping group in Devon provide the impetus and narrative material for the five poems. In her last summer with Hughes, she had purchased a beehive and decided to become a beekeeper herself. Both Plath and Hughes have recalled her decoration of the newly acquired hive: like "a teacup, / White with pink flowers on it" ("Stings," lines 8–9); "you painted it, / White, with crimson hearts and flowers, and bluebirds" ("The Bee God," lines 3–4). Both poets recognize a retrospective irony in the con-trast between the domestic optimism of these decorations and the ferocity, the "black asininity" ("Wintering," line 17), denied by the painted facade.

The subsequent drama of her personal life is exemplified by an incident in which Hughes was stung by a swarm of bees, and both poets read sig-nificance into the recollected scene. Here the bees act as metaphors for a natural moral force, adjudicating on Hughes's infidelity, whereby the bees "found him out / Molding onto his lips like lies."[18] In this context, the image of the beehive with its contained energy becomes for Plath an apt metaphor for the struggle between an attempt to control events in her life and the lack of control that positions her as a bystander to the breakdown of her marriage. "The Arrival of the Bee Box," for example, recounts this struggle in terms of a conflict of ownership ("I am the owner," "sweet God" [lines 25, 35] of an uncontrollable force ("a Roman mob" [line 19]).

The poet's imaginative and psychological engagement with her father, who was an entomologist and the author of a book on bumblebees, obviously compounds the significance of bees in her work. Her father's area of professional expertise, his own writing, and the fact that he died when Plath was young become a potent combination for Plath in her relation to men and as a writer. The psychological narrative relating to her father is evident in poems such as "Lament" (from the juvenilia) and "Beekeeper's Daughter." The earlier poem chants a refrain of regret—"the sting of bees took away my father"—while the "maestro of the bees" (line 5) in "Beekeeper's Daughter" is at once "father" and "bridegroom" (line 19), and the speaker is clearly enthralled to this figure: "My heart under your foot" (line 7).

A substantial amount of criticism devoted to Plath's late poems delineates a personal mythology around a figure of transcendence or escape, often read as a feminist figure of triumph. In a number of biographical readings, the figure is baldly identified as the "poet-as-bee."[19] Linda Bundtzen, for one, contends that the final lines in "Wintering"—"Will the hive survive" (line 50)—remain inconclusive as a direct consequence of Plath's actual circumstances: "Plath did not know what flight to London would bring." I would argue that the poetic potency of the bee image is understated in Bundtzen's focus on less-menacing traits: "swarming and clustering . . . to brood and commune."[20] Such social and nurturing connotations belie the drive toward conceptualization of the self indicated in the bee imagery. More radical than the accuracy of Plath's bee knowledge is an imagined spatial composition of the self projected in the poetry.

The personal vision Plath articulates through the bee image has been a source of comment for its exclusivity. An early review suggests this myth is so specifically personal as to be solipsistic: "The persona of the late poems is 'All-Mouth' [from "Poem for a Birthday"] muttering and mythologizing to itself."[21] Though a singular vision, the persona reveals a metaphoric shape; for Plath, the "I" describes a spatial dimension in its reference to a body and the nonbody. Having regard for this duality and for a common sensibility in their work, we can begin to explore Maher's and Plath's trope of the bee in relation to each other. Each comes to the iconography of the bee from her own context, yet both imagine a female self, and both arrive at this figure by means of the gothic.

Where the gothic is evident in the work of twentieth-century writers and artists, a number of themes emerge relevant to the present discussion, among them: girlhood (in relation to danger and virginity), the grotesque, the figure of a "familiar," and a ghostly "presence in absence." While no critic has read Maher's work in relation to the gothic, it is not unprecedented to think of Plath's poetry in these terms: Ellen Moers, for instance, locates Plath in a tradition of "female gothic," and Victor Sage has brought to light the relationship between the genre and Catholicism in her work.[22] Certainly one can find in the bee cycle scenes espousing classic gothic elements. In "Wintering," for example, there is a sense of enclosure ("this is the room I could never breathe in") and a distinctly gothic scheme of "black," "bat," "no light," "appalling objects," "decay," and "possession."

Among such gothic features is the figure of the adolescent girl, which Moers argues marks the female gothic.[23] Certainly throughout *Ariel* a fear of the beekeeping father (conflated with the sexual figure of Hughes) replicates the gothic scenario of brooding male presence and female victim. The persona of "Daddy" operates as a gothic figure ("Herr Doktor, Herr Lucifer"), and accordingly Plath's own girlhood (recalled perhaps in the girlish decoration of the hive) becomes relevant to this scenario. The poems "Swarm" and "Wintering" contribute to the characterization of the father as fascist and broaden the poet's rejection of the unfaithful spouse into the speaker's ultimate endorsement of the female bee's action: "they have got rid of the men" ("Wintering," line 40). This stance might be read as feminist, yet the poet also mines the gothic imagery of brides, virgins, and violence. For Plath, this imagery engages with the emergence of a female self and undercurrents of fairy tale while arguably sharing the sexual and murderous drama of the life cycle of actual bees (in which the queen's female rivals are killed and male drones die in the act of copulation).

In response to the traditional gothic figure of the virgin impaled (sexually or murderously or both), the bee poems provide two possible, and differing, accounts. The first of these replicates the emblematic gothic scene and, indeed, the gothic colors of black, white, and red, colors also recognized as "Plath's colors."[24] References to virginity and violence appear in the cycle of poems, but it is "Bee Meeting" that most closely follows the gothic paradigm: the poem opens with a sense of impending initiation, the journey to the place of initiation bears telltale warnings ("blood clots," "bored hearts"), pain is experienced ("gorse hurts me"), and the "bride flight" (by the occupant of the virginal hive) leads to an inference of death ("white box," "cold").

Furthermore, reading "Bee Meeting" against David Punter's notion of the "ceremonial gothic" confirms Plath's uncritical reproduction of a gothic model.[25] The scene in this poem clearly belongs to the ceremonial: there is the procedural "taking out of veils"; the speaker is passive as her cuffs are buttoned for her; "everybody is nodding," yet she does not know the meaning of this; and membership is conferred: "they are making me one of them." The setting correlates to that of ritual event: "shorn grove," "circle of hives." The tension of this initiation culminates in the announcement "here they come," followed by a gradual deceleration and relief: "there will be no killing," and "I am exhausted." Yet any relief is short-lived, as the speaker cannot decipher the conclusion ("they are shaking hands"), followed by the dawning realization of innocence lost in "why am I cold?" Punter's proposition that in the structure of ceremony "two devices, the welcome and the expulsion, are perhaps one and the same" is borne out in Plath's poem by the initial welcome of the speaker to the group *and* the sense that she remains the one outsider following the conclusion of the event.[26]

A similar tropic cluster of girlhood, initiation, and violence characterizes aspects of Maher's work as gothic and generally follows the replication of gothic narrative that we find in "Bee Meeting." The appearance of girl figures in Maher's work reflects the anarchy and pleasure the artist discerns in what she calls the "rich wild time of girlhood." Expanding on this theme, Maher suggests that "the image of the little girl bursting out into the world is as much about the liberation of the female imagination as it is about a personal story [her own childhood in the Irish countryside]."[27] In addition to any biographical resonance, the debauched and anarchic girls found in Dorothea Tanning's work of the 1940s provide the wild girls in Maher's *The Thicket* with a surrealist precedent.

One might argue that Maher's two "dress" pieces create a gothic effect as the clothes of such imaginary, anarchic girls. *Berry Dress* is made of bloody

rosehips individually pinned to the small dress, the interior of which reveals the steely sewing pins that have been stuck through from the outside.
The contrast between the little-girl dress with its puff sleeves and pleated
hem and the staining color of the stuck berries evokes a gothic configuration of danger, wounds, and the virginal. The dresses' small scale and
maidenly detail indicate the gender and age of their imagined owners. An
allusion to the gothic virginal girl in *Bee Dress* suggests that here "death,"
rather than any bloody death, appears to have been occasioned by the male
bees stinging her, as if the dress stands as the aftermath of a deathly swarm.
This reading accords with the gendering of the gothic's female victim and
male impaler, and the bee in Maher's piece consequently comes to represent
the murderous rapist: as male bees die once they have mated, the viewer
speculatively imagines that they have all sacrificed themselves in attaining
the virgin embodied by the dress.

An alternative account of the gothic narrative can be read in Plath, one
that focuses on the fact that the male bee dies after mating with the queen.
The bees on Maher's dress have seemingly sacrificed themselves for an
alleged sexual dominance, and in Plath this inversion of the gothic paradigm
is an expression of feminist triumph. In "Stings," the male bees "thought
death was worth it" (line 51), but the queen survives "more terrible than she
ever was" (line 57). Her flight "over the engine that killed her" (and here
we start to see the projection of an idealized female self) exceeds the sexual danger posed by the male. Here the *queen* is the murderer and sexual
predator. Accordingly we might conclude that the queen bee's triumph over
the "wax house" (an image read variously as patriarchy and representation)
can be read as a feminist turn from generic, and gendered, convention.

If Plath's configuration of the gothic genre hinges on a "compulsion to
visualize the self,"[28] then rather than a strict biographical identification of
the poet with the figure of the queen bee—an identification often too easily
made—it is possible to consider the figure instead as an imagined female
"familiar" of the speaker. We know that Plath had an interest in the figure of the double (the topic of her undergraduate thesis), and the figure of
a doubled Other appears in many of *Ariel*'s poems. In the bee poems, the
relationship between the speaker and the bees (particularly the queen bee)
suggests the extension of self in the form of a familiar. It is not surprising
that the image of the bee works so effectively as an embodiment of the
poet's self or voice, as among other characteristics its ability to fly can

render mobility of thought. In fact the figure of an insect as a familiar has antecedents, albeit esoteric, in literary history.[29] Familiars explicitly belong to Maher's work; the artist applies this term to the figure of a little girl in *Familiar I* (1994). This piece includes a painting in which a small girl appears on a red background with her golden hair streaming upward, while next to the painting long strands of flax hang from a peg, amplifying the image of the stream of virginal hair. The girl here is again reminiscent of Tanning's girls—both artists depict girls with their hair standing on end in apparent response to surmised fear, surprise, or a sexual event. This arresting figure belongs to Maher's visualized "alter egos,"[30] a term equally applicable to the treatment of the bee figure in Plath.

In her surrealist self-portrait *Birthday* (1942), Tanning pictures herself in a dress partially made of twigs while a monkeylike creature with claws and wings sits at her feet. This portrait depicts the familiar as grotesque, not as a perfected or ideal form of the self. Certainly many of Plath's images of an alter ego also epitomize the grotesque, a mode that arises from "the juxtaposition or clash of the ideal with the real, the psychic with the physical, or the concrete with the symbolic."[31] The relationship between a "new absolutely white person" and an "old yellow one" neatly articulates such oppositions in the poem "In Plaster": "She lay in bed with me like a dead body / And I was scared, because she was shaped just the way I was" (lines 6–7). The scarred, decaying, and bandaged body becomes the scene for negotiation between the self projected as transcendent ("I gave her a soul" [line 16]) and the self as immanent. The speaker does not rest in either condition of self but constantly negotiates both as its mode of being. As Rose rightly points out, "Transcendence appears here not as solution, but as repetition."[32] Bound up with this process, the grotesque ultimately articulates a sense of frustration, even a sense of disgust, at the self's own physical constraints—and yet, at the same time, our pleasure as Plath's readers derives from the staging of this compelling act of repetition itself. This tension between the psychic and the physical is similarly central to the function of Plath's bee image, wherein disembodied transcendence is pitched against grotesque materiality.

Connotations of the grotesque in *Bee Dress*, meanwhile, arise from its constitutive material. Transformed into the raw material of art, the bees reveal architectural and textural properties. The tactile quality of the textural bees arouses a sense of fascination in the viewer; yet the implicit fact that the artist has intimately handled the bees, the thorns, the bloody berries, and, in the more recent work, several lambs' tongues may also elicit a sense of repulsion. Nature here is both fascinating and sinister, not least because the work is composed of dead objects. In *Bee Dress* the assemblage of bee torsos creates a "plushness," as the collected softness invites the urge to touch, even as we sense that such an urge would ordinarily involve a degree of danger. Maher's objects then engage with taboos of touch—in her choice of material, as *art* in a gallery space, and in her declared interest in "transformation": "There are a lot of stories and fairy tales where it is often the touch of something sharp like a thorn or sword which has the power to transform."[33] Here, then, the visual is imbricated with its associative sense of touch,[34] and the grotesque is acquainted with spectacle. The spectator is drawn by the allure of difference even as he or she is simultaneously appalled; such a reaction to Maher's dress is akin to that aroused by the traditional sideshow character of the "Bee Man," who was known to perform the spectacle of "wearing" clusters of bees on his arms and head.[35] Plath also emphasizes the visual, as in "The Arrival of the Bee Box," in which the speaker is curious voyeur: "I put my eye to the grid" (line 11). The speaker is both drawn to the hive ("I can't keep away from it" [line 8]) and feels "appall[ed]" (line 17). The imagined spectacle of the old queen is reminiscent of an exhibit in a natural history museum: "Her wings torn shawls, her long body / Rubbed of its plush" ("Stings," lines 17–18). The latter phrase again invokes the uneasy combination of the luxury of "plush" and the disconcerting contact implied in "rubbed." Signaled by such abject materiality, this highlighted sense of embodiment emerges as the foundation for a figuration of the self in the bee image.

Despite the prominence of this material embodiment invoked by the bee's body, the resonant effect of *Bee Dress* and the bee poems is in fact its antithesis: immateriality or absence. In both cases, the presence of a projected self seems to reside "elsewhere." While in part produced by the connotations of death,[36] this effect relies on an interpretation of the dress as the actualized effect of an imaginary event. *Bee Dress* in a sense *embodies* the fate feared by Plath's "magician's girl," who stands as a "Pillar of white in a blackout of knives" and "hides" as an "invisible" "tree" to avoid becoming the focus of the swarm's attention.[37] One can read the imagined narrative of the dress as the bees having attached themselves to the now "missing" girl—having clung to her dress—and the work captures the moment after her death. This lends the piece a gothic irony; its almost defiant carapace of suffering combined with its little-girl sweetness creates a disturbing vision.

Just as *Bee Dress* presents an invisible or absent inhabitant (of the dress), so Plath's poems invite us to consider the position of the poems' speaker. The final line of "Bee Meeting," which ends with "why am I cold," suggests the death of the speaker, through a probable identification of the lyric "I" with the image of the bee. While references to death occur elsewhere in the bee cycle, the voice in this poem most clearly articulates a version of prosopopoeia or an act of "defacement," as Paul de Man would have it.[38] Plath's poetry works to actualize the lyric voice but also achieves an apparently opposite effect here as the poem's ending begs the question of who is speaking and from where.

The mystery, or "coagulation around a secret" (to use Punter's account of a gothic effect), that resides in *Bee Dress* is occasioned by a similar, though fanciful, question: who wore this dress? Morrison has observed a similar effect in Maher's *The Twins* (two bronze wigs): "An actual person to animate the hair is absent. Did she die? Did she change state and walk through the wall. . . . Was it even a woman?"[39] This "impossible appearance," impossible in its figuration of death, impossible because unimaginable in concrete terms, is gestured by the "remains" of the dress. And it is this implied absence at the core of the projected image of self to which I now turn in an exploration in Maher and Plath of this figuration, composed of material embodiment, but fascinated by a sense of "absent" disembodiment.

As we have seen, we can read *Bee Dress* and the bee poems in terms of narrative: each carries a "story" of myth, biography, or genre. Maher's and Plath's figures of the girl and the familiar point to an articulation of a self, whether fantasized Other or autobiographical reflection. As characteristics of actual bees inform both the poems and artwork, attention to the constituents of the insect image may alert us to the conceptualized duality of this self. The dichotomy of embodiment and disembodiment is the rubric through which female subjectivity has most often been read by feminist theory. "Corporeal feminism" has focused on the effects of the Cartesian mind-body dualism on the representation of the feminine, whereby female subjectivity is predicated on both "aggressive solidification of the object-body" and the "decorporealization of the flesh."[40] It is sufficient here to reiterate that feminism has challenged the hierarchization implicit in the mind-body split, where the body is gendered feminine and serves primarily to facilitate the achievement of (masculine) transcendent subjectivity. In their critique of Western metaphysics, several theorists attempt to rethink the body as something other than the negation of thought created by the mind-body dualism.[41] I would like briefly to point to the expression of this dichotomy in relation to the bee image before turning to consider whether aspects of the image help us to postulate a female figure independent of old dichotomies.

The bee image is just one of the metaphors in Plath's work that emphasize a contrast between these two constituents of the self—embodiment and disembodiment—and the consequent operation of transcendence whereby mind (or the "external soul")[42] ascends and exceeds the body (thereby "negating" the body). In Plath's intended order of the collection *Ariel,* poems situated before the bee sequence firmly establish this dynamic. When the female speaker in "Lady Lazarus" proclaims, "Out of the ash / I rise with my red hair" (lines 82–83), her "success" is to overcome the "ash" of mortality (embodiment) and "rise" to an unspecified, transcendent plane. "Ariel" inscribes a similar drive or arc in the speaker's renunciation of the bodily sphere in favor of a form of dissipation: "I unpeel— / Dead hands, dead stringencies. / And now I / Foam to wheat, a glitter of seas" (lines 20–23). In the intended order, "Fever 103°" immediately preceded the bee poems (although it was written some days later), and this poem clearly illustrates a potent sense of transcendence aligned with purity, disembodiment, flight, and elevation; and the implied success of this transcendence is based on the repression or rejection of what is immanent: "fat," "the weak," "hanging" (an earthbound trajectory), that which "will not rise," the "retch" of bodily sickness, and the sexual ("whore petticoats").[43]

The reader then turns to the bee poems with this visual construction already accented. In "Wintering," the image of "Black / Mind against all that white" (lines 32–33), where white is identified with death (the material corpse), echoes the preceding dynamic. Even draft versions of the bee poems demonstrate a tension between the embodiment of "corpses" and the gesture toward disembodiment in "glass."[44] The relation is given quintessential expression in "Stings" in the following description of the queen bee: "her lion-red body, her wings of glass" (line 55). The association of lion and body lends a sense of heaviness to that side of the equation; the transparency of the bee's wings suggests a lightness and fragility that, while still dependent on the tangible, gesture toward the immaterial.

A similar conception of self appears in an essay from 1962 depicting Plath's childhood. "Ocean 1212W" offers a perception of her young self as "a fine white flying myth." This aspirational projection, while announcing its purity ("white") and sense of transcendence ("flying" and "myth" as that which exceeds the ordinary), still remains tied to an embodied self, as the speaker explains, "I felt the wall of my skin: I am I."[45] The articulation of Plath's encounter with this "I" (and its dependence on the body's *surface*) is immediately relevant to our reading of the bee poems. An arc is sketched in these poems that has its origins in the body before moving up and away. In "Stings," for instance, the "dew" describes an upward evaporation *from* the body: "dew from dangerous skin" (line 27). "Dew" acts as an apt metaphor for the body "distilled" into air, nothingness, invisibility.

In response to such singular symbolism, Plath's critics have given varying attention to each term of this ontological equation, thereby declaring their own critical ethos. Bundtzen's "embodied" criticism, for example, contrasts with Jacqueline Rose's textual or representational emphasis. In her reading of "Ariel," Bundtzen argues that Plath "lets it [her body] take fiery flight," a literal-minded reading that seems to overlook the metaphorical complexity of Plath's use of imagery.[46] Bundtzen's reading operates within the tradition of a corporeal feminism that seeks to reinstate the body (including that of the critic herself) as a site of liberation, for as recent theorists have observed, "the body has been targeted as the redemptive opening for a specifically feminine site of representation."[47] Rose, on the other hand, concentrates on the *figure* of transcendence in Plath's poetry, her focus being on Plath's representational practices.

In Maher's *Bee Dress,* the embodied-disembodied dichotomy principally resides in the tension between its physicality and the impression of an absent body suggested by the form of the dress. While it figures the body, it also points to an excess of representation. The dress *remains* present— its imaginary occupant elsewhere—and displays a defiance through its own materiality, in accordance perhaps with Maher's avowed concern with "places of immanent resistance." Yet the dress arguably also figures the "remains" of a representational event, as an effect of discursive representation. Concurrent attention to the body and the absence of a body occurs in part because its subject is clothing. Clothes are both a disguise for, and an outline of, the body, and inherent to *Bee Dress* is the notion of showing versus hiding. Maher is drawn to material that "decorates the body or encases the body."[48] A sense of being sealed, and concealed, accords with the artistic appeal of bee imagery and its "strange hermetic world."[49]

Certainly disguise and encasement are relevant to the bee poems. The speaker in "Bee Meeting" dresses in strange clothes to keep her safe from the bees. The image shares the paradox belonging to other coverings, dressings, and clothes in Plath: they act as "skins" in which to hide, but they must also ultimately be escaped. Often the "narrative" drive results in an escape from such "clothing," a triumph over encasement, and this escape usually involves flight. What is escaping, of course, is the incorporeal element, which leads us to read the figure, and indeed this membrane of skin separating the corporeal and incorporeal, in terms of Grosz's view of "the body and mind relation as a complex interweaving of both 'outside' and 'inside.'"[50]

However, in response to such a view, feminist theorists have recently argued that "as long as representation is seen as a negation of corporeality, dualism can only ever be complicated and never overcome."[51] Locating the dualistic relationship of embodiment and disembodiment in Plath and Maher illustrates their engagement with a figuration of the female self, but it can also lead us into just such an interpretive or critical cul-de-sac. It is for this reason, indeed, as Moira Gatens has recognized, that "many feminists are working on the creation of an alternative *topos* from which to reject or work through these dominant dualisms of the mind and body."[52] Accordingly, the new move in feminist theorization of "incorporeality" includes readings of the self as event, trajectory, and "machinic assemblage," where "the self is nothing other than the performances it effects or the connections it makes." Claire Colebrook demonstrates how "possibilities, responses, purposes and actions" may come to articulate "the incorporeal gap that separates any *thought* of the body from any biological given."[53] Reading the bee imagery closely, we begin to glean signs of disruption to the interpretive models grounded in Cartesian dualism.

The power of the bee image, as we will see, in fact does not derive solely from knowledge of narrative context, or through the strategy of imagining the self as disembodied (though both are valuable avenues of criticism). Rather, close attention to the figural that does not depend on the familiar dichotomy of embodiment and disembodiment leads us to Deleuze's distinction of "affect" or "sensible force."[54] Two aspects of the bee imagery that offer an alternative to an exegetic reliance on a dualist model are the features of sound and kinesis, affects that bear out Deleuze's argument about the very basis of art's power: art "is not a matter of reproducing or inventing forms, but of capturing forces."[55]

Sound does not fall neatly into the category of mind or body; related to the senses, sound is experienced through the body, yet the act of imagining sound involves a mental activity. The loud buzzing generated by bees is conspicuous through its silence in *Bee Dress* and is similarly an imagined component of the psychic space of Plath's poems. The conglomeration of bees in Maher's piece looks capable of considerable, and frightening, noise. The dress seems to carry an aural reverberation of the sound of bees; the bee bodies appear uncannily silent, and the viewer's experience of the work may vacillate between fascination and fear. An imaginative re-creation, however conscious, of the sound of the bees—a sound that many people find startling, if not alarming—contributes to the dress's repelling effect. The mass of bees here suggests not the "uncertain stumbling buzz" of Dickinson's solitary fly but rather the ferocity, volume, and intent recognized by Plath in her phrase "black intractable mind." Moreover, a recognition of sound irrevocably alters one's perception of the work: once the viewer "sees" the sound, it is no longer possible to look at the reverberating body of the dress as a quiet aesthetic object. The projection of sound in this regard transforms *Bee Dress* into an object of "sensation," whereby a "spasm" or vibration is communicated to the viewer.[56] In a reading where the object is relieved of its representational functions and stands as a "Figure," as Deleuze argues, sound works as a kind of rhythm that itself becomes "sensation."[57]

If an operation inherent to poetic language means that silence can strengthen the presence of an image to become a strongly moving presence, then this is doubly true in Plath's bee poems, where the metaphor that achieves this effect turns on a relationship between noise and silence.[58] Perceiving the figured self as a body exceeded by an invisible but palpable consciousness, voice, or ghostly presence, the sound of the bees negotiates these two spheres (the embodied and the disembodied) as discernible in *Bee Dress* and in the bee poems. The association of a self with the bee image means that the noise—created by the body *and* associated with the ephemeral wings—expresses an event of the self as something resistant to the binary. In Plath the speaker hears, adding to the sense of embodiment of the speaking "I." "Arrival of the Bee Box" explicitly highlights the bees' sound,

their "noise" (line 17) made of "unintelligible syllables" (line 18) and "furi-
ous Latin" (line 21). Indeed it is the "din" (line 5) coming from the box
that indicates that there is life inside the coffinlike container. Unable to see
the bees (they are "black on black" [line 15]), the speaker detects a presence
through the noise; here it is the bees' sound itself that signifies a self or
selves. Allusions to muteness serve to maximize this "presence" of sound
in the poems. A phrase such as "The dumb, banded bodies" ("The Swarm,"
line 47) makes the silence all the more palpable, an effect that is also in part
created by the speaker's sense of isolation and distance (as in "The Bee
Meeting").

Plath creates a similar inversion in "Wintering" with her account of the
sluggish bees inching their way to an "unnatural" source of sugar: "the bees
/ So slow I hardly know them, / Filing like soldiers / To the syrup tin" (lines
22–25). This picture is strikingly different from more immediate associations with the bee of speed, power, and flight. Attending to the spectrum
of movement from complete inertia to near-invisible velocity inherent to
the bee itself reveals a sense of kinesis that is crucial to the application of
the bee image. If we think of the appearance and function of a fly in the
tradition of still life painting, we remember its indication of the decaying
"life" of the fruit or other object on which it is poised, but we also notice
its kinetic effect: whereas the objects in still lifes are inert, the fly, on the
other hand, gives the impression that it might move, thereby heighten-
ing the picture's sense of realism and lending it a tremulous quality. An
impression of energy accrues around the image of the fly as the locus of
potential movement (even though the viewer logically knows that it will
not move).

In *Bee Dress* a comparable effect is at work. The bees are clearly fixed
to the dress and, being dead, are perfectly still. Yet a sense of fear is nevertheless created by their seeming potential for movement. When dead, bees
continue to elicit a gothic sense of fear and excitement. We may visualize
their previous flight or even their swarm onto the dress, even as we witness
the visceral effect of their stillness and rigidity. The latter effect too does
not preclude a sense of horror in imagining that the bees might yet take
flight again. The oscillation in this response is initiated by the highly visual,
even tremulous, nature of the bee image. Relying on the mechanics of a
body in air, the trope of flight negotiates the terms of the embodiment-
disembodiment dichotomy. In the function of the image in the dress and

the poems, flight is not determined by either category but is an act of imagining a corporeal entity sketching an abstract trajectory. Visualizing this
arc, we do not imagine a material body so much as an arrow, one never
fully seen because of the speed of insect flight. In Maher's dress, the bee
image expresses a sense of restrained energy, a force that the dress threatens to release. Applied to the form of the girl, this visual impression presents a female figuration composed of movement, desire, potential power,
even defiance.

Tension between stillness and dynamism also informs the figuration of
a self in Plath's poems. Acting as the poet's metaphor for transcendence as
it does, the flight of the bee visualized by the reader is a crucial element
in the reader's experience of the poems. The pleasure in the freedom, and
danger, of the bee's flight derives from the sense of imprisonment established in advance of their release. Images of confinement—"the white
hive," "the box of maniacs"—emphasize the kinetic energy latent in the bee.
When freed, this energy embarks on a skyward trajectory, the beginning
and ending of which are indeterminate, reminiscent of "the arrow" (line
27) in "Ariel" (where the energy is in tension with "stasis" [line 1]). Once the
bees take flight in Plath's poems, we "picture" their movement. It is in this
visualization of an elusive "arrow" (always returning in its repetition of the
attempt at transcendence) that we try to locate Plath's impression of a self.
This can prove a disorienting task for the reader; the sense of agency in the
bee poems often remains fugitive.[59] Rather than a negation of corporeality
within the logic of dualism, the trajectories we perceive here can be understood as "lines of new becoming." The notion of "becoming-animal" gives
these lines of flight a dimension that liberates their imagery from conventional female figuration and points up the potential of art "to render
visible."[60] The insect image expresses this idea of "becoming-animal" for
Deleuze and Guattari (hence their engagement with Kafka), an idea that
they use "to describe the positivity and multiplicity of desire and affect,"
as Colebrook explains. Put simply, we can imagine seeing the world from
a perspective unknown to us, and not a single perspective "so much as a
collection or swarm."[61]

In the sound and kinetic flight of the bee image, Maher and Plath ultimately comment on the process and limitations of figuration itself. Recognizing that the "*thought* of the body," and indeed of the mind or consciousness, gives rise to numerous shapes, their iconography of the bee endeavors

to give a "face" to the unrepresentable, to map out lines of becoming. Each use of the bee gestures toward an incorporeal presence, a state of being that is irreducible to direct representation.[62] The bee image, in its synthesis of plush body and ephemeral wings, proves at first glance to be well suited to the picturing of the dual nature of selfhood but in fact overcomes this duality in its affective sensations and imaginary avenue to new perception, a figure seemingly as intangible and provisional as a "red / Scar in the sky, red comet" ("Stings," lines 57–58).

NOTES

1. Leila Brosnan, *Reading Virginia Woolf's Essays and Criticism* (Edinburgh: Edinburgh University Press, 1997), 144–45. Brosnan shows how the figure of the swarm suggests a new kind of subjectivity, one located in language itself.

2. Emma Tennant, in *The Pleasure of Reading,* ed. Antonia Fraser (London: Bloomsbury, 1992), 143–47.

3. Mieke Bal, *Reading "Rembrandt": Beyond the Word-Image Opposition* (Cambridge: Cambridge University Press, 1991), 179.

4. Ibid., 1. Maher has complained that most criticism of her work is descriptive; she is in fact complaining about the traditional form of art criticism itself. *Circa* 83 (1998): 16–19.

5. Ted Hughes, "The Bee God" (lines 15, 20), in *Birthday Letters* (London: Faber and Faber, 1998); Plath, "Arrival of the Bee Box" (line 18), *Collected Poems,* ed. Ted Hughes (New York: Harper and Row, 1981).

6. Medb Ruane, "A Sting in the Tail," in *Alice Maher,* ed. John O'Regan (Cork: Gandon Editions, 1998), 7. Ruane suggests that Maher's use of these materials is a "forensic device."

7. For instance, *Knot* (a series of drawings and installations about hair) is reminiscent of the Rapunzel fairy tale, while *Nettle Coat* refers to the Irish folktale "The Children of Lir." Maher herself fuels such an interpretation by work such as *Fairytale Wall*—her contribution to the Integrated Artworks Project at the Royal Victoria Hospital in Belfast (2002).

8. Angeline Morrison agrees that Maher's work cannot be classified simply as folk art: "It isn't folk art—although it is heavy with folk associations." See Morrison, "Fetched in from the Wild," *Circa* 83 (1998): 20–22. For a discussion on feminist revisions of fairy tale and identity formation, see Ellen C. Rose, "Through the Looking Glass: When Women Tell Fairy Tales," in *The Voyage In: Fictions of Female Development,* ed. Elizabeth Abel, Marianne Hirsch, and Elizabeth Langland (Hanover, N.H.: University Press of New England, 1983); and Kay Stone, "Feminist Approaches to the Interpretation of Fairy Tales," in *Fairy Tales and Society: Illusion, Allusion, and Paradigm,* ed. Ruth Bottigheimer (Philadelphia: University of Pennsylvania Press, 1986), 230–33.

9. Considering the title of her 1989 exhibition *Tryst*, Peter Jordan speculates that it "might equally have been called 'The Adventures of Alice in Wonderland.'" *Circa* 49 (1990): 36.

10. Maher is also "tired of people referring to them in an Alice in Wonderland fashion . . . that's just an easy take on my name." Interview, *Circa* 83 (1998): 18–19. Morrison observes that such a reading (Alice in Wonderland) is "redundant or based on a reading of surface alone" ("Fetched," 21).

11. Whitney Chadwick, *Women Artists and the Surrealist Movement* (Boston: Little Brown, 1985), 122–23. Notably, I have not read any comparisons of her work to female surrealist artists; Jordan invokes Delvaux and Magritte. Jordan, *Circa* 49 (1990): 37. It is worth remarking that insects appear in the surrealist world of Dalí, who repeatedly painted ants and grasshoppers, and insects also feature in some gothic writing such as Franz Kafka's *Metamorphosis* (1916), in which the central character himself is transformed into an insect.

12. Chadwick, *Women Artists*, 123. Chadwick points out that the erotic content of the teacup arises from the richness of visual associations and language of furry tongue. Just as Oppenheim herself considered *Object* a "joke," so the element of play in Maher's work should also be acknowledged.

13. Morrison, "Fetched," 21.

14. Contrary to Marian Lovett's review of *Bee Dress* suggesting an opposition between its "surreal concerns" and "references to childhood," a number of young, anarchic girls appear in the work of the surrealist Dorothea Tanning (for example, in *Eine kleine Nachtmusik* [1946] and *Palaestra* [1947]). Lovett, *Circa* 80 (1997): 41.

15. Little Red Riding Hood, for instance, can be read as a quintessential gothic heroine (with the fairy tale's labyrinthine forest and sexual initiation).

16. *Circa* 83 (1998): 16–19. Maher: "Collected objects have a life of their own."

17. Kroll reads against Robert Graves's *White Goddess*, following Hughes's guidance about Plath's reading list. Judith Kroll, *Chapters in a Mythology: The Poetry of Sylvia Plath* (New York: Harper and Row, 1976).

18. "Stings," lines 48–49. As Jacqueline Rose notes, much of Plath criticism has been preoccupied with questions of blame in regard to the poets' personal lives. The complexities of Plath criticism have been rehearsed elsewhere: see particularly the introduction to Rose, *The Haunting of Sylvia Plath* (London: Virago Press, 1991); and Janet Malcolm, *The Silent Woman: Sylvia Plath and Ted Hughes* (New York: Vintage Books, 1995).

19. In her study *The Other Ariel* (Amherst: University of Massachusetts Press, 2001), Linda K. Bundtzen gives a sustained reading of the bee poems.

20. Ibid., 158, 160.

21. Review by P. N. Furbank (1965), cited in *The Art of Sylvia Plath*, ed. Charles Newman (Bloomington: Indiana University Press, 1970), 293–94.

22. Ellen Moers, *Literary Women* (London: Women's Press, 1978), 107; Victor Sage, *Horror Fiction* (London: Macmillan, 1988), 115–22. Furbank's review of *Ariel* briefly mentions the gothic (cited in Newman, *The Art of Sylvia Plath*, 293–94).

23. Moers, *Literary Women*, 107. Suggesting that Victorian gothic could portray a darker side of children's lives, Moers proposes that "the savagery of girlhood accounts in part for the persistence of the Gothic mode into our own time."

24. This color scheme frequently appears in Plath's poetry, for example, in the poems "Tulips" and "Three Women," where they are associated with gothic experiences of self-haunting and self-loathing.

25. David Punter, "Ceremonial Gothic," in *Spectral Readings: Towards a Gothic Geography*, ed. Glennis Byron and David Punter (New York: Macmillan, 1999), 37–53.

26. The sense of alienation is partially cultural: the characters at the beekeepers' meeting are stock English types such as the vicar.

27. Maher's reflections on girlhood appear in the *Circa* 83 interview (17); and in "A Conversation with the Artist," in *Alice Maher* (Cork: Gandon Editions, 1998), 14. Medb Ruane briefly discusses the figure of the "girl-child" ("A Sting in the Tail," 6–7).

28. Moers, *Literary Women*, 107.

29. *OED*, 2nd ed. (1989): "1584 R. Scot *Discov. Witchcr. III xv. 65* 'A flie, otherwise called a divell or familiar'; 1830 Galt, *Lawrie T. I vii (1849) 22* 'The garret was alive with musquitoes, domestic familiars.'"

30. *Circa* 49 (1990): 37.

31. Margot Northey, *The Haunted Wilderness: The Gothic and Grotesque in Canadian Fiction* (Toronto: University of Toronto Press, 1976), 6.

32. Rose, *The Haunting of Sylvia Plath*, 148.

33. *Circa* 83:16–19. Morrison points out that the work is menacing as well as fascinating.

34. As Elisabeth Bronfen reminds us, "Freud has argued that the touch is both derived from and a natural extension of the gaze, so that the relation between hand and eyes is contiguous, not oppositional." *Over Her Dead Body: Death, Femininity and the Aesthetic* (Manchester: Manchester University Press, 1992), 10.

35. Helen Stoddart, *Rings of Desire: Circus History and Representation* (Manchester: Manchester University Press, 2000), 90.

36. Both women acknowledge images of death in nature such as the yew: Maher's *Limb* and Plath's image of the "black yew" in "Little Fugue" ("Gothic and barbarous"; "Death opened, like a black tree, blackly"). Speaking about her choice of materials, Maher has noted that objects such as the yew branches in *Limb* are "already dying," a reference to her avowed engagement with the process of metamorphosis, and, it might be argued, a process that concludes in the incorporeal.

37. "The Bee Meeting," lines 53, 52; "The Arrival of the Bee Box," line 28.

38. Paul de Man, *The Rhetoric of Romanticism* (New York: Columbia University Press, 1984), esp. "Autobiography as De-Facement," 75–76.

39. Morrison, "Fetched," 22.

40. Francis Barker, *The Tremulous Private Body: Essays on Subjection* (London: Methuen, 1984), 103.

41. Abigail Bray and Claire Colebrook summarize the work of Elizabeth Grosz, Moira Gatens, Judith Butler, and Rosi Braidotti and identify corporealist arguments and discursive perspectives among feminist theory's "attempts to overcome dualism." "The concepts of 'disembodiment' and 'embodiment' function dichotomously such that 'disembodiment' is frequently coded as phallocentric fantasy articulated through a dualist and specular representational economy that finds its most perfect expression in the Cartesian cogito." Bray and Colebrook, "The Haunted Flesh: Corporeal Feminism and the Politics of (Dis)Embodiment," *Signs: Journal of Women in Culture and Society* 24, no. 1 (1998): 36, 41, 47.

42. Kroll, *Chapters in a Mythology,* 136.

43. Lines 4, 18, 21, 15, 33, 53.

44. From "Wintering" (quoted in Bundtzen, *The Other Ariel,* 158).

45. Plath, *Johnny Panic and the Bible of Dreams* (New York: Harper and Row, 1979), 23.

46. These poems are not only biographical—about *her* body—but also a poet's expression of the inexpressible: what it is to be. There is an act of imagination, conceptualization, that is sidelined in readings that focus exclusively on the facts of Plath's life. Bundtzen feels that Plath's manuscripts, and the reverential treatment that they receive in the special collections room of the library at Smith College, easily invoke her physical presence; however, the hushed atmosphere and rules governing use of manuscripts apply to all special collections rooms and all archived manuscripts—Bundtzen's experience surely cannot underpin an understanding of Plath's "textual body" in particular. It is true that Plath's late poems are acutely embodied, in that they involve a great deal of bodily imagery, but relating all the images to the poet's body alone veers toward the reductive.

47. Bray and Colebrook, "The Haunted Flesh," 35. In feminist theory generally, they argue, "there is an insistence on the negating, repressive, and limiting character of representation set against a putatively more authentic corporeality" (54). Bray and Colebrook further underline the redemptive quality assigned to the body when they observe that "the representation/material dichotomy [or incorporeal/corporeal] . . . organizes many theories of sexual difference and leads to the uncritical celebration of the body as an inherently liberatory site" (56).

48. Ruane, "A Conversation with the Artist," in *Alice Maher,* 15.

49. Bernhard Baer, introduction to *Bees,* by Graham Sutherland (London: Marlborough Fine Art, June–July 1977), 3.

50. Grosz's *Volatile Bodies* (1994), cited in Bray and Colebrook, "The Haunted Flesh," 45.

51. Bray and Colebrook, "The Haunted Flesh," 45.

52. Moira Gatens, *Imaginary Bodies: Ethics, Power, and Corporeality* (New York: Routledge, 1996), 58.

53. Bray and Colebrook, "The Haunted Flesh," 64; Colebrook, "Incorporeality: The Ghostly Body of Metaphysics," *Body and Society* 6, no. 2 (2000): 27.

54. Colebrook, *Gilles Deleuze* (New York: Routledge, 2002), 24.

55. Deleuze, *The Logic of Sensation* (1981; New York: Continuum, 2002), 56.

56. I am indebted here to a Deleuzian reading of Brockden Brown's work by Marc Amfreville in a paper presented to the European Association of American Studies, Prague, April 2004. See Amfreville, "The Theater of Death in Charles Brockden Brown's *Arthur Mervyn*," *Litteraria Pragensia: Studies in Literature and Culture* 28, no. 14 (2004): 40–49.

57. Deleuze, *The Logic of Sensation*, 73.

58. Karsten Harries, "Metaphor and Transcendence," in *On Metaphor*, ed. Sheldon Sacks (Chicago: University of Chicago Press, 1978), 88.

59. As Rose has demonstrated, discussing "Poem for a Birthday," "the poem disperses the agency or source of negativity across the text; like the body of the speaker, it can appear almost anywhere" (*The Haunting of Sylvia Plath*, 56).

60. Paul Klee, quoted in Deleuze, *The Logic of Sensation*, 56.

61. Colebrook, *Deleuze*, 133–34.

62. Rose has certainly recognized this in Plath's poetry: "By representing this figure [of female transcendence], Plath pushes it to its own vanishing point." Rose continues: "She exposes the conditions of possibility of this figure *even* as she affirms it in her work. This problem seems to me to be far more important than any discussion of the positive or negative, creative or destructive attributes of this figure of female transcendence in Plath's poetry" (*The Haunting of Sylvia Plath*, 149).

8

Voices of the Least Loved

The Cockroach in the
Contemporary American Novel

MARION W. COPELAND

Besides Kafka's *The Metamorphosis,* with its satiric morph of a man to a giant insect (a cockroach in the popular imagination), finding literary cockroaches may seem a stretch for even the most avid readers—at least until they stop to consider how often they have encountered cockroaches on the printed page as details of realistic settings, particularly in urban settings but also in the semitropical and rain forest settings where wild cockroaches are most diverse and numerous.[1] And then there are the cockroaches encountered in horror novels (and, of course, films). And in science fiction. And in fantasy, that genre related to science fiction in that neither is usually set in what we often refer to as the "real world," and both support characters who are not found in, or behave differently from, the characters we encounter in "real life."

Actually, in generic animal fantasies, where setting or habitat—wild or domestic—is almost always naturalistic in detail, representing the actual environment in which the animal or insect protagonist exists, the characters themselves *are* nonhuman and tell their stories either in their own voices (as writers imagine them to be) or through the intervention of a human narrator who has insight into the animal's or insect's thoughts and feelings (and assumes that the protagonist has both).

Animal fantasy preexisted the publication of Anna Sewell's *Black Beauty* in 1877, but it was that autobiography of a horse that ensured the genre a place in literature as well as the hearts of the adult reading public. In the novel, Beauty, as an old horse fortuitously reunited with the humans he knew as a youngster, tells his own story, widening it with the experiences of the horses he has met along the way as fate moves him from the life of a stylish driving horse to increasingly less well-to-do situations. Inherent in Beauty's tale is a plea for a better life for the powerless, human and nonhuman, a theme common to novels in the animal fantasy genre. In later animal fantasy novels, the thematic emphasis often moves beyond the welfare of the individual or species (though neither becomes an unimportant concern) to a concern for the health of the environment essential to the survival of both.

The number of cockroach encounters to be found in contemporary and American literature in general is as startling as appearances of the real creature when the kitchen or bathroom light suddenly goes on at night. The subgenre of animal fantasy I have come to call the "cockroach novel" and those characters in it who are cockroaches are my sole object of study in this essay. I focus still more narrowly on four contemporary mainstream novels in which cockroaches appear as subjects: Donald Harington's *The Cockroaches of Stay More* (1989), Daniel Evan Weiss's *The Roaches Have No King* (1994), Penny Perkins's *Bob Bridges: An Apocalyptic Fable* (1999), and Marc Estrin's *Insect Dreams: The Half Life of Gregor Samsa* (2002).[2]

While animal fantasy protagonists, if they are accurately and authentically depicted, may convince the reader to respond to their dramas with empathy and compassion, in the case of cockroach novels, there's always

Catherine Chalmers, *Hanging* (2000), from "American Cockroach."

a little extra of what Rachel Carson called "a sense of wonder" required because so many humans are conditioned to react to the cockroach with revulsion.[3] Who, unaided, would acknowledge that cockroaches might think and feel and wonder and live through dramas not unlike our own night-mares and dreams as they go about their business of living and surviving as cockroaches? On the other hand, when successful in convincing readers to identify with their cockroach characters, cockroach novels succeed, as we shall see, in a more radical questioning of cultural assumptions and value systems than do other animal fantasy or fantasy novels.

Probably for that reason, cockroaches in literature are nothing new. All the novels discussed draw on an ancient and venerable tradition of cock-roach symbol and allusion found in the lore and traditions of cultures worldwide. Cockroaches have been part and parcel of human story since humans began telling stories. Certainly they have figured in the mainstream Western tradition at least since Aeschylus and Aesop and, if folklore is any indication, undoubtedly in the oral tradition that preceded them as well. Cockroaches are equally ubiquitous in the oral and written literatures of non-Western cultures past and present.

Right now cockroaches seem particularly at home in two American tra-ditions, the so-called mainstream (I suppose that means "white") tradition represented by the novels this essay focuses on and the Hispanic tradition. Oscar Zeta Acosta, for instance, names his exposé of the plight and retali-ation of the Chicano American *The Revolt of the Cockroach People* (1973). Cockroaches are at home in the Hispanic tradition because much of this tradition is either urban or emerges from tropical or semitropical climates, both favorite habitats of many of the extant species of cockroaches.

Cockroaches serve in both traditions, but particularly in the Latino, largely as symbol and metaphor rather than as character as they do in these mainstream cockroach novels. However, it is important to note that when cockroaches do appear as actual characters, and especially when cockroaches are the protagonists, the works in question have a thematic emphasis dis-tinct from that found in works in which the cockroach is only a symbol or background detail. The symbolic value of the cockroach to marginal liter-atures comes from the insect's reputation as both survivor and victim. No creature more elegantly illustrates the degree to which mainstream culture despises and fears marginal peoples or how determined those marginal peoples are to survive and prosper.

Something of that symbolic value functions as well in literature that evokes the cockroach not only as symbol but primarily as character, in other words, not as object but as subject. In *The Roaches Have No King*, Daniel Evan Weiss "tried to write . . . as a roach would write." Most of his roach characters take the same negative view of humans that most humans take of cockroaches. Persons "of every racial and ethnic stripe [are] skewered according to his or her group's worst stereotypes."[4] However, Weiss's novel is, as we shall see, also strongly rooted in world traditions that draw on the cockroach's tendency to prefer dark and hidden places, both linked in the modern mind to the chthonic, the earthly powers associated with the feminine as well as with eroticism and fertility.

The earliest extant example evoking this thematic emphasis comes in the opening scene of Aristophanes' *Peace,* an antiwar play first produced in 422 BC.[5] Until the modern period it was, as Davies and Kathirithamby note in *Greek Insects,* the only "scene composed in Greek (or indeed in any nation's drama)" that focused on a cockroach character (11). Although unnamed, Aristophanes' dung beetle or cockroach cooperates with the farmer Tygaeus to save the country from the ravages of the Peloponnesian War. The giant cockroach, collected from the environs of Mount Etna, serves as Tygaeus's mount as the two ascend Olympus to release the goddess Peace from the pit in which Zeus has buried her.[6] Together the farmer and his chthonic mount suggest, as is so often true with Aristophanes, a particularly modern thematic twist, as much environmental as social. Not only is war bad for humans; it is bad for the earth on which the well-being of both farmer and cockroach depends. That this thematic emphasis is intended seems certain when the connection to Aesop's cockroach fable is recollected: both Aristophanes' Zeus and Aesop's eagle are familiar symbols of war, while Aesop's victimized hare, fallen victim to the eagle, and vengeful cockroach are, like Aristophanes' farmer and his cockroach mount, reminders of the pre-Olympian world ruled by natural (here chthonic) forces instead of by anthropomorphic gods. Thus the ancient fable too acquires what might be called a biocentric or an ecocentric thematic force.[7]

The presence of what many probably assumed to be a late-twentieth- or twenty-first-century theme—bio- or ecocentricity—in the classical cockroach literature of the mainstream Western tradition suggests that another aspect of the cockroach's association with the chthonic has to be acknowledged. Such bio- and ecocentric themes are highlighted in the Chicano novelist Anna Castillo's short story "Christmas Story of the Golden Cock-roach."[8] Even though these are themes rarely evoked in the North Ameri-can Chicano tradition to which Castillo belongs, they exist in this story because it is narrated by a young mother, giving it what might be con-sidered if not an ecofeminist then a maternal (feminist) perspective. The narrator's concern for her child's nurture, in turn, heightens her concern for a healthy environment as well as for the cultural heritage she would like to remain meaningful to her child.

Rare golden cockroaches—perhaps genetic throwbacks to Mexico's rain forest roaches—mingle among the dark-hued "pest" species of roaches that infest the housing available to Mexican immigrant workers in Chicago, where the story is set. Although they have come to have only monetary worth to the rest of the story's humans, the narrator's first sight of a golden roach leads her to associate it with her gold wedding band.[9] Motherhood leads her to further connect that golden band (and, with it, the golden roach) with fertility—birth and nurture. Because she makes that connection, she values the golden roach more for its symbolic associations than because it can be traded for money from the pawnbroker. For her, the golden roach is a "mini-king in some ancient, sacred ritual."[10]

Most significant is that she understands the relationship of that ritual to her ancestors' association of golden roaches, inhabitants of the semitropi-cal rain forest, with the golden maize used in their ritual observance of the sun's power over the biotic community. They had revered the roaches as one of the chthonic powers, not unlike D. H. Lawrence's reverence for "The Snake," and equally associated it with darkness and light, death and life—the natural cycle. Joanne Luack comments that

> the pairing of gold, that enduring essence that symbolizes the soul, with the ancient insect that has both preceded and accompanied us in our evolution-ary journey signifies that some great work is underway—a deep recognition and healing called forth from the primordial wisdom that is held in the heart of creation.[11]

Despite the strength of the ecocentric theme in her story, Castillo does not seem tempted to develop the golden cockroach from symbol to char-acter.[12] That metamorphosis does take place, however, in the mainstream cockroach novels that share Castillo's thematic thrust. Donald Harington's novel *The Cockroaches of Stay More* (even though the roaches are one of the most ubiquitous of "pest" species, the American cockroach rather than rare golden rain forest roaches) is told by a female narrator, Tish Dingledoon, as is Castillo's short story. Tish, however, is also a cockroach, and the novel's central theme, like Castillo's and like that of so many late-twentieth-century animal fantasies, is clearly bio- and ecocentric.

Harington, in fact, suggests that empathy and compassion, attributes usually associated with the feminine and in the novel most strongly possessed by the narrator and at least peripherally by its human female, Sharon, are essential to the survival of any species, cockroach or human. Thus Harington's novel is at heart ecofeminist.[13] Appropriately, Tish's empathy is suited to her cockroach nature. Like Castillo's young human mother, Tish is most concerned for the welfare of her own family, mate, and offspring. What is noteworthy is that Tish easily extends her concern to the two humans who share the otherwise deserted (by humans, not roaches) Stay More. As we will see, it is questionable whether the human female, Sharon, can do the same.

Although few critics have commented on Tish as narrator, and the novel's narrator does not explicitly identify herself, Harington has Tish provide supportive evidence. Well into the tale, after her parents have disappeared, Tish is left to care for her forty-two siblings. After assessing their condition, "almost absently," by taking their "sniffwhips [antennae] into her mouth" (67),[14] Tish gathers her brothers and sisters around her for one of the story sessions she is known for. All her stories begin, as does *The Cockroaches of Stay More* itself, "One time . . ." because "such a beginning carried the suggestion not only that the story being told had occurred once upon a time long, long ago, but also that it had occurred only once, a one-time-only unique event" (69). That echo of the novel's opening words reinforces that Tish is, in fact, the narrator of both the story she tells her siblings in the novel and, like Black Beauty, of the novel itself, the story of the survival crisis faced by Tish herself as well as by her human and cockroach neighbors.

The novel itself opens with the words "One time [at] the beginning of night in the latter part of May . . ." (1). It is night because we think of roach activity as chthonic, restricted to the nocturnal hours, despite the fact that there now is evidence that many species are, in the wild, diurnal or can function either during the day or at night.[15] In urban areas where habitat is shared with humans, cockroaches have adapted by becoming largely if not exclusively nocturnal, as have Stay More's cockroach citizens. Being survival experts means that cockroaches must be adept at weighing the alternatives offered, a fact Tish builds into the interactive story she tells her siblings just as Harington builds choice into his novel.

Her siblings, being young and inexperienced, choose the forbidden and therefore tempting (and dangerous) alternative when, in the story, the Mockroach (a real insect, distinct from the cockroach, used both in the tale and at the end of the novel itself as a kind of demi-demon) offers the story's young roaches the choice of being one of the fable's two sun-dwelling insects, a herbaceous grasshopper or a predator praying mantis (both close enough relatives of the cockroach to make the metamorphosis almost possible). Offering her listeners the same choice, Tish is disappointed, though not surprised, when all but one yell, "The mantis! The mantis!" Following their direction, the Mockroach turns the young "roosterroach" in Tish's story into a mantis, tells him that now he must pray to him, "hop[s] on his back and [says], 'Giddyup! You've got to be my horsey!'" (71).[16]

The metamorphosis in the story may remind the reader of the novel's debt to Kafka's "Metamorphosis," but the form it takes in Tish's fable alludes specifically to the metamorphosis that takes place in African American "voodoo" ritual when the worshipper, believed to be literally possessed by the spirit rider, becomes the earthly manifestation of and speaks for the spirit invoked. While the former allusion serves to tie *The Cockroaches of Stay More* still further to the larger tradition of cockroach literature, the latter ties these Ozark *Periplaneta* (American cockroaches) to the African roots they share with those humans who accompanied the cockroaches from their native Africa to the shores of the Americas on slave ships. With them came ties to the earth and earth deities that, in turn, underlie whatever form those rituals took in this new habitat.

Spring is met with ritual and rites—ancient ceremonies—by all human cultures, not just those originating in Africa. In her *Village Voice* review, Pagan Kennedy pointed out that Harington's roaches are meant to "evoke backwoods culture," the mountain people who have, if not disappeared from their habitat in the Ozarks, become themselves an endangered species.[17] Tish tells us:

In certain isolated coves of the Ozark Mountains, up until the most recent times, the folk (both humanfolk and roosterroach folk) still celebrated,

particularly in May as the earth began to grow, what can only be called
Cerelia, rite in honor of Ceres, the godhead above the god of Roman Man, or
rather goddesshead: Mother Earth herself, protectress of all the fruits of earth
from whom the sacred word "cereal" comes. (30–31)

She goes on to describe the form in which the cockroaches of Stay More
continue to celebrate Ceres' reign.

That the novel begins in springtime becomes, in this light, significant. First, it is significant that the cockroach senses spring in ways it cannot be—or is not—perceived by humans. Both, of course, hear the usual
spring sounds: "Choral groups of katydids . . . serenading in four-part harmony; . . . and in the distance . . . a background of countless *Hylae* [peep-
ers] peeping and piping," as well as the more "ominous overtones and . . .
discordant noises" that are also part of the "Purple Symphony," Tish's name
for the harmony of nature. For the cockroach narrator, however, the Symphony consists of scent as much as of sound: the "flowering cacophony
of sounds"—"the strident bloom of seeking odors, . . . the purple smell of
boisterous desires, the lascivious essences of unfolding tones, . . . and per-
fumes of swollen lust" (6). This is music, much like pheromonal essences,
meant to stimulate the creation of new life among all of nature's creatures.

However, Stay More's humans—particularly its single human male,
Larry—are deaf to its call. Tish's intended, Squire Gregor Samsa Ingledew
(Sam), his ears (cockroach "ears" are located in their knee joints!) rendered
useless by the tolling of the human clock on the mantel of the Woman's
house where he resides, proves as deaf as Larry to the prelude Tish hears
and re-creates so effectively in her story. Hence the plot and challenge of
the novel become healing Sam's and man's separation from (deafness to)
the call of the natural world, a healing that, in turn, would return fecundity, sexual and creative (Larry used to be a writer), to Stay More's human
and cockroach citizens.

Since Harington's reader is more likely to be human than cockroach,
and since Harington obviously feels humans have more need of acquiring
an ecocentric perspective than cockroaches, who—except for Sam—have
never completely lost such a perspective, it is essential to extend the theme
to the human realm as well. For Sam, as for Weiss's cockroach protagonist Numbers, rising to the challenge means shedding human influence.
(Once Sam comes to that realization, the Mockroach restores his hearing.)

Harington's human Woman, Sharon, is shown to possess, albeit unconsciously, biocentric empathy. She is able to guess Tish's name once she has been led to see Tish not as a pest but as an individual in distress. Her naming of the cockroaches reinforces Harington's readers' growing empathy with his cockroach protagonists and is meant, I think, to lead readers to make a positive choice between the two scenarios that seem likely conclusions when, at the end of the novel, Tish and her cockroach lover Sam are left trapped in the Woman's toilet. Where the knee-jerk human response would be to flush, the reader, like the Woman, has been allowed to encounter and empathize with Tish and Sam as individuals with life stories, not just as—ugh!—cockroaches. And like the Woman, therefore, by the end of the novel, Harington's reader is meant to have developed the consciousness required to choose between murder and rescue, extermination and compassion.

Opting for the life force, symbolized in the novel by nature's Purple Symphony, carries with it a myriad of ramifications. One of them, clearly biocentric, leads to the reader's recognition of the cockroach as kin. On a deeper level, seeing that we are kin involves understanding that the roaches in the novel are more than allegorical figures, symbols standing for man, understanding that real roaches live lives essentially similar to the reader's human life. Most of all, readers are to understand that they are dependent on the same habitat that the cockroaches' lives depend on. In the "Song of the Mockroach," which serves as a kind of epilogue for Tish's narrative, readers are told:

If roach were man and man were roach,
   The subjects both would brood and broach
      Are love, dependency, survival.

By "re-ken[ning] . . . our [cockroach] kin," recognizing that each species needs the other, and even more by remembering our own role in the Purple Symphony, humans might at least "keep the world from getting worse" (336–37). Thus the lesson taught by *The Cockroaches of Stay More* embraces ecocentrism as well as biocentrism.

Unlike Harington's cockroach characters, Daniel Evan Weiss's cockroach protagonist "Numbers" in *The Roaches Have No King* needs to be considered allegorical, object, as well as protagonist, subject. Unlike the roaches

of Stay More, but like modern Western man, Numbers has become unnatural (more like man than cockroach), not by accident but by nurture.
Because he was born in the binding of a copy of the Old Testament and
consumed the whole of the book of Numbers while he was maturing,
Numbers has developed into a patriarchal thinker (when the novel was first
published in England, its title was *Unnatural Selection*): "Among his brethren
is Columbo, who came of age inside the Columbia Encyclopedia."[18] In light
of this aspect of Weiss's novel, "one of the first lessons" baby cockroaches
are taught in Harington's Stay More is "to leave alone the tempting glue
in the binding of [Man's] books" (93). Instead they are turned loose in the
natural world to consume its "glue." As a result, they grow up as cockroaches in a natural environment despite being American cockroaches, an
imported "pest" species, whereas Numbers, confined to the insides of an
apartment or the depths of New York City's sewers and bars, is denied this
nourishment as are so many human urbanites.

The reviewer Matthew Flamm notes that the importance of nurture is
only one of the details about cockroach natural history that Weiss absorbed
as he "devoured books on roach biology while writing the novel. His research came in handy for" the novel's realistic "roach sex scenes, which
involve a hefty supply of pheromones and foolproof, interlocking parts."[19]
Although Numbers's sex drive is at first totally in keeping with aeons of
roach experience, when his fellow German roaches (*Blattella germanica*)
begin to be exterminated by the humans with whom they have shared
an apartment in relative peace for generations, Numbers's nurture, rather
than his nature, responds. Like a human raised on Old Testament ethics
might, he retaliates and, when that fails, takes an awful revenge. Both are
uncockroach-like behaviors. Roaches faced with danger flee and, if fleeing
proves futile, trust to future generations adapting to new environments.

Long before the crisis that occasions Numbers's retaliation and revenge
on the Legal Aid lawyer Ira Fishblatt and his live-in partner Ruth Grubstein,
the reader sees other examples of equally unroachlike behavior. Before Ruth,
Ira had been intimate with "the Gypsy . . . every cockroaches' dream of a
slovenly housekeeper."[20] The Gypsy provided the cockroaches with an ample
supply of food, but with the advent of Ruth, that supply diminishes, and
"Numbers wonders if perhaps it wouldn't be wise for the roaches to start
storing food somewhere." Ruth intends to redo the kitchen, threatening to
"sheetrock [the roaches] in and starve [them] out." Sensible as Numbers's

plan seems to human readers, Bismarck, one of Numbers's fellow bookcase roaches, responds to it in horror: "Ants do that [store food]. They're so obsessed with protecting themselves against a bad day that they never have a good one." Even though cockroaches aren't quite as blasé as the grasshopper in Aesop's "The Grasshopper and the Ant," they know regimented behavior like the ant's would be, for cockroaches, "not living" (Weiss, 59). Numbers's unnatural behavior here (recommending hoarding) foreshadows his later, even more unroachlike action.

Once Numbers's revenge has been precipitated by the insecticide poisoning of his girlfriend Rosa, the only sex that Numbers experiences is with the water bug (American cockroach) queen four times his size (as well as another species) who reigns in a neighboring apartment. In Harington's novel, by contrast, sex and the survival of the species are natural and play major roles. Whatever Tish's and Sam's fate, they take comfort in the knowledge that their egg case (significantly called "easteregg" by the cockroaches looking to it for salvation) has been safely located outside Stay More and their offspring are therefore destined to live solely in the wild and to survive independent of man even if their parents cannot (or choose not to, having come to value the company of humans).

Numbers's unnatural revolution leads not to victory or marriage or fertility but to a lethal application of Raid, which creates a holocaust in which almost his entire tribe perishes. It does, however, shock Numbers out of his reliance on Old Testament wisdom. In despair, he falls back on the three and a half million years of cockroach wisdom (which advocates flight, not fight, and survival, not revenge) stored in his genes. Harington's and Weiss's novels, then, share the antiwar theme of Aristophanes' *Peace* and anticipate the ecocentric themes and emphasis of Perkins's *Bob Bridges* and Estrin's *Insect Dreams,* both of which take further the suggestion that man has become a creature as unnatural as either Weiss's Numbers or Harington's Sam.[21]

Indeed, like Numbers, Estrin's cockroach protagonist (who is quite literally, as the novel's title suggests, Kafka's Gregor Samsa saved, like Smiley's Gregor, from the dustbin) tells us that war stands as proof of man's "profound failure . . . to find a right way to live" (26). Gregor finds himself, cockroach though he remains, living almost exactly as men do. He has become, because of his close alliance with humans, a victim of unnatural selection very much as Weiss's Numbers had. This is emphasized throughout as he is drawn sexually not to other cockroaches—largely because there seem to be no female giant cockroaches around despite the legions developed by horror film special effects artists since the 1940s—but to human females.

It is because Kafka's own ecocentric message has either fallen on the deaf ears of our anthropocentric culture or been muted by its critics that writers who are quite literally his descendants (Harington, Weiss, Perkins, and Estrin, as well as other writers less literally so) feel compelled to reinforce the biocentric and ecocentric themes of Gregor's story, elaborating on precisely those themes that critics have overlooked or silenced in Kafka since the publication of "The Metamorphosis" (1917). Not all of Kafka's followers share either Kafka's or Estrin's or, with a decidedly ecofeminist twist, Perkins's sense that salvation requires Gregor to sacrifice himself.

Jane Smiley's 1992 short story "My Life as a Bug," for example, imagines Gregor surviving the dustheap not as a giant insect like Estrin's but as a regulation-size cockroach liberated from ties to human family, job, and apartment.[22] Here again is the suggestion that Kafka intended Gregor to be understood as an allegorical exposure of what was happening to humans as we became "company and corporate men and women"—but that he meant more, as well.[23] What is natural is swept out with the trash in the society that Kafka (and Smiley and Harington and Weiss and Perkins and Estrin) satirizes. As Margot Norris notes, all of Kafka's "putatively transcendent heroes," human and nonhuman, "end like dead animals thrown into ditches and garbage dumps (Gregor, the hunger artist, and Joseph K)."[24]

Perhaps even closer to the point, Smiley has a professor of creative writing, a main character in her 1995 novel *Moo,* provide a reassessment of Kafka's cockroach novella:

> When I was teaching Kafka in my class a week or two ago, I realized that the reason Gregor Samsa is redeemed by being turned into a bug is that he learns to live in the physical world, and take pleasure in simple actions like running over the walls of his room or hanging from the ceiling and rocking back and forth. Being turned into a bug is a step UP for him.[25]

In "My Life as a Bug," Smiley further identifies such simple pleasures (as well as the bug Gregor has become) with the natural world. When Smiley's Gregor realizes he is a real cockroach, not a monster bug-man, he grasps that his life is now full of possibility. This miracle occurs as "the silver light" of the moon transforms both Gregor and the landscape. In that light, the dustheap melts into the natural world (which it had always inhabited, of course), and the moon itself becomes "not flat [like a stage setting] but full of facets like a great diamond," a possible allusion to Sexton's "The Cockroach," and Gregor himself becomes the possessor of a virile "young body." In recognition of this metamorphosis, Smiley's Gregor "lifted his back legs and gave a triumphant buzz of joy. Sure the world held dangers, but hell so what? What was that compared to setting out? Compared to the actual, authentic, bona fide transformation that lay ahead of him now?"[26]

Smiley's cockroach has a more powerful voice, is more alive to his surroundings, more responsive to his own nature and to the natural world he now lives in than was Kafka's Gregor Samsa as man or insect. Similarly the cockroach voices in Harington's *The Cockroaches of Stay More*, Weiss's *The Roaches Have No King*, Estrin's *Insect Dreams*, and Perkins's *Bob Bridges* are more powerful than the human voices their novels articulate to emphasize that, like Smiley's Gregor, they—even Numbers and Estrin's Gregor— have not totally lost touch with the natural world as humans have. Those cockroach voices echo, as well as the spirit of Kafka's Gregor, the voice of another seminal cockroach character, Don Marquis's memorable cockroach poet "archy."[27] Most especially, archy's satiric vers libre resonates in the voice of Harington's Mockroach.

Harington alludes specifically to both Kafka and Marquis, the former in the name of Tish's cockroach swain, Gregor Samsa Ingledew (Sam), and the latter in the name and actions of another of his young male cockroaches, Archy, who, like Marquis's archy, figures out how to write messages to the world on a human typewriter. [28] The machine in *The Cockroaches of Stay More*, an IBM Selectric, is considerably more modern than the one on which archy wrote his lyrics in Marquis's office at the *New York Sun* in the 1920s and 1930s. Where archy's lyrics often appeared in place of Marquis's own column and were ultimately published in numerous volumes still in print, Harington's Archy types a brief but potentially lifesaving message to Sharon, the Woman, informing her that Larry, the Man, has shot himself in the foot while shooting at cockroaches, has contracted gangrene, and will die unless he gets help.

Unfortunately, unlike Marquis's archy's urban success story, Archy's attempt proves a failure in interspecies communication, although it did inspire the sociologist Jay Mechling to title his essay on the prevalence of

cockroaches in American folklore and personal narrative (what I've come
to call cockroach encounter tales) "From archy to Archy: Why Cockroaches
Are Good to Think" (1992). Mechling argues that "Marquis' archy and
Harington's Archy . . . represent the same tradition in 'serious' American
literature, and they share with African American folklore an attraction to
the cockroach as a character who can speak truly from the margins."[29] The
difference is that the margin from which Harington's Archy—or, to be
accurate, his narrator Tish—speaks is the margin between what is usually
(if inaccurately) referred to as civilization and the wild.

In his *New York Times* review of Harington's novel, Harry Middleton
concludes that the novel "probes the transitory and fragile worlds of man
and cockroach alike," essentially by viewing each species through the eyes
of the other: "As Sam Ingledew says, 'You have to see everything in a different language to understand it.'"[30] But it is the cockroach view that Middleton finds most valuable, largely because, as he writes, "There hasn't been
much useful news from the natural world since E. B. White gave us Charlotte, the spider who spun messages in her web."[31] Middleton's point is not
that *The Cockroaches of Stay More* is a delightful tale for children, which it
is not, but that Harington's country roaches are nurtured more by nature
than by human culture. However charming the tale of Wilbur the Pig's
escape from the culinary fate of pigs in the modern world, White's message
in *Charlotte's Web* is about something his child readers may have to grow
up to understand. Charlotte entreats Wilbur to understand that although
she must die, what is important is the survival of "the egg sac and the five
hundred and fourteen little spiders that would hatch in the spring."[32] What
is important is not mourning for what must die but protecting what must
be born.

Wilbur returns Charlotte's friendship by protecting her egg sac during
the cold winter (much as does the Great White Mouse in *The Cockroaches
of Stay More*), waiting for the spring when she has told him the eggs would
hatch. Although Wilbur loses Charlotte, "Charlotte's children and grandchildren and great grandchildren, year after year, lived in the doorway. Each
spring there were new little spiders hatching out to take the place of the
old" (White, 183). White's ecocentric message here is as clear as Harington's
and is very similar: Wilbur's barn, like the wild surrounds of Stay More in
the Ozarks, have much in common, namely, that each is the ideal habitat for
the species in question, spider and cockroach: "this warm delicious cellar,

with the garrulous geese, the changing seasons, the heat of the sun, the passage of the swallows, the nearness of rats, the sameness of sheep, the love of spiders, the smell of manure, and the glory of everything" (White, 183).

Harington's roaches have, toward man's extinction, an attitude not dissimilar to Charlotte's attitude toward her own death. It will sadden them because they like man's company, but they also know that life will survive when humans, as they are sure they will, cause a nuclear holocaust and exterminate themselves as well as many others. Like Perkins, Harington suggests that cockroaches "would lead Stay More through the post-Bomb period and pave the way for a new Golden Age" (198). However, as hard as the cockroaches try, Stay More's humans are unwilling to listen as White's Wilbur did to news from the natural world brought to them by other-than-human voices, and consequently the era to emerge from nuclear disaster will deprive cockroaches of a valued neighbor, man, not of life itself.

Weiss's Numbers is by nurture a totally urban cockroach, as is Estrin's Gregor; Perkins's Cock, however, inhabits a world vastly altered by a cosmic catastrophe more devastating than the ones that finished off the dinosaurs and many of the planet's other life-forms at stages along Earth's evolutionary journey. In part the escalation is caused when cosmic shock sets off humankind's nuclear arsenal, escalating already lethal radiation fallout and global warming. The only life-forms to survive are cockroaches and bacteria, both of which evolve to become radiation synthesizers after the catastrophe. In the fullness of geologic time, these seemingly trivial—compared to man, of course—life-forms will restore to the planet an oxygen-based atmosphere capable once again of supporting diverse life-forms.

Perkins's human hero, Bob Bridges, has, as the novel opens, failed to warn his fellow humans even of the danger of the Y2K crisis predicted to end the world as the twentieth century bowed to the twenty-first. Like the nuclear holocaust Harington's and Estrin's cockroaches fear, Y2K has not occurred. (Both apocalyptic prophecies seem all but faded from human consciousness now that the twenty-first century is under way.) But it is Bob's bio- and ecocentric concern that leads Cock to choose and transport him to a future that has rendered Earth incapable of supporting mammalian life just as he predicted might happen as a result of Y2K. Ironically, Cock comes to him first just as Bob wakes from a nightmare that pits him against giant cockroaches very like those spawned by nuclear fallout in the 1940s horror films he saw as a child.

Of course, irony is the dominant mode in most of these novels, so the world Bob wakes up in is exactly his nightmare world except that no humans, in fact no warm-blooded creatures, exist in it, and the cockroaches are saviors rather than the dangerous monsters of his nightmares. Although the plot is far more complicated than this, what is of major importance here is, first, that Bob rethinks his assumptions about roaches and, second, that the evolution experienced by the cockroaches since the cataclysm "will, in the fullness of geologic time—something cockroaches have more reason to understand than humans do—return to Earth an atmosphere in which diverse [though not necessarily human] life forms may [again] evolve."[33] However, the full ecocentric message of the novel lies not as much in the cockroaches' replenishing oxygen to Earth's atmosphere as in their knowledge that, once they have succeeded, they themselves will be unable to survive. Thus they seal their own extinction, a sacrifice they willingly make because they feel they owe their lives to the planet that has supported them for such an unprecedented span.

Marc Estrin is the most recent of those writers who have found Kafka's giant insect an apt metaphor for what modern man has become as well as for what he must be if the human species itself is to survive. In his final metamorphosis, as an adviser to the researchers at Los Alamos (the half-life of the title refers, of course, to the life of atomic matter), Estrin's Gregor finds himself drawn to the animal gods of the Taos peoples. They seem to waken in him something far older than any of his previous experiences, something primordial out of the earliest eras of the cockroach's long evolutionary journey. It is an appropriate setting for the ending of a novel with such an important message for modern man because, as Estrin has written, "The story of the Manhattan Project, the final setting of *Insect Dreams* is, in my opinion, the culmination and apotheosis of the last five hundred years of human history."[34]

It comes to Gregor that by "suspending human thought"—perhaps all the years since the agricultural revolution—"a surge of divinity might come streaming through him," and his first impulse is to express it as the Taos themselves might through a Roach Dance.[35] Caught by this impulse, he is ripe for the experience when an Indian friend takes him to see the petroglyphs his ancestors had created. What Gregor sees determines the novel's dramatic ending:

At about five-thirty, the figure on the stone began . . . to grow . . . antennae! Gregor was doubtful at first, but as the sun sank lower, there could be no doubt: two lightly feathered antennae slowly appeared from the previously unadorned head. Next—*guck mal!*—a third pair of limbs, growing high out of the thorax, reaching in praise to the sky! The final touch—at six-thirty— little hooks appeared at the ends of all the limbs, and a set of cercae emerged at the bottom of the abdomen. Six forty-five—the metamorphosis was complete: a man had turned into an insect! (340)

To be specific, into a roach, and not perceived as a nightmare because it is a roach. Rather, the figure is perceived as the sacred image the roach has come to symbolize in eco- and biocentric works like those that emerge as well in the cockroach novels of Perkins, Weiss, and Harington.

When Estrin's Gregor subsequently immolates himself at ground zero of a volcanic, indeed chthonic, pre-Hiroshima bomb test at Los Alamos, he does so to acknowledge his willingness to give up his life: "I AM THE ROACH OF THE GOD CARBONIFEROUS, A LIVING RUMOR OF ETERNITY" (Estrin, *Insect Dreams*, 426). He intends his sacrifice to teach man to seek redemption by the path he has shown them. In other words, he directs us to rediscover our own animal evolutionary roots and with them our place in the natural world. After Gregor's death, the hospital director at the Manhattan Project summarizes the theme of *Insect Dreams* as well as of *The Cockroaches of Stay More, The Roaches Have No King,* and *Bob Bridges:* "The really 'new frontier' of our age will not be defined politically. It will be delineated only by a revolution in our instinctual lives comparable to the Industrial Revolution. This is why Gregor's life, his example, held such great promise. . . . We may still be saved by obscure efforts of heroic individuals whose passion it is to redeem the world" (Estrin, *Insect Dreams,* 461).

The ultimate irony, Estrin suggests, goes beyond our deafness to the voices of the least loved. Like Perkins, he questions whether the heroic individual destined to be our savior is, in fact, not, as modern human religions assume "*he*" will be, human, but nonhuman, a voice from the natural world—and, of all the unlikely beings, the voice of a cockroach, that most hated, most reviled, least loved, most instinctively stomped-on by humans of all living beings. How many chances at redemption, Estrin's narrator seems to taunt, have you slaughtered in a lifetime? As each of the cockroach

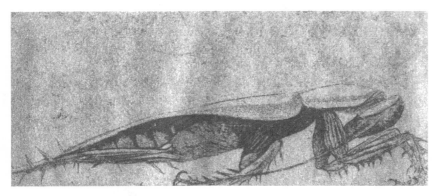

Drawing by Leonard Baskin taken from *Diptera: A Book of Flies and Other Insects,* published by Baskin's Gehenna Press in 1983. Reproduced by permission of the Estate of Leonard Baskin. Copyright the Estate of Leonard Baskin.

novels and the associated works explored have asserted, the necessity of humans drastically altering our current cultural and personal assumptions about ourselves and the rest of the living world (and, of course, of altering the behavior such assumptions foster) is critical if we hope *Homo sapiens sapiens* is to enjoy anything approaching the long, successful life story of the cockroach.

NOTES

1. Franz Kafka, *The Metamorphosis and Other Stories,* trans. Joachim Neugroschel (New York: Scribners, 1993). My own interest in cockroaches as cultural symbol as well as fascinating creature has spawned, among other works, an extensive annotated bibliography, *appROACHES to literature* (www.hnet.org/~nilas/bibs/appROACHES.html#index), and the book *Cockroach* (London: Reaktion Books, 2003). Both attest to how prevalent human-cockroach encounters actually are in the "real" world as well as in both the art and literature of cultures worldwide. See also David George Gordon, *The Complete Cockroach: A Comprehensive Guide to the Most Despised (and Least Understood) Creature on Earth* (New York: Ten Speed Press, 1996); and Richard Schweid, *The Cockroach Papers: A Compendium of History and Lore* (New York: Four Walls Two Windows, 1999).

2. Harington, *The Cockroaches of Stay More* (New York: Vintage, 1990); Weiss, *The Roaches Have No King* (New York: High Risk, 1994); Perkins, *Bob Bridges: An Apocalyptic Fable* (Albany, N.Y.: Chrome Deco, 1998); Estrin, *Insect Dreams: The Half Life of Gregor Samsa* (New York: Penguin Putnam–Blue Hen Books, 2002). These works are cited hereafter in the text.

3. Stephen Kellert of the Yale School of Forestry and Environmental Studies published reports on American attitudes to wild and domestic animals in the twentieth century between 1979 and 1988. He found that "the least-favored animals were the bat, rattlesnake, wasp, rat, and mosquito, with the cockroach finishing last [or first, depending on your point of view]." Kellert, "Human-Animal Interactions: A Review of American Attitudes to Wild and Domestic Animals in the Twentieth Century," in *Animals and People Sharing the World*, ed. Andrew R. Rowan (Hanover, N.H.: University Press of New England, 1988), 137–75. The entomologist Howard E. Evans subtitled his well-known essay on the cockroach "Why Man Has Much to Learn from the Most Adaptable if Least-Loved Species on Earth." See "The Intellectual and Emotional World of the Cockroach," *Harper's*, December 1966, 50–55, reprinted in Evans, *Life on a Little-Known Planet: A Biologist's View of Insects and the World* (New York: Nick Lyons, 1993), 48–61.

4. Matthew Flamm, "A Bug's-Eye View of the World," *Entertainment Weekly* 22 (July 1994): 47.

5. The earliest use of the cockroach in the written tradition of the West was in fifth-century BC Attic comedy. Satyr plays like Aristophanes' *Sisyphus* and Sophocles' *Trackers* and *Daedalus* count on the insect's appetite for dung occasioning laughter; see Malcolm Davies and Jeyaraney Kathirithamby, *Greek Insects* (New York: Oxford University Press, 1986), 12. "Aristophanes' comedies include animal choruses," and animals and insects figure in Greek Old Comedy, generally as chorus (Davies and Kathirithamby, 11). The first appearance of the cockroach in Greek tragedy was in Aristophanes' *Peace* (422 BC). His cockroach character, central to the plot and theme of the play, gains resonance from the one extant Aesopian fable that includes a cockroach character. Aesop's cockroach takes revenge on an eagle for killing his friend the hare first by soiling the eagle's nest and then, after the eagle has secured his eggs in the lap of Zeus, by flying "up to Olympus [exactly like Aristophanes' roach] and deposit[ing] dung on the god's lap." In a predictably human reaction, Zeus leaps up to brush away the dung, also dumping the eagle's eggs on the ground and breaking them (Davies and Kathirithamby, 3).

6. Mount Etna was so famed "from the first third of the 5th century onwards" for its enormous cockroaches that the insect became a symbol of that volcano in particular and the powers of volcanoes in general (Davies and Kathirithamby, 86–87). The association is of relevance in several contemporary mainstream American novels including Thomas Page's *The Hephaestus Plague* (New York: Putnam's, 1973) and the by now classic horror film based on it, *Bug* (dir. Jeannot Szwarc, 1975), as well as Marc Estrin's *Insect Dreams*, an association to which I will return later. In *Feasts* Plato wrote: "How big Mt. Etna is said to be can by judged from the fact that there are beetles there no smaller than a man" (quoted in Davies and Kathirithamby, 860). Davies and Kathirithamby translate Aristophanes' insect, instead of as a dung beetle as it is in the translation they refer to, as a cockroach. The translator's reluctance to admit that a cockroach could be the hero of a classical Greek drama speaks to current rather than to Greek attitudes toward the creature. For the Greeks,

the cockroach was not a pest species but a powerful symbol of the chthonic or natural earthly powers, an association, as Camille Paglia points out in *Sexual Personae:
Art and Decadence from Nefertiti to Emily Dickinson* (New York: Vintage, 1991),
often overlooked after the "imaginative realignment of western male will toward
female [chthonic] powers" that led to "Kafka's crippled cockroach, Gregor Samsa"
(301).

7. "Ecocentric" and "biocentric" have become literary jargon in recent years.
They are applied to works that show concern for the health of the biotic community (of the environmental, of wildlife, and of the planet) and for championing
humans' acceptance of their own membership in, and therefore their responsibility
to, that community. See Lawrence Buell, *The Environmental Imagination: Thoreau,
Nature Writing, and the Formation of American Culture* (Cambridge: Harvard University Press, 1995); Max Oelschlaeger, *The Idea of Wilderness: From Prehistory to
the Age of Ecology* (New Haven: Yale University Press, 1991); Marian Scholtmeijer,
Animal Victims in Modern Fiction: From Sanctity to Sacrifice (Toronto: University
of Toronto Press, 1993); Patrick D. Murphy, *Literature, Nature, and Other: Ecofeminist Critiques* (Albany: State University of New York, 1995); Randy Malamud, *Poetic
Animals and Animal Souls* (New York: Macmillan Palgrave, 2003).

8. Castillo, "Christmas Story of the Golden Cockroach," in *A Gathering of
Flowers: Stories about Being Young in America,* ed. Joyce Carol Thomas (New York:
Harper Keypoint, 1990), 65–78.

9. There is in this an implicit reference to Anne Sexton's poem "Cockroach" in
which a young woman protects a cockroach in her hand "like a diamond ring," her
age and status limiting her association to engagement and the promise of fertility
rather than marriage and its fulfillment as in the Castillo story. See Sexton, "Cockroach," in *45 Mercy Street* (Boston: Houghton Mifflin, 1976).

10. Castillo, "Christmas Story," 71.

11. Joanne Luack, *The Voice of the Infinite in the Small: Revisioning the Insect
Human Connection* (1998; Boston: Shambhala Publications, 2002), 309. Luack's
thesis has been a major influence on my reading of these cockroach novels and is
essential reading for anyone who admires insects and is interested in cultural entomology and the human-insect bond.

12. Janelle Cannon's *Crickwing* (San Diego: Harcourt, 2000), a picture book
for children, has, as far as I know, the one tropical cockroach protagonist extant.
Others may flourish in oral traditions I have no access to. Not golden but pale
green, Crickwing begins as a cripple, but when he proves a good neighbor to the
leaf-cutter ants who share his environment, he is, like Harington's Sam, healed.
Cannon's pictures and story include well-researched cockroach natural history as
well as environmental themes, qualifying the book as a cockroach novel.

13. Ecofeminism, which was experiencing its birth pangs when Harington was
writing *The Cockroaches of Stay More,* can in part be defined by its concern for the
welfare of animals and the environment as well as for the welfare of humans. In
fact, it sees, as it rightly should, that the health of each depends on the health and

balance of the other two. Its usefulness as literary criticism is explored in some detail in Murphy, *Literature, Nature, and Other*.

14. By "'counting the beads' on it," Tish is able to assess "her environment: the temperature (73 degrees and falling), tomorrow's forecast (partly cloudy, scattered thunderstorms), the present location of each of her brothers and sisters, what they were eating, which ones had intestinal . . . or mental problems, which ones had constipation or diarrhea, and how many worms, crickets, and katydids were in the vicinity" (67–68). Such accurate knowledge of cockroach natural history, anatomy, and behavior informs each of the cockroach novels discussed and is an essential part of the best cockroach art.

15. See John Kricher, *A Neotropical Companion: An Introduction to the Animals, Plants and Ecology of the New World Tropics*, 2nd ed. (Princeton, N.J.: Princeton University Press, 1997).

16. They prefer to be called "roosterroach" not because they realize humans have an immediate and adverse reaction to the mention of cockroaches but because their "religion," a peculiar blend of Ceres worship and Christianity called, not without humor, Crustian—I have underplayed the rich humor in the novel in order to emphasize theme—is as prudish as a Victorian parlor and hides an equally Victorian love of the bawdy and downright pornographic. Sam notes that for them "'cock' is one of the unmentionable words," although he is aware the Spanish root for cockroach, *cucaracha* "has nothing to do with the male member or even male chickens" (22).

17. Kennedy, "Roach Clip," *Village Voice*, May 23, 1989, 57.

18. Flamm, "A Bug's-Eye View," 47.

19. Ibid.

20. Marion Copeland, review of *The Roaches Have No King*, by Daniel Evan Weiss, *Interactions Bibliography* 6, no. 1 (March 1995): 25–26.

21. An earlier and not unrelated reference to this development is found in *The Fate of a Cockroach*, a play by the Egyptian Tewfig Al Hakim (in *The Fate of a Cockroach: Four Plays of Freedom*, trans. Denys Johnson-Davies [London: Heinemann, 1973], 2–76). Here too the cockroach inhabitants of an apartment in urban Cairo have taken on a social structure decidedly human with a king and queen advised by a minister, learned savant, and priest. As a result, when the cockroach king slips into the tub, neither he nor his court have any idea how he is to survive. In point of fact, he cannot, for he, like Harington's Tish and Sam stranded in the Woman's toilet, has become dependent on "someone up there who hears our voices, understands our language, and pays attention to our entreaties." Even the cockroach queen, although she insists that "only he can save himself," adds, "or a miracle from the skies" (25). But Samia, the woman in the play, although she seems at first quite unlike Harington's Woman, has the same basic gift for empathy and compassion. When directed by the doctor to "show affection to the roach" because her husband so clearly identifies with it, her at first "feigned interest" grows, the struggle the men are watching without intervening comes to seem heartless, and she urges them to

rescue "the poor thing!" so that it can "get out alive" (63), at which point the doctor explains that because men are incapable of such compassion, the cockroach's
"whole hope now lies in your compassion" (70). Unfortunately, in the play, it is a
force not up to the challenge. Also unfortunately, Al Hakim's men are far too much
like Harington's Man. Although Adil hasn't, like Harington's human male, literally
shot himself in the foot, Adil has himself become very like the cockroach king, "like
someone following a game of chess" rather than someone involved in a struggle for
life (55). All these humans seem the result of an unnatural selection, and once that
becomes clear, so is the rest of the thematic message: rediscovering, reclaiming our
animal nature, its "very core and essence," is "the heart of the matter" (47).

22. Smiley, "Gregor: My Life as a Bug," *Harper's Magazine,* August 1992; reprinted
in *The Story and Its Writer,* ed. Ann Chartres (Boston: St. Martin's Press–Bedford
Books, 1995), 1495–97.

23. It is instructive here to note a parallel between Kafka's *Metamorphosis,*
Weiss's *Roaches,* and the 1991 Japanese animation-plus-live-action film *Twilight of
the Cockroaches* (*Gokiburi-tachni no Tasogare*), written and directed by Hiroaki
Yoshida. The movie is set in an apartment in Tokyo, occupied by a bachelor "salary-
man" and a host of contented cockroaches. Disaster strikes when the man introduces
a determined "office lady" (parallel to Weiss's Ruth) to the mix. She immediately
begins to clean, employing "increasingly deadly . . . poisons and bug bombs in a full
scale war to wipe out the roaches." After a brief (and unnatural) attempt to retali-
ate, the roaches fall back on their fail-safe survival skills: the cockroach general
yells, "For every one they kill, we'll breed a hundred more!" Japanese movie audiences, unlike American ones, cheered him wildly. The *Washington Post* Asia Bureau
head T. R. Reid explains the difference in terms of Japanese respect for the cockroach "as a survivor . . . a creature that can take everything the world throws at
it and keep on keeping on" (42–43). "Earth Spiders and Caretigers," *International
Wildlife* (March/April 1992): 40–47.

24. Norris, *Beasts of the Modern Imagination: Darwin, Nietzsche, Kafka, Ernst,
and Lawrence* (Baltimore: Johns Hopkins University Press, 1985), 1.

25. Smiley, *Moo* (New York: Ivy Books, 1998), 237.

26. Smiley, "My Life as a Bug," 1497.

27. Marquis, *archy and mehitable,* illustrated by George Harriman (1927; New
York: Doubleday Anchor, 1990).

28. Archy types on the journalist Marquis's typewriter in his office in New York at
night when there are no humans there by jumping from key to key. Since he cannot
work the shift, his vers libre poems lack capital letters. They are, nonetheless, powerfully satiric, establishing even more clearly than does Kafka's "Metamorphosis" the
themes of alienation, victimization, survival, and speciesism on the human and nonhuman levels he observes. His mode, as is the case in so much cockroach literature,
is irony; his humor, though ample, dark; his themes, deeply bio- and ecocentric.

29. Mechling, "From archy to Archy: Why Cockroaches Are Good to Think,"
Southern Folklore 48 (1992): 136.

30. Middleton, "Bugging Out," *New York Times Book Review,* April 23, 1989, 17.

31. Ibid.

32. White, *Charlotte's Web* (1952; New York: Harper and Row, 1980), 166.

33. Marion Copeland, "Fables, Imposters, and Dreams: A Cockroach Totem Update," *NILAS [Nature in Legend and Story] Newsletter* 1, nos. 3–4 (Fall 2002–Winter 2003): 21. NILAS Cockroach Totem, a group established in 1995, appears both on the organization's Web site (www2.h-net.msu.edu/~nilas) and in most issues of its newsletter. The NILAS Web site also includes a section on bibliographies on individual animals in story, legend, folklore, myth, art, and media that includes my extensive *appROACHES to literature.*

34. Estrin, "An Essay," January 12, 2005, http://www.bookbrowse.com/index.cfm?page=author&authorID=727&view=Interview.

35. Estrin, *Insect Dreams,* 335.

PART II

Rhetorics and Aesthetics

9

Reading as a Close Encounter of the Third Kind

An Experiment with Gass's "Order of Insects"

BERTRAND GERVAIS

The monstrous is unsettling because it appears to belong nowhere but its own boundless category.

—RIKKI DUCORNET, *The Monstrous and the Marvelous*

How can we describe the relationship between the reader and the text? Is it a form of work, of communication, of play? And what can be said about the object we are trying to read and, ultimately, understand? With what kind of being or form can we identify it? Is it the expression of a consciousness that can be grasped despite its distance, as hermeneutics tells us? What if it was something fundamentally different? What if the text was an entity of a completely different nature, needing to be tamed before being understood?[1]

In the following pages, I will explore the idea that reading is an encounter between a reader and a fundamental otherness, that it is an encounter with an insect, an arthropod, a being with which we share neither the same body structure nor the same subjectivity. To play with this idea of the encounter with an insect as a metaphor to describe how texts are read,[2] I will offer a close reading of a short story by William H. Gass, "Order of Insects," taken from the collection *In the Heart of the Heart of the Country* (1981).[3] I will examine the fascination generated by the dead cockroaches in this text as they hypnotize and manipulate the narrator, a woman who dares to look at them and experiences a complex epiphany.[4] This analysis will lead me to reflect on the cognitive and affective processes in reading, on our general relation to fictions and characters, as well as on our usual definitions of texts and their nature.

A CLOSE ENCOUNTER

In *Thomas the Obscure* (1973), Maurice Blanchot provides a fascinating representation of reading. In the fourth chapter of the novella, Thomas is sitting in his room, his hands joined over his brow with his thumbs pressed against his hairline, totally absorbed in and captivated by the words on the page:

> He was reading with unsurpassable meticulousness and attention. In relation to every symbol, he was in the position of the male praying mantis about to be devoured by the female. They looked at each other. The words, coming forth from the book which was taking on the power of life and death, exercised a gentle and peaceful attraction over the glance which played over them. Each of them, like a half-closed eye, admitted the excessively keen glance which in other circumstances it would not have tolerated.[5]

The metaphor of the mantis becomes literal: the text for Thomas starts to behave as a female praying mantis about to consume its mate, which it can do after or even during copulation. Thomas is therefore in a position of both strength and vulnerability. As with the male mantis, his strength comes from his role in the reading process, from the fact that he is the one who awakens a spark of life in the text; and his vulnerability comes from the fact that the embrace that brings him closer to it leaves him defenseless. For this spark of life that he incites, he must pay. Thomas does not die literally as a result of his encounter with the text, but he nevertheless allows it to take him and ultimately to transform him (26). Reading is described as bringing about a double metamorphosis: that of the text, which the reader constructs with his own eyes, and that of the reader himself, whom the text, now awakened by his glance, alters. Their union forces them to converge, to acquire otherwise alien qualities, which ultimately make them "similar."

Reading, Blanchot proposes in *Thomas the Obscure,* is a complex experience, defined less as the reunion of two consciousnesses, or of similar entities, than as an experience of a complete otherness. It is a migration, a kind of metempsychosis.[6] This extreme relationship with the text, inscribed here by the figure of the praying mantis, appears elsewhere in Blanchot's work, above all in the form of a "relation of the third kind." Far from the various stages in the process of encounters with extraterrestrial life-forms, which have made this particular typology so popular, the third relationship designates the fundamental otherness (or *altérité*) that can exist between human beings. As Blanchot writes in *The Infinite Conversation*:

> What is now in play, and demands relation, is everything that separates me from the other, that is to say the other insofar as I am infinitely separated from him—a separation, fissure, or interval that leaves him infinitely outside me, but also requires that I found my relation with him upon this very interruption that is an *interruption of being*. This otherness, it must be repeated, makes him neither another self for me, nor another existence, neither a modality or a moment of universal existence, nor a superexistence, a god or a non-god, but rather the unknown in its infinite distance.[7]

William Gass also believes that the encounter with the text is an experience of fundamental strangeness, a relation of the third kind that substantially changes whoever engages in it. A text is not simply something that we read but, in a Blanchotian way, something that reads us, a monad that is interpreting us, altering us in an essential way. Gass, who has written extensively on literature and language, on aesthetic experience, and on fiction and the reading process, offers a similar view when he explains: "I cannot have in my consciousness the actual consciousness of another, so there is no direct way for me to know if we are seeing or feeling the same things—you causing the doorslam, I hearing it, both inferring and fearing divorce, both lost and out of love in that instant, cutting an aquatint in two with a lawyer's shears—because we are wholly windowless with regard to one another, to use Leibniz's wonderful word."[8] That we are windowless is to say that there can be no simple relation, no comprehension that is not an attempt to bridge a gap, no communion that is not also interpretation. Language is not transparent but essentially opaque. It is a frontier we must learn to inhabit, where identities coalesce, constituting a new entity, hybrid, transitional, but all the more necessary.

A fiction is, for Gass, a "mind like a monad aware of the world."[9] His short story "Order of Insects" tells us this mind is not sound or stable, and the world it is aware of is made not of facts and data but of desires and disorder, of chaos and metamorphoses. Like the text that Blanchot's Thomas is reading, "Order of Insects" moves "through the mind like a procession of speech; and as it does so it largely replaces, like music, our own interior life."[10] And it opens up a world within its words that forces us to explore the limits of our imagination.[11] The limits of our act of reading.

A Fundamental Otherness

"Order of Insects" deals with cockroaches or, to be precise, with the fear caused by their discovery. To briefly describe what is at stake in the story, we could say that this narrative, of some ten pages or so in length, finishes off where Franz Kafka's "The Metamorphosis" begins. When Gregor Samsa wakes up that first morning, he has already been transformed into an enormous insect. It is a fait accompli, a fact with which he must live or die.[12] In "Order of Insects," on the other hand, the metamorphosis has hardly begun: indeed, it is difficult to know whether or not it has actually taken place. Is it a case of a physiological process or a simple hallucination, the ravings of a distressed housewife or an actual modification of her metabolism, the arthropodization of her body? The signs and symptoms of her metamorphosis are scattered throughout the text; the traces point toward it but do not really conclusively identify it as such. Of course, the narrator provides certain clues indicating the appearance of an exoskeleton, of a new body shape. For example, she mentions her growing nails, a supposedly radical change in her existence that leaves her with frightening eyes that seem to pop out of her head. And at night, when she lies, like a rod, stiffly sleeping next to her husband, strange ideas shake her up from within, leaving her the impression that she possesses a heavy, constricting carapace, mummifying her. She even imagines that her husband compares her to a small snail, as though her children's building blocks have finally surrounded her, thus caging her.

The clues, then, are there, increasingly obvious as the text progresses, but present as nymphs or larvae: intermediate, inchoate shapes, never definite. They are there, tenacious, glued to the text, but they do not draw a clearly defined shell. Each time the ambiguity persists. Her eyes are not literally popping out of her head; her imagination leads her to believe this, just as her carapace would seem to be an extreme expression of dorsal stiffening, of a tension that is as much psychological as it is physiological. But at the same time, her children have become afraid of her, and the thoughts that inhabit her have nothing to do with being a housewife. The ambiguity is repeated throughout the story, as in a tale of fantasy: these bodily changes swing constantly between metaphor and metamorphosis, between the displacement of meaning and corporeal transformations. To read this story, in fact, is to live this ambiguity, to make it our own. And the text provides a locus for our most gnawing fears: cockroaches, madness, and death.

So the story follows a woman as she attempts to tame the disorder that insects have brought in her life and her mind. And it all begins with the discovery of dead insect shells on her carpet. Her initial reaction is one of disgust, to reject these lifeless creatures scattered over the rug. Where do they come from, why are they dead? Did the house cat kill them? After having leaned over, horrified, to look at them, the narrator hurries to vacuum them up. From this moment on, she will incessantly remember this initial encounter, reliving it in her mind, seeing once again those dead cockroaches, the fine dust surrounding them, the disorder they introduced into the household world of this woman who describes herself as being "terribly meticulous" (164). Then her attitude toward the Dictyoptera slowly begins to change, going from disgust and repugnance to curiosity, to sympathy, and finally to obsession. She starts to look at them more attentively, distinguishing the nymphs from the adults, using a magnifying glass to better appreciate the shape of their shells, the lines, the veins, the spurs. She even goes so far as to touch them, sliding her nail between their mandibles, holding them in her hands, beginning a collection not only of cockroaches but of all kinds of insects—ants, worms, crickets, caterpillars. The study of cockroaches opens up a new world of which she had been ignorant: a world of inordinate otherness where what she learns is not entomology, with all its classes, its etiquette of descriptions and collecting, but rather, beyond this, a world without end, divine, of Oriental mysticism where bodies are no longer the same, where logic no longer resembles itself.

The dead cockroaches open up the path to what she calls "the dark soul of the world" (169), where she seems to lose herself, to become empty and hard. Her imagination, she says, no longer belongs to her (167), which is like saying that she has been banished from its domain, exiled in an ecstasy, which again leaves the body behind mummified. Her point of view is no longer that of a housewife but of a god, wandering wherever it sees fit, freed from the restraints of domestic life. But she has not yet completely adopted this new possibility. She is hesitant, fearful; she cannot let herself go all the way. The story tells of her hesitations, the discovery of this other world amid the fabric of her everyday life, without ever really making explicit its true nature, or the consequences of its eruption.

> My hobby's given me a pair of dreadful eyes, and sometimes I fancy they start from my head; yet I see, perhaps, no differently than Galileo saw when he found in the pendulum its fixed intent. Nonetheless my body resists such knowledge. (171)

Is the narrator going mad, is she dying, or, following some unheard-of process, is she being transformed, literally, into an insect? What has she discovered, what movement, akin to Galileo's pendulum? The text does not tell us but allows its readers to draw their own conclusions, to complete the journey on their own. It is up to them to find the cockroach wherever it may be hiding and to pursue it to the heart of the heart of their own originality.

Gass's story allows itself to be read in the same way that the cockroaches allow the narrator to tame them. The text is the insect that frightens us first of all, even disgusts us, which at the least causes a syncope similar to that suffered by the narrator; then, insofar as we are sensitive to its mysteries, to the web it weaves between two worlds, it seduces us, even obsesses us slightly and calls for an investment of ourselves that is no stranger to the loss of self experienced by the narrator. Wanting to find the very quick of the word, our imagination ends up no longer belonging to us. To live in the space opened up by reading the text means being like the cicada; we must shed our old skin and acquire a new one, made to measure. It is not a matter of saying that to read is to identify and lose oneself totally in the other, to be a Gregor Samsa of reading, but rather to lose a part of oneself in order to leave room for the other, to assimilate it like the ancient Egyptian gods—half-human, half-animal hybrids. Gass's cockroach-text, then, is like Thomas's praying mantis–text in that both of them seduce and absorb the reader, the link between them being all the easier to forge given that the mantis and the cockroach are members of the same order of insects (Dictyoptera); they are, so to speak, cousins.

Reading Gass's text causes a cognitive syncope that is a mirror image of the one suffered by the narrator when she discovers the carcasses on the carpet. The two are even closely linked, appearing in the same sentence, the first one:

> We certainly had no complaints about the house after all we had been through in the other place, but we hadn't lived there very long before I began to notice every morning the bodies of a large black bug spotted about the downstairs carpet; haphazardly, as earth worms must die on the street after a rain; looking when I first saw them like rolls of dark wool or pieces of mud from the children's shoes, or sometimes, if the drape were pulled, so like ink stains or deep burns they terrified me, for I had been intimidated by that deep rug very early and the first week had walked over it wishing my bare feet would swallow my shoes. (163)

This long, winding sentence, increasingly muddled, ends with what can only be considered a cognitive blackout: a complete blank in our understanding, a fundamental inability to grasp what is being said, rather like a pleasure born with terror. How are we, in fact, to understand the final "had walked over it wishing my bare feet would swallow my shoes"? Already the numerous convolutions of the sentence may have led us astray as the narrator covers up with successive layers the initial perception, which she is unable to explain. The design formed on the carpet by these large dead black insects scattered here and there cannot be understood in itself but must be grasped by way of increasingly domestic analogies: earthworms, rolls of wool, dried mud, ink stains, burn marks. If the list is dizzying with its approximations and startling logic, it is only to better prepare us for the final segment, which leaves us flabbergasted. Already the words did not seem to be able to correctly describe reality; now they no longer correspond to anything at all. Intimidated by the too-deep carpet, the narrator makes a wish that even a genie in a lamp could not grant. This wish expresses a tension clearly underlined by the elision of the personal pronoun (it is not "the first week I had walked over it" but "the first week had walked"). Faced with the uneasiness of the situation, the stress of this experience, the narrator seems to disappear, holding her breath, leaving behind nothing but words, small, hard-to-understand ink stains. This loss of self, of the mark of her subjectivity in midsentence, is also the loss of a certain kind of rationality. From this moment on, nothing for the narrator will be the same.[13]

But the experience is shared in some way. The narrator's holding her breath translates into an equivalent blackout for the reader. We too cannot understand what is presented to us. How can bare feet "swallow" shoes? Here indeed is a many-sided logical error. In the first place, a bare foot is not a shod foot; it is therefore a foot, which is no longer or has not yet been in contact with a shoe, a foot that is, indeed, separate from a shoe. That is why it is a bare foot. Then there is an inversion of the relationship of inclusion between the two terms. It is the shoe that contains the foot, not the other way round. To this we must add the fact that a foot does not swallow: if need be, we could say that a shoe does, if by such a metaphor we mean that it takes in, it contains, it receives a foot. The foot is the object and not the agent of such an act. In fact, this proposition twists the relationship established between the three terms of the equation, that is, the feet, the shoes, and the carpet. From the actual putting on to the final wearing, we would normally say that the deep carpet swallows the shoe, which swallows the foot. Here, however, the chain is broken into pieces that cannot be put together again. The effect of the carpet on the feet is such that, even bare, they enter into an inverse relationship with the shoes.

Although it may well have been perfectly normal up to this point, our relation to the text now finds itself necessarily modified. Such a conclusion to a sentence leaves us the choice of stopping and attempting to resolve the ambiguity or letting it take life in us. As in Blanchot's *Thomas the Obscure,* where reading started out by being a test of will between the text and the reader, before becoming a form of subtle exchange, we are in a situation where the words cannot be literally understood. We cannot look them in the eye to grasp their meaning, to find the core that would justify our glance, this piercing of their intimacy; on the contrary, we must let them look at us, we must close our own eyes and allow their particular logic to take hold of us, to mold us, until these figures impose themselves and become that secret intelligence which represents our only real grasp of the text. The estranging image of a foot swallowing a shoe, which by its topsy-turvy logic slips through our fingers, resembles the narrator's experience when she almost manages to take hold of one of the cockroaches, which, however, takes off at high speed, "tossing its shadow across the starch like an image of the startle in my hand" (164).

In "The Medium of Fiction," Gass ironically declared that "it seems a country-headed thing to say: that literature is language, that stories and places and the people in them are merely made of words."[14] Much of his fiction aims at making us never forget this truth: that novels are "made of words, and merely words."[15] Unsurprisingly, then, "Order of Insects" does not permit a distracted reading, one based on a simple progression through the text, a reading that forgets the text, its words and sentences, in order for a reader to project himself into the fictional world created. The story is not a tale with clear edges, precise actions, and simple facts. The narrative slows down to a point where it almost stops altogether. Of course, there is the discovery of the insects and a metamorphosis, but the latter is never more than begun, and the former returns continuously, a leitmotif. The time frame is not the linear one of facts and actions but rather the cyclical one of a consciousness losing touch with reality, turning over the same events again and again. Gass's text is a story of words; his argumentation does not set out from a logic of actions but proceeds from a symbolic nucleus that is so heavily invested in as to become saturated, which constitutes its own space, a reading space with its tensions, effects, and logic. A space where monads interact and proceed to swap sounds and views:

Made of concepts and their connections, of vestigial twitches in the larynx, gray paradigms of sound, the novel moves through the mind like a procession of speech; and as it does so it largely replaces, like music, our own interior life—those little vistas of bed sheet, table, and freeway, our immodest mumblings of self-justification and praise, our low heats and frosts of absent feeling—with its grander avenues of interest, its lucent objects and eloquent emotions; for a novel is a mind like a monad aware of a world; and as we, while reading, live it, we live within a metaphorical model of our own, even though the two may seem as distant as my life is from Sancho Panza's.[16]

Words inhabit the mind, transforming it the same way as the insects invade, in "Order of Insects," the narrator's imagination, to the point where she feels she doesn't own it anymore. Reading asks us to live the story, not just to be part of it, but to replace our own interior life with its own, blending words and thoughts, until we do not know anymore which belongs to whom. The short story manages to do it, with its cyclical form; but all fictions, Gass suggests, work in the same way, creating hybrids, metaphorical beings. A text is something that reads us.

ORDER AND FAMILY

That "Order of Insects" follows its own linguistic logic is apparent from the first sentence. Its disorder refers us directly to the title, which announces quite explicitly the order of its insects. Order is, of course, the opposite of disorder, which is, for its part, chance, the unknown, the unstable. The appearance of the dead cockroaches signals the arrival of disorder in the house. Something is out of place, and everything suddenly begins to move. Order must be reestablished, and the narrator hurries to do so. Indeed, she will spend the whole story reflecting on her relationship to order, her situation as a housewife dazed by life's disorder. But the order she eventually manages to reestablish has nothing in common with the one she was forced to leave behind.

A meticulous and feminine housewife, she begins with a spotless home and well-stocked cupboards, a mother anxious about the good behavior and health of her children, a woman happy to please her husband. Under the impact of the cockroaches, she will first become masculine, "I took up their study with a manly passion" (170), before undergoing an apotheosis: "This point of view I tremble in is the point of view of a god" (171). The insects, which appeared first of all as pure disorder, pure otherness, ugly armor-plated entities that forced her to look away, which inspired terror and haunted her dreams, have gradually become the object of her admiration. Their shape becomes something to marvel at: she notes the regularity of the lines of their shells, as well as their mahogany color, the differences between nymphs and adults, between males and females, the regular segmentation of their abdomens, the geometric precision of their compound eyes. And this precision is such that it prevents the horror initially felt, as the narrator tells us herself: "It isn't possible to feel disgust toward such an order" (167). Once their presence has been assimilated and their being tamed, the cockroaches acquire a new value. As suggested by chaos theory, the insects' apparent disorder was only ever a facade, hiding a more important and more fundamental array:

> All along I had the fear of what it was—something ugly and poisonous, deadly and terrible—the simple insect, worse and wilder than fire—and I should rather put my arms in the heart of a flame than in the darkness of a moist and webby hole. But the eye never ceases to change. When I examine

my collection now it isn't any longer roaches I observe but gracious order, wholeness, and divinity. (169)

Ugliness, fear, and poison become order, wholeness, divinity. The cockroaches are no longer an object of fear but are part of a collection, of an ordering of specimens, of taxonomy. For the order of cockroaches, above all, refers us to a category of classification. In taxonomy, various groups are distinguished one from the other, going from the largest to the smallest, from the kingdom to the species by way of class, order, and family, with their multitude of prefixes. So the cockroaches identified in the story, the *Periplaneta orientalis*, are members of the Blattidae family, which belongs to the suborder of Blottodea, which is itself part of the order of Dictyoptera, of the superorder of Orthopteroids, and so on until the animal kingdom. But the story's cockroaches have this additional particularity: they are the result of crossbreeding. There are no *Periplaneta orientalis* at the moment. There are *Blatta orientalis* and *Periplaneta americana*, but no cross between the two. It is as though Gass's cockroaches are duty bound to provide the union of the Orient and the Occident, a point to which I will return.[17]

In taxonomy, the order is hierarchically superior to the family. This conceptual superiority of one over the other is one of the main themes of the story. The order not only opposes disorder but also distinguishes itself from the family, which is seen both as a taxonomic category and as the family nucleus. By taming the insect universe, the narrator passes from one category to another. She moves up the hierarchy, leaving the family with its clearly defined social roles where she is completely subordinate, enslaved by an imprisoning framework, the four walls of her house or even the children's building blocks marking its boundaries; she leaves all of this, then, to join the order and the new freedom it gives her, a freedom based on the opening up of a new world, shadowy, perhaps, but divine in essence, where Oriental mysteries roam far from domestic banality. The dark soul of the world, which is unlocked by the cockroaches, is light-years away from the subdued jinni of the house. This coming to order marks the birth of a new subject, different, reincarnated, a subject disposed to immortality, to the infinitely large: "a soul so static and intense, so immortally arranged, I felt, while I lay shell-like in our bed, turned inside out, driving my mind away, it was the same as the dark soul of the world itself" (168).

Order and family, then, are presented as categories whose values have been inverted. One is divine just as the other is mortal; one is freedom, infinity, eternity, the other restrictions, limits, precariousness. Order is reason, that of the natural world and all its regularity; it is truth, transcendence, beauty; the family is madness, niggling fears, phobias ("the ordinary fears of everyday life" [168]). In the same way, if the family is life, order is death, but a death with inverted values. For in the narrator's logic, truth is invested in death. The cockroaches only open up the world once they are dead. Alive, they were merely pests that we fear and try to get rid of; it is only in death that they become ferrymen who can deliver us to a new way of life. In the beginning of the story, the narrator's cat amuses itself by knocking the insects' inert bodies into the air with its paws. For the narrator, this image of shells fluttering about here and there with no fixed trajectory, moving only at the whim of the cat's gestures, replaces the cockroaches' actual jumping. To such a point that "even if I actually saw those two black pairs of legs unhinge, as they would have to if one leaped, I think I'd find the result unreal and mechanical, a poor try measured by that sudden, high, head-over-heels flight from our cat's paw" (164). A point of contact with a divine and mysterious world opens up in the wake of these dead creatures. And it is their death, too, that initiates the metamorphosis and unites these two opposing universes—the world of vertebrates and that of arthropods. This ascent toward order is, for the narrator, the acquisition of an exoskeleton, of which the growing nails, the stiffening body, and the eye development are the first symptoms. If, in life, the exoskeleton seems hideous, surplus, obscene, in death it becomes the only possible vessel. The beauty of the dead cockroaches comes from the fact that they mummify quite naturally, that they preserve their shape intact even though their bodies dry up and their insides decompose (166). They are protected from the effects of death by their outer covering: they remain immutable, intact, even in decay. Their skeleton is not that which reemerges once their flesh has rotted away, as is the case with vertebrates, but it is always already there, clearly visible, it is maintained regardless. The narrator's endoskeleton was adapted to family life, but unless it is mummified, it quickly becomes a burden in death and its order.

It has perhaps become apparent with these last remarks, which link cockroaches and mummification, that Gass's story crosses two domains, two realms of the imagination: a local one, made up of the fears and phobias of American society, and an exotic one, full of the distant, glorious mysticism of the Egyptian pantheon. As with the *Periplaneta orientalis*—an imaginary hybrid of the Orient and America—the story unites this very American phobia, which is the fear of cockroaches, with the conception of death, or of life after death, so present in pharaonic Egypt.

The narrator's fears are not hers alone; she shares them with the rest of her culture. According to certain American studies on our relationship with insects, it would seem that the cockroach is the least favorite creature, far more unpopular than mosquitoes, rats, wasps, rattlesnakes, bats, and vultures, not to mention all the other invertebrates that are generally dreaded.[18] Even if this fear is easily understandable, insects have always been associated with death and disease.[19] We need only think of the relationship between fleas and the bubonic plague, lice and typhoid disease, tsetse flies and sleeping sickness (or trypanosome), mosquitoes and malaria, to name but the most common, to see that the fear of cockroaches is overdetermined.[20] They are marginal creatures operating at the limit of our territory, they fear light, they appear dirty and are destructive parasites whose mere presence within our walls is threatening, because they are a sign of unhealthiness, of contamination, of the loss of control of our space. Since cockroaches have existed for 320 million years without any major evolutionary change, the risk they pose seems immemorial. As they manage to infiltrate everywhere, in cupboards and pantries, under home appliances, in bookshelves, even in books, as they are gregarious and swarm in all these places, their presence hits at the very heart of our territory, of our extended selves. Jay Mechling notes:

> Human reactions to the cockroach are startling enough to alert us that we are in the presence of a powerful symbol, and we know that the power of that symbol derives in part from the "objective" character and behavior of the cockroach itself and in part from the meanings we humans project upon the creature. The cockroach nicely condenses into one symbol a great many social and psychological anxieties, some of which are human but most of which may be characteristically (if not uniquely) American.[21]

The narrator's reactions to the invasion of cockroaches are therefore representative of the American unease when faced with this insect associated with a loss of integrity, control, and power.[22] But equally representative, and perhaps even more surprising, is the destiny of this phobia, of this terrible fear of terrifying insects. It does not remain fixed; it even has a tendency to reverse itself, as the narrator's metamorphosis has shown.

Mechling goes on to discuss the avatars of this fear of cockroaches, saying that the average American associates the roach with dirt, danger, darkness, disorder, disease, death, and evil:

> But there is another traditional American view of the cockroach, one that *inverts* the valorization found in most folklore and mass media and that draws its own power from the energy it inverts. Not surprisingly, the cockroach often becomes the cultural hero to people who are themselves marginalized by dominant American culture.[23]

Mechling talks about Afro-American and Mexican minorities, and about children too whose fascination for insects is well known; but we are tempted to add to the list our housewife, this mistress of the house who believes herself to be master of nothing, not even of her own life, imprisoned in a domestic yoke that is too tight, subordinate to the demands of daily life, reduced to the status of maid. For her, too, cockroaches become a source of power, since they are a source of fear. And after their initial rejection, they play a liberating role, becoming the soul of the world, the initiators into mysteries undreamed of until now.

A second domain takes ancient Egypt as its symbolic counterpoint.[24] This surpassing of oneself into which the narrator is initiated, the Oriental mysteries she discovers, her acquisition of an exoskeleton following the example of the cockroaches, who are described, indeed, as being Egyptian mummies, this shadowy world she takes hold of for the first time—all these things point in this direction.[25] Ancient Egypt was a culture where death was not the morbid taboo subject we now know, where the cult and ritual of dying was highly developed, if not indeed hypertrophied. We need only consider the pyramids, the funeral chambers or halls of eternity, mummies—those living corpses surviving on to the next world, the sarcophagi and effigies, the *Pyramid Papers* or even the *Book of the Dead* whose chapters are so many prayers offered up to the gods to facilitate life in the deep beyond. Françoise Dunand and Christiane Zivie-Coche remark that the importance of "death and, even more so, of all the paraphernalia which surround it is so strong that it has caught our imaginations, if not fascinated, in a sometimes morbid way, our Western minds."[26] And what was so fascinating was that, for the initiated in the Egyptian temples, death corresponded not merely to the dissolution of the human body, as our materialistic conception teaches us, but to a stage in a series of supraphysical phenomena, the metamorphosis of consciousness. Death was a birth, a rebirth of the mind. And the place where the deceased emerged was an area where nothing is limited, fixed, and stable. The realm of the beyond was a place of hybrids, gods being as we all know a mixture of anthropo- and zoomorphism: an animal's head on a human body, the union of the head and the body of two different animals, a human head on an animal's body. By reaching this place, the deceased participates in these possible movements, in this game of transforming bodies:

> After death, when the earthly body is only just eliminated, the possibilities for the human being, compressed during his earthly passage, shoot up, overflow from the personality's framework; and this limitless transforming, this function of the universe's potentiality, comes to reign. The deceased now finds himself in the "Region of Metamorphoses" characterized by the extreme rapidity and variety of its transformations.[27]

Mummification, metamorphosis, and immortality: the Egyptian tradition describes death as a threshold to be crossed, beyond which a new existence begins. The cockroaches in "Order of Insects" set out quite clearly this threshold by their own death, their natural mummification, the predisposition to immortality accorded them by their exoskeletons. The dark soul of the world opened up by their order is that region of metamorphoses where the narrator's body discovers new forms for itself, hybrid forms, halfway between reality and possibility: the reality of the family, profane in nature, and the possibility of the order, divine in essence. Gregor Samsa became a living cockroach, waiting for death to free him from his situation; Gass's narrator is transformed into a dual figure, already dead although still breathing, a living corpse—part cockroach, part woman; half god, half human; both exo- and endoskeleton—whose death is not a liberation but the realm she already inhabits. If the metamorphosis remains constantly at work, if the story that relates this process is above all circular, never ending, engaged in a cyclical and nonlinear time frame, it is because the narrator's state is not a phase quickly over, but a new state, her own version of immortality.[28]

The dead cockroaches in "Order of Insects" are thus at the junction of two worlds: as cockroaches, *Periplaneta americana,* they take on a very American phobia; as carcasses and corpses, *Blatta orientalis,* they open up the way to a night world whose values and contours are Egyptian. The story is to be read in suspension: the suspension of time, which has become as static as the cockroaches' souls; the suspension of meaning, which forces us to get over our initial disgust in order to look more closely; and the suspension of the body, elusive in the fluidity of its alterations.

EXOSKELETONS

I have tried, in this analysis, to sustain the metaphor of reading as an encounter with an insect, a being whose otherness is great, and whose body answers to different formal principles.[29] The presence of an exoskeleton was the most obvious sign of its otherness. Such an equivalence between text and insect throws new light on reading. Usually, reading is described as an encounter between two consciousnesses, the reader's and the text's, behind which hides, more or less successfully, the author. What is at stake with this conception is the equality of the two participants. Both are of the same nature, able to maintain a relationship of comprehension. This position, generalized throughout contemporary literary studies, presents the work as being an equal, the result of a consciousness, against which we may sometimes stumble, but with which we learn to cooperate. It is hard to argue against it.

However, we can play with the idea that the reader and the text possess a profoundly different nature one from the other. If I must let the text live in me to understand it, then it is above all different to me. It is not a rival consciousness but an entity belonging to a different order. To understand a text means to tame it, to work to decipher it; it means to listen to it, not as we would hear another person's words, in a simple act of communication, but as we listen to the cicada's song or the humming of a mosquito. There is no equality between the reader and the text; there is only a distance that reading tries to reduce. Reading is work, exactly because the mystery of the text is equal to the challenge posed by the dead cockroaches; it is a battle against the self, as the narrator in Gass's story shows us. The text is an insect that I must learn to be close to, to understand, and that ends up by being as seductive as a monarch butterfly in flight.

All this calls for a final reflection. For to identify the text with an insect rather than with a human being, with an invertebrate rather than a vertebrate, means somehow to maintain that the text, too, possesses not an endoskeleton but an exoskeleton. By this logic, the text and the words that make it up must not be perceived as bodies whose skeletons are hidden behind a fictional illusion upheld by linguistic and stylistic strategies, but bodies with an obvious skeleton, an inescapable presence that offers itself up to be seen and to be read as it is. Gass's story, by constantly bringing the reader's attention to the text, by proposing a narrative with blurred edges marked by an ambiguous metamorphosis and atypical logic, does not allow the text to fade from our view but rather imposes it on us and makes its materialness an essential dimension of our reading. They are, for that matter, examples of antirealism.

Realism, as a mode of representation, favors an endoskeletal conception of the word, the signified prevailing over the signifier, which fades away to benefit the former and its conceptual articulations. What the text is about, realism tells us, is to be found not on the page but below or above it, where the text's core is lodged, temporarily hidden beneath an easily detached layer of skin. The page is just an envelope, which quickly vanishes when we want to move on to the essential, which is hidden out of sight. Characters, places, emotions, and actions appear when the sign becomes transparent and the referent imposes itself as the sole object of attention.[30]

However, there is nothing that stipulates a text must be conceived as an endoskeleton. It would even be most advantageous to combat such a habit and to favor theoretical and critical undertakings that take into account the concrete relationship to the text and all those acts required to get to know it, which do not forget the surface of the text with its tropes, its figures, its accidents. We must pursue these endeavors, which give precedence to an exoskeletal conception of text and words, where the signifier does not find itself being devalued. Because it is the latter that holds the word together, which gives it its being, instead of being just its complement; it does not limit itself to introducing the word and then disappearing once the word is known in the so-called transparency of its designation; it is that which must be known in the word, that which keeps the word present. If, as the narrator in "Order of Insects" tells us, we must love what dies in vertebrates—that is, the muscles and humors, the fleshy parts—then when it comes to the text, we must learn to love that which is permanent: the words and sentences, all those marks written on the page that enable us to know it.

NOTES

1. Translated by Jean Valenti and Nancy Costigan. The French version of this article appeared as a chapter in my essay *Lecture littéraire et explorations en littérature américaine* (Montreal: XYZ Éditeur, 1998), 147–69.

2. George Lakoff and Mark Johnson, in *Metaphors We Live By* (Chicago: University of Chicago Press, 1981), have theorized metaphors as initial forms of conceptualization, and one can find a marvelous example of such a metaphorology in Hans Blumenberg's *Shipwreck with Spectator: Paradigm of a Metaphor for Existence* (1979; Cambridge: MIT Press, 1996). In *Lecture littéraire*, I play extensively with the concept of a "grounding metaphor," a form of initial conceptualization, which serves as a basis for interpretation or, to be more precise, as the hypothesis required to establish a rule, which enables an interpretation to be accomplished (39–44).

3. Gass, *In the Heart of the Heart of the Country*, 4th ed. (Boston: David R. Godine, 1981). Hereafter cited in the text. William Gass's other fictions are *Omensetter's Luck*, 2nd ed. (New York: New American Library, 1972); *Willie Masters' Lonesome Wife* (New York: Dalkey Archive, 1968); and *The Tunnel* (New York: Knopf, 1995).

4. Strangely enough, "Order of Insects" follows the same path of loss and discovery as Clarice Lispector's novel *The Passion According to G. H.* (1964; Minneapolis: University of Minnesota Press, 1988). Written in the 1960s, both books can be said to define the same allegory of experience or, for that matter, the same "allegory of reading." On the latter, see Paul de Man, *Allegories of Reading* (New Haven: Yale University Press, 1979).

5. Blanchot, *Thomas the Obscure* (New York: David Lewis, 1973), 25. Hereafter cited in the text.

6. In his short narrative *Le lecteur* (Paris: Gallimard, 1976), Pascal Quignard described reading exactly as an abduction of the soul, writing that "this being devoured by books, I see it, if you will, as a second type of metempsychosis between the absence of soul and the absence of meaning" (13; translation mine). And this is what we find at work with Blanchot: reading as metempsychosis, as transmigration, but a migration that makes the book not only a receptacle, that in which we invest ourselves, but a living being in which we transform and reincarnate ourselves.

7. Blanchot, *The Infinite Conversation* (Minneapolis: University of Minnesota Press, 1993), 77.

8. Gass, *Habitations of the World* (Ithaca: Cornell University Press, 1985), 108–9.

9. Ibid., 109.

10. Ibid.

11. See *The World within the Word*, 2nd ed. (Boston: David R. Godine, 1978).

12. In "Representation and the War for Reality," Gass identifies an image that is apparently the basis for this character: "Normally, we might have said of Gregor Samsa that he was a little no-account man who lived in the cracks of life like a bug

between boards, but Kafka causes the image to become the character. . . . In Gregor Samsa's situation, the interpretive system succeeds in abolishing its object, in taking its place. But a bug of what kind, we might ask. Why, a bug in a bed—a bedbug— the sperm that Samsa's name suggests in German, and the immediate meaning of 'bedbug' to the imagination. Hence in Kafka's *Metamorphosis* not only does the interpretive term become the agent of the action, it then receives its own appropriate figuration" (*Habitations of the World*, 107). Dee Drake, who quotes this passage in "William Gass and the Alchemy of the Text," in *Criticism in the Twilight Zone: Postmodern Perspectives on Literature*, ed. Danuta Zadworna (Stockholm: Lennart Bjork–Almquist and Wiksell, 1990), develops the relation to the nymph, present in Gass's short story and linked both to the insect and to a goddess. She notes the sexual connotation implied by the presence of the nymph and goes on to propose optional titles for the story: "Hors d'Oeuvres in Sex" or else "Order of Intersex," and so forth (139).

13. Furthermore, her soliloquy tends toward solipsism, as Eusebio L. Rodrigues has remarked in "A Nymph at Her Orisons: An Analysis of William Gass's 'Order of Insects,'" *Studies in Short Fiction* 17 (1980): 348–51; as well as Lucy Wilson in "Alternatives to Transcendence in William Gass's Short Fiction," *Review of Contemporary Fiction* 11, no. 3 (1991): 79.

14. "The Medium of Fiction," in *Fiction and the Figures of Life*, 3rd ed. (Boston: David R. Godine, 1989), 27.

15. Ibid., 27. It is, for Gass, an essential element of his aesthetics. In "The Soul inside the Sentence," he will argue that "we should never forget, then, that from the very beginning, when the word made the world, the word has been one of the most important 'objects' in human experience. We were born into language as into perception, pain and pleasure" (122).

16. Ibid.

17. It is of course possible that Gass simply reproduced the typology used in the old insect manual mentioned in the short story. Thus, in the *Larousse du XXième siècle*, dating from 1932, we find *Periplaneta orientalis* in a now out-of-date typology.

18. See Stephen R. Kellert, "Values and Perceptions of Invertebrates," *Conservation Biology* 7, no. 4 (1991): 845–55.

19. The relationship between insects and death, or even the afterlife, has been noted as early as the seventeenth century, as made clear in the *Dictionnaire historique de la langue française*, ed. Alain Rey (Paris: Dictionnaire le Robert, 1992): "In the seventeenth century, were called *insects* those animals which, it was thought, stayed alive even after they had been cut in two (snakes, for example) and those whose body was either divided into rings (worms, arthropods) or apparently unorganized (oysters, mollusks in general)" (1031; translation mine).

20. J. L. Cloudsley-Thompson, *Insects and History* (London: Weidenfeld and Nicholson, 1976).

21. Mechling, "From archy to Archy: Why Cockroaches Are Good to Think," *Southern Folklore* 48, no. 2 (1991): 122.

22. André Siganos's findings tend to generalize this fear of cockroaches (and other insects). Quoting Jung, he notes that cockroaches represent the darkest aspects of the personality, and proposes, by way of several examples, "a psychological schema of the insect assimilated with the liberating forces of hidden evil, with the terrifying shadows, with the cruelest torment" (98; translation mine). See *Les mythologies de l'insecte: Histoire d'une fascination* (Paris: Librairie des Méridiens, 1985). For some relationships between popular culture and insects, see Kenneth Alan Adams, "Arachnophobia: Love American Style," *Journal of Psychoanalytical Anthropolgy* 4 (1981): 157–97; James W. Mertins, "Arthropods on the Screen," *Bulletin of the Entomological Society of America* 32 (1986): 85–90; as well as James Hillman's conference on the psychoanalytical impact of insects, *Going Bugs* (New York: Spring Audio–Gracie Station, 1991). Ilan Stavans, in "Kafka, Cortazar, Gass," *Review of Contemporary Fiction* 11, no. 3 (1991): 131–36, concludes with these remarks: "Because while man believes himself intelligent enough to control nature, an ancestral terror inhabits him, one which pushes him to understand insects as rivals. Their strength, he knows, lies in their communal purposefulness, so sophisticated, so methodically structured. Better to kill, collect, or ignore them. Our aggression against mosquitoes, spiders, ants, bugs, flies, bees, cockroaches . . . is nothing but the hidden anxiety of eventually losing the supremacy of power" (135).

23. Mechling, "From archy to Archy," 132.

24. On this topic see also Vanessa Haley, "Egyptology and Entomology in William Gass's 'Order of Insects,'" *Notes on Contemporary Literature* 16, no. 3 (1986): 3–5; and Drake, "William Gass and the Alchemy of the Text."

25. There are no cockroaches in the Egyptian pantheon; there is a scarab beetle, but it does not play the same role.

26. *Dieux et hommes en Egypte, 3000 av. J. C.–395 apr. J. C.* (Paris: Armand Colin, 1991), 159.

27. Grégoire Kolpaktchy, introduction to *Livre des morts des anciens Égyptiens* (Paris: Stock, 1993), 47 (translation mine).

28. In Clarice Lispector's *The Passion According to G.H.*, the contact with a cockroach, which initially causes fear, leads in much the same way to a revelation expressed in terms of metamorphosis; there too, a prolonged contact concludes with a dehumanization as well as with a new knowledge whose effects are irreversible. In fact, the correspondences between Lispector's novel and Gass's short story are major. Both seem to answer to a common encounter scenario. In Lispector's novel, for instance, we move from initial archaic terror and from the impression, right from the start, that something irreparable has just happened, to a form of superior consciousness, if not even a superior existence. And once more we find the same conception of the insect as being both immemorial and current, threatening and primordial, an object not only of transfer but also of transit. Even Egypt reappears as a troubling leitmotif: the narrator also describes the cockroach in terms of hieroglyphs: "I sense that all this is ancient and immense, I sense in the hieroglyphic of the slow cockroach the writing of the Far East" (53). The convergence of these

two stories stemming from two distinct cultural universes points toward a shared imagination.

29. Texts that explore our relationships with these skeletal creatures, our fantasies and phobias, our projections, are numerous in literature, as Siganos's essay illustrates so clearly with its review of poetic works and novels where insects reign. And these encounters are both with insects possessing a great lyrical capacity, to use Roger Caillois's expression, which designates those insects that, like butterflies, have "a remarkable appearance, movements which awaken man's attention and excite his imagination, in such a way that these animals become the bearer of a rich symbolic signification and a universal value" (Siganos, *Les mythologies de l'insecte,* 28); and with arthropods, which are basically repulsive, such as cockroaches, earwigs, centipedes. If fiction is a laboratory where we put life's possible configurations to the test, then the order of insects would seem to provide fertile ground for the exploration of life's limits: death, madness, dreams, metamorphoses.

30. We could easily accumulate examples based on an endoskeletal conception of the text, which has imposed itself quite naturally as a theoretical and critical presupposition. For instance, the slight importance accorded to the materiality of the text, seen as an accident that must be passed by in order to arrive at the essential, was a major element of structuralist semantics and the semiotics derived from them, where the word's skeleton, its elementary semic structure, is hidden or buried, so that it becomes necessary to kill it, to stop and dissect it, to find out what it is made of.

10

A Sacred Insect on the Margins

Emblematic Beetles in the Renaissance

YVES CAMBEFORT

Even if pagan images had not been forgotten in the Middle Ages, the tendency to study pagan sources, in order better to understand both Christian religion and the structure of the natural world, was a characteristic of the Renaissance.[1] Some humanists, like Erasmus, went so far as to give more weight to pagan allegories than to Christian scriptures: "Perhaps we may find more profit reading poetic fables and looking for allegorical sense, than Holy Scriptures, if we content ourselves with the external [i.e., literal] meaning."[2] The word "poetic" is here almost synonymous with "false," as opposed to the "true" realities of Christianity, and "fables" refer to any text neither biblical nor historical. Our words "fable," "fabled," and "fabulous" have the same root: the Latin *fabula,* which had a much broader sense than our "fable." Ancient Greeks, too, had no word exactly expressing our "fable."[3] They usually said "Aesopian *logos,*" since Aesop was for them the most illustrious author of this literary genre.[4] In Aesopian fables, insects play their role despite, or perhaps because of, their small size: the main characteristic of fables is the condensation of significant teaching into a small form.[5] This method became especially prominent in the Middle Ages, with the invention of the *exemplum,* a sort of Christian fable.[6] The Renaissance followed with its *loci communes,* but also, in a more symbolic, allegorical style, with the invention of devices, *impresse,* and other "emblems."[7] In these productions, humanists have both hidden and discovered the fundamental relationships, the shared elements, they had found in pagan and Christian thoughts.

One of these emblematic elements, which regularly recurs in art and literature in the years 1500–1650, is an insect that had been placed by ancient Egyptians in the rank of the gods: the beetle.[8] The beetle is the smallest of these antique "gods" whose images never ceased to be present in European art and thought. Contrary to all the other pagan gods, the beetle also possesses an authentic Christian significance, which gives it a unique, ambiguous status. But this religious ambiguity is not the only one. Beetles, like many other insects, or perhaps more than most of them, may provoke uneasiness. Such discomfort is due to multiple reasons, but especially the fact that insects are often related to dirt, pollution, and decay.[9] This is more specifically the case of the so-called sacred scarab of the Egyptians, which belongs to a coprophagous genus of beetles.[10] Its unattractive habits bizarrely contrast with the scarab's sacredness and give the insect a disturbing, even dangerous, character. But scholars have pointed to the ambiguity of the holy itself, which is always vaguely sinister.[11] Here I will explore the various connotations of the beetle in the Renaissance, from Christian meaning in Dürer's work, to pagan ambiguity in Erasmus, and, through the coexistence of both Dürer's and Erasmus's heritages, to the emblematic works of Rudolfian Prague and its intersections with seventeenth-century science and literature.

The Beetle's Christian Melancholy

Dürerian Margins

Albrecht Dürer's *Stag Beetle* is probably the most famous artistic study of an insect ever made. According to its monogram and date, this watercolor— now in the Getty Museum, Malibu—was painted in 1505.[12] The German artist was thirty-four and at the climax of his life and talent. This particular subject had retained him during a brief period: around 1503–5, he introduced it in the three drawings of the *Madonna with a Multitude of Animals* (1503) and especially in the painting of *The Adoration of the Magi* (1505).[13] There is a small bronze of the Italian sculptor Andrea Riccio, representing a stag beetle of natural size, which seems almost exactly contemporaneous with Dürer's study: might one of these works have inspired the other?[14] Contrary to watercolor and bronze, where it represents the principal subject, the stag beetle was introduced in the three drawings and the painting as a mere "marginal element," as it had already been the case in illuminated manuscripts as well as in large paintings of the fourteenth and fifteenth centuries. For example, the stag beetle was figured in the Book of Hours of Giangaleazzo Visconti (c. 1390),[15] as well as in the altarpieces of Stephan Lochner's *The Saint Patrons of Cologne* (1440)[16] and Michael Wolgemut's *The Apostles' Departure* (c. 1485).[17] Very often, these marginalia give a clue as to the true and profound meaning of the works.[18] So what was, in Dürer's mind—as far as we might imagine it—the beetle's meaning? Indeed, since classical times, the creature had been equated with the stag, venerated as a sacred animal whose horns could subdue the dragon, in the same way that Christ subdues Satan.[19] Various saints had seen a stag with a Christian cross between its horns, especially Saint Eustathius, whom Dürer had depicted twice before 1505.[20] But the potential meanings of the stag beetle in Dürer's

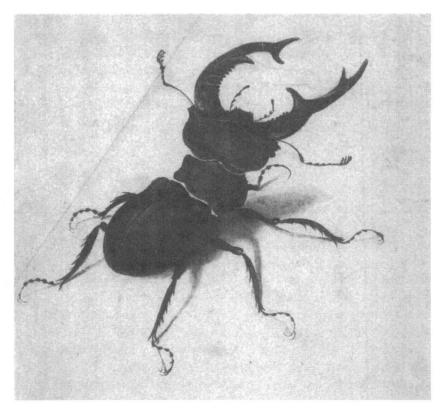

Albrecht Dürer, *Stag Beetle* (1505). Watercolor. Courtesy of the J. Paul Getty Museum, Los Angeles, California.

work were equally motivated by the beetle's close relationship with the sacred scarab (*Scarabaeus sacer*), a species restricted to the Mediterranean area. Among notable pagan sources there was at least one outstanding text of which Dürer was aware: Horapollo's *Hieroglyphica*. This fifth-century Greek text had been famous since its rediscovery in 1419 and provided explanations of some ancient hieroglyphs that modern studies have con-firmed in part. Dürer became interested in Horapollo around 1500 (maybe later) through his friend the Nuremberg scholar Pirckheimer, with whom he prepared an illustrated German version of *Hieroglyphica* for Emperor Maximilian (curiously enough, Dürer's supposed illustration for the scarab does not figure a beetle but a sort of millipede).[21] Horapollo described the scarab as *monogenes*, "only begotten," that is, a unique son, and *autogenes*, "self-begotten, unborn of the female."[22] The Greek word *monogenes* is like-wise used five times in John's gospel and first epistle as characteristic of Christ, unique Son of one Father. The same word, in its Latin form (*unige-nitus*), appears also in the Nicene Creed, the Latin *Credo*. But it is not clear whether "self-begotten" refers to divine filiation or to some sort of sponta-neous regeneration, as in the case of the phoenix.[23]

We cannot speculate whether Dürer knew other pagan sources. The most important one, Plutarch's *Treatise on Isis and Osiris*, was published only in 1509, a few years after the aforementioned works of art. We do not know whether Dürer had heard (from manuscript sources) about this book, where Plutarch referred twice to the beetle, explaining that this species was honored by the Egyptians because it preserved a faint trace of the powers of the gods. In particular, the beetle's habit of rolling its dung ball back-ward, Plutarch said, resembled the way in which the sun seems to turn the sky around in the opposite direction when moving from west to east.[24] On the other hand, an important Christian source was surely available to Dürer: Saint Ambrose of Milan's writings.[25] In at least five different texts, Saint Ambrose introduced the scarab as an equivalent for Christ, as in the following excerpt from his *Treatise on St. Luke's Gospel*:

[Jesus Christ] was on the cross like a worm, on the cross like a scarab. But how good a worm attached to the wood, how good a scarab shouting from the cross. . . . How good a scarab who changed into virtue the shapeless ordure of our body, how good a scarab who exalted the poor from his dunghill.[26]

It is very likely that Dürer was aware of this sound basis for a Christian interpretation of the beetle, possibly in addition to that of Horapollo. Such an equivalence (stag beetle for Christ) is clear in *The Adoration of the Magi*. In respect to Horapollo's and Ambrose's texts, the beetle in this painting—which overtly depicts Jesus as a child—covertly alludes to the Passion and suffering on the cross of God's unique Son. Hence the "marginal" beetle changes an important, but anecdotal, scene of Jesus's childhood into a striking summary of the whole Christian faith.

Erasmian Proverbs

For the Renaissance humanistic public, however, the word *scarabeus* (beetle) alluded not to Dürer's works of art but to a writing famous during this epoch. In Erasmus of Rotterdam's collection of *Adages*, or proverbs, edited by John Froben in Basel in 1515, a rather long text drew the humanists' attention. Entitled *Scarabeus aquilam quaerit* (The beetle searches for the eagle), it was soon generally known by its mere first word, *Scarabeus*. It is not necessary here to detail the genesis of Erasmus's *Adages*: the British scholar Margaret Mann Phillips has presented it well in her book *The "Adages" of Erasmus: A Study with Translations*.[27] They were published for the first time in Paris in 1500 (Erasmus was thirty-three), in the form of a slim book, briefly explaining some 818 proverbs drawn from Greek and Latin authors; they became a huge volume in 1508, when they were published again in Venice by Aldus Manutius, in whose workshop Erasmus was staying. The 1508 volume contained 3,285 adages, hence its name *Chiliades*, or "thousands" of adages. From this time on, the book had an enormous influence and established Erasmus's reputation as the leading "teacher of Europe."[28] In spite of its size and price, the book was reissued by his favorite printer, John Froben, seven times during Erasmus's lifetime (in addition to pirated editions). Its final version, published in March 1536 (four months before his death), contained 4,151 adages.[29] In the 1515 edition, nine adages that had appeared in 1500 or 1508 were developed into longer texts, becoming sorts of "essays" anticipating those of Montaigne. One very long development was added to *Scarabeus aquilam quaerit*, the first number of the seventh century of the third *Chilias* (3.7.1 or 2,601). The text became widespread among humanists, separately reprinted in 1517 by Froben (with *scholiae* by Beatus Rhenanus), and again by other printers in 1517, 1521 (twice), and 1522. Its argument is straightforward: it develops the famous Aesopian fable *The Eagle and the Dung Beetle.*

According to this text, once upon a time, a hare chased by an eagle found refuge in a dung beetle's hole. The beetle pleaded for the hare in the name of Zeus; but in spite of it, the eagle captured and devored the hare. The dung beetle got very angry, looked for the eagle's nest, and smashed its eggs. The eagle begged its patron, Zeus, to protect its eggs, and laid them in the god's lap. But the beetle flew up to Olympus, carrying a big ball of dung right in front of Zeus. The god leaped to his feet, and the eagle's eggs were smashed again. Then the beetle told him the whole story. Zeus invited it to relent, but, as the beetle did not agree, he changed the eagle's and beetle's time of activity so that they could no longer meet and interact.[30] In Greek, the word for eagle (*aetos*) is masculine in gender; but it is feminine in Latin (*aquila*), and the beetle is masculine (*scarabaeus* or *scarabeus*). This changes completely the spirit of the story and renders it more convincing and more interesting, which probably motivated Erasmus.

Erasmus managed to transform Aesop's fable into a philosophical tale of no less than 818 lines in the reference edition, a masterpiece of the serio-comic style.[31] First he describes both protagonists. As the favorite emblem of kings and other crowned heads, the (she-)eagle is identified with them, and Erasmus undertakes against her an attack both ferocious and joyful. His satire of princes' ferocity, rapaciousness, and even cowardice is the most severe he ever wrote, so violent it was censored: the comparison of eagles with princes was eliminated in the post-Tridentine editions of the *Adages,* changing it into a mere chapter of natural history comparable to those of Pliny.[32] Meanwhile Erasmus celebrates the beetle; because Aristophanes, in his comedy *Peace,* introduced a large beetle living on Mount Etna, Erasmus also places his scene in this area.[33] The beetle, he says, lives in dirt and nevertheless keeps a neat and clean appearance (playing on the two Greek words *kantharos* [beetle] and *katharos* [clean, pure]), whereas the eagle is soiled with the carrion she does not disdain to eat, and "stinks even in the air." Much smaller in size, the beetle is not afraid to battle against such a dreaded enemy: wasn't he, among ancient Egyptians, the emblem of the warrior? (All scarabs were regarded as virile males, a peculiarity reported in various classical texts, especially Plutarch's treatise *On Isis and Osiris.*[34] It is of course biologically incorrect, but the natural history of dung beetles was completely unknown until the nineteenth century and the observations of Jean-Henri Fabre.)[35] Yet another reason for beetle worship, Erasmus explained, was their courage, which is due to their young age: "Every year they slough off their old age and immediately renew their youth."[36] The belief, drawn from Aristotle, was used by Erasmus to justify the reissues of such a big and costly book as the *Adages:* "But when snakes and some insects slough away their old age and are, as it were, reborn several times a year, surely it is no scandalous matter for a book to reappear in fresh guise from time to time, so long as it is purified, revised, and enriched?"[37]

In addition to these qualities, the beetle is sympathetic and charitable. He welcomes the hare in his Mount Etna hole and attempts to mollify the raging eagle, but she kills and eats the poor animal. Such a barbarous deed fills the beetle with rage and indignation. From this moment on, his only goal will be to avenge his guest's death. First "he went to Vulcan [and] begged him to hammer out a suit of armour, not too heavy to fly in, but strong enough to protect him against an average attack. Vulcan armed the beetle from top to toe, in the very armour which he still wears (for before that he was unarmed, like a fly)."[38] The beetle then proceeds toward his enemy's citadel. In a story that is animated and full of spirit, Erasmus narrates the successive attacks of the insect against the eagle, whose eggs he manages three times to smash. The whole of Olympus is divided about the quarrel. On the beetle's side range the "smaller ones," all the minor deities, but also Juno, "out of hatred for Ganymede," the young boy whom the eagle had kidnapped by order of Jupiter. At last the beetle's victory is so complete that Jupiter has to reserve a place on earth, a sanctuary where the eagle can be safe from a beetle's attacks.

At this point in the story, it would seem that Erasmus's sympathy goes to the beetle, representing feeble and small ones, *parvuli* who gain victory because of their intelligence, since they lack strength. But matters are not so simple: certainly, Erasmus hates the unconscious ferocity of the greats in this world, and he would like to side with the beetle against them.[39] However, he cannot simply accept that base creatures gain victory over superior beings. Thence the conclusion of the adage:

> The story teaches us that no enemy is to be despised, however humble he may
> be. For there are some tiny men, of a very low sort but extremely pernicious,
> no less black than beetles and no less evil-smelling and contemptible, and
> yet by the persistent cunning of their hearts (although they can do no good

to any mortal creature) they can often bring trouble even to great men. Their blackness is terrifying, their stridency drowns everything, their stench is a nuisance, they fly round and round, won't be shaken off and wait their chance—so that it is far preferable to compete with great men sometimes than to irritate these beetles, whom one is ashamed of mastering; it is impossible either to shake them off or to struggle with them without coming away defiled.[40]

This conclusion seems ill adapted to the rest of the adage: in these last lines, Erasmus appears to have taken the eagle's part and rejected that of the beetle. As it is the final word of the story, one can think that here lies Erasmus's true and profound feeling, and that this conclusion put the beetle back in its true place in his mind and in his world: in spite of some remarkable traits and qualities, this base insect provokes contempt.

The idea is expressed more strongly in adage, 1,905, *Abominandus scarabeus* (The abominable beetle). But why is the beetle so odious? For Erasmus, the main reason seems to have been because it generates a sort of ill-defined fear, especially through the noise it makes in flying. This particular trait, which is already in Pliny (*Natural History*, XI) is quoted four times in *Scarabeus:* the insect is "horridest of all by its buzzing noise"; "some make a terrifying buzz and dreadful booming noise as they fly, and frighten the unwary quite badly"; they have a "terrifying and Panic hum and screech"; and "their stridency drowns everything."[41] The idea recurs in adage 2,145, *Scarabei umbrae* (Beetle shades), where the very title provides some explanation: it refers to the infernal shades, ghosts, and other specters, but also to a motiveless fear. The expression *umbras timere,* for example in Cicero, means "to fear false ghosts and specters, to get alarmed without a motive." As a matter of fact, however unpleasing a beetle's hum or buzz might be, it is not something to be feared. This disproportionate reaction refers also to another recurrent concept in Erasmus's writings: *decorum* (convenience, appropriateness). In every matter, thoughts and acts should be appropriate to their cause. For example, it is not suitable to invoke God when you are bitten by a flea: adage 2,304 (*In pulicis morsu deum invocat*), where Erasmus refers again to people who fear small and inoffensive animals and explains that Aristotle called such a fear "bestial" (*theriodes*). It may be bestial because such an anxiety is hard to suffer and painful, despite its being motivated by nothing, exactly like the fear of death; but it is also bestial because it is not as refined as might be expected from a civilized person, or even from a man, and this too is shocking.

There appears to be no classical text referring to any fear provoked by the beetle's hum. Therefore it is likely that Erasmus speaks out of his personal experience.[42] Should we then conjecture that this particular feeling affected him personally and that he suffered from it? He was a great traveler, riding across the whole of Europe in spite of his frailty and bad health. One can imagine that such a small adventure as a beetle humming close to his ears would have happened to him more than once, or even only once, causing him a big shock that he would have remembered for the rest of his life. Indeed, such a strong and sudden hum is likely to provoke a surprise, but is it reasonable to be shocked, or even frightened? This would be precisely a case of that "bestial" fear referred to by Aristotle. But *bestia* also evokes theriomorphic gods, and this fear might be related to sacredness, to the divine power that, at that time yet, impregnated the whole world. Whatever this fear's origin, perhaps one might invoke here the *timor de re non timenda* (the fear of something not likely to be feared), a characteristic of the melancholic and Saturnine temper, very important in the Renaissance. The permanent uneasiness of this temper—it is always wary and never relaxes—is the principal cause of that "generous melancholy," that melancholy of the scholar, the artist, the genius.[43] This permanent and causeless disquiet may find some justification not only in the beetle's—or other insect's—noise but in their mere existence. Indeed, and despite the apparently ironic and humorous way in which Erasmus deals with beetles, he seems to perceive them as insects representing everything that, in nature, is opposed to man in some obscure or "sacred" way.

THE BEETLE EMBLEMATIC

Alciato, Camerarius, and Others

Another famous collection of *exempla* was the *Emblems* of Andrea Alciato (or Alciati).[44] This book founded the genre of emblem books, or *emblemata*, which became extremely favored in the sixteenth and seventeenth centuries.[45] The main difference between an adage and an emblem is that the emblem contained a picture. In fact, Alciato's original concept did not comprise illustrations, but they were introduced in the first edition, and from the beginning each emblem was composed of a title, an engraving, and a text (often poetry). As Alciato's book was published for the first time in 1531, it might have been influenced by Erasmus's *Adages*. The heroic beetle is to be found in emblem number 169, entitled *A minimis quoque timendum* (One ought to fear even the tiniest creatures), whose text reads:

> The beetle wages war and provokes his enemy of his own accord; even though inferior in strength, he surpasses her in cunning. For he hides himself in secret and unknown in the feathers of the eagle, to reach his enemy's nest through the highest stars. By breaking the eggs, he puts an end to the hope of the young growing up: and, having avenged in this way the shame inflicted on him, he departs.[46]

The detail of the beetle hiding in the eagle's feathers is not included in Aesop's fable, and Erasmus makes slight allusion to it. But it is part of a widespread European tale, where the eagle's enemy is sometimes not the beetle but a small bird, the "petty king" (*regulus*), as opposed to the eagle, the "great queen." However "petty" (i.e., small), the little bird, as well as the beetle, acts as a male and "mounts" his big queen—a meaning perceivable also in Erasmus's text. In fact, beetle and eagle are not so different as it would seem at first sight. They may compose a couple, a pair, bound by mysterious but profound ties. Returning to Horapollo, we find such a pair, or even a double pair: one of a beetle and a vulture, and another of a vulture and a beetle, "for the universe seems to them [Egyptians] to be made up of the male and the female."[47] It seems then that Erasmus's story is not merely about a rivalry between the small and the big; it might also refer to the eternal opposition between male and female. This opposition-conjunction reminds us of one of the favorite *topoi* of the Renaissance: *concordia discors*, which Nicolas Cusanus called *coincidentia oppositorum*.[48] Indeed, this coincidence of opposites is also present in the very beetle's character, both the lowest of creatures and almost the only (mortal) one able to reach Jupiter's throne.

In other books of emblems, the beetle is sometimes good, sometimes bad, according to the author's sensibility and perception. For example, in his first volume of emblems (1590), the naturalist and poet Joachim Camerarius (1534–98) evokes together the rose, beetle, and Spanish fly.[49] The latter insect is not a fly but a beetle of a bright metallic green color.[50] It has been used since antiquity to make medicines used for lubricious and lascivious purposes.[51] In this emblem, Camerarius refers to a classical topos according to which beetles hate, or are even killed by, "suave odors," especially roses' perfume.[52] On the contrary, Erasmus explained in the adage *Scarabeus* that—despite its generally bad tastes—"the beetle has a particular love for roses, and covets them above everything."[53] This was drawn from Erasmus's own version of Pliny.[54] But the passage is unclear, and Pliny's modern editors generally understand, in accordance with most of the antique authors, that beetles are killed by roses,[55] an idea insisted on and moralized by Camerarius:

> Destruction of the depraved:
> The Rose is death for the Cantharis.[56] Thus luxury and delights
> Enervate the spirit and terminate the man.

The engraving shows a rose tree, from which a beetle falls upside down. Then follows one page of commentary:

> Cantharides, beetles and other insects of this sort like very much vile and sordid places, where they originate and delight. On the contrary, they faint and perish in suave odors. For this reason, beetles and cantharides getting into roses are told to collapse and die. In the same way, depraved and voluptuous men ruin not only their bodies, but their spirits and souls.

In his third volume, Camerarius came back to the subject, this time comparing the beetle to the bee:[57]

> The one's salvation, the other's destruction:
> As Rose is death for you, O Scarab, it is delight for you, O Bee.
> Virtue is joy for the good, and foe to the bad.

In a later collection of emblems, another author comes back to the heroic and virtuous beetle.[58] The engraving depicts the daring beetle flying up to Jupiter, who floats on a cloud cushion and holds his dear eagle close. The title, *Animus nobilitat* (Spirit makes noble), is accompanied by eight verses that contrast body and spirit, earth and sky, and, according to the beetle's model, exhort men to escape terrestrial heaviness. The beetle here symbolizes the highest spirit, as opposed to the basest earthly powers. This is in opposition to Camerarius's opinion. But one cannot avoid thinking of a possible occult, more precisely alchemical meaning of this emblem, because the word "spirit" is very significant there, and Schoonhovius's book was produced at the peak of European alchemy.[59] But the word can refer to Christian Sacred Spirit as well.

From Emblems to Still Lifes: Joris Hoefnagel

In 1576, Rudolf II (1552–1612) was crowned German emperor. He settled in Prague and soon established his reputation as one of the most important protectors ever of all the arts and sciences. Although a Roman Catholic, he was especially interested in occult and hermetic knowledge. But he was first of all a passionate collector. In his palace in Prague he established the most important cabinet of curiosities ever. It contained thousands of works of art (often incorporating or illustrating natural objects, animals, or plants), whether antiques or made for him by an army of artists attached to his court.[60] Especially fond of Dürer, Rudolf sent emissaries to buy every work of his they could find and also commissioned artists able to work in Dürer's style, either copying his works or making originals inspired by him. This was the main cause of the so-called Dürer Renaissance, which took place beginning about 1580. The most important artist of this revival, Joris [Georg] Hoefnagel (1542–1600), was a specialist in miniature painting.[61] But Hoefnagel's most interesting idea was to renew Dürer's iconographic models by adding to them short sentences extracted from the Bible or Erasmus's *Adages,* thus transforming them into a sort of emblem. Hoefnagel did not use the word "emblem," but he styled himself *inventor hieroglyphicus et allegoricus,* which gives a good indication of the symbolic and emblematic character of his works, even if not accompanied by texts.[62] Around 1580 he realized one of his masterpieces: a group of four volumes, each of them containing eighty exquisite watercolors on vellum, and referring to one of the four elements: fire, earth, water, and air. They were presented to the emperor, who rewarded Hoefnagel with the huge sum of four thousand gold crowns. These small but brilliant works of art, depicting a number of insects, were in harmony with Rudolf's tastes and character, fondness for everything of beauty, and imperial melancholy.

Number 6 in the first volume of the collection (fire) is a remarkable copy of Dürer's *Stag Beetle,* with the title *Scarabei umbra* (Beetle shadow).[63] Although lacking the terminal *e* of the plural (*umbrae*), it is easy to recognize here the Erasmian adage alluding to irrational fears. On the opposite page, a longer sentence reads: "The beetle armed with horns generates itself; the man Christ was himself his sole origin."[64] This is an explicit reference to an analogy of Christ and (stag) beetle, both being "self-begotten." But analogy does not mean equivalence: it is of a symbolic, emblematic nature, and the beetle's inauspicious value is impossible to attribute to Christ. In addition, if this resemblance is only apparent, and if—as it seems—the beetle has no divine qualities, by what mysterious power is it able to generate itself? This question may contribute to explaining the subtle uneasiness one feels toward this insect, beyond the fear comparable to that referred to by Erasmus. Hoefnagel's iconographic models were engraved by his son Jacob (1575–1630) in an album of four parts (with frontispiece and twelve plates each) and published by him at the tender age of seventeen (1592).[65] This time, each plate contains one or two sentences that give the album the character of a book of emblems, not without touches of humor. Plate 2.1 includes the stag beetle, again with the caption *Scarabei umbra,* and a second sentence, "Seek no more for the rose which is overblown," also drawn from Erasmus, dealing with a classical topos of the Renaissance about the passing nature of things and beings, as exemplified by roses.[66] Written just below a beetle, the sentence also refers to the supposed love (or hate) the beetle feels for roses.

Another miniature by Joris Hoefnagel, belonging to the same collection and volume, introduces a variant on Dürer's iconographic pattern: the stag beetle's elytra and wings are opened as if the insect was flying.[67] It is here accompanied by a scorpion, and the inscription refers to biting and stinging creatures. The 1592 engraving (plate 1.6) has a different comment: "Neither a male engendered me, nor a female conceived: I am myself the sole author of mine and of my breed."[68] This is again Horapollo's "self-begotten" beetle, with a Christian connotation, added to some obscure and occult meaning, and for this reason—at least it might be supposed—particularly appreciated at Rudolf's court. More precisely, this picture might refer to the phoenix, the fabled Egyptian bird that was burned and reborn from its ashes, which has also been taken in a Christian sense.[69] Indeed, the first volume in this group of four contains representations of creatures belonging to the two categories of *animalia rationalia et insecta,* which clusters, under the "fire" label, both human beings and insects.[70] Men and insects are of the nature of the fire, and the beetle seems, by certain aspects, closer to Christ than to ordinary men. Surprising as it may seem at first sight, this association was supported by the hermetic belief that "the smallest is the same as the greatest, the lowest as the highest," by the *concordia discors* concept, which found its last period of glory in Rudolfian Prague.

In addition to painters, a number of other artists worked for the emperor Rudolf's court, among them goldsmiths, jewelers, and makers of precious objects. For in addition to the two main items of the cabinet of curiosities (natural and artificial objects), a third category was sometimes differentiated: the "marvels," which belong to the *Schatzkammer,* or treasure room. One of the most famous goldsmiths of the time was Wenzel Jamnitzer (1508–85). Although he worked for the emperor for only a few years, at the end of his life, he nevertheless had the opportunity to produce a few artifacts for the court, including his last masterpiece: a fountain that was one of the most famous curiosities in the Prague Castle.[71] This monument, which has unfortunately been destroyed (only a few parts have been kept), was some three and one-half meters tall and made of massive silver with parts in gold. It represented the theme of the four seasons, with the same purpose as the whole *Kammer:* to give a complete description of the world—both perceptible and imperceptible. The seasons were represented by four deities: Flora, Ceres, Bacchus, and Vulcanus, who symbolized the

Wenzel Jamnitzer, *Writing Casket* (c. 1570). Silver. Courtesy of Kunsthistorisches Museum Wien.

four elements as well. As an example of the paradoxical tastes of the court, the god of the fire, Vulcanus, represented the winter (probably due to the fact that the cold can "burn" as severely as flames). As Jamnitzer's works were made of precious metals, most of them have been melted down. Among the few that have survived, there is a writing casket made of silver for Archduke Ferdinand II of Tyrol (1525–95), uncle to the emperor.[72] It is typical of the naturalistic "style rustique," introduced by the Frenchman Bernard Palissy, where nature was represented in every detail without artistic license, sometimes even in the form of casts from natural objects. On the lid of the casket there are ten compartments with life casts of small animals: a locust and a cicada, two shells, two beetles (a stag beetle and a rhinoceros beetle, *Oryctes nasicornis*), a crayfish and a mouse, a toad and two lizards. Garlands of flowers, leaves, and blades of grass enlivened with insects and other small animals decorate the sides of the casket. Although the small animals are placed tidily on the lid—as if in the boxes of a collection of *naturalia*—the central position of the two beetles, in the middle of the lid, gives them a special importance. The rhinoceros beetle figures in Jacob Hoefnagel's album (plate 3.1), with the title "It is not given to everybody to have a nose,"[73] which refers to Erasmus: "In a proverb, 'nose' means judgment."[74] If it alludes to the purpose of the casket, namely, to contain small writing objects (pens, knives, etc.), it was an elegant way to remind the writer that he had to use all his judgment in the text he would be writing. In the same sense, the stag beetle might here refer to another of Erasmus's adages: "More astute than a beetle" (2,142, *Cantharo astutior*). The two beetles might thus refer to some intellectual and mental conditions necessary to a writer before he takes up his pen. More subtly, applying here again the *concordia discors* framework, one notices that the two beetles have been molded with their wings and elytra closed. But they can open them and fly. For the important thing is not to fasten words on paper or another material but to be able to have them fly in the sky, like spirits, "for the letter killeth but the spirit giveth life."[75]

From Still Lifes to Entomology

Joris Hoefnagel had a strong influence on some painters in the so-called Prague school, and he is likely to have played a major role in the creation of the genre known today as the still life. Already some of his works appear as small still lifes, arranging together flowers and insects, with a religious or moral (or emblematic) meaning. But the first authentic canvas of this genre is generally acknowledged to have been painted in 1603 by Roelandt Savery.[76] It is probably due to Joris Hoefnagel's influence that Savery, a painter of the Prague school, introduced insects, and especially beetles, into his still lifes. After this first impulse, the genre—which sometimes merges with so-called vanity[77]— spread across Germany, Holland, and especially Flanders. During the whole seventeenth century, it was one of the genres produced by Protestant artists who no longer recognized saints and did not accept representations of God, Christ, or the Sacred Spirit.[78] Among the many artists who have produced these paintings and included insects in them, some have remembered Hoefnagel's iconographic models of the stag beetle, and, before him, Albrecht Dürer's. The German painter Georg Flegel has often figured the stag beetle, and other beetles as well, in oil paintings and in watercolors, obviously with both Christian and melancholic meanings, which somehow give his still lifes the character of vanities.[79] The Dutch Jacob Marrell and Peter Binoit, both Flegel's pupils, must also be cited, together with Jan Brueghel the Elder, Otto Marseus Van Schrieck, Marrell's pupils Abraham Mignon and Maria Sibylla Merian, as well as more recent masters, like Verbrugghen the Younger and Rachel Ruysch. In still lifes, the beetle returns to a marginal position. But when looking at a glorious flower bouquet, or a richly served table, we notice a crawling beetle, both surreptitious and obvious (especially in the best paintings), we immediately think about the transient status of creatures, including men, which are nothing more than "bubbles" compared with God,[80] but we also think of Christ, who is supposed to redeem and save at least some of these creatures.

In addition to gallery paintings in oil, most of these artists also produced watercolors destined for portfolios of the cabinets of curiosities. Some of these cabinets specialized in natural objects and became the first natural history museums. They also gave birth to the first natural history monographs, with the same purpose: ordering the world's data.[81] The first major entomological monograph that may be called scientific is that of Ulisse Aldrovandi, *De animalibus insectis libri septem* (Bologne, 1602).[82] The stag beetle is illustrated on page 451, but the engraving seems not to be derived from Dürer's model. In addition to Aristotle and Pliny, Aldrovandi quoted heavily from Erasmus. The second large treatise of entomology, published in London in 1634 under the title *Insectorum sive minimorum animalium theatrum*, is attributed to the physician Thomas Mouffet (who had been dead since 1604). It has a long and complicated story, combining data gathered by the Swiss Gesner, the British Wotton and Penny, and Mouffet himself in the 1590s, all of that being assembled and published by the French-born physician Sir Théodore de Mayerne.[83] An English translation was published in 1658.[84] Even more than in Aldrovandi's book, Mayerne depends heavily on Erasmus and the emblematic books. He insists on the beetle's black color and noise, as well as its base habits, although the author adds some moralizing considerations directly drawn and interpreted from Erasmus:

> When we see the beetle, though in the dung, alwaies clean, and his shell alwaies neat; compare him with men polluted and infected with stews and bawdy houses, and I shall ask which of the two is most cleanly? And I think it had its name *kantharos* a Beetle from *katharos* pure and clean.[85]

But, in fact, they are not always so pure:

> Of all plants they cannot away with Rose trees, and they hate them as the destruction of their kinde; for they dye by the smell of them but on the contrary they take great pleasure in stinking and beastly places.[86]

Here Mouffet refers to the topos on the beetle's supposed aversion to roses, or rather on the danger the roses are supposed to pose for beetles, as we have seen. This is in accordance with his time's science, which had not yet been freed from obsolete knowledges of ancient times.

Around 1650 the Jesuit Athanasius Kircher (1602–80) made an attempt to decipher Egyptian hieroglyphics.[87] While correctly supposing that the language was related to Coptic, he nonetheless failed in his interpretations of the signs.[88] Rather, he related the beetle hieroglyphic to what was familiar: Saint Ambrose's interpretation of the scarab as Christ:

> What does the beetle's body mean, if not the Unique Son whom the Father has established as principle, rest, and end of everything, by whom everything is done, and without whom nothing is done? . . . Let those, who get nauseous by this comparison of God to the vilest, basest, most horrible and most stinking of all beings, remember that this merely expresses the human condition's baseness, which God's infinite majesty has accepted to dress.[89]

He accompanied this text with an engraving of a beetle showing the word "love" (Greek *philo*, which he wrote *phylo*). At this point, the buckle is buckled. The sacredness of the beetle is permanently circumscribed by what the French linguist Émile Benveniste has termed the positive and negative values of holiness.[90] The first conveys a notion of "something impregnated by divine presence"; the other suggests "something forbidden to man's contact," and both are subsumed, Benveniste said, in the Latin word *sacer* (contrary to *sanctus*, which conveys only the favorable meaning). Dürer's Christian/pagan beetle, filtered through Erasmus and the emblematists, persists as "vile," "base," "most horrible," and yet full of grace. Shakespeare captures these diverse discourses in his plays: a reference to Erasmian *Scarabeus* is evident in *Cymbeline* (3.3.19–21)—"And often to our comfort shall we find / The sharded beetle in a safer hold / than is the full-wing'd eagle"—and in *A Midsummer Night's Dream* (2.2.20–23), we find the beetle in rather bad company:

Weaving spiders, come not here;
Hence, you long-legg'd spinners, hence.
Beetles black, approach not near;
Worm nor snail do no offence.

The Tempest suggests their occult potency when Caliban invokes his mother to threaten his master, Prospero: "all the charms / Of Sycorax, toads, beetles, bats, light on you" (1.2.339–40). The beetle, then, which appears both saint and sullied, familiar and dangerous, seems an authentic—even if marginal—résumé of sacredness. In 1758, when the first taxonomist, Carolus Linnaeus, named the most illustrious of the many species of beetles *Scarabaeus sacer* (a name it has maintained), he thus returned not only to the religion of the ancient Egyptians but to all the discordant harmonies of the creature's symbolic past.

NOTES

Thanks to Roy Rosenstein, who very much improved the English of this chapter, and to Eric Brown, who made important suggestions.

    1. Jean Seznec, *The Survival of the Pagan Gods: The Mythological Tradition and Its Place in Renaissance Humanism and Art* (original French edition, 1940; reprint, Paris: Flammarion, 1993; New York: Pantheon Books–Bollingen, 1953).

2. "Immo fortasse plusculo fructu legetur fabula poetica cum allegoria, quam narratio sacrorum librorum, si consistas in cortice." Erasmus, *Enchiridion militis christiani*, quoted in Seznec, *Survival of the Pagan Gods* (1993), 118.

3. The word *ainos*, which seems the closest to "fable," was no longer used in classical times. Daniel Loayza, introduction to his edition of *Aesop* (Paris: GF-Flammarion, 1995), 20.

4. See Laura Gibbs, trans., *Aesop's Fables, a New Translation* (New York: Oxford University Press, 2002).

5. Malcolm Davies and Jeyaraney Kathirithamby, *Greek Insects* (New York: Oxford University Press, 1986), 1–16.

6. See, for example, Claude Brémond, Jacques Le Goff, and Jean-Claude Schmitt, *L'exemplum* (Turnhout: Brepols, 1982), fasc. 40 in *Typologie des sources du moyen âge occidental*.

7. Jean-Marc Chatelain, *Livres d'emblèmes et de devises: Une anthologie (1531–1735)* (Paris: Klincksieck, 1993).

8. Cf. Yves Cambefort, *Le scarabée et les dieux* (Paris: Boubée, 2006).

9. See Mary Douglas, *Purity and Danger: An Analysis of the Concepts of Pollution and Taboo* (1966; Ark Paperbacks, 1985).

10. See Ilkka Hanski and Yves Cambefort, eds., *Dung Beetle Ecology* (Princeton, N.J.: Princeton University Press, 1991).

11. See Rudolf Otto, *The Idea of the Holy* (Oxford: Oxford University Press, 1968).

12. George R. Goldner (with the assistance of Lee Hendrix and Gloria Williams), *European Drawings 1: Catalogue of the Collections* (Malibu: J. Paul Getty Museum, 1988), plate 4, 287–90.

13. Fritz Koreny, *Albrecht Dürer and the Animal and Plant Studies of the Renaissance* (Boston: Little, Brown, 1988), esp. 112–27.

14. Berlin State Museum. Colin Eisler, *Dürer's Animals* (Washington: Smithsonian Institution Press, 1991), 124 and fig. 5.19.

15. National Library, Florence. Giorgio Taroni, *Il cervo volante* (Milan: Electa, 1998), 113.

16. Cologne Cathedral. Koreny, *Albrecht Dürer*, 112–13.

17. State of Bavaria Collection, Munich. Eisler, *Dürer's Animals*, 120, fig. 5.1.

18. Michael Camille, *Image on the Edge: The Margins of Medieval Art* (Cambridge: Harvard University Press, 1992). See also Thomas DaCosta Kaufmann, "The Sanctification of Nature," in *The Mastery of Nature: Aspects of Art, Science, and Humanism in the Renaissance* (Princeton: Princeton University Press, 1993), 11–48.

19. Koreny, *Albrecht Dürer*, 113; Hans Biedermann, *Dictionary of Symbolism: Cultural Icons and the Meanings behind Them* (New York: Meridian Books, 1994).

20. Copper engraving of 1500/1503, with a complete stag; Paumgartner altarpiece (Munich Alte Pinakothek), c. 1498/1504, with only stag's head on a banner.

21. National Library, Vienna. Eisler, *Dürer's Animals*, 137 and fig. 5.61.

22. George Boas, *The Hieroglyphics of Horapollo*, with a foreword by Anthony Grafton (1950; Princeton: Princeton University Press–Bollingen, 1993), 48–49.

23. This is different from Aristotle's idea of insects born spontaneously from larvae, themselves issued from rotting materials (Aristotle, *History of Animals*, 758a–759a). There is no original material or larva in the cases of both the phoenix and Christ. Later on, a larval stage was introduced in the story of the phoenix. Yves Cambefort, "Le scarabée et le phénix," *Mémoires de la Société Royale Belge d'Entomologie* 35 (1992): 45–53.

24. Plutarch, *Isis and Osiris* (*Moralia* 28), sec. 10 and 74. The apparent movement of the sun from west to east was taken from, and explained in, Plato's *Timaeus*, sec. 38d (comments in Christian Froidefond's edition of *Isis and Osiris* [Paris: Les Belles Lettres, 1988], 317–18; and Albert Rivaud's edition of *Timaeus*, [Paris: Les Belles Lettres, 1925], 55–56).

25. In 1505 there had already been a number of editions of Saint Ambrose, including his complete works (*Opera omnia*), printed in Basel in 1492, reprinted in 1500. The *Treatise on Saint Luke's Gospel* was printed as early as 1476.

26. Saint Ambroise de Milan, *Traité sur l'évangile de Saint Luc*, ed. and trans. Dom G. Tissot (Paris: Cerf, 1976), 2:193–94 (translation mine). The worm of this text comes from Psalm 22:6, "But I *am* a worm, and no man," and the scarab from Habakkuk 2:11 in the Greek Bible (*Septuaginta*); the poor exalted from his dunghill is an allusion both to Psalms 113:7 and Job's book. See F. J. Dölger, "Christus im Bilde des Skarabäus: Der Text *Scarabaeus de ligno* in Habakuk 2, 11 nach der Auslegung von Ambrosius und Hieronymus," *Antike und Christentum: Kultur- und Religionsgeschichtliche Studien* 2 (1930): 230–40.

27. Mann Phillips, *The "Adages" of Erasmus: A Study with Translations* (Cambridge: Cambridge University Press, 1964).

28. Jean-Claude Margolin, *Érasme précepteur de l'Europe* (Paris: Julliard, 1995).

29. After Erasmus's death, the collection was reprinted more than forty times (some editions affected by censorship); it was also published in shorter versions (epitomes) as well, of which at least sixty-two were published between 1521 and 1759. Modern edition: *Opera omnia Desiderii Erasmi Roterodami, Ordo secundus*, 7 vols. (out of eight) (Amsterdam: North Holland, 1981–99).

30. Gibbs, *Aesop's Fables*, 79–80.

31. *Opera omnia*, 6:395–424. English translation in Mann Phillips, 229–63; French translation with notes by Jean-Claude Margolin in *Érasme*, collection "Bouquins," (Paris: Robert Laffont, 1992), 155–99.

32. Jean Céard, "La censure tridentine et l'édition florentine des *Adages* d'Érasme," in *Actes du Colloque international Érasme, Tours, 1986* (Geneva: Droz, 1990), 337–50.

33. Aristophanes made use of Aesop's fable, to which he added Mount Etna for historical reasons (see also Davies and Kathirithamby, *Greek Insects*, 86–87).

34. Sec. 10, 74.

35. See Jean-Henri Fabre, *Souvenirs entomologiques*, First and Fifth Series (Paris, 1879 and 1897); English translation by Alexander Teixeira de Mattos, *The Sacred Beetle and Others* (New York, 1918).

36. Mann Phillips, 249.

37. Preface to the *Adages* (editions of 1515, 1517, 1520, and 1523), in *The Correspondence of Erasmus, 2, Letters 142 to 297*, trans. R. A. B. Mynors and D. F. S. Thomson (Toronto: University of Toronto Press, 1975), 242.

38. Mann Phillips, 257. Spenser might have remembered this passage when he described the fly prince Clarion's arming in his *Muiopotmos* (1590), line 54 and following (Eric Brown's suggestion). In fact, beetles and other insects are often referred to as "flies" in some European languages.

39. Erasmus was very concerned by war in general, and by crimes and offenses committed in war by princes against peoples. See Jean-Claude Margolin, ed., *Guerre et paix dans la pensée d'Érasme* (Paris: Aubier Montaigne, 1973).

40. Mann Phillips, 262–63 (modified).

41. Ibid., 247, 248, 252, 263 (modified).

42. *Opera omnia*, 5:131, note of the volume editors F. Heinimann and E. Kienzle.

43. *Timor de re non timenda*: Raymond Klibansky, Erwin Panofsky, and Fritz Saxl, *Saturn and Melancholy: Studies in the History of Natural Philosophy, Religion, and Art* (London: Thomas Nelson and Sons, 1964), 83.

44. There were about seventy editions of this work during the sixteenth century. Modern facsimile of the edition of Lyons: Mathias Bonhomme, 1551, in André Alciat, *Les emblèmes* (Paris: Klincksieck, 1997).

45. The anthology of Chatelain, *Livres d'emblèmes*, mentions ninety titles.

46. From the online translation of the Memorial University of Newfoundland (modified) at http://www.mun.ca/alciato/e169.html; Latin text and illustration from the Lyons 1551 edition in Alciat, *Les emblèmes*, 182.

47. Boas, *The Hieroglyphics of Horapollo*, 52.

48. See, for example, Jean-Claude Margolin, "Sur un paradoxe bien tempéré de la Renaissance: *Concordia discors*," *Medioevo e Umanesimo* 84 (1993): 405–32.

49. *Symbolorum et emblematum ex re herbaria desumtorum centuria una, a Ioachimo Camerario, medico Norimberg.* (Nuremberg, 1590), 56–57, emblem XLVI, *Turpibus exitium*.

50. At least in the European species *Lytta vesicatoria* L. (Meloidae).

51. P. V. Taberner, *Aphrodisiacs: The Science and the Myth* (London: Croom Helm, 1985).

52. Davies and Kathirithamby, *Greek Insects*, 85, quoting Aristotle, Aelian, Theophrastus, Plutarch, et cetera.

53. Mann Phillips, 251.

54. Pliny, book 11 of *Natural History* (Basel: Froben, 1549), 216, a reprint of Erasmus's edition: "Omnia [insecta] olei aspersu necantur. Vultures unguento qui fugantur, alios appetunt odores: scarabei rosam."

55. For example, in H. Rackham's version in *Pliny: Natural History* (Cambridge: Harvard University Press–Loeb Classical Library, 1967), 3:608: "Omnia [insecta] olei aspersu necantur, vultures unguento (qui fugat alios appetunt odorem), scarabaei rosa."

56. The word *cantharis* (plural *cantharides*) is a Latin version of the Greek *kantharis*, a feminine variant of *kantharos*, often used for Spanish fly (French *cantharide*).

57. *Symbolorum et emblematum ex volatilibus et insectis desumtorum centuria tertia* (1596), emblem XCII, *Uni salus, alteri pernicies.*

58. *Emblemata Florentii Schoonhovii I. C. Goudani, partim moralia, partim etiam civilia* (Goudae: Andreas Burier, 1618), emblem LVI.

59. See, for example, Alexander Roob, *The Hermetic Museum: Alchemy and Mysticism* (Los Angeles: Taschen America, 1997).

60. See, for example, Thomas DaCosta Kaufmann, *The School of Prague: Painting at the Court of Rudolf II* (Chicago: University of Chicago Press, 1988); and Kaufmann, *The Mastery of Nature.*

61. See Kaufmann, *The School of Prague;* Lee Hendrix and Thea Vignau-Wilberg, eds., *Mira calligraphiae monumenta, Inscribed by Georg Bocskay and Illuminated by Joris Hoefnagel* (Malibu: J. Paul Getty Museum, 1992); Thea Vignau-Wilberg, *Archetypa studiaque patris Georgii Hoefnagelii, 1592: Nature, Poetry, and Science in Art around 1600* (Munich: Staatliche Graphische Sammlung, 1994).

62. Thea A. G. Wilberg Vignau-Schuurman, *Die emblematischen Elemente im Werke Joris Hofnagels* (Leiden: Universitaire Pers, 1969).

63. National Gallery, Washington. Koreny, *Albrecht Dürer,* 124–25.

64. "Cornubus armatus generat se cantharus ipsum Christus homo suimet, solus origo fuit."

65. The four parts of the album do not correspond to the four volumes presented to the emperor (for a facsimile of, and comments on, the album, see Thea Vignau-Wilberg, *Archetypa studiaque*).

66. *Rosam quae praeterierit ne quaeras iterum* (adage 1,540), inspired by the ode *De rosis nascentibus* of the Latin poet Ausonius.

67. Berlin State Museum, extracted in the seventeenth century from the collection now in Washington (Koreny, *Albrecht Dürer,* 126–27).

68. "Me neque mas gignit, neque fœmina concipit: autor ipse mei solus seminiumque mihi."

69. See Cambefort, "Le scarabée et le phénix."

70. The other sections were (2) *Animalia Quadrupedia et Reptilia (Terra);* (3) *Animalia Aquatilia et Cochliata (Aqua);* and (4) *Animalia Volatilia et Amphibia (Aer).*

71. Gerhard Bott, ed., *Wenzel Jamnitzer und die Nürnberger Goldschmiedekunst, 1500–1700* (Munich: Klinckhardt und Biermann, 1985), 231–35.

72. Now in the Vienna Museum. Bott, *Wenzel Jamnitzer,* 226–27.

73. *Non omnibus datum habere nasum.* The album was published after Jamnitzer's death, but he might have known Joris Hoefnagel's model of the rhinoceros beetle (figured, for example, in Hendrix and Vignau-Wilberg, *Mira calligraphiae monumenta,* 138–39).

74. "Denique nasus ipse in proverbium abiit pro judicio" (adage 581, *Odorari*).

75. 2 Corinthians 3:6 (Authorized King James Version).

76. Kaufmann, *L'École de Prague*, 268–69; Jan Briels, *Peintres flamands au berceau du Siècle d'Or hollandais, 1585–1630* (Anvers: Fonds Mercator, 1997), 248–53, 375–80.

77. Alain Tapié, Jean-Marie Dautel, and Philippe Rouillard, eds., *Les vanités dans la peinture au XVIIe siècle: Méditations sur la richesse, le dénuement et la rédemption* (Caen: Musée des Beaux-Arts, 1990).

78. Charles Sterling, *Still Life Painting from Antiquity to the Twentieth Century* (New York: Harper and Row, 1981); Claus Grimm, *Natures mortes flamandes, hollandaises et allemandes aux XVIIe et XVIIIe siècles* (Paris: Herscher, 1992); Norbert Schneider, *Still Life* (New York: Taschen, 1994).

79. Kurt Wettengl, *Georg Flegel, 1566–1638: Stilleben* (1993; Ostfildern: Gerd Hatje, 1999). See also Kurt Wettengl, *Maria Sibylla Merian, Artist and Naturalist, 1647–1717* (Ostfildern: Gerd Hatje, 1998).

80. *Homo bulla* (adage 1,248).

81. Michel Foucault, *Les mots et les choses* (Paris: Gallimard, 1966).

82. See, among others, Adalgisa Lugli, *Naturalia et mirabilia: Les cabinets de curiosités en Europe* (Italian ed., 1983; Paris: Adam Biro, 1998); and Lorraine Daston and Katharine Park, *Wonders and the Order of Nature, 1150–1750* (New York: Zone Books, 1998).

83. Michael A. Salmon, *The Aurelian Legacy: British Butterflies and Their Collectors* (Colchester: Harley Books, 2000), 95–98.

84. *The Theater of Insects: or, lesser living creatures, as bees, flies, caterpillars, spiders, worms, &c. a most elaborate work* (London, 1658; reprint, New York: Da Capo Press, 1967).

85. Ibid., 1011.

86. Ibid., 1005.

87. Joscelyn Godwin, *Athanasius Kircher: A Renaissance Man and the Quest for Lost Knowledge* (London: Thames and Hudson, 1979).

88. Athanasius Kircher, *Prodromus coptus sive aegyptiacus* (Rome: Typis Sacrae Congregationis de Propagatione Fidei, 1636).

89. Kircher, 239 (translation mine).

90. Émile Benveniste, *Le vocabulaire des institutions européennes. 2. Pouvoir, droit, religion* (Paris: Éditions de Minuit, 1969), 179–207.

11

Made without Hands

The Representation of Labor in Early Modern Silkworm and Beekeeping Manuals

ERIKA MAE OLBRICHT

In "The Preface to the Reader" of his beekeeping manual, *The Feminine Monarchie* (1609), Charles Butler acknowledges England's nascent involvement in the silkworm industry. He writes that "although the delicat Silk-worme . . . is now setting foot in this land," she must "yeelde the precedence to the laborious Bee, as to hir elder sister; which as in time, so in vertue is before her."[1] Butler's sense of the competing insects and their products is an important logic through which to gauge the early seventeenth century's printed material treating sericulture and apiculture. The distinction Butler makes lies in the use and value of the insects' products as well as between the kinds of work they do to create their product. According to Butler, the medicinal and culinary uses of honey and wax practically—but also morally—outweigh the vanity of silk: "For the fruite of the Silke-worme serveth onlie to cover the bodie; but the fruite of the Bee to nourish and cure it: that is to bee applied outwardly, this to be invvardly received: that for comlinesse and conveniency, this for health & necessitie" (a2r). In this case, however, Butler's reservation also has to do with the chronology of the two trades and their cultural efficacy: he recognizes that sericulture brought with it not just a competing insect but—both literally and representationally—a competing mode of industry, an early capitalism glimmering with promises of the consumption of goods for mere "comlinesse and conveniency."

Linda Levy Peck notes that in the first decade of the seventeenth century, the initiation of an English silk industry was motivated by "a clamor for luxury goods" and a recognition that satiating the current fashion taste for

silk depended on imports from the Continent.[2] Various economic strategies were enforced, from blocking imported silk from the Continent to
royal encouragement for the domestic industry, including James I's offer
of subsidized mulberry seeds and saplings for planting and providing the
worms' food, announced in his November 16, 1609, letter to the "Lords
Liefetenants of the seuerall Shieres of England" and printed as a preface to
an early sericulture manual. The potential for the silk industry to revolu-
tionize the nation's economy was expressed by John Bonoeil (the keeper of
the king's silkworms), who wrote two sericulture manuals in the 1620s:
"For by this meanes great store of Clothes may be vented there, multitudes
of poore set on worke, and England inriched, and made in time the Maga-
zin for silkes."[3] Bonoeil's belief in silk's wide-reaching ameliorative powers
would be reiterated over and over in his own manuals, as well as in other
seventeenth-century sericulture writing, where silk is considered a "reall-
royall-solid-rich-staple commodity."[4]

On the other hand, as represented in beekeeping manuals, honey and
wax were not the profit makers that silk was considered to be. For most
seventeenth-century apiculturalists, these products were still part of a
localized economy, one more closely tied to rural subsistence production
and consumption, not one that sought to inveigle the international import
and export trade.[5] Joyce Oldham Appleby has suggested that in early modern England, while the market economy increasingly provided "new net-
works of buyers and sellers [that] replaced the isolated economies of local
consumption,"[6] food production nevertheless stood conceptually outside
the commercial market and was seen as a "principally social rather than
economic" activity.[7] Butler writes that he hopes the information in his beekeeping manual will be of use "to my neighbours and country-men, which
I haue since found so beneficiall to my selfe: so that the Reader may now
freely reape the fruit of that, which the Author hath deerely sowen vnto him"
(A4r). While not every beekeeping manualist places himself in the position
of fatherly caretaker, Butler's tone toward his readers clearly presumes that
they will benefit in ways other than "profit."

Sericultural and apicultural manuals themselves manifest a distinction
among forms of economy signaled by competing models of labor; they
establish the terms on which the efficacy of their industry and viability of
their products are judged. Therefore they are an important record of the
discourse surrounding these two industries. Several authors hoped to spur

on English silk production as a new economic project in the first part of the seventeenth century by providing instruction for keeping silkworms, growing mulberry trees, and processing the silk cocoons (called "cods" or "bottoms" in the manuals) from the insects. In 1599 Thomas Moffet published a long poem titled *The Silkwormes and their Flies*, which provides more legendary and poetical knowledge than practical information about raising silkworms. However, it lauds sericulture and encourages the production of English silk. In 1607 Nicholas Geffe translated into English the first and most substantial sericulture manual, *The Perfect Use of Silk-wormes, and their benefit*, from Olivier de Serres's French original, which was followed quickly by William Stallenge's *Instructions for the Increasing of Mulberrie Trees*, where James I's 1609 letter appears.[8] In 1622 James took up the pen again, this time addressing the Earl of Southampton in the colony of Virginia to urge silkworm raising as a more desirable alternative to tobacco, which, as James famously wrote, "besides much unnecessary expence, brings with it many disorders and inconueniences"[9]—an objection he registered in other texts as well.[10] The letter appeared as the preface to Bonoeil's second sericulture manual, titled *His Majesties' Gracious Letter to the Earle of South-hampton*, which was Bonoeil's follow-up to his 1620 sericulture manual, *Obseruations to be Followed, for the making of fit roomes, to keep silkwormes in*. The 1650s saw another spurt in silkworm manuals, this time focused on the industry's possibilities in the colonies. Edward Williams's *Virginia's Discovery of Silkworms* (1650) showcased the colony's climate and resources for successful raw silk production. Samuel Hartlib also concluded that the colonies were the best place to raise silkworms, and his curiously titled *A Rare and New Discovery . . . found out by a young lady in England* (1652) was reprinted in 1655 along with the text of Stallenge's *Instructions* to make up part of Hartlib's *The Reformed Virginian Silkworm*. At the heart of each of these manuals is a recognition of how much money the nation stood to gain from a domestic silk industry, even one that only provided raw materials to the Continent.

While national commercial profit may not have been the motivating factor of beekeeping manuals, their authors still desired their readers to be able to "profit" from the skillful production of honey and wax, though in a much broader sense of "profit." As the numerous printings of beekeeping manuals show, both by the fact of their existence and because their prefaces tell us so, there were many people keeping bees in order to produce honey and wax for personal or familial use in medicinal and culinary recipes, of which the manuals contain examples. The two earliest of these English manuals, Edmund Southerne's *A treatise concerning the right use and ordering of Bees* (1593) and the first edition of Butler's *The Feminine Monarchie* (1609), both exhorted their readers to pay the tithe of their honey and wax honestly—a curious detail that implies that beekeepers, small though their contributions may be, were nevertheless enmeshed in the local economy of tithe payments. Among the manualists helping beekeepers to succeed in their craft in the early seventeenth century, Butler was the best known and the most highly praised by both contemporary and subsequent apiculturalists for his practical skills and also his scientific observation, in particular for his claim printed in English for the first time that the "king" bee is actually female (thus Butler's controversial book title). His manual was printed in a second edition in 1623, again in 1634 with a dedication to Queen Henrietta Maria, in Latin in 1673 and 1682, and, though significantly altered, was translated into English from the Latin in 1704. It remained the standard beekeeping manual for almost two hundred years from its first printing. John Levett's *Ordering of Bees* (1634) and Richard Remnant's *A Discourse or Historie of Bees* (1637) both provide instructions on beekeeping and its uses. Levett reminds his readers of the numerous uses of bee products, which are perhaps easy for twenty-first-century readers to forget: "And although that hony and wax may seeme to be matters of small estimation in the eyes of many, yet to the poore Countryman, good Housholder, well traded Merchant, expert Apothecary, and lerned xperienced Physitian and Chirurgian, they are known to bee commodities well worth the looking after."[11] In fact, so important is the skill of beekeeping that instructions for the care of bees and production of honey and wax appear in practically every gardening and husbandry manual in the early modern period—even if only a page or two are dedicated to it.

Both sericulture and apiculture manuals are directed at increasing the keeper's ability and skill in profiting by the labor of his insects. They have in common the need to successfully control and maintain a population of insects that create raw goods that humans then process. In the manuals, therefore, one finds serious consideration of what type of society the insects organize (particularly so for bees), and in what ways they are like humans, or how humans should be like them. However, in terms of the labor, production, and economic effect theorized in their manuals, the two industries appear quite different. Each presumes a different relationship between the insects and their keepers, and each targets a different type of audience, at least insofar as that audience is rhetorically addressed in the manuals: while silkworm manuals presume that the owner hires the workers, beekeeping manuals presume that the reader is also the keeper and laborer. The effect sees a parallel between the worker and the insect in apiculture, but sericulturalists tend to align the worm with the upper-class consumer of its goods. This essay considers not the strict references that serve to *analogize* human and insect life (though numerous examples could be given in beekeeping manuals, particularly Butler's), but rather how the organization of the insects into an *economy* illustrates anxieties about human labor and its economic proficiency.

It may seem a conceptual imposition on early modern entomological manuals to read them for how their insect is like a human. And yet such a trope is central in poetic, political, and even instructional representations of the insects. The most clearly stated of these is Butler's often-quoted pronouncement that "bees abhorre as well polyarchie, as anarchie, God hauing shewed in them vnto men an expresse patterne of a perfect monarchie, the most natural & absolute forme of government" (A3r). In addition to their role as political model, bees are also considered a pattern for human industry, since they are awake early and stay constantly busy through the day, collecting honey (as early modern apiculturalists believed) and bringing it back to be stored in their perfectly constructed wax houses. Echoing their political efficacy, Butler writes that bees "in their labor and order at home and abroad . . . are so admirable, that they may be a patterne vnto men" (A1v). Their qualities and virtues are extolled and the keeper admonished to follow their example of "an orderly Common-wealth, consisting of an amiable, loving and gentle Queene, and of proper, comely, able, attentive and diligent guard and commanders, with loyall and laborious, provident and valorous Commons: all worthy admiration and serious observation."[12] In their industriousness, social organization, and political responsibility, bees have much to teach their keepers through "serious observation."

Likewise, Moffet's *Silkwormes* also establishes a relationship between humans and silkworms. While not a manual per se, Moffet's poem works to reclaim the somewhat negative cultural understanding of worms as insects: they devour good and useful plants in the same way that they devour human corpses—a trope that some manuals rely on to praise the longevity of the manual long after the author has been devoured by the worms he writes about. Moffet establishes that the worms' fate is linked with that of humans, in part because the fall of humans caused the worms' particular diet: "Then [i.e., after the Fall] wormes in common fed with vs, and tore / Our trees, our fruits, yea eu'n our selues therefore."[13] Moffet's trope of the worm who consumes is also the other manuals' characterization of the worm, whether implied or explicit.[14] Only occasionally are silkworms to be the model of human behavior, for example, in their chastity (the same is true of bees).[15] He writes that silkworms "onely keepe themselues to one, / Who being dead, another chuse they none" (28), concluding clearly that the insects model this behavior for us: "let little flies teach great men to be iust, / And not to yeeld braue mindes a prey to lust" (33).

While bees are portrayed as serious laborers rarely dissuaded from their work, silkworms are shown to be luxuriant consumers set up in their private homes, waited on by their keepers, who must bring them their food. Indeed, the labor of the industry falls to the keepers of the worms rather than to the insects—a marked difference from the industrious bees. Much work goes into the feeding of the worms, including the labor of planting a new species of tree in England and the gathering of thousands of mulberry leaves, not to mention the actual time-intensive processing of the silk cods. Sericulture manuals therefore offer a much different model of industry than beekeeping manuals, because the silkworm's labor is figured as consumption of human labor (particularly the gathering of leaves) before it finally spins its cod or bottom that human workers then process. The labor of the silkworm and the labor of the keeper are therefore each implicated in the other. In fact, Nicholas Geffe provides a particularly fascinating example of the silkworm's potential for consumption. In his silkworm manual, he illustrates his own experience raising worms:

These seauen yeeres together my selfe haue kept of the seede of Silk-wormes, and the Wormes themselues, where they haue multiplied so farre forth, that their encrease hath so much surpast the meanes of feeding them, that *the leaues of a million of trees would not haue satiated the Wormes I might haue nourished;* hauing this same yeere been constrained to burne infinit numbers of the egges vnhatched, & to bury millions of new hatcht ones, putting them rather to the massacre in their first beginning, then to suffer them to languish and pine hereafter with miserable famishment.[16]

This image of a horrifying ravishment of "the leaues of a million of trees" is an image of insatiability and rampant consumption rather than productivity. Such reminders of the destructive power of worms seem to offset the labor of the humans to ensure the silkworm's productivity. Images included in sericulture manuals illustrate this human and insect division of labor: while the worms are shown eating leaves, there is a detailed and instructive image of a man and woman boiling and spinning the cods.

Generally speaking, the manuals spend more time discussing soil preparation, planting, and care of the trees, including descriptions of extensive pruning and dressing, than they do the care of the actual insect itself, which shows the extent to which this was a labor-intensive industry that had to be started from scratch in England. The quantity of leaves needed necessitates the planting of more and more trees, as noted in *Observations to be Followed* (1620), attributed to John Bonoeil. He advises that

> for one that is a good husband to reape good profit, they prescribe the quantity of two or three thousand trees; for with a lesse number a man that will bee a master of this worke, ought not to enterprise this businesse; for here is no question of good profit which must grow out of a sufficient number of trees. Therefore it is necessary to imply this worke heere in a great volume, or else the play will hardly be worth the candle. . . . If you minde to be very rich indeed in this commodity, you must not stay at that number of trees aboue-named, but alwayes still augement your Mulbery yard, adding thereto certaine hundreds of trees yeerly.[17]

This passage shows not only how much land the keeper needs to have at his disposal (an indication of his wealth) but also the labor that goes into preparing the soil for planting and subsequent care of the trees, including keeping them pruned and dressed, in addition to stripping the leaves for the worms. Likewise, Edward Williams suggests in *Virginia's Discovery of Silkworms* that "it will bee absolutely necessary for our Master of the silkeworm, to have such a proportionable number of trees, that the halfe may alternately repose unpluckt every second year."[18] Where Bonoeil advises an already extensive two to three thousand trees, Williams suggests that a keeper would need to double that figure to let half of the trees regenerate every year.

But the need for all this labor created opportunities as well. A common theme in the sericulture manuals—indeed, in seventeenth-century

By this figure is shewed the order, to ranke the tables on the skaffolde, & to lay the leaues on, to feed the Wormes there.

Images from *Geffe's Perfect use of Silke-Wormes*, 445.c.25(2), 1607. Reproduced with permission of the British Library.

By this figure is shewed the fashion of the Engine, how to winde off the silke from the cods, with the furnaces and cauldrens for that purpose.

economic policy—is an insistence that "cottage" industries like the silk industry will solve the country's poverty problems. Joan Thirsk, in *Economic
Policy and Projects*, treats such schemes dating from the early seventeenth
century. She writes that domestic production of luxury goods "did not at
the outset provide full-time jobs, but offered a by-employment, especially
in rural areas where they afforded an additional source of cash to supplement what people got from their land and rights of common. But that extra
bit of cash could turn a mere pittance into a tolerable living. . . . A new project in a village could thus transform a miserable collection of beggarly poor
into a self-respecting community."[19] While raw silk production was never
successful in England,[20] silk weaving and fabric making did indeed have a
place in London's history, particularly in the Spitalfields district, where
Huguenot silk weavers found refuge from their native France and brought
their skill in silk with them. Indeed, the promise of an economic project
such as a new silkworm farm would potentially provide labor for those in
the community. Moffet, for example, promises that the labor opportunity
provided by keeping silkworms will benefit various tradesmen: "winders . . .
twisters . . . and weauers thriue / Vppon this trade,"

> Which foode doth daily giue
> To such as else with famine needes must strive:
> What multitudes of poore doth it relieve,
> That otherwise could scarce be kept alive?" (69)

The lucrative promise of the silk trade depends on rather extensive human
labor and therefore seems to solve several problems at once: how to compete with France and other countries in the international silk trade, how
to provide raw silk to the English without in fact relying on other countries
to provide either the raw material or the finished product, as well as what to
do with the unemployed.

The expression of sericulture's efficacy echoes a larger economic discourse
in the seventeenth century, namely, that "the poor" are never a simple economic group but are rather considered morally problematic and dysfunc-
tional. In his 1609 letter in which he requests the widespread planting of
mulberry trees in England, James I gauges the success of the burgeoning
silkworm industry by the work it would provide the people of England. He
hopes that because of the care of silkworms, English workers "may be both

wained from idelnesse & the enormities therof, which are infinite, and exercised in such industries and labours, as are accompained with euident hopes, not onely of preseruing people from the shame and greefe of penurie, but also of raysing and increasing them in wealth and aboundance."[21] As Thirsk would note, the concern here for the poor is acknowledged with a recognition not only that their labor will create a good desired by the English (noble) population, but that their own status will ameliorate: they will have "wealth and aboundance."

Subsequent sericulturalists seem to take their cue from James's outlook that the silk industry would cure "idelnesse & the enormities thereof." Nicholas Geffe, in his own *Discourse*,[22] notes that England provides a profusion of happily available labor: "Multitudes of poore necessitous people may be relieued, where with our countrie will in time be too much pestred, vnlesse some new inuented necessarie imployment, supplie their wants; than which the making of silke in England (vnder reformation) cannot giue better occasion, seeing that thereby themselues shal be enabled to liue, and the weale publike aduantaged by their proper handlabors to the great contentment of vs all" (12–13). The poor are thus the linchpin for the success of the "weale publike," and for the benefit of the citizenry who are contented by the labors of the poor rather than "pestred" by them. Geffe insists that the employment of the poor in the silk industry will also fix moral problems and crime altogether: "We shall see infinit numbers of our owne contrimen, winding silke of our owne countrie; and weauing Sattins, Veluets, Taffatas, and diuers sorts of other silken stuffes, by which disposing them the industrious will bee readie and willing to worke, or being idle loyterers may be compeld, whereby the wretched well disposed, shall be farthered to liue better, and the miserable ill disposed by their example may endeuour the like, that the hungrie may be satisfied with bread, the begger bee ashamed to beg, and the thiefe to steale" (13). Geffe's hope is not just that crime will stop but out of moral compulsion the very consciousness that compels the criminal will be changed. The implication is that labor will bring poor citizens docilely into the economic community in a way in which they had not been present before.

The English concern for the welfare of the poor continues to develop in the varied writings of members of the Hartlib circle in the middle of the seventeenth century. Taking their name from their central organizer, Samuel Hartlib, the circle comprised a group of men concerned particularly with economic schemes involving agricultural reform and technology improvement. Hartlib, in his *Legacy of Husbandry* (1651), no doubt took his cue from James's letter, which he reprints in the *Legacy*'s section on silkworms. Also recognizing the labor intensivity of the industry, Hartlib reassures his reader that England has its own population of slaves: "Here in *England*," he writes, comparing the potential of England's participation in the silk trade with plantations in the colonies, "we have plenty of women, children, old folkes, lame, decrepite &c. who are fit to be overseers of this worke. . . . I hope if that particular men will not endeavour to advance this worke, for their private profit; yet the *State* will for the *Publique Good;* it being the best way I know, to set all the poor children, widowes, old and lame people on worke: and likewise will save this Nation many 100. thousand pounds *per annum.*"[23] Here labor is still a necessary ingredient to leaven the economic project, the establishment of which would alleviate England's dependence on other nations for the supply of silk—this is one reason it would save England money, another being that it would alleviate spending funds on poor relief. Hartlib indicates the need to make unproductive bodies productive in the name of the "Publique Good."

Ideas about labor are even more pointed when the scene shifts to the New World and its readily available labor. John Bonoeil makes use of everyone except the actual owner of the silkworms, from the "naturally born slaues"[24] of Virginia to "many Families (especially of the poorer sort) [who] join hands together, for the speedy setting vp of these Silke-lodgings, and for the gathering and sorting of the Mulbery leaues, and for the helping and teaching one another to feed and order the Wormes, and so worke, and liue together, all the Silk-haruest time" (78). He also establishes the use of those other than men for the menial work of stripping leaves and dealing with the insects themselves: "For the feeding, and shifting of the Wormes, and other imployments, women, children, and impotent persons may be vsed" (73). He even admits that such profit occurs at no expense for the owner: "Thus you see, what rich benefits I affoord you, for your small labour onely" (79)—the irony, of course, being that according to the logic of his labor recipe, the ones laboring are not the ones achieving the "rich benefits." Furthermore, these suggestions are written in Bonoeil's manual in the persona of Nature, who "speaks" the conclusion of his work, thus literally *naturalizing* both the poor underclass and the indigenous people of Virginia as slaves as she talks about them and their particular contributions to this economic project.

This desire to help the poor (and the public) through their docile labor seems to be negated by the middle of the seventeenth century, when apparently the goal of sericulture seems to be the excision of all human labor from the process. In his colonially oriented *A Rare and New Discovery . . . found out by a young lady in England,* Samuel Hartlib reveals a "secret" that will make the silk industry appeal to everyone. The "young lady" is Virginia Ferrars of Little Gidding, who allows her silkworms to stay on the tree for their forty-five-day maturation rather than coddling them in bespoke houses that require the intensive labor of the tree being brought to the worms—a new way of raising silkworms that significantly cuts back on human labor, at least until the cods must be boiled and spun.[25] Hartlib concludes: "And what can any of you now wish for more incouragement? the full proof is made, the work (or rather let me call it) the pleasure is effected with so much ease, so little cost, hazard, or pains, as all may admire it."[26] Work and labor are here replaced by pleasure: the keeper has no more to do than be "ravished" by the sight of the silk bottoms in the trees (3). Indeed, Hartlib concludes his manual with a contrast between easy silk and labor-intensive tobacco, asserting that "what will be the gain and profit by the wormes feeding and spinning on the Trees is more considerable. . . . What a Treasure then will this be, and no labour, cost, hazard, expence of time at all, a Boy onely to keep away the Birds from eating the Silkworms on the Trees" (A2v). James's desire to employ the poor has gone the way of capitalism: the least amount of expenditure (of both money and labor) for the highest profit. Such miraculous production is encapsulated in Moffet's work, which insists in fact that silk is "a Quintessence, / Made without hands byond al humane sense" (67). Undoubtedly, we understand what he means: the silk thread is itself seemingly magically created by the worms alone. On the other hand, that cocoon requires significant amounts of human intervention and labor before it becomes a consumable product, and yet that part is strategically elided from Moffet's account. Consider, for example, the case of the woodcuts mentioned earlier. A group of the same four woodcuts, two of which are reprinted here, is included in many of the manuals, but the third woodcut in the series, which shows a man and woman boiling and spinning the cods (pictured earlier in this essay), is missing from both editions of Stallenge's *Instructions.* The effect of the "missing" woodcut (whether or not it was purposefully left out) is the elision of human labor; the work process is then focused completely on the work of the worm: eating, spinning, and reproducing.

Because the early modern silk industry was meant to edify the wealthy, or the owners of the silkworms and not those who labor for the silkworms, it is clear that the manuals were not written for the laborer to read but written for the owner, who is pointedly not one of the laborers. For example, while Bonoeil's manual addresses responsibilities to the owner of the worms, it is assumed that that person will be *hiring*, and not *working*. He writes: "Your chiefe charge will be, for the gathering of the leaues to feed the Wormes. A man and boy will feede the Wormes. . . . But for the last fortnight, because the Wormes must be then carefully and often fed. . . . Then you must adde three or foure helpers, to the other two aforesaid" (K4v–L1r). Workers are added by the owner, who remains outside the actual labor completed. The silk trade, in a very real way, therefore requires an organized base of laborers, whereas beekeeping does not.

Even Moffet's work, arguably the most class-sensitive sericulture manual in this time period, quietly presumes that the people using the product are the wealthy. Consider, for example, his recipe for a "cordial medcin" for curing melancholy using silk-cod infused apple juice mixed with "graines of muske and Ambres flake": "O what a Balme is made to cheere the heart, / If pearle, and gold, and spices beare a part" (69). Clearly the use of silk to obtain this brew solidifies its economic value, as does the use of pearl and gold to amend the infusion. They are real ingredients (and common enough ones in contemporary medicines) that carry symbolic power, especially in their particular combination here. The passage seems to suggest that the wealth signified by these ingredients is the means to happiness—indeed, it is a recipe to cure the melancholy. Likewise, the silk that is created is not an equal-opportunity clothing; rather, the silkworm "is ordiened of God to clothe Kings and Princes" (Geffe, 70). In fact, Queen Anne, James I's wife, perhaps in support of her husband's political bid to create a domestic silk industry, was painted in the early years of the seventeenth century wearing a silk dress embroidered with silkworms.[27]

The expense of the end product of silkworm keeping exhibits the economic profit to be had by the owner and reveals an economy based in conspicuous consumption. In fact, the worms themselves begin to seem more like class-specific versions of their owners rather than insects in their own right. They are (unsurprisingly) anthropomorphized in the manuals, the most striking instance of which is in Geffe's translation of de Serres. Geffe creates a strict social hierarchy as he discusses the care of the worms. He warns that the "governor" (or keeper) of the worms cannot be offensive in any way and notes that access to the worms should be tightly controlled because they are sensitive to visitors: "Wherefore the entring of their lodging is not to be indifferently permitted to al sorts of persons, by that shunning the harme that too free frequenting brings to the creatures; which the supersticious vulgar, sottishly attribute to the eye, beleeuing that there are people which by their lookes brings ill lucke to the Wormes; but it rather is, nay, assuredly, the breathing of the ill breath which causeth them, indispositions" (60). He insists that the worms are negatively affected by the smells around them, which come "not of these noble creatures, the which of themselues smels nothing at all, no not their very dung" (61), but rather from molted skins that are not cleared away by "slothful" governors. Since the worms "loue sweete and good smelles, . . . one shall not onely gouerne these delectable cattell with profit, but their habitation made pleasant, and sweete smelling as the shop of a perfumer shall be found a place agreeable for good conditioned folkes. So will it be fore Ladies and Gentlemen, for whom these excellent creatures trauaill" (61–62). The silkworms' rooms and the perfumer's shop are connected in the logic of this passage, both of which need to be clean to support the shopping habits of "Ladies and Gentlemen." The clear connection here is in the class of the people for whom products are made. The worms are thus anthropomorphized with a keen sense of smell, equivalent to that of the nobility, and offended by dirt and the poorer classes who work for them in the same way that ladies and gentlemen were. A consonance is therefore established between the insect and the *consumer* of the product, bypassing those who labor for the insect, calling in fact for the governor to "giue commande to the gatherers neuer to goe to worke before they haue washed their handes" (62).

While the silkworm manual creates a consonance not between the worker and the insect but between the consumer and the insect, beekeeping manuals link the insect to ideal human behavior, especially that of their keeper. Toward the beginning of his book, Butler gives explicit instructions to beekeepers about what they must be like in order to be approved and accepted by their bees:

> If thou wilt haue the favour of thy Bees that they sting thee not, thou must not be (1) vnchast or (2) vncleanly: for impurity & sluttishness (themselues being most chast and neate,) they vtterly abhorre: thou must not come among

them (3) smelling of sweat, or having a stinking breath caused either through eating of leekes, onions, garleeke, and the like; or by any other meanes: the noisomnes whereof is corrected with a cup of beere; and therefore it is not good to come among them before you haue drunk: thou must not be given to (4) surfeting & drunkennes: thou must not come (5) puffing & blowing or sweating vnto them, nether hastily stirre among them, nor violently defend thy selfe when they seeme to threaten thee; but softlye mouing thy hand, before thy face gently put them by, and lastlie thou must be (6) no stranger vnto them. In a word thou must bee chast, cleanelie, sweet, sober, quiet, and familiar: so will they loue thee, and know thee from all other. (A7v–A8r)

No doubt we find this unscientific moral instruction quaint. But in context, it shows not only the *possibility* of imitating the bees to live a good life but also the *necessity* of it to successfully profit from beekeeping *and* to avoid being stung—the mark of moral failing, according to the logic of this passage, which prefaces its list with "if thou wilt haue the favour of thy Bees that they sting thee not."

As part of their exemplary labor, bees have a built-in guard against inappropriate consumption. The drone, configured in the manuals as a lazy male bee who consumes egregious amounts of honey without helping to gather it, is used to show the extent to which the worker bees abhor idleness. Consider Butler's anthropomorphized description of the drone (note that he refers to him as a "person" and not a bee): "The Drone, which is a grosse hiue-bee without sting, hath been alwaies reputed for a sluggard, & that worthily: how soeuer he braue it with his round velvet cappe, his side gown, his great paunch, and his lowd voice; yet is he but an idle person living by the sweat of others brows. For he worketh not at al, either at home or abroad, and yet spendeth as much as two labourers" (D5r). As a person, his consumption of leisure goods like velvet caps and side gowns (perhaps made of silk?) denotes his perverse participation in a local economy. Butler clearly draws on class markers to distinguish between those who labor and those who profit from that labor. In a way, therefore, this section in Butler's manual (especially when linked with his assertions about "comlinesse and conveniency" quoted at the beginning of the essay) is a critique of industries like silkworm raising whose owners profit from the luxury goods that they have achieved by means of others' work. The female worker bees eventually kill the drones after they have mated with them (according to Butler and others). They are punished on the grounds of their lack of productivity, which is exactly the worker bees' motive; as Richard Remnant explains, "the males are exceeding great eaters and wasters of the winter provision, therefore the females kill them for necessity" (4).

The fastidiousness of the bees' labor would have justified titling this essay "with industrious hand," which is Butler's description of the human labor needed to prepare honey and wax from the beehive. The contrast between the idea of the "industrious hand" of the beekeeper and the insistence that silk is magically "made without hands" indeed defines two poles of labor representation in early modern entomological manuals. But differences in the representation of economic systems can also been seen in the difference between the addressee of beekeeping manuals and those of sericulture manuals. The promise of any manual is the proficiency needed to ensure the successful (and profitable) exercise of the trade under instruction. Whereas sericulture manuals are almost always addressed to the owner of the worms and not the laborers, beekeeping manuals assume rhetorically that owner and laborer are one and the same—that the reader of the volume is also the keeper of the insects and labors to create a product from their raw goods. Prefaces to apicultural manuals note that the manual is written for the express purpose of teaching people to raise bees most efficiently—the people who actually look after the insects. For example, John Levett writes that "the greatest use of this book will be for the unlearned and Country people, especially good women, who commonly in this Country take most care and regard of this kinde of commodity . . . because sometimes they want help, sometimes diligence, but most time knowledge how to use them well."[28] In addition to Levett's fascinating claim that women number the most among beekeepers, he makes it clear that ideally, the people who gain from his book will be those actually keeping the bees. This detail points to a significant way the owners of the manuals participate in their various economies—one directly and the other as an employer.

Entomology manuals' representation of the labor and consumption the insects perform is filtered through ideas of human labor and consumption. Such representations of human labor are best contextualized in a nascent capitalism still characterized by an overlap, "with people from the old agrarian order living at the same time as those who had already been absorbed in the new commercial system."[29] Beekeeping manuals depend on a local vision of a subsistence economy with their insistence on the virtue and moral profitability of their product. Sericulture, on the other hand, perhaps because of its newness in England and its consumer base, gauges its success by standards of consumption of luxury goods. Indeed, sericultural manuals show the relationship between the labor used to create the silk and the ideas of labor in an early capitalist mode; the manuals help to establish the discourse surrounding labor in early modern England, particularly labor surrounding the creation of a luxury good. While the beekeeping manuals point toward an idealized vision of a laboring society of bees (and, by expressed extension, their keepers), sericultural manuals represent their rewards as the elision of all human labor, creating a self-contained natural process that tends to obscure its material conditions. The difference is not a matter of capitalism replacing local economies with its increasing presence in the seventeenth century. But the differing representational landscapes of these industries and their labor help us to see the shifting poetics of the economy through the poetics of the insect.

NOTES

I would like to thank Caroline Bowden, Eric C. Brown, and Ariel Hessayon for reading and commenting on earlier drafts of this essay.

1. Charles Butler, "*The Feminine Monarchie*" *or a treatise concerning bees, and the due ordering of them* (London, 1609), a2r. Hereafter cited in the text.

2. Linda Levy Peck, "Creating a Silk Industry in Seventeenth-Century England," *Shakespeare Studies* 28 (2000): 225.

3. [John Bonoeil], *His Maiesties Gracious Letter to the Earle of South-Hampton, treasurer, and to the Councell and Company of Virginia heere* (London, 1622), 63.

4. Samuel Hartlib, *A rare and new discovery of a speedy way and easie means, found out by a young lady in England, she having made full proofe thereof in May, anno 1652* (London, 1652), 4.

5. Samuel Hartlib's manual *The Reformed Commonwealth of Bees* (1655) is an exception. In the 1650s, the Hartlib circle was particularly adamant about honey's ability to save the nation from reliance on the import sugar trade, but the desire for sugar—silk's culinary analogue—far outweighed the Hartlib circle's proposed scheme. See Timothy Raylor, "Samuel Hartlib and the Commonwealth of Bees," in *Culture and Cultivation in Early Modern England: Writing and the Land,* ed. Michael Leslie and Timothy Raylor (Leicester and London: Leicester University Press, 1992).

6. Joyce Oldham Appleby, *Economic Thought and Ideology in Seventeenth Century England* (Princeton: Princeton University Press, 1978), 3.

7. Ibid., 28.

8. There are two editions of *Instructions* printed in London in 1609, a translation of Jean-Baptiste Letellier's *Memoirs et instructions pour l'establissement des meuriers*. The text is largely the same in the two printings, as are the woodcuts. However, in the edition with "New Printed" on the title page, the reader may find instructions for locating cheap mulberry saplings and seeds in London in the final paragraph. One would therefore assume that the promise from James in the prefatory letter had in fact been put into effect. William Stallenge also holds the assignment of Geffe's translation of *Perfect Use*.

9. Bonoeil, *His Maiesties Gracious Letter*, A3v.

10. In addition to various state proclamations against the production and use of tobacco, see James's *A Covnterblaste to Tobacco* (London, 1604). See also Susan Campbell Anderson, "A Matter of Authority: James I and the Tobacco War," *Comitatus: A Journal of Medieval and Renaissance Studies* 29 (1998): 136–63.

11. John Levett, *The ordering of Bees: Or, the Trve History of Managing them From time to time, with their hony and waxe, shewing their nature and Breed* (London, 1634). The quotation is from the preface, n.p.

12. Richard Remnant, *A Discourse or Historie of Bees* (London, 1637), 13.

13. T[homas] M[offet], *The silkewormes, and their flies: liuely described in verse, by T.M. a countrie farmar, and an apprentice in physicke. For the great benefit and enriching of England* (London, 1599), 22. Hereafter cited in the text.

14. The threat of the consuming worm is echoed from Thomas Nashe's *The Unfortunate Traveller* (1593). Nashe writes that before the Fall, nature existed in a perfection that did not admit blemish or consumption: "the rose had no cankers, the leauues no caterpillers" (k1v).

15. For a brief source history on the bee as a symbol of chastity, see Sarah Plant, "Shakespeare's Lucrece as Chaste Bee," *Cahiers Elisabethains: Late Medieval and Renaissance Studies* 49 (1996): 51–57.

16. Nicholas Geffe, *The Perfect Use of Silke-wormes, and their benefit*, trans. de Serres (London, 1607), 7 (italics mine). Hereafter cited in the text.

17. [John Bonoeil], *Obseruations to be followed, for the making of fit roomes, to keepe silk-wormes in* (London, 1620), 16.

18. Edward Williams, *Virginia's Discovery of Silkworms* (London, 1650), 7.

19. Joan Thirsk, *Economic Policy and Projects: The Development of a Consumer Society in Early Modern England* (Oxford: Clarendon, 1988), 3. See also Margaret James, *Social Problems and Policy during the Puritan Revolution, 1640–1660* (London: Routledge and Sons, 1930). James writes: "The relief of the poor was not primarily a religious duty and a moral obligation, but an urgent practical necessity, the evasion of which would be followed by disastrous political and economic consequences" (275).

20. Prudence Leith-Ross writes that James's design to populate England with mulberry trees for the purposes of silkworm raising was "doomed to failure because silkworms do not thrive on the red [or black] mulberry, which grows well

in Britain, while the white mulberry, on which they do flourish, is much less happy with the English climate. Although the silkworms' preference was understood at the time, the surviving trees that are supposed to date back to this order all seem to be of the red variety." *The John Tradescants: Gardeners to the Rose and Lily Queen* (London: Peter Owen, 1998), 42.

21. [William Stallenge], *Instrvctions for the increasing of Mulberie Trees*, trans. Letellier (London, 1609), A3r.

22. Geffe appends his own observations about silkworm keeping to his translation of de Serres's *Perfect Use*.

23. Samuel Hartlib, *Samuel Hartlib his Legacie: or An enlargement of the Discourse of husbandry used in Brabant and Flaunders* (London, 1651), 73.

24. Bonoeil, *His Maiesties Gracious Letter*, 86.

25. Little Gidding was a religious community active in the middle of the seventeenth century. It was founded by Nicholas Ferrars and included many members of his immediate and extended family. For a contemporary account of the activities of Little Gidding, see *The Arminian nunnery: or, A briefe description and relation of the late erected monasticall place, called the Arminian nunnery at Little Gidding in Huntington-shire, 1641*. See also the work of A. L. Maycock, including *Nicholas Ferrar of Little Gidding* (1938), *The Chronicles of Little Gidding* (1954), and *The Story of Little Gidding* (1947), all published in London by the Society for Promoting Christian Knowledge.

26. Hartlib, *A rare and new discovery*, 3.

27. Peck, "Creating a Silk Industry," 227.

28. Levett, preface, n.p..

29. Appleby, *Economic Thought*, 274.

12

Through a Flea-Glass Darkly

Enlightened Entomologists and the Redemption of Aesthetics in Eighteenth-Century France

MARC OLIVIER

One of the most striking plates of Robert Hooke's *Micrographia* (1665) portrays a flea that seems ready to leap from its large fold-out page and demand reassessment from its human observers. Formerly depicted as no more than a black dot, formerly regarded as an annoyance best pulverized rather than pondered, the insect emerges from the tome a fearsome and beautiful presence, in the words of Arthur Danto, "a creature as ornamental and intimidating as a warhorse in Nuremberg armor."[1] Hooke's rendering stands as a testament to a radically altered aesthetics born from artificially enhanced vision. The facilitator of that vision, the microscope, also commonly called a *pulicarium,* or "flea-glass," functions as an advocate for the lowly, the overlooked, and even the despised inhabitants of the natural world. Throughout *Micrographia*, the gnat, the fly, the mite, the louse, and other physical minima enjoy representation as seen through the instrument and rendered in exquisite detail on costly plates, many of which exceed the standard page size of the already-large-folio work. The author's choice of objects, while not limited to insects, fosters an association between the new discipline of microscopy and the emerging subdiscipline of natural history that was formalized as "entomology" a century later.[2] This essay looks at how, in the aesthetic tradition of Hooke, eighteenth-century entomologists sought to promote the observation of insects as a cure for degenerate taste. In France, in particular, authors such as Noël-Antoine Pluche (1688–1761), Gaspard-Guillard de Beaurieu (1728–95), and Gilles Augustin Bazin (1681–1754) endorsed entomology as a noble, pastoral science—an enlightened substitute for corrupt urban pleasures. The study of insects, they argued, produces admiration better than a visit to an art museum, satisfies curiosity better than travel literature, provides spectacles superior to the opera, and stirs up more worthy passions than the romance novel.

Most historians of science regard the eighteenth century as a stagnant era for microscopy, a century-long lull following a few important discoveries by pioneers such as Jan Swammerdam (1637–80), Marcello Malpighi (1628–94), and Antony van Leeuwenhoek (1632—1723). Brian J. Ford christens the period after Leeuwenhoek's death "the lost century," a time in which "the progress of microbiology came to an almost total halt."[3] Equally critical, Gerard Turner writes, "It can scarcely be claimed that any research was done [during the eighteenth century], and the only thin sections that were cut were of wood."[4] In retrospect, Hooke's own work was limited by its preoccupation with the surfaces of his new visual world, and with no

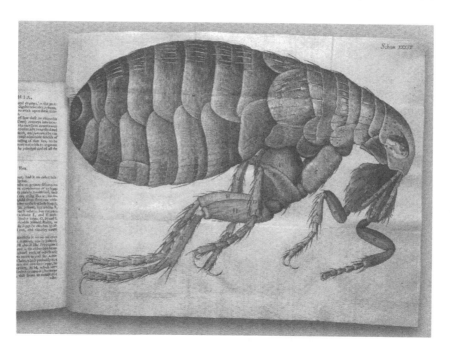

Flea from Robert Hooke's *Micrographia* (1665). Copyright Octavo and the Warnock Library. Reprinted with permission. Image by Octavo (www.octavo.com).

common standards of microscopic measurement, his observations proved more likely to capture the imagination of a wide audience than to advance a clear research agenda.[5] Yet although Hooke's promotion of microscopy may have resulted in a century of failure according to the standards of modern science, the broader impact of his work extends beyond the concerns of microbiology and to the rehabilitation of both subject and object, observer and observed.

As the instrument transformed the flea into a monumental creature, so too did it change the status of the viewer. In a declaration that reads like an early modern cyborg manifesto, Hooke suggests that the microscope brings its user closer to prelapsarian perfection:

> By the addition of such artificial Instruments and methods, there may be, in some manner, a reparation made for the mischiefs, and imperfection, mankind has drawn upon itself, by negligence, and intemperance, and a wilful and superstitious deserting of the Prescripts and Rules of Nature, whereby every man, both from a deriv'd corruption, innate and born with him, and from his breeding and converse with men, is very subject to slip into all sorts of errors.[6]

Hooke claims that through technological enhancement, humans can make amends for the physical deficiencies brought on initially by the Fall and furthered by social intercourse. The microscope, he hopes, will be only one of many "artificial Organs" added to the natural as part of a cure for body and mind. Acting out of optimism, or arguably hubris, Hooke proposes to redeem humankind (at least in part) from the consequences of our biblical parents' actions by offering a technological solution to a theological problem: "And as at first, mankind fell by tasting of the forbidden Tree of Knowledge, so we, their Posterity, may be in part restor'd by the same way." That is, we may partake of the "fruits of Natural knowledge" with our extended organs and, in so doing, refashion ourselves as a new Adam or Eve in a "new visible World discovered to the understanding." The plates of *Micrographia* give the reader a glimpse into that new Eden—a terra incognita populated by majestic lice, terrible and noble fleas, jewel-eyed flies, and other amazing creatures, many waiting to be named.[7] Paradise could be found, in Hooke's plan, with the help of artificial eyes.

An eighteenth-century microscope designed by Gerrit Cramer visually expresses the continuation of Hooke's discourse into the Enlightenment.

The ornamental tripod microscope is adorned with a representation of a magnified insect beside a man who is being touched by the hand of God while performing observations, perhaps of that same insect. The painted instrument reinforces the ties between microscopy, entomology, and the salvation of the human mind. Equal to the man in size and detail, the insect stands as testament to the microscopic gaze, a page in the book of nature as read through godly eyes. The instrument itself acts as an intermediary between the man and nature's bible (or *biblia naturae*, as Swammerdam called it), while the finger of God accords a divine seal of approval to the endeavor. The ornate exterior echoes Hooke's theological perspective and conveys the enthusiasm felt by a new generation of microscopists.

Detail of microscope by Gerrit Cramer, circa mid-1700s. Museum Boerhaave, Leiden.

Exuberant praise of the microscope was a standard feature of many eighteenth-century natural history writings. Pierre-Louis Moureau de Maupertuis (1698–1759) felt that microscopes gave mortals the senses (although regrettably not the reason) of superior beings.[8] Henry Baker (1698–1774) and André François Deslandes (1690–1757) both referred to "new senses," Deslandes going so far as to state that men were blind before the invention of the microscope.[9] Jean-Antoine Nollet (1700–1770), like Hooke, called the instruments "new organs," and Friedrich-Christian Lesser (1692–1754) wrote of a "new world" opened by the lens.[10] Yet another commonplace made the microscope the weapon in a war between moderns and ancients, as seen in Baker's assertion that "we now see objects 600 times more distant and thousands of times smaller than the most distant and the smallest that could once be observed by the most piercing eye of antiquity."[11]

Also reminiscent of Hooke were comparisons between human objects of refinement and nature's handiwork that shocked and delighted polite society.[12] Martin Frobene Ledermüller (1719–69), whose copiously illustrated observations were published in German, Dutch, and French, found his comparison of a bee's stinger to a needle so well received that unnamed "people of high rank" quickly commanded more.[13] He soon followed up by pitting the finest-quality lace against half of a small spiderweb, the former a "masterpiece of the fair sex" and the latter "the daily work of the most vile of insects."[14] With the enlightened vision of the microscope, the victor is clear: the product of the arachnid suggests "equality, design," and, adds Ledermüller, "intelligence," whereas the lace becomes a laughable and confused tangle of knots.[15] The disorder of the human product debases not only the skill of the lace maker but also her judgment, and more crucial to the well-bred reader, the taste of any woman who proudly decorates her décolletage with the suddenly barbaric rope. The transformative gaze of the lens raises the standard of taste, and with it the status of entomology as a potential wellspring of refinement. Those who still prefer what Ledermüller calls "simple sight" risk appearing outmoded next to those who can appreciate the finesse of the spider.[16] Thanks to the comparison, the spider gains intelligence and generates envy from a public now wondering how a spiderweb might become a fashion accessory.[17]

Comparisons such as that of the lace and the spiderweb typify the dissemination and transmutations of Hooke's dream throughout enlightened Europe. Theology continued to color descriptions of the minute—for in admiring the perfection of a web, the stinger of a bee, or the wings of a dragonfly, the naturalist unfailingly claimed to honor the creator—but the benefits vaunted by popularizers of both microscopy and entomology rarely included a return to Eden. In France, where matters of taste and distinction often overshadowed concern for salvation, the biblical garden was displaced by a less temporally distant and more politically charged ideal: the noble pastoral.[18] The discourse of reparation and redemption, and the longing for an idealized past, resonated more strongly among the elite when cast as a critique of urban and courtly life. Naturalists urged their readers to practice the study of insects in the country, away from the distractions of the city and the intrigues of the court. They created their own brand of pastoral literature—not of sheep, shepherds, and shepherdesses but of insects hidden in the fields encircling a provincial estate. Their depictions of noble independence surrounded by nature drew freely from the mythos of feudal nostalgia more than from a biblical paradise. In contrast to the waning courtly power and the decadent pleasure of the city noble, the ideal naturalist of Enlightenment texts enjoyed free rein among the insect nations of the meadows.

The writings of Gaspard-Guillard de Beaurieu typify the pastoral ideal promoted by most French naturalists. In his *Abrégé de l'histoire des insectes* (1764), Beaurieu gives the reader the entomologist's version of Rousseau's Emile: a young man of rustic simplicity whose noble purity contrasts with the corruption of his urban counterparts. Beaurieu, however, mentions no preceptor other than Nature herself, and leaves the reader to imagine the boy's upbringing. Unlike Rousseau, Beaurieu is less concerned with pedagogy and process than with fabricating an ideal. His imaginary young naturalist embodies all the characteristics his young readers can aspire to imitate: he displays intellectual curiosity, devotion to God, a sense of adventure, and refined taste. And although Beaurieu does not show the reader *how* his protagonist acquired those attributes, he repeatedly mentions *where* he gained them: "Far from the city, far from the court, he spends peaceful nights and happy days."[19] There, in the country, he is untouched by Augustinian *mala curiositas*—that unholy curiosity that drives life in the city. Instead of distractions, the boy finds satisfaction in daily contemplation. As he looks at an insect, his mind is drawn to God and back again to himself without shame or fear, for "his heart is pure."[20] Every day he attends the spectacles offered by nature and savors even dreary weather "as one in the city loves a beautiful tragedy" or tempestuous music.[21] Equally innocent is his choice of sport. Rather than hunt game, he chases butterflies and adds them to a collection that shames commercial luxuries: "Let an artist come boast to him of the beautiful fabrics he makes, let a woman display before him the most beautiful dress she wears; he shows them some butterflies, and they despair."[22] As in the spiderweb and lace comparison, Beaurieu demonstrates that the products of civilized refinement fall short next to insect goods. Impotent as tempters, and horrified by their defeat, the artist and the finely dressed woman are left to return to a less-discriminating courtly audience.

In addition to the portrayal of his exemplary yet fictional young student of nature, Beaurieu reinforces his preference for the noble pastoral through brief biographical sketches of famous naturalists. The account of Swammerdam's life, in particular, emphasizes the naturalist's rejection of court and city in favor of country retirement. Beaurieu relates his version of a meeting between Swammerdam and the Grand Duke of Tuscany in which the duke offered to purchase Swammerdam's entire natural history collection, but only on the condition that Swammerdam leave Holland and come to the court in Tuscany to care for it. Swammerdam refused, according to Beaurieu, because he was "too wise to leave a city in Holland for a court in Italy."[23] In this account, a longing for a peaceful life in the country supersedes not only the temptation for glory to which a lesser man would have succumbed but also the perfectly honest pleasure of possessing a cabinet of curiosities. In the context of Beaurieu's lengthy introduction, Swammerdam represents a true historical parallel to the encounter between his ideal student of nature and the tempters from the city. As in the fictional episode, the naturalist and his collection triumph over the allure of courtly opulence.

The biographies of the great naturalists lead Beaurieu to conclude that those who live nobly in the country are the most worthy of admiration. Praiseworthiness, however, is not dependent solely on one's choice of residence. To be included among the estimable few, one must "lead in the country a life as simple as and less vulgar than that of our laborers and our shepherds."[24] One must share all the virtue and none of the vulgarity of common folk and live away from courtly grandeur by choice, not by necessity. If those qualifications are met, one can expect to experience pleasures that are as invisible to the laborer in the fields as they are to the courtesan at the opera. In the case of the commoner, however, the defective taste that prevents access to those pleasures appears inborn, whereas for the courtier, a voyage to the country and an open mind will quickly provide a cure. As proof, Beaurieu proposes that the reader imagine two men out in nature: the first vulgar and not well educated, and the second of good breeding and distinction. The first, Beaurieu claims, "will stare blankly and distractedly at everything around him and will see nothing," while the other will see "a thousand beauties at once."[25] The "unfortunate laborer," although arguably in closer contact with nature through his work, shares none of the delights of an "attentive observer, a man who has a soul."[26]

The possession of a soul in Beaurieu's phrasing is synonymous with the possession of taste. Just as Descartes deprived brute beasts of souls a century earlier by equating *anima* (soul) with *anima rationali* or *mens* (mind), Beaurieu reflects a common attitude of his own time that ensures class divisions by equating soul with taste. As Daniel Cottom has observed, "taste is a domain of the upper classes and is ultimately a property exclusive to the purest aristocracy."[27] In Voltaire's words, "The man of taste has different eyes, different ears, and a different touch than the coarse man has."[28] To the post-Hookean aesthete, Voltaire's statement can be understood quite literally: the man trained in the art of observation has sufficiently transformed the workings of his senses that his mind no longer receives information in the same manner as the commoner. Even without the use of the microscope, the enlightened entomologist enters new worlds where others see only a field to plow. The promotion of both microscopy and entomology as tasteful pursuits for the upper classes appeals to the aristocratic "belief that their unique pleasures are imperceptible to outsiders."[29] The noble young naturalist, therefore, can wander the provincial landscape knowing that he or she is *in* the country, but not *of* the country. A hobby that could otherwise have been advertised as a democratic luxury—a wealth available to all—instead creates allure as the leisure pursuit of the elite. The appeal of entomology for the well-bred resides in its ability to subvert courtly structure while preserving class distinction. In finding superior objects of refinement in the country that are visible only to the trained observer, Beaurieu questions the supremacy of court or salon as generators of good taste and simultaneously guarantees the preservation of privilege. Beaurieu guarantees that the common man, the man without a soul, is no more likely to savor the hidden spectacle of nature than he is to acquire box seats at the opera.

Noël-Antoine Pluche's immensely popular *Spectacle de la nature* (1732–42) also maintains a class-biased approach to natural history. The nine-volume opus functions as a training manual for noble young would-be naturalists, inviting them to act out the roles of ideal student and tutors when reading the dialogic work. The reader imaginatively participates in the country vacation of a young student and can acquire the attitudes, if not the direct experience, that will lead to his initiation into the realms of superior taste. In Pluche's words, the principal actors in this dramatization are "interlocutors of different estates"—a phrase that the student of French history would typically understand to be a reference to the three Old Regime orders of society: the nobility, the clergy, and the massive third estate that includes both bourgeois and peasant.[30] In Pluche's configuration, however, the commoner is replaced by "a young man of quality" called the Chevalier de Breuil, the role with which the young reader is meant to identify.[31] The other characters include a distinguished gentleman named Monsieur le Comte de Jonval, his wife, Madame la Comtesse, and the local prior. Although the dialogue takes place around the country estate of the count, Pluche never introduces any peasants into the discussion. Inclusion of the lower classes, even members of the bourgeoisie, would simply muddy his pedagogical goal, which is above all to instruct "our young nobility."[32]

Among the first implicit lessons in the book is the need for the fledgling person of quality to retreat to the country. When introducing the characters, Pluche informs the reader that our young chevalier has come to the country during his school vacation, accompanied by his older brother and his father. While the boy's father helps set up the older brother in his own lands, the boy befriends the count and begins a long series of discussions, the first of which centers around a comparison of country and city. To the count's delight, the boy finds the country "a thousand times more beautiful than Paris with its splendor and its gildings."[33] In Paris, the boy claims to find life monotonous and tiresome, but in the country he discovers endless amusement in the spectacle of insects kept living by the count in elaborate glass and crystal housing. The count's massive collection and the lens of his microscope give the chevalier an immediate desire to delve deeper into entomology. "Since you showed me those lenses that magnify small objects, I have seen admirable things in insects. The head alone of a fly is full of bouquets and diamonds."[34] But before continuing, the count wants the boy to understand the difference between urban activities and their own pastoral studies. In a rhetorical vein reminiscent of Erasmus, the count contrasts the reasonable routine of city life with his own rural folly: "Tell me, I pray you, Chevalier, do you find a person in the world amusing himself with the study of insects? People crush them, or at least do not look at them."[35] Adding to the subversive appeal of the mentorship, he warns the chevalier against choosing him as a role model. Reasonable city pleasures, he explains, include finding the right snuffbox, ordering a proper table setting, making social calls, gambling, or going to the opera.[36] The critique of city reason and praise of pastoral folly set the tone for Pluche's work and prepare the reader to view the spectacle of nature as the antidote for all that ails the city noble.

Nature endlessly generates new pleasures, provided that the spectator is qualified to discern them. Courtly experience and proper breeding notwithstanding, Pluche demonstrates that only those trained in the art of observation come to know what the others are missing. The young student's dismissal of Paris, his description of urban ennui, and his eagerness to emulate the count prove him a worthy apprentice. "We will make of you an observer," announces the count, just before giving his first lesson on insects.[37] Not surprisingly, the microscope plays a key role in the boy's initiation. Through the lens, the chevalier hopes to understand how the count can speak of insects whose clothing, weapons, and tools rival those made by the most skilled French laborers. A good natural theologian, the prior clarifies that in fact, human production cannot compete with "the infinite superiority that shines in those [products] of nature."[38] In support, the three recall their own observations of a sewing needle and bee stinger under the microscope. Although both needle and stinger appear perfectly smooth to the naked eye, only the stinger retains its polish under magnified scrutiny. The lesson for the apprentice observer is clear: refined vision, like refined taste, favors the invisible. Common errors in judgment regarding quality or beauty expose the shortcomings of the unschooled eye. And while the preeminence of the insect specimen takes its claim on human pretense, the defeat is savored as a victory for the arbitrator of the contest—the keen observer who can see success or failure where others sense no difference.

A more striking comparison given by the prior paraphrases scripture and asks that rather than consider the lilies of the field as suggested in the celebrated passage from Matthew, one should consider the head of a common fly through a lens. "One cannot tire of seeing such a profusion of gold," proclaims the man of God.[39] Should one continue to meditate, says the prior, the mind will inevitably be drawn to compare the glittering image to "other heads which affect similar adornment" but do not attain favorable results.[40] Still speaking of flies, he concludes: "Solomon in all his glory was not adorned like the least of these."[41] The prior's inscription of the fly into sacred verse coupled with his derision of human self-beautification puts theology in the service of entomology and implies that refined taste leads to hidden truth. In this case, meditation focused on the head of an insect leads to riches not recognized by others (the profusion of gold covering the fly) and debases as feigned and vulgar the conventions of human embellishment. The study of insects, like the reading of scripture, leads the prior to compare the work of a divine creator with that of a less-than-divine society. The young chevalier, Pluche's model student, quickly learns to make similar testimonials, thereby setting the example for other young, privileged, and bored city dwellers.[42] In spite of the theological tone of the work, Pluche makes no promise of an Eden regained. Instead he evokes a pastoral hidden within the pastoral and invites his converts into a realm more exclusive than heaven itself.

A final and more detailed dramatization of a student's metamorphosis into naturalist and observer can be found in the works of Gilles Augustin Bazin. Whereas Beaurieu presents the already-formed student of nature, and Pluche introduces the young man eager to learn, Bazin stages a dialogue with more reluctant learners—well-bred women who question the use, pleasure, and appropriateness of entomology as a hobby. Bazin's *Histoire naturelle des abeilles* (Paris, 1744) and its four-volume sequel, *Abrégé de l'histoire des insectes pour servir de suite à l'histoire naturelle des abeilles* (Paris, 1747), trace the transformation of two very different women into enlightened entomologists. The first, Clarice, lives peacefully in a provincial estate rather than in the city and consequently already possesses many of the qualities promoted by naturalists. She is devoted to the well-being of her children, to her lands, and to her own self-improvement. She demonstrates an interest in the admirable economy of bees from her first dialogue with Eugène (Bazin's alter ego) and worries only that social norms and the complex language of science must prevent her from accepting lessons. Bazin resolves her concerns by framing the study of insects as a domestic science and by converting the means of delivery into literary form. The story of bees, Eugène tells Clarice, is the account of a people "whose dominant passion is the prosperity and the good of the family; in a word, a people who seem to have modeled themselves after you."[43] Her interest in bees therefore becomes wholly compatible with family life. As for the language, Clarice rejects the style of Réaumur's *Mémoires pour servir à l'histoire des insectes* (Paris, 1734–42) and proposes a dialogic and novelistic adaptation as a more suitable alternative. "I only ask you for the novel, but for the true novel of the history of bees."[44] Eugène complies with Clarice's request, and their subsequent dialogues become the novelistic adaptation of the book of nature. The *true* novel of insects replaces and improves on both jargon-ridden scientific texts and pleasurable but frivolous fictions. The hybrid form appeases Clarice's initial anxiety, justifies her curiosity, and grants her access to knowledge formerly gendered as male.

In Bazin's sequel, Eugène and Clarice are joined by a second woman: a vacationing young widow and Parisian socialite named Hortense, who finds the very names of insects disgusting.[45] Accustomed to city amusements, Hortense represents an unlikely convert. In Eugène's eyes, Hortense is the product of an environment where "nature is obfuscated, masked, and often corrupt," and therefore she holds little promise as a future student.[46] Clarice insists, on the contrary, that her friend is a truth-loving woman of good taste and judgment, and consequently a suitable "proselyte of natural history."[47] Yet of the two views, the former is most validated by Hortense, who warns Eugène that only lovely stories of the rare and unseen interest her and that she will yawn the minute she gets bored.[48] Unlike the young chevalier of Pluche's work, so quickly disenchanted with city life, Hortense genuinely enjoys fairy tales, nights out at the theater, social events, and all the glitter of Paris. She has no experience with the aesthetics of microscopic vision, nor any idea of nature's invisible beauty. Her primary motive is pleasure, and her ultimate acceptance or rejection of her friend's proselytizing will determine the appeal of entomology as a substitute for her usual activities.

At the beginning of the first lesson, Eugène manages to pique Hortense's curiosity by making entomology a form of exotic travel. "Without leaving this park, we will pass, so to speak, into a foreign land," he announces.[49] Hortense will soon learn "that she lives amid an infinity of different nations," some analogous to French society, but many others strange, exotic, and even barbaric.[50] Eugène will show her "peoples" who dress in nothing but silk and others who wear only wool, shells, or sticks: "She will see some who spend half of their life in the water in the form of fish, and the other half in the sky like birds."[51] With Eugène as guide and Clarice as traveling companion, Hortense will participate in a tour of the microcosm. She will learn to explore firsthand, to visit and speak knowledgeably of other cultures. In essence, she will come to generate her own travel literature. Even her interest in fairy tales will wane as she discovers real beings whose lives are stranger than fiction. But Hortense will see none of those wonders until she becomes an observer. So while the more experienced Clarice can enthusiastically declare, "Take us away, Eugène, into this new world. Let us travel in this park. Let us go from nation to nation," Hortense will find the journey disappointing until her sight passes through the flea-glass.[52]

Hortense quickly learns that the success of her so-called travels depends on her ability to observe. As the three seek out mason bees along the facade of Clarice's chateau, Hortense sees nothing. Even when Eugène shows her the nests all along the walls, she sees only spots of mud thrown by some vulgar country man. "It wasn't worth the bother to make us come all the way out here to see such things," she objects.[53] Eugène takes her response as an example of youthful haste and, like the microscopists, bemoans that those not trained in the art of observation tend to overlook the marvels that surround them. Having failed to impress Hortense with mason bees as witnessed by plain sight, Eugène's next lesson revisits the nests—this time with flea-glass in hand. Eugène offers the lens to Clarice, who describes the actions of the bees while the other two listen. Hortense never takes the lens herself, yet this doubly mediated encounter with mason bees succeeds in giving her a passion for insects that her insufficiently mediated first lesson did not.

Hortense's means of passage through the flea-glass into new worlds follows the same route taken by admirers of sumptuous picture books such as Hooke's *Micrographia* or Ledermüller's *Amusements microscopiques*. She learns that the road to becoming a direct observer begins with indirect spectatorship. Because the beauties of nature are veiled and inaccessible to the untrained eye, the would-be observer must first experience the natural object as part of a well-orchestrated mise-en-scène. As Danto suggests, "Just think about Hooke's flea once more: it instructs us in how the flea looks, but it does more than that in instructing us how to think and feel about the flea and about a world which has such creatures in it."[54] Hooke's engraving tells its viewer how a man with perfected vision sees the flea, and changes that viewer's perception of the creature and of the world even if it does not transform the viewer into a true observer. Just as the chevalier in Pluche's *Spectacle de la nature* first becomes interested in insects by witnessing the ornate staging of specimens living under crystal in the count's magnificent cabinet of curiosities, Hortense first develops a love of bees only after experiencing the performance given by her friend Clarice.

In the course of only two lessons, Hortense progresses from questioning the existence of the mason bees to performing her own observations. By day five, she has become a convert, a traveler. Like the count in Pluche's work, she is proud of her pastoral folly and happy to distinguish herself from her urban counterparts. As she embarks on her daily outing with Eugène and Clarice, she wistfully declares her desire to surprise an acquaintance with their curious pilgrimage:

> It would please me, for the singular effect it would produce, that someone of our acquaintance stumble upon us presently in this park, making our way as we are, running through fields. He would not miss the chance to ask us where we are going in this manner, and we to answer him: make way, good man, we are traveling, we are about the discovery of unknown peoples. We would speak truthfully, and yet at such a response, he would not hesitate to treat us as fools.[55]

By the eleventh meeting, Hortense has become a seasoned traveler among the insect countries. Her eyes have been opened, and she has become an observer: "My eyes seem clearer, more piercing; it seems that I see better that which I see as well as a thousand things that I didn't see before."[56] The revulsion she once felt for insects has long since disappeared, and she now adopts the language of a romantic heroine as she declares, "I see [insects] in dreams, I think about them when I'm awake."[57] The following afternoon, Hortense announces that she must return to the city on business. She expresses once again her enjoyment and promises to come back the following year to pursue her studies with Clarice and Eugène. As she prepares to leave, she acknowledges the divide that now separates her former self from the observer she has become. She delights in the change and takes pleasure in imagining the surprise of her friends—"all occupied with games, parties, spectacles, feasts, ambitious intrigues, visits, errands"—when they learn how she spent her time in the country.[58] "I thought like them on arrival," she adds, "and I will return thinking like you."[59] She is now ready to become a teller of true tales, anxious to share stories of the rustic slumber, the crystal waters, the rocks, the forests, and the observations made on the banks of the Rhine.[60] Her stay with Clarice has made her a citizen of a hidden pastoral community, a proud convert to the folly of rural entomological exploration. She knows that as she shares her stories with her circle of socialite friends, they will be shocked, amazed, but unchanged in their thinking. Unlike Hortense, their taste is still trapped in the city.

The conversion of Hortense and her subsequent return to Paris represents the sort of compromise that allows all three of the authors discussed here to popularize entomology for the urban elite. As the reader experiences the transformations of the vacationing protagonist (whether it be a young chevalier or widowed socialite) the narrative-propelling binaries such as city–country, simple sight–microscopic sight, and human product–natural product are recast as the peripheral views bordering a hidden vista of refined taste. Otherwise stated, Hortense and the chevalier never choose between city and country because they will henceforth belong to both and to neither. Their sight is no longer informed by the naked eye alone, yet they do not routinely perform microscopic observations. In popular comparisons, the ostensible preference for the natural product over human artistry is mitigated by the use of the latter to promote the former.[61] The status of the enlightened observer resembles Leo Marx's formulation of the pastoral ideal as "located in a middle ground somewhere 'between,' yet in a transcendent relation to, the opposing forces of civilization and nature."[62] In a similar fashion, the popularization of entomology in eighteenth-century France occupies a middle ground between science and aesthetics. Ultimately the works of writers such as Beaurieu, Pluche, and Bazin cannot be judged on their success or failure to produce a nation of entomologists but, like Hooke's *Micrographia*, are best evaluated by their ability to transport the reader to a superior state at the sight of a flea.

NOTES

1. Arthur C. Danto, "Aesthetics and Art Criticism," in *Embodied Meanings: Critical Essays and Aesthetic Meditations* (New York: Farrar, Straus and Giroux, 1994), 376.

2. For more on how microscopy inevitably led to increased praise of the insect world among natural theologians during the eighteenth century, see Jacques Roger, *Les sciences de la vie dans la pensée française du XVIIIe siècle: La générations des animaux de Descartes à l'Encyclopédie* (Paris: Albin Michel, 1993), 233–38.

3. Brian J. Ford, *Single Lens: The Story of the Simple Microscope* (London: Heinemann, 1985), 68.

4. Gerard L'Estrange Turner, *Essays on the History of the Microscope* (Oxford: Senecio Publishing Society, 1980), 216. Edward G. Ruestow contends that the social setting of the eighteenth century can be blamed for its failure to properly institutionalize microscopy as a legitimate discipline. Ruestow, *The Microscope in the Dutch Republic: The Shaping of Discovery* (New York: Cambridge University Press, 1996), 291.

5. Catherine Wilson notes that Hooke's *Micrographia* "exercises a fascination which cannot be well accounted for by reference to its role in any direct or orderly line of scientific development." Rather than dismiss Hooke's observations as useless from the vantage point of modern science, Wilson contextualizes the fascination with surface as crucial to seventeenth-century struggles against occultist views of nature. In her words, "The microscope leads to a kind of displacement, attention to visual surface substituting for attention to the symbolic meaningfulness of the object." Catherine Wilson, "Visual Surface and Visual Symbol: The Microscope and the Occult in Early Modern Science," *Journal of the History of Ideas* 49, no. 1 (1998): 85, 100.

6. Hooke, *Micrographia: Or Some Physiological Descriptions of Minute Bodies Made by Magnifying Glasses with Observations and Inquiries Thereupon* (London: Martyn, 1667), preface.

7. Hooke, *Micrographia*, preface.

8. "Les microscopes & les lunettes nous ont, pour ainsi dire, donné de nouveaux sens au-dessus de notre portée; tels qu'ils appartiendroient à des intelligences supérieures, & qui mettent sans cesse la nôtre en défaut." Pierre-Louis Moureau de Maupertuis, *Vénus physique*, 6th ed. (n.p., 1751), 69.

9. Baker writes, "En un mot les Microscopes nous fournissent en quelque sorte de nouveaux sens, propres à nous faire connoître les opérations les plus surprenantes de la nature, & ils nous mettent sous les yeux des prodiges qu'on n'auroit pas même soupçonnés dans les premiers siécles." Henry Baker, *Le microscope à la portée de tout le monde, ou description, calcul & explication de la nature, de l'usage & de la force des meilleurs microscopes; avec les méthodes nécessaires pour préparer, appliquer, considérer & conserver toutes sortes d'objets, & les précautions à prendre pour les examiner avec soin* (Paris: Jombert, 1754), 1:ix. Deslandes states, "Les hommes étoient des espéces d'aveugles avant la découverte des Microscopes & des Télescopes." André François Deslandes, *Recueil de differens traités de physique et d'histoire naturelle, propres à perfectionner ces deux Sciences* (Paris: Quillau, 1748–50), 1:202.

10. Nollet declares, "Ces nouveaux organes ont dévoilé les secrets de la nature." Jean-Antoine Nollet, *Leçons de physique expérimentale* (Paris: Guerin, 1745–64), 5:558. Lesser sees new worlds emerging from an abyss: "Il nous fait pénétrer dans une espèce de Néant, & étale à nos yeux un nouveau Monde, composé d'un nombre infini d'Etres animés." Friedrich-Christian Lesser, *Théologie des insectes, ou*

démonstration des perfections de Dieu dans tout ce qui concerne les Insectes, trans. Pierre Lyonnet (La Haye: Paupie, 1743), 2:20.

11. "Nous voyons à présent des objets 600 fois plus éloignés, & des objets mille fois plus petits, que les plus petits & les plus éloignés qui pussent être autrefois apperçûs par l'oei[l] le plus perçant de l'antiquité." Baker, *Le microscope,* 368. All translations, unless otherwise noted, are mine.

12. Hooke did not make side-by-side comparisons, but he did show the imperfections in human products such as a needle, a razor, fine linen, and silk. Hooke, *Micrographia,* plates 2 and 3.

13. Martin Frobene Ledermüller, *Amusement microscopique tant pour l'esprit que pour les yeux; contenant estampes dessinées d'après nature et enluminées, avec leurs explications par Monsieur Martin Frobene Ledermüller conseiller de justice & inspecteur du cabinet de curiosités naturelles de S.A.S. Monseigneur le Marggrave regnant de Brandenburg-Coulmbac; de l'Academie Imperiale des Naturalistes, et de la Société Teutonique d'Altorf* 3 vols. (Nuremberg: Winterschmidt, 1764).

14. "La prémière réprésente un Chef d'oeuvre du Beau Sexe; & l'autre l'Ouvrage journalier du plus vilain des Insectes." Ledermüller, *Amusement microscopique,* 2:11. Though not technically an insect, the spider was categorized as such by eighteenth- and even nineteenth-century naturalists.

15. His comment on the lace is as follows: "L'on ne voit qu'une Enlaçûre grossière & confuse de *Noeuds* & de *Lacqs* de Ficéle & de Corde d. . . . On n'y reconnoît ni Dessein, ni la moindre Ordonnance; de sorte qu'on ne le peut voir sans rire," whereas for the web, "Dedans & dehors du Microscope, rien qu'Egalité, que *Dessein,* et si j'ose le dire, qu'Intelligence." Ledermüller, *Amusement microscopique,* 2:11.

16. He speaks of "certaines Gens, à qui rien ne paroit beau, que ce qu'ils aperçoivent par la simple Vüe," and calls them "Timons"—misanthropes of low social rank. Ledermüller, preface to *Amusement microscopique,* 1:1.

17. The promotion of spider silk for the fabrication of luxury goods fascinated eighteenth-century readers. The story of Monsieur Bon, author of a dissertation on the usefulness of spider silk, made its way into several publications, even decades after the failure of his project. According to reports first published in 1710, Monsieur Bon presented a pair of stockings and gloves crafted from spider silk to the Montpellier Assembly along with instructions for their production. Claude-François Lambert, *Bibliothèque de physique et d'histoire naturelle, contenant la physique générale, la physique particuliere, la méchanique, la chimie, l'anatomie, la botanique, la médecine, l'histoire naturelle des insectes, des animaux & des coquillages* (Paris: Chez la Veuve David Jeune, 1758), 5:201–10; Lesser, *Théologie des insects,* 2:1540. Although Bon never lived to see spider farming become commonplace, his dream may soon be realized thanks to Nexia Biotechnologies of Montreal, whose scientists have injected the spider-silk-protein gene into goats. The new fiber extracted from the goat milk is said to be five times stronger than steel. Cathy Newman, "Dreamweavers," *National Geographic,* January 2003, 60.

18. The French literary pastoral, which reached the zenith of its popularity

during the first half of the seventeenth century, often stages the tensions between collective and individual existence. In the words of Jean-Pierre van Elslande, the shepherd figure comes to embody the impossible union of competing ideologies: "Les bergers parviennent à satisfaire aux exigences de la vie en société tout en préservant leur liberté individuelle." Jean-Pierre van Elslande, *L'imaginaire pastorale du XVIIe siècle: 1600–1650* (Paris: Presses Universitaires de France, 1999), 197. A more thorough comparison of the seventeenth-century French pastoral and the eighteenth-century popular natural history writings exceeds the purpose of this essay but merits further exploration.

19. "Loin de la Ville, loin de la Cour, il passe des nuits tranquilles & des jours heureux." Gaspard Guillard de Beaurieu, *Abrégé de l'histoire des insectes, dédié aux jeunes personnes; Orné de figures en taille-douce. Par l'auteur du Cours d'histoire* (Paris: Panckoucke, 1764), 1:v.

20. "Son coeur est pur." Beaurieu, *L'histoire des insects*, ix.

21. "Comme on aime à la Ville une belle Tragédie, une Musique tendre & languissante, ou furieuse & terrible." Beaurieu, *L'histoire des insects*, xii.

22. "Qu'un Artiste vienne lui vanter les belles étoffes qu'il fait, qu'une femme vienne étaler devant lui la belle robe qu'elle porte; il leur montre des Papillons, & les désespere." Beaurieu, *L'histoire des insects*, viii–ix.

23. "Trop sage pour passer d'une Ville de *Hollande*, dans une Cour d'*Italie*." Beaurieu, *L'histoire des insects*, lxxi.

24. "Ceux qui menant à la campagne une vie aussi simple & moins grossiere que celle de nos Laboureurs & de nos Bergers." Beaurieu, *L'histoire des insects*, lxxxix.

25. "Le premier regardera d'un oeil fixe & distrait tout ce qui sera autour de lui, & ne verra rien. L'autre enlevé à lui-même, par mille beautés à la fois." Beaurieu, *L'histoire des insects*, xx.

26. "Malheureux laboreur," "un observateur attentif, un homme qui a une âme." Beaurieu, *L'histoire des insects*, xx.

27. Daniel Cottom, "Taste and the Civilized Imagination," *Journal of Aesthetics and Art Criticism* 39, no. 4 (1981): 368.

28. Voltaire, quoted in Cottom, "Taste and the Civilized Imagination," 370.

29. Cottom, "Taste and the Civilized Imagination," 370.

30. "Des Interlocuteurs de différens états." Noël-Antoine Pluche, *Le spectacle de la nature, ou entretiens sur les particularités de l'histoire naturelle, qui ont paru les plus propres à rendre les jeunes-gens curieux, & à leur former l'esprit*, 6th ed. (Paris: Desaint, 1739), 1:xiv.

31. "Un jeune homme de qualité, que nous appellerons le Chevalier de Breuil." Pluche, *Le spectacle*, xvi.

32. "Notre jeune noblesse." Pluche, *Le spectacle*, xvii.

33. "Mille fois plus belle que Paris avec son faste & ses dorures." Pluche, *Le spectacle*, 2.

34. "Depuis que vous m'avez montré ces verres qui grossissent les petits objets,

j'ai vû dans les insectes des choses admirables. La seule tête d'une mouche est pleine de bouquèts & de diamans." Pluche, *Le spectacle*, 3.

35. "Dites-moi, je vous en prie, Chevalier, trouvez-vous quelqu'un dans le monde qui s'amuse à étudier les insectes? On les écrase: du moins on ne les regarde pas." Pluche, *Le spectacle*, 3–4.

36. Pluche, *Le spectacle*, 4.

37. "Nous ferons de vous un observateur." Pluche, *Le spectacle*, 12.

38. "La supériorité infinie qui brillent dans ceux de la nature." Pluche, *Le spectacle*, 13.

39. "On ne se peut lasser de voir une telle profusion d'or." Pluche, *Le spectacle*, 13.

40. "D'autres têtes qui affectent une semblable parure sans en pouvoir approcher." Pluche, *Le spectacle*, 13.

41. "Salomon dans toute sa gloire n'étoit pas couvert comme la moindre d'entre elles." Pluche, *Le spectacle*, 13.

42. In a later lesson, for example, the chevalier expresses a preference for the architecture of wasps' nests over that of the most beautiful palaces. Pluche, *Le spectacle*, 128.

43. "Dont la passion dominante est la prospérité & le bien de la famille; d'un peuple, en un mot, qui semble avoir pris modéle sur vous." Gilles Auguste Bazin, *Histoire naturelle des abeilles; avec des figures en taille-douce* (Paris: Guerin, 1744), 1:4.

44. "Je ne vous demande que le Roman, mais le Roman vrai de l'histoire des Abeilles." Bazin, *Histoire naturelle des abeilles*, 1:7. For more on the problematic and hybrid nature of dialogic narrative, see Daniel Brewer, "The Philosophical Dialogue and the Forcing of Truth," *MLN* 98, no. 5 (December 1983): 1234–47; and Maurice Roelens, "Le dialogue philosophique, genre impossible," *CAIEF* 24 (May 1972): 43–58. For a useful historical overview that includes the Italian tradition, see Sidney L. Sondergard and Madison U. Sowell, "Bruno's *Cabala* and Italian Dialogue Form," foreword to *The Cabala of Pegasus*, by Giordano Bruno, trans. Sidney L. Sondergard and Madison U. Sowell (New Haven: Yale University Press, 2002), xxxviii–xlix.

45. Gilles Auguste Bazin, *Abrégé de l'histoire des insectes pour servir de suite à l'histoire naturelle des abeilles*, 4 vols. (Paris: Guerin, 1747), 1:16. One can imagine Hortense's expressed fear of names and Clarice's subsequent response as a much abbreviated reenactment of Plato's dialogue "Cratylus." Hortense, like Cratylus, posits a direct connection between name and thing, whereas Clarice, like Hermogenes, sees no natural relationship between signifier and signified. Bazin's treatment of the problem, however, is resolved as a question of maturity and social status rather than philosophy. The enlightened Clarice declares: "How young you are, my dear Hortense! You still sound like your governesses. Who told you that names are disgusting? Names are only sounds, and sounds are not made to affect smell or taste" (Que vous êtes neuve, ma chère Hortense! Vous avez encore le ton de vos gouvernantes. Qui vous a dit que des noms sont dégoûtans? Les noms ne sont que des sons, & les sons ne sont point faits pour affecter l'odorat & le goût). Bazin, *Abrégé de l'histoire des insectes*, 1:16. Hortense's viewpoint is characterized

as a naive residual belief taken from the superstitions of her socially inferior care-takers, a belief that must now be abandoned. Eugène further adds that these "friv-olous fears, and these ridiculous aversions" are best left "to the people, to the ignorant, and to the weak-minded" (Laissons au peuple, aux ignorans, & aux esprits foibles, ces craintes fivoles, & ces aversions ridicules). Bazin, *Abrégé de l'histoire des insectes*, 1:20.

46. "La Nature y est offusquée, toujours fardée, & souvent corrompue." Bazin, *Abrégé de l'histoire des insectes*, 1:5–6.

47. "Prosélyte de l'Histoire Naturelle." Bazin, *Abrégé de l'histoire des insectes*, 1:10.

48. Bazin, *Abrégé de l'histoire des insectes*, 1:14–15.

49. "Sans sortir de ce Parc, nous allons passer, pour ainsi dire, dans une terre étrangère." Bazin, *Abrégé de l'histoire des insectes*, 1:21.

50. "Qu'elle habite au milieu d'une infinité de nations différentes." Bazin, *Abrégé de l'histoire des insectes*, 1:22.

51. "Elle en verra qui passent la moitié de leur vie dans les eaux sous la forme de poisson, & l'autre moitié dans l'air sous la figure d'oiseau." Bazin, *Abrégé de l'histoire des insectes*, 1:23.

52. "Menez-nous, Eugène, dans ce nouveau Monde. Voyageons par ce Parc. Allons de nations en nations." Bazin, *Abrégé de l'histoire des insectes*, 1:25.

53. "Il n'étoit pas nécessaire de nous donner la peine de venir jusqu'ici pour voir de pareilles choses." Bazin, *Abrégé de l'histoire des insectes*, 1:31.

54. Danto, "Aesthetics and Art Criticism," 383–84.

55. "Je voudrois bien pour la singularité du fait, que quelqu'un de notre con-noissance nous surprît à présent dans ce Parc, cheminans comme nous voilà, & courans à travers champs. Il ne manqueroit pas de nous demander où nous allons de cette sorte, & nous de lui répondre: Passez votre chemin, homme de bien, nous sommes en voyage, nous allons à la découverte de Peuples inconnus. Nous dirons vrai, & cependant sur pareille réponse, il n'hésiteroit pas de nous traiter de folles." Bazin, *Abrégé de l'histoire des insectes*, 1:87.

56. "Mes yeux me paroissent plus nets, plus perçans; il me semble que je vois mieux ce que je vois, & mille choses que je ne voyais point auparavant." Bazin, *Abrégé de l'histoire des insectes*, 2:79.

57. "J'en vois en songe, j'y pense en veillant." Bazin, *Abrégé de l'histoire des in-sectes*, 2:80.

58. "Ces gens tout occupés de jeux, de fêtes, de spectacles, de festins, d'intrigues ambitieuses, de visites, de courses." Bazin, *Abrégé de l'histoire des insectes*, 2:176.

59. "Je pensois comme eux en arrivant, & je m'en retournerai pensant comme vous." Bazin, *Abrégé de l'histoire des insectes*, 2:177.

60. Bazin, *Abrégé de l'histoire des insectes*, 2:178.

61. In Pluche's work, the countess praises paintings for their ability to make even the most hideous objects pleasing. Pluche, *Le spectacle*, 96.

62. Leo Marx, *The Machine in the Garden: Technology and the Pastoral Ideal in America* (Oxford: Oxford University Press, 2000), 23.

13

The Force of the Entomological Other

Insects as Instruments of Intolerant Thought and Oppressive Action

CRISTOPHER HOLLINGSWORTH

I

That individuals sometimes use metaphors to label persons whom they see as different is neither news nor a pressing subject for scholarly investigation. However, when such labels are used *instrumentally,* as tools of collective aggression, understanding metaphor and its relationship to action becomes imperative. Michael A. Sells, author of *The Bridge Betrayed: Religion and Genocide in Bosnia,* illustrates why one should be concerned with aggressive, instrumental metaphors:

> Dehumanizing labels were . . . important in motivating genocide. In Serb-occupied areas, Bosnian Croats were invariably called Ustashe, in reference to the fascist units of World War II. Muslims were called Turks (a term of alienation and abuse when used by Serb and Croat militants), Ustashe, and "balije." The origin of the term "balija" (plural "balije") is obscure. Some believe it is related to the South Slavic term for spit or mucus (*bala*); others suggest different etymologies. Bosnian Muslim survivors of the "ethnic cleansing" reported that nationalist Serbs would "spit" the term out at them. A popular song in Belgrade was based on the rhyme "Alija" (the first name of Bosnian President Alija Izetbegovi) and "balija."[1]

These details confirm Gregory H. Stanton's analysis of genocide, which he describes as a process having a structure of eight related stages.[2] Of these stages, the first three—classification, symbolization, and dehumanization—directly involve the work of metaphor.

But not all instrumental metaphors are as historically and culturally specific as those Sells describes. In particular, metaphors that figure a human group as insects have much wider currency. This is so for at least the following two reasons. First, the insect metaphor's terms imply a set of differences that are readily grasped and apparently natural. Second, because the differences on which the metaphor's sense depends are extreme, the figure easily meshes with a variety of absolutist thinking. Thus the metaphor is particularly useful for the conversion of ideology into self-justifying acts of aggression and oppression—a process that is this essay's primary subject.

Consider, for instance, the following instrumental comparisons between human beings and lice. On November 29, 1864, Colonel John M. Chivington, while commanding a unit of the Colorado territorial militia, thus exhorted his troops to massacre a Cheyenne community, including women and children: "We must kill them big and little . . . Nits make lice."[3] The same comparative logic is found in a similar context, this time formulated as a metonymy between lice and Jews in a speech delivered to German personnel on December 16, 1941, by Hans Frank, the Nazi governor of occupied Poland:

In all these weeks, they [his audience's families in Germany] will be thinking of you, saying to themselves: my God, there he sits in Poland where there are so many lice and Jews, perhaps he is hungry and cold, perhaps he is afraid to write. It would not be a bad idea to send our dear ones back home a picture, and tell them: well now, there are not so many lice and Jews any more, and conditions here in the General Government have changed and improved somewhat already. Of course, I could not eliminate all lice and Jews in only one year's time. But in the course of time, and above all, if you help me, this end will be attained. After all, it is not necessary for us to accomplish everything within a year and right away, for what would otherwise be left for those who follow us to do?[4]

It is obvious that Chivington and Frank understood and used the lice metaphor with striking similarity. However, since there is no indication that Frank—or any other Nazi who used this or other related human-animal metaphors for genocidal purposes[5]—was aware of Chivington, much less a student of his rhetoric, how do we account for these nearly identical figures? What is the "logic" that subtends and therefore links these metaphors (similarly informs their structures, their cognitive and dramatic potentials) and their contexts? Is this logic historically and culturally specific? What is the relationship between this logic and oppressive actions?

Alex Bein, author of "The Jewish Parasite," a much-cited historical and semantic investigation of the metaphor of parasitism in European culture and Nazi discourse, would view Chivington's and Frank's similar use of the insect metaphor as unique to postromantic Europe.[6] Bein argues that romantic organicism was the primary and essential ground for the irrational, mystical perspective (5) that eventually made possible the literalization of originally scientific human-animal comparisons, which were thereby empowered to play a decisive role in the Final Solution's prosecution.[7] To clarify: it is Bein's position that, before the convergence in the late nineteenth century and the early twentieth of "biological, technological, and mythological" thinking and, in particular, the "infiltration" of biological concepts into other discourses (5), any given comparison between humans and animals was, to one degree or another, understood "in the manner of an analogy rather than a scientific definition" (19). From this perspective, then, aggressive instrumental metaphors are best studied as recent, culturally specific linguistic and political forms.

According to Bein's theory, Chivington's and Frank's lice metaphors ultimately derive from, and refer to, the power of scientific discourse. In that Frank was an educated member of a scientifically advanced culture, no argument need be made concerning the influence of biological concepts—specifically the pathogenic theory of disease—on his thought and language. Chivington's case, however, is less clear. Though we may assume that by 1864, biological concepts had "infiltrated" what Bein would call America's "language of popular politics" (18), thereby establishing a quasi-scientific foundation for racist, mythical thinking, it was not until Ronald Ross's 1897 study of malaria that a connection between insects and sickness was proved.[8] The scientific connection between these men and their metaphors now seems more tenuous.

Fortunately there are several certainties that enable a broader path of understanding. For one thing, Chivington and Frank were members of a bourgeois culture that equated cleanliness with virtue, civilization, and the mastery of nature.[9] For another, there is little doubt that each man felt himself to be a warrior for this culture and its ideology. Each was a supervising "frontier" agent of his civilization's seemingly necessary expansion and was tasked with controlling and eradicating members of a weaker, cultur-ally Other, and therefore undesirable population. Scientific thinking is, of course, part of their shared bourgeois culture, and a vital source of its tech-nological superiority and entitlement to aggression. But science is not as cognitively, emotionally, and metaphorically crucial as the genocidal con-text itself. Chivington and Frank were commanders who needed metaphors that were equal to their motives, capable of expressing and, as important, justifying the use of otherwise immoral force against other human beings.

Certainly Bein's theory illuminates. However, its dependence on a pre-cise sequence of unique historical, philosophical, and cultural events limits its ability to account for the variety of instrumental human-animal compar-isons—particularly human-insect metaphors—that are common features of the language of oppression as it presents itself in historical texts and across a range of present-day situations of cultural conflict, few of which are entirely defined by the European cultural tradition. Another related problem with his theory is its foundational assumption that science is a uniquely rational and therefore transparent and value-free discourse. This notion enables his argument's key principle (behind which we might sense the influence of a drama of corruption and fall), namely, that the "infil-tration" of biological (rational) concepts into nonscientific (irrational) dis-courses is necessary for the formation of "mythical thinking" (18).[10]

A better model of the relationship between metaphor, ideology, and action—one capable of relating instrumental uses of the insect metaphor as historically and culturally disparate as, for instance, Virgil's description of Carthage as a beehive ripe for Trojan harvesting and the figuring of Tutsis as cockroaches by Hutus during the recent Rwandan genocide—may be had through treating the instrumental insect metaphor as the visible aspect of an ideologeme. Writing in *The Political Unconscious*, Fredric Jameson defines the ideologeme as "a historically determinate conceptual or semic complex which can project itself variously in the form of a 'value system' or 'philosophical concept,' or in the form of a protonarrative, a private or col-lective narrative fantasy."[11] One example that Jameson treats is the binary opposition of good and evil, a simple, highly structured, and apparently moral way of thinking that has tremendous psychological and cultural influence. As I understand Jameson's thought, it is fair to speak of his ideologeme as a false consciousness given conceptual solidity and, there-fore, cultural agency. Especially when modeled by the good/evil binary, the

Jamesonian ideologeme is a psychosocial entity that has the agency to "project itself variously," forcing its starkly oppositional logic on public thinking and individual fantasies alike—a strategy that is furthered by this ideologeme's apparent ahistoricity and seeming cognitive naturalness.

Jameson's notion of the ideologeme allows for, and to a degree explains, an intuition about many insect metaphors that is almost certainly shared by all observers of symbolic insects and challenges the entrenched doctrine of historical and cultural uniqueness. Beneath the variety of insect metaphors lies a subtending logic, simultaneously evasive and determinate, that springs less from historical and cultural particulars than from a powerful and morally charged contrast of opposites. Indeed, when viewed as a lens for this logic's force, the lice metaphor economically and unequivocally accomplishes the first three of Stanton's eight, mutually reinforcing genocidal stages. Through its *symbolization* as a noxious insect (a metaphorical vehicle that simultaneously expresses alterity, powerlessness, and worthlessness), a group of human beings is *classified* as Other and thus *dehumanized*. But the product of this tripartite process is not merely the apprehension in a reader's or auditor's mind that a group is nonhuman. The metaphor also functions as a dramatic syllogism whose proper conclusion is the application of necessary force against a physically insignificant and verminous pest. It is in this light that I conceive the instrumental insect metaphor to be a machine of the imagination that converts (clarifies, simplifies, amplifies, and organizes) ideological abstractions into a simple and powerful mentally staged drama—what amounts to a blueprint for action in the world.

Several of Wolfgang Iser's key observations about the psychology of reading further clarify how and why the insect metaphor may be used instrumentally to convert ideology into a mentally staged drama. To Iser, reading is an experience realized through what he suggestively calls the "virtual dimension."[12] It is in and through this virtual dimension—which Iser speaks of as both a creative response to textual language and a mental space—that highly shaped verbal forms such as metaphors are "ideated," experienced as internal images.[13] From the phenomenological perspective, one does not "see" an ideated image in the optical sense; one inhabits or *lives* this sort of image, unfolding its terms, translating them into the virtual dimension's dramatic language of relative size, position, and proximity, and apparent similarity and difference. Given that a metaphor has sufficient ideational agency, this unfolding is an act of construction that evokes and orchestrates a virtual space, within which concepts may function as actors.

Whether read or heard, the insect metaphor is one such figure that enjoys this order of agency. The act of conceiving—ideating—a human group as an insect swarm or society, primarily carried out by the cognitive unconscious, is at the same time an act of spatial construction. To ideate the insect metaphor—which, again, is to inhabit, to live through and according to its laws—is to assume the role of a singular subject whose raison d'être is to see and thus to know the entomological object of its gaze as the Other. Hence the conventional pattern of the insect metaphor: a human subject positioned above and gazing down on an insect collective.[14] It is through this pattern that the abstract substance of ideology is given flesh, made available to the mind as a dramatically charged situation that narrowly defines subsequent imaginative or physical action.

The sum of this necessarily involved analysis is that, far from being an innocent bit of posy, a mere metaphor that is sometimes made to serve unsavory purposes, the insect metaphor is inherently political—but not in the abstract sense. What the figure is "about" is the feeling that attends a dramatic confrontation of self and Other in the context of targeted power. In Aristotelian terms, the insect metaphor's operation, its "working out of a motive," may be conceived as a specific praxis that involves, and dramatizes, a purposeful and self-justifying application of power against the Other.[15] And it is its special praxis, I am convinced, that accounts for the metaphor's popularity with persons from different times and cultures who share a fascination with the process and application of power that they wish to represent as natural.

II

If one focuses on contemporary instances of the instrumental insect metaphor, elements of a general poetics of imperialism and genocide may be proposed. Some insect metaphors are strikingly simple, horrifying in their directness. These may be called *blatant*, because their subtending ideology is simple enough to be expressed entirely through the insect metaphor's structural implications, its power to mentally stage a confrontation between antithetical modes of being that concludes with the necessary and therefore satisfying extermination of the Other. Donald E. Miller, a scholar of religion and genocide, provides us with an example of a blatant insect metaphor that serves this present argument in two ways. First, because this metaphor was instrumental in the recent genocide in Rwanda, it confirms that neither Western historiography nor scientific categories are essential for the development of extreme forms of the insect metaphor. Second, the following example illuminates the instrumental insect metaphor's utility as an easily grasped dramatic experience that bridges the gap between thought and action:

> In Rwanda, the majority Hutus regularly referred to Tutsis as cockroaches— one of nature's lowest and most tenacious life forms. A well-educated Rwandan told me [Miller] that his Hutu pastor refused to serve Communion to Tutsis prior to the genocide, because he did not think insects were worthy to eat and drink the body and blood of Christ.[16]

Here the instrumental formulation is embodied through the cockroach (in Kinyarwandan, the native language of Rwanda, *inyenzi*)[17] and used to symbolize the Hutu's view of the Tutsis in such a way as to unequivocally dehumanize them and imply a clear and self-justifying praxis: the Tutsis' extermination. But it is the Hutu pastor's individuation of the figure that underscores its power to convert ideology (in this instance, religious belief) into action, transforming it from shared, often unconscious, assumptions and feelings into a conscious and therefore manipulable pattern. Almost certainly this pastor would have refused the Tutsis communion under any condition. However, that he uses the insect metaphor to justify this action, which we may assume runs counter to his religious training and faith, strongly suggests that, to the ideologically prepared, this metaphor is no ordinary figure of speech.

This metaphor's rhetorical currency and capacity to evoke and shape action within the Rwandan context are further illustrated by language urging the Tutsis' extermination that was broadcast over RTLM (Radio Libre Des Mille Collines, a Hutu-run radio station): "The Inyenzi [cockroaches] have always been Tutsi. We will exterminate them. One can identify them because they are of one race. You can identify them by their height and their small nose. When you see that small nose, break it."[18] Given my argument thus far, I think it is more than speculation to hold that, to the ideologically prepared, including educated professionals, the blatant insect metaphor exerts a discrete and compelling cognitive presence that is inseparable from a disturbingly aggressive emotional appeal. The figure's praxis creates a role and script for action appealing enough to negate or at least corrupt alternative, humanistic codes, such as Christian values and professional ethics.

Owing to a superior congruence between ideology and embodying figuration, the blatant instrumental metaphor offers its user clarity of motive and action. But there are other situations of greater rhetorical, social, and ideological complexity, where a genocidal motive cannot be expressed so clearly, either because such an expression is politically unadvisable or because genocide *in itself* is not a primary goal. Such complex situations call for complex—*nuanced*—versions of the insect metaphor, which, as I will demonstrate, tend to moderate genocidal images and patterns of action through embedding them within a nexus of more acceptable ideologies of progress.

Take, for example, the following passage from Freud's *Civilization and Its Discontents,* a singularly rational argument that seeks to expose and counter unreason: "The bees, the ants, the termites—strove for thousands of years before they arrived at the State institutions, the distribution of functions and the restrictions on the individual, for which we admire them to-day."[19] We are now so used to this evolutionary comparison of human and insect sociality that its metaphorical nature is hardly obtrusive; but that Freud is using the evolutionary perspective, as Bein theorizes, to literalize his insect metaphor, should give us reason to examine it more closely. In contrast to the blatant instrumental formulation, this nuanced version expresses motivational complexity, some of which is not entirely available to its author. On the one hand, Freud wishes to subordinate the insect metaphor to science. Through hybridizing an inherited literary pattern and biological theory, Freud attempts to eliminate the qualitative differences between subject and object that are essential to the poetic form. At the same time, however, Freud is drawn to and requires the insect metaphor's praxis, its ability to stage and naturalize power that is targeted at a collective. Freud cannot, therefore, break entirely with the metaphor's traditional pattern. His actual strategy is to alter this pattern by increasing the conceptual distance between the position of knowing observer and observed collective, to such a degree that it is possible to visualize humans and insects as comparable, equally animals. Here the metaphor threatens to converge with others we associate with absolutist or even genocidal thinking. Freud's target is not, however, actual human beings. Instead he directs his metaphor's force at Western culture's idea of itself, which his purpose is to undo. However much his science may be said to camouflage this metaphor's motive, cloaking motivated force in dispassionate natural law, by its extremity and aggression this figure shows both its modernity and its generic kinship to other instrumental formulations.

In Freud I sense a struggle between the insect metaphor's praxis, the locus of this textual moment's imaginative power, and the rational argument and humanistic purposes that the figure is supposed to serve. That Freud prefaces this metaphor with a statement of human singularity, the claim that the human struggle for survival is unique because of its cultural component, strikes me as a moment of unintentional irony.[20] Altered by Darwinian perspective, which implicitly defines *all* labor (action) as competition and *any* sort of progress as a struggle for survival, the metaphor's extremity collapses the human into a disenchanted, disinterested nature. Heroism, duty, and the search for love and salvation (all human justifications for struggle—and reasoned argument itself) are negated, replaced with necessity in the form of the impersonal principle of competition. If this metaphor may be said to give form to an ideology, then it is one that, against its containing argument's better nature, seems capable of fully naturalizing, justifying a staggering range of immoral cultural practices and their attendant ideologies and motives: colonialism, imperialism, unrestrained capitalism, war, and genocide.

As I have suggested, Freud is probably not aware of the mixed motives his language reveals. One might say that his argument manages to repress his metaphor's fantastic aggression. Uzi Landau, however, does not seem to share Freud's ambivalence concerning the instrumental insect metaphor's implications. Landau's formulation, though nuanced, deals with these implications more directly and for an overt political purpose. According to an unnamed reporter for *Arabic News,* while Israeli minister of internal security, Landau more than once "described the Palestinians as insects that should be eliminated after drying the swamps they live in." The journalist further reports that Landau used this comparison to Palestinians in regard to "demolishing the Palestinian cities, villages and camps."[21] It is arguable that Landau is drawn to the insect metaphor because it enables him to dehumanize the Palestinians in such a way as to justify their extermination.

However, Landau's motives and hence his insect metaphor are more complicated. Similar to Frank, Landau wishes to displace, camouflage, and justify
his genocidal motive and the application of power it assumes. Interestingly,
his "compromise" instrument is a close relative of the praxis that we have
seen in Freud. This dramatic path's evolutionary logic enables Landau to
embed a morally reprehensible motive within an apparently natural narrative of progress, thereby partially transforming it.

While I sense that Landau shares Chivington's and Frank's desire for
already occupied territory, he clearly cannot admit to their methods. I hes-
itate to think that the terrible irony of a Jew using a blatant insect metaphor
to model and justify genocide is lost on Landau.[22] Regardless, it is significant that Landau expresses this metaphor in such a way as to de-emphasize
its analogical and potentially blatant aspect (the comparison between Palestinians and insects) in order to foreground and complicate the metaphor's
true ideological work. Rather than extermination, this insect metaphor's
primary action is "drying the swamps," which implies a natural and necessary expansion into unimproved land. What Landau has done is evoke the
insect metaphor's apicultural associations, a cultural memory of a bucolic,
honeyed relationship between human and insect (a *natural* imperialism),
which he fuses with a politicized evolutionary process. This complex metaphor offers the members of its Israeli audience the role of heroic agricultural laborer, which reacts back on the aggressive and disturbing image of
Palestinian insects, moderating and usefully redefining their Otherness.

These Palestinian "insects" are Other not because they are biologically
different from the Israelis. Rather, they are Other because they are economically useless, "incapable" of improving the swamps they live in and therefore cannot lay claim to. Through embedding his genocidal motive in a
complex of assumptions that hinge on an economic definition of man that
he believes is ethically neutral and is subtended by a fusion of evolutionary
and nationalistic ideologies, Landau recasts genocide as resettlement, a secondary consequence of Israel's progressive conversion of wilderness into
the Promised Land.

Landau's nuanced metaphor suggests that the economic definition of man
adds to the insect metaphor's utility as an instrument of intolerant thinking and action. We may therefore expect similar versions of the insect metaphor to appear in other situations where human value and interaction are
understood through an economic lens. In the southwestern United States,

for instance, Mexican immigrants are frequently described as cockroaches.[23] As one should expect, a good number of these cockroach metaphors are blatant, similar to the Rwandan instances quoted earlier. Others serve as evidence that the economic definition of human beings and society does not always result in nuanced metaphors. I would have the following insect metaphor (transcribed without corrections), which "William" has posted on the *Rush Limbaugh Campfire,* an Internet discussion board, serve as an example of an insect metaphor that has become increasingly common with the spread of capitalist ideology and its instrumental definition of human beings.

> The garbage on here are running their pieholes because everything that the whites are saying is true and they know it. Wetbacks are good for nothing. They are so stupid that they will work for a lot of time and have nothing to show for it exept to stay drunk and reck the cars that they have. Mexicans arent even good enough to lick our boots and I wouldnt let them anyway. It should be legal to shoot them on sight. They breed their filthy race like the cockroaches that they are.[24]

This language is an unappetizing stew of influences, and though it shares much with Landau's description of the Palestinians, the degree of intolerance it expresses is more pronounced. Moreover, I sense that it contains a heightened and therefore shaping presence of capitalist ideology. In comparison with William's metaphor, Landau's seems old-fashioned. Landau casts the Palestinians as Other because they cannot make the *land* productive. In contrast, William's core objection to Mexicans is not either that they are Mexican or invaders or even that they do not work hard (he admits they do). Rather, to William, what makes Mexicans Other and authorizes their killing is that they cannot make themselves productive within the American capitalist system. As racist as William is, the root "logic" of his intolerance is neither scientific nor imperialistic. One may speculate that William is angered that he and other middle-class whites will have to support these (in William's eyes) unproductive, illegal immigrants. But the logic of his instrumental insect metaphor, which he presents as argument, clearly derives from a belief that the degree of one's humanity is determined by, and measurable through, success in the laissez-faire economic system.

Fortunately, since ideology is transmitted through form, its influence may be identified and at least a measure of its power opposed. And in the case of the instrumental insect metaphors used by William and his ilk, it is being countered by its mirror image. Figuring a human group as a horde of cockroaches has obvious ideational and rhetorical power. But this metaphor belongs to no particular person, group, or ideological position. Moreover, because the comparison between human beings and insects is an ideated (visual-spatial) elaboration of a binary opposition, it is easily reversible—especially in the context of the U.S.–Mexican immigration debate. To Mexicans, the cockroach is more than a pest. Celebrated in folklore and song, this durable creature is associated with survival and successful opposition to oppression.[25] It is therefore no small irony that the historical and cultural ignorance that enables bigoted anti-Mexican rhetoric also vitiates its force.

Elena Poniatowska, a leading Mexican journalist and writer, uses the Mexicans-are-cockroaches metaphor to dramatize the power and progress of Mexican immigration: "The common people—the poor, the dirty, the lice-ridden, the cockroaches—are advancing on the United States, a country that needs to speak Spanish because it has 33.5 million Hispanics who are imposing their culture." "Mexico is recovering the territories yielded to the United States by means of migratory tactics."[26] Here virtue and agency belong to the cockroaches. What many Americans would probably regard as an invasion expressed through inverted rhetoric is to Poniatowska the simultaneous recovery of culture and territory appropriately symbolized. Interestingly, although Poniatowska's instrumental insect metaphor shares the structure of all the examples I have examined, both the type of action that her metaphor proposes and the degree of oppression this figure advocates are distinct from, especially, William's rhetoric of economic dehumanization and extermination. Poniatowska's idea of historical and political progress—and hence her metaphor's path of action—is cultural, not scientific or economic; its terminus is a "recover[y of] . . . territories" through immigration. While Poniatowska's figure recognizes and, indeed, embraces cultural difference and pursues conflict over territory, the targeted extermination of any particular group is not even implied. I further suggest that while the Hispanification of "white" America may be interpreted as aggression, or even genocide, the terms and processes of Poniatowska's insect metaphor do not traffic with this order of violence because its author does

not define human beings, Mexican or American, according to imperialistic, scientific, or economic logic. Even though Poniatowska's instrumental
metaphor was created within a context of oppression and conflict and responds to a rhetoric far more intolerant, it expresses an ideology that should
give us hope. Perhaps the growing inequalities and conflicts that attend the
expansion of capitalism and its nexus of dehumanizing ideologies do not
in every instance determine that the magic of metaphor to covert ideology
into action must serve the intolerant and thus play a role in oppressive and
genocidal actions.

NOTES

1. Sells, *The Bridge Betrayed: Religion and Genocide in Bosnia* (Berkeley: University of California Press, 1996), 75–76.

2. Stanton, "The Eight Stages of Genocide," *Genocidewatch,* http://www.
genocidewatch.org/8stages.htm, April 18, 2003. The eight stages are as follows: classification, symbolization, dehumanization, organization, polarization, preparation,
extermination, and denial. For an authoritative definition and discussion of genocide, see Frank Chalk and Kurt Jonassohn, *The History and Sociology of Genocide:
Analyses and Case Studies* (New Haven, Conn.: Yale University Press, 1990), 5–53.

3. Chivington, quoted in "Tragedy of the Plains Indians: The Sand Creek Massacre," *Gilder Lehrman Institute of American History,* http://www.gliah.uh.edu/
database/article_display.cfm?HHID=563, April 1, 2003.

4. Frank, quoted in "Statements by Leading Nazis on the 'Jewish Question,'"
A Teacher's Guide to the Holocaust, http://fcit.coedu.usf.edu/holocaust/resource/
document/DocJewQn.htm, March 30, 2003.

5. In "The Language of Manipulation," Henry Friedlander observes that "the
Nazis used two languages. One was the public language, the language of the propagandists. The other was the bureaucratic, hidden language, the language of the
technicians. While the language of the technicians remained hidden from public
view until the postwar years, the language of the propagandists stood for all Nazi
language during the twelve years of the Third Reich. Hitler pronounced it, Goebbels
refined it, and every Nazi functionary copied it. This public language—used to
guide the followers, convince the subjects, and intimidate the opponents—eventually penetrated all aspects of public and private life." Friedlander, "The Manipulation of Language," in *The Holocaust: Ideology, Bureaucracy, and Genocide,* ed. Henry
Friedlander and Sybil Milton (Millwood, N.Y.: Kraus International, 1980), 103.
Because the lice metaphor was a commonplace of Nazi rhetoric, Frank's use cannot be treated as a personal, independent formulation—nor should Chivington's.
Each such instrumental metaphor is simultaneously an element of a unique public
rhetoric of intolerance and a representative member of a class of metaphors that

are present—even if only as a potential—in every situation of cultural contact. Thus, and because metaphors such as these also mediate between propaganda and individual action, I choose to emphasize these figures' rhetorical liminality, their power as shaping catalysts that participate in both public and private discourses.

6. Bein, "The Jewish Parasite: Notes on the Semantics of the Jewish Problem, with Special Reference to Germany," in *Leo Baeck Institute Year Book* 9 (London: Horovitz, 1964), 3–40.

7. Bein recognizes his argument's indebtedness to Victor Klemperer, a professor and philologist who fell prey to Nazi oppression, whose diaries—*Lingua Tertii Imperii*—singularly illuminate the Nazi use and abuse of language. See Klemperer, *The Language of the Third Reich (LTI—Lingua Tertii Imperii): A Philologist's Notebook,* trans. Martin Brady (New Brunswick, N.J.: Athlone, 2000). Although its focus is Nazi linguistics, aspects of Klemperer's analysis are highly useful for developing a wider understanding of the relationship between language and oppression. Several other important treatments of Nazi language available in English include Karin Doerr, "Nazi-Deutsch: An Ideological Language of Exclusion, Domination, and Annihilation," in *Nazi-Deutsch/Nazi German: An English Lexicon of the Language of the Third Reich,* ed. Robert Michael and Karin Doerr (Westport, Conn.: Greenwood, 2002), 27–46; Christopher M. Hutton, *Linguistics and the Third Reich: Mother-Tongue Fascism, Race, and the Science of Language* (New York: Routledge, 1999); Robert Michael, "The Tradition of Anti-Jewish Language," in Michael and Doerr, *Nazi-Deutsch/Nazi German,* 1–25; Heinz Paechter, "The Spirit and Structure of Nazi Language," in *Nazi-Deutsch: A Glossary of Contemporary German Usage,* ed. Heinz Paechter (New York: Frederick Ungar, 1944), 5–15; and Leni Yahil, "Sprachregelung," in *Encyclopedia of the Holocaust,* ed. Israel Gutman (New York: Macmillan, 1990), 4:1398–99.

8. Deborah Z. Altschuler, "Zinsser, Lice and History," *HeadLice.Org,* http://www.headlice.org/news/classics/zinsser.htm, April 2, 2003.

9. Jonas Frykman and Oscar Löfgren, *Culture Builders: A Historical Anthropology of Middle-Class Life,* trans. Alan Crozier (New Brunswick, N.J.: Rutgers University Press, 1987), 157–73.

10. Another factor shaping Bein's analysis is the position that the Holocaust was culturally and historically unique. In this regard, Inga Clendinnen's *Reading the Holocaust* (New York: Cambridge University Press, 1999) will provide the interested reader with a bold but responsible introduction to the Holocaust's changing and complicating historiography. This study's bibliography is current and well selected.

11. Jameson, *The Political Unconscious: Narrative as a Socially Symbolic Act* (Ithaca, N.Y.: Cornell University Press, 1981), 115.

12. Iser, "The Reading Process: a Phenomenological Approach," in *Reader-Response Criticism: From Formalism to Post-Structuralism,* ed. Jane P. Tompkins (Baltimore: Johns Hopkins University Press, 1980), 54–56.

13. Iser, *The Act of Reading: A Theory of Aesthetic Response* (Baltimore: Johns Hopkins University Press, 1988), 137.

14. For a more detailed explanation of the insect metaphor's spatial-dramatic construction and its implications, see Cristopher Hollingsworth, *Poetics of the Hive: The Insect Metaphor in Literature* (Iowa City: University of Iowa Press, 2001), 2–16.

15. I derive this meaning of the word *praxis* from Francis Fergusson's introduction to *Aristotle's Poetics* (New York: Hill and Wang, 1961), 4, 8–13. The quoted phrase appears on page 9.

16. Miller, "April is the Cruelest Month," *Sightings*, May 2, 2002, Martin Marty Center, University of Chicago Divinity School, http://marty-center.uchicago.edu/sightings/archive_2002/0502.shtml.

17. Philip Gourevitch, *We Wish to Inform You That Tomorrow We Will Be Killed with Our Families: Stories from Rwanda* (New York: Farrar, Straus and Giroux, 1998), 32.

18. Mary Kimani, "Media Trial: 'Hate Radio' Urged Hutus to Break 'Small Noses,' Expert Witness Testifies," *Internews Reports of the International War Crimes Tribunal for Rwanda*, March 30, 2002, http://www.internews.org/activities/ICTR_reports/ ICTRnewsMar02.html.

19. Sigmund Freud, *Civilization and Its Discontents*, trans. James Strachey (New York: W. W. Norton, 1961), 70.

20. Ibid., 69.

21. "Israel severs contacts with Arafat, five Palestinians killed, 70 wounded," *Arabic News*, December 14, 2001, http://www.arabicnews.com/ansub/Daily/Day/011214/2001121415.html.

22. Bein, who was writing in the early 1960s, observed that "Zionists, especially socialist Zionists," were not averse to using the word "parasite" to describe other Jews: "to mark the unhealthy professional structure of the Jews in the Diaspora, and to motivate the necessity for them to return to Palestine and to basic production." In the same footnote (25n64), Bein paraphrases A. D. Gordon's description of "a Jewish national economy, based on Jewish domination over Arab workers, as 'national parasitism.'" Bein views these uses of dehumanizing metaphors by Jews against other Jews as unconscious, evidence that "language penetrates so deeply the consciousness . . . that the word 'parasite' is being taken over unthinkingly." Perhaps there is something like this at work in Landau's rhetoric; however, I think his motives are largely distinct from the Nazis' and clear to himself and all others who are involved in the contemporary Israeli-Palestinian conflict.

23. Through collecting metaphors for an earlier version of this essay, I was reacquainted with the commonplace of American anti-immigration rhetoric that associates Mexican immigrants and the so-called Africanized or killer bees. I first became aware of this association through the "Killer Bees" sketches that began airing in 1975 on NBC's *Saturday Night Live* ("Killer Bees," http://www.tvacres.com/insects_killerbees.htm). As I recall, these sketches revealed and savaged the racist ideology of the Mexican–killer bee association and lampooned the popular hysteria surrounding the anticipated invasions of both Mexicans and hyperaggressive killer insects. Regardless, a generation later it is apparent that together the presence

and power of the metaphor and its context of fear have increased. Moreover and relatedly, there is evidence that the killer-bee metaphor has become abstracted from its origins, becoming a fixture in the American popular consciousness. For instance, when describing the motivation behind the recall of California governor Gray Davis, "Democratic strategist Darry Sragow . . . said Republicans favoring the recall 'are like a hive of Africanized killer bees. They have a mission and a target.'" Sragow, quoted in Patrick McMahon, "Latinos May Make or Break Election," *USA Today,* October 6, 2003.

Because the metaphor tends to be used by American conservatives against a targeted group (usually Mexican immigrants), Sragow's inversion, the figuring of Republicans as mindless and nonhuman Africanized killer bees, doesn't work: his formulation's obvious irony is overwhelmed by unproductive rhetorical incongruity. In contrast, Michael Moore's ironic use of the same abstracted metaphor—in visual form—is highly effective. In *Bowling for Columbine* (2002), his award-winning documentary exploration of, and argument about, contemporary American violence, Moore places images that evoke Africanized killer bees in a new and wider context, that of White America's media-fueled culture of fear, particularly the fear of African American males. Moore's transplantation of what many Americans regard as a geographically and racially specific metaphor to a novel but metaphorically congruent situation succeeds in several ways. It foregrounds the constructedness of metaphorical knowledge and reveals the ideological irrationality that subtends both the killer bee metaphor and the conjoined myths of African and African American savagery. Moore's success in this regard, however, cannot be ascribed entirely to either his genius or the powers of cinematic montage. Swift and Twain are only two of many precinematic satirists who achieved similar results through dropping the commonplace into the uncommon.

24. William, "Mexicans are human garbage," posted March 6, 2002 on the *Rush Limbaugh Campfire,* http://killdevilhill.com/conservativechat/shakespearew/31.html.

25. Lois Marie Jaeck, "'Viva México/Viva la Revolución'—One Hundred Years of Popular/Protest Songs: The Heartbeat of a Collective Identity," *Ciencia Ergo Sum* 8, no. 1 (2001), http://ergosum.uaemex.mx/marzo01/corridos.html. The reader who is interested in the cockroach's wider political symbolism may wish to compare Oscar Zeta Acosta, *The Revolt of the Cockroach People* (New York: Vintage, 1989), with Tewfik al-Hakim, *The Fate of a Cockroach,* in *The Fate of a Cockroach and Other Plays,* trans. Denys Johnson-Davies (London: Heinemann, 1973), 1–76. See Hollingsworth, *Poetics of the Hive,* 214–24, for a reading of al-Hakim's *The Fate of a Cockroach* as a response to Sartre's *The Flies* (trans. Stuart Gilbert, in *No Exit and Three Other Plays* [New York: Vintage, 1955], 49–127) and its author's antagonistic version of existentialism.

26. Poniatowska, quoted in "Mexico Reconquering U.S. Territory? Writer Says Emigration Imposing Hispanic Culture on North America," *WorldNetDaily,* August 15, 2001, http://www.worldnetdaily.com/news/article.asp?ARTICLE_ID=24059.

PART III

Unsettling Insects

14

Inside Out

The Unsettling Nature of Insects

CHARLOTTE SLEIGH

Insects are all wrong. There is a good case for regarding them as zoology's Other, the definitive organisms of *différance*. We humans have skeletons; they keep their hard parts on the outside and their squishy bits in the middle. We humans celebrate intelligence as our defining feature; they form almost equally complex societies by instinct. No wonder we are disgusted and fascinated when we find them in the kitchen.

The origins of such representations are complex, but the early twentieth century is an identifiable transition period in the history of entomology, when insects were reconstructed as modernist bogeys. Their physiology and senses were reconsidered in the light of evolutionary theory; in particular, a reassessment of their psychology allied them to the savagery of the unconscious. Doubt and anxiety attended the question of where they should be posed on the evolutionary tree: at the topmost twig of an offshoot alternative to that of vertebrates, or lower down on the selfsame branch? In short, were insects protohuman or antihuman by nature? Drawing on historical, literary, and psychoanalytic sources, this essay explores insects' representational metamorphosis into truly *creepy* crawlies.

My high school biology class held many horrors. Preserved primitive sea creatures that had been gently disintegrating over many years were unbottled annually, releasing shreds of gray flesh into their thin formaldehyde gruel as they were poked and prodded by queasy teens. Ox eyes were stored unrefrigerated through a hot June day to be dissected in last period; their pale, strawlike lashes were—paradoxically—the only part that appeared to gaze at us, balefully, as we sliced through the hard yellow fat and into the viscous fluid bags. Worse yet, two pickled human fetuses at differing stages of development stood on the shelves. Yet of all these experiences—of which at least the latter can no longer be considered appropriate to inflict on students—the memory that has stayed with me most strongly is that of the bluebottle.

We were studying the life cycle of the bluebottle and had before us some of their pupae: red brown, shaped like fat cigars about of seven millimeters' length, and segmented in appearance. Then we cut into them. I will never forget the horror as a thick, puslike yellow goop oozed out. Something struck me as profoundly wrong. I could understand how a vertebrate could grow from a homunculus embryo, but how could a fly assemble itself, life-size and ready to go, from a soup? These seemed like the properties of a science-fictional beast so far as I was concerned. How could a liquid possibly organize itself into an animal? Here was nature at its most perverse.

The roots of the disgust felt by my classmates and me lie in a variety of cultural norms and expectations quite specific to twentieth-century Western culture. Not the least of these is the notion, drummed into us from childhood, that flies are "dirty." Around 1910, the U.S. government scientist L. O. Howard rechristened the housefly—previously considered a friendly visitor to the home—the "filth fly" or "typhoid fly."[1] The *Nature-Study Review,* aimed primarily at schoolteachers of Howard's day, exhorted its readers to transmit this message to their pupils, suggesting a mass "fly-killing crusade" as a suitable object lesson for one whole day.[2]

The aspirations of would-be professional entomologists like Howard are responsible for a lot of our antipathy toward insects. In their eagerness to persuade governments and universities to fund their work, these men (and a handful of women) needed to convince their audiences that insects were a serious problem requiring professional intervention.[3] Economics formed a major part of their argument (crop damage by insects), as did human disease (malaria, typhoid), and, in more general terms, the cultivation of a negative image for insects.

Historically, however, the majority of insect students were not pest-control professionals but amateur natural historians and collectors. During the day they might work as physicians or teachers or even attend school themselves; on weekends the gardens and prairies became their hunting grounds as they sought out and captured exotic new specimens for the cabinet drawer at home. From the latter part of the nineteenth century there were guidebooks to help them identify their prizes, but even so there was often a good chance of finding something as yet undescribed by science, such was (and is) the vast number of insect species. But in the wake of Howard and the others, the bugs they collected took on a different edge; they became more suspect. The joy of "beetling" was now tinged with an edge of perversity; what was desirable might also be dangerous. For children in particular, this was excellent news. They no longer needed to pull the wings off flies to elicit a satisfyingly strong reaction; merely collecting insects was now enough.

In each of the following two sections, a phylogenetic transformation of the insect is mapped onto a cultural metamorphosis of Western civilization in the twentieth century. The theme was a common one in the early twentieth century. Alerted to the existence of a "plagiarized" human-turns-into-animal story by a friend, Franz Kafka replied: "Oh no! He didn't get that from me. It's in the times. We both copied it from that."[4] The comparisons echo the then-prevalent "law of recapitulation"—posited by Ernst Haeckel—that ontogeny recapitulated phylogeny.[5] In other words, the development and growth of the individual organism fast-forwarded through the evolution transitions undergone by its ancestors. In the following instances, the development of humans is seen to reflect in some way (not always straightforwardly) the evolutionary metamorphoses of insects. The essay thus dwells on the ambiguity of the term "imago." This was first used frequently in the nineteenth century, when it referred to the adult or "perfect" form of an insect having completed all its metamorphoses. In the twentieth century it was adopted as a psychoanalytic term, referring to the image of another person, most usually a parent, in an idealized form that exerted a powerful influence over the subject's own behavior. These external and internal imagoes were held in tension, producing a fruitful if disturbing source of metaphor that combined the insect and the human.

Metamorphosis 1: Adult ↔ Child

For Carl Jung (1875–1961), as for many others, the unconscious was an insect. The childish instincts that furnished the desires of the id were seen by daylight in the evolved behaviors of the six-legged. By the time of Jung's writing, insects had long been regarded as displaying the most impressive demonstration of instinct in the animal kingdom. Unlike, say, dogs, which can *learn* to perform certain tricks, insects appeared to do everything by instinct—some of it astounding. The Provençal hermit and popular science writer Jean-Henri Fabre (1823–1915) produced the most influential description of these "wonders of instinct" at the beginning of the twentieth century. In his hot, dry garden, he watched for hours the equally patient labors of solitary wasps.[6] After laying her eggs in their little dry-mud, cup-shaped cells, the mother wasp *Philanthus* killed a bee to leave with each of her eggs, ready for her larvae to eat when they hatched. Instinctually she "knew" that the honey of the bee she provided for her offspring would make it inedible to them. Thus she emptied the bee of its honey by squeezing its stomach before leaving it for the grubs. However, her stomach-squeezing action could not be performed if the bee were paralyzed, being prevented by the rigidity of the bee's stomach muscles. Many solitary wasps, as Fabre elsewhere described, paralyzed their prey rather than killing it, but this would be no good for the fussy *Philanthus* larvae. There were many gaps in the bee's chitinous armor where a sting would result in paralysis, but only one pin-sized chink in the throat enabling an instant killing. The mother *Philanthus* possessed an unerring instinct to pierce the bee's chitin, accurately and every time, at just this point.

The other standard illustration of the heights that instinct reached in the insect world was the social organization of bees, wasps, and most particularly ants. Surely it would be ridiculous to impute rationality to these tiny bugs, and yet their activities embraced many of which humanity itself was proud. They practiced agriculture, of both the animal and plant varieties; certain ants kept aphid "cattle," and others had their fungus "gardens." Ants nursed their young and performed marvelous feats of architecture. Less admirably, they also went to war and took slaves. How did ants know to do all these things, and especially to do them in concert? The answer, astoundingly, was "by instinct."

As the ideas of Darwin and others on evolution were incorporated into, and reinterpreted within, various areas of science and culture, the question arose as to whether instinct were not the forerunner to human intelligence, rather than its animal analogue. And assuming that instinct was present in the human psyche—whether far or near from the surface—the next question was whether or not that was desirable.

Jung answered both these questions in the affirmative. He concurred with standard accounts of instinct and its exemplification in the life of insects:

> I have already mentioned that Freud established the existence of archaic vestiges and primitive modes of functioning in the unconscious. Subsequent investigations have confirmed this result and brought together a wealth of observational material. . . . Instinct and the archaic mode meet in the biological conception of the "pattern of behavior." . . . Always it fulfils an image, and the image has fixed qualities. The instinct of the leaf-cutting ant fulfils the image of ant, tree, leaf, cutting, transport, and the little ant-garden of fungi.[7]

Moreover, he identified these instincts in the life of humans; their particular "images" were manifested as archetypes, inherited memories from the evolutionary past of the race.[8]

It being established that instincts were the vestiges of the animal psyche present in humans, the question arose as to whether or not this was a desirable state of affairs. Jung's response was unambiguous: "Modern investigation of animal instinct, for example in insects, has brought together a rich fund of empirical material which shows that if man sometimes acted as certain insects do he would possess a higher intelligence than at present."[9] It was, appropriately enough, an insect that provided Jung with his most famous confirmation of the value of the "irrational" in human life. The story concerns a difficult patient, whose resolutely "rational" attitude made her resistant to therapy. Jung went on to recount that the young woman

> had at a critical moment a dream in which she was given a golden scarab. While she was telling me this dream I sat with my back to the closed window. Suddenly I heard a noise behind me, like a gentle tapping. I turned round and saw a flying insect knocking against the window-pane from outside. I opened the window and caught the creature in the air as it flew in. It was the nearest analogy to a golden scarab that one finds in our latitudes, a scarabeid beetle, the common rose-chafer . . . which contrary to its usual habits had evidently felt the need to get into a dark room at this particular moment.[10]

The chance incident of "synchronicity" punctured the woman's rational carapace and allowed progress to be made at last. Jung's beetle performed exactly the same function as the gold bug of Edgar Allan Poe's tale. Poe's scarab, though a cause of consternation to the hyperrational narrator of the tale, eventually yields an imaginative corrective to the excessively inductive reason characteristic of mid-nineteenth-century science.[11]

Jung was unusual in his outright enthusiastic welcome for insectile transformation, as most contemporary responses to Kafka's *Metamorphosis* indicated.[12] But when "instinct" was connected with the human larva, it was easier to concur with Jung. The imago of the entomologist was a child.

It was again Fabre who was largely responsible for the appointment of the child as the ideal entomologist. He employed his many ragged but happy children as his assistants in his Sérignan garden. (At least, this was the picture he painted.)[13] He portrayed himself as a humble, childlike observer of nature and encouraged his readers to adopt the same attitude. Fabre was certainly successful in his aims; his ten-volume *Souvenirs entomologiques* (1879–1907) was purchased by the thousands around the globe, bowdlerized specifically for children, and sold over again.[14] The series reached its peak of sales between 1910 and 1930, but even today a remarkable number of people remember these books as staples of their childhood reading.

Fabre, though influential in his own right, was part of a general trend to encourage children in the study of insects. The nature study movement in North America reached its height at the same time as Fabre's sales; its proponents recommended the keeping of artificial formicaries and beehives in the classroom to teach children the values of housekeeping, braveness, love of fellows, and so on.[15] Teachers and educationalists debated the presumed suitability of children for nature study in general and study of the insect realm in particular.[16]

The trend also extended to more professional entomology. In early-twentieth-century America, amateurs George and Elizabeth Peckham involved their children in entomological research that had considerable academic credibility. They were explicit about their debt to Fabre's ethos, and even in their most specialist book they credited their young son with helping them in their labors.[17] William Morton Wheeler (1865–1937), the world's preeminent ant specialist in the first third of the twentieth century, also chose to ally his craft to the child's talents and capacities, claiming that "no facts or theories in entomology . . . transcend the understanding of any fairly intelligent lad of fourteen."[18] His claim is all the more remarkable when one considers the unlikelihood of a Harvard professor in any other discipline saying the same thing. But Wheeler was convinced that besides being comprehensible to young minds, science was actually indebted to them for all its most important ideas.[19]

The majority of entomologists over the last century have made a point of tracing their interest in insects to an incident during their early youth.[20] Perhaps to reinforce their own memories, they have often been keen to encourage the young to follow in their footsteps. Between about 1920 and

This boy, almost certainly the young Graham Fairchild, gazes upon his fate. From David Fairchild and Marian Fairchild, *The Book of Monsters: Portraits and Biographies of a Few of the Inhabitants of Woodland and Meadow* (Washington: National Geographic Society, 1914), 12. The original caption reads, "The monsters . . . imprisoned in one museum case. They are all pinned in the box and have dried out and changed almost beyond recognition, but the impression which their portraits have made will, I hope, be lasting."

1927, Wheeler's correspondence with his amateur entomologist friend David Fairchild centered on Fairchild's son Graham, who seems to have figured for them as a sort of Peter Pan of entomology, "the ... enthusiastic boy we hope he will always remain." Graham's young, inquiring mind apparently put adults on entomological expeditions to shame. Fairchild wrote of Graham: "He was so delighted to be made a member of the Cambridge [Mass.] Entomological Society. I think it puts the last pin through him which will fasten him to an entomological box for the rest of his life. He has been mounted."[21] Although the image is somewhat chilling, it was appropriate that the state of childhood should be captured on a pin like an insect. The entomologists' imago was a child; it was the desirable face of the untrained unconscious.[22]

METAMORPHOSIS 2: MALE ↔ FEMALE

Alert readers may have noticed that both the paradigmatic examples of instinct cited earlier concern female insects: a mother wasp in one case, and the all-female ants' nest in the other. This was a familiar construal of instinct: females as being closer to nature, further down the great chain of being that had rational males at its peak. It suggests a second imago for consideration: the insect as woman.

Nina Pelikan Straus has highlighted a second metamorphosis implicit in Kafka's tale; as Gregor's verminous body wastes away, his sister Grete's develops from a child's to an adult's and finally, in the last sentence of the story, to that of a blooming young woman ready for marriage.[23] There is something more than a little repulsive in Grete's efflorescence at the expense of her brother. Her transformation resembles that of a young ant into a winged queen, ready to fly off and start the whole cycle again.

Early-twentieth-century writers were curiously obsessed with this stage of the life cycle, and indeed with the sexual lives of insects in general. Fabre, that most child-friendly of authors, was particularly taken with the behavior of the female mantis. When she reached maturity, he found that she would duel her peers to the death ("the swelling of the ovaries perverted my flock, and infected them with an insane desire to devour one another"). But this was just the start; a "yet more revolting extreme" of their behavior was displayed after fertilization. After their "lengthy embrace," the insect couple was "made one flesh in a much more intimate fashion" as the female "methodically devour[ed] [her husband], mouthful by mouthful, leaving only the wings." Fabre found himself wondering about the reception of a second male.

> The result of my inquiry was scandalous. The Mantis in only too many cases is never sated with embraces and conjugal feasts. . . . In the course of two weeks I have seen the same Mantis treat seven husbands in this fashion. She admitted all to her embraces, and all paid for the nuptial ecstasy with their lives. . . . Insects can hardly be accused of sentimentality; but to devour [the husband] during the act surpasses anything that the most morbid mind could imagine.[24]

Scandalized, yes, but Fabre was also clearly delighted by his observations. Though his writing can now appear mawkishly sentimental, it was in its context remarkable for its expression of deism in place of conventional Catholic moralization. Fabre, in fact, was sacked from an early teaching post for teaching science in an overly secular manner.[25] His anthropomorphism was not of a Sunday school variety, and he could afford to enjoy the perverse in the insect realm.

Fabre's promoter, the symbolist writer Maurice Maeterlinck (1862–1949), saw the insect feminine in altogether darker terms.

> The king—or let us call him the prince-consort—is shabby, undersized, punitive, fearful, furtive, and always in hiding underneath the queen. . . . She is merely a gigantic belly, crammed to bursting point with eggs . . . [an] enormous flabby inert greasy whitish mass; [an] appalling idol. Thousands of worshippers are incessantly licking and fondling the monster.[26]

In a final insult to the male of the species, it was thought that reproduction did not even take place through physical union; the "prince consort" had to be content with scattering his sperm over the eggs. Maeterlinck saw a greater degree of kinship than did Fabre between the insect and the human. So while Fabre's use of the word "husband" in connection with the mantis was knowingly and playfully anthropomorphic, for Maeterlinck, interspecific comparisons were laden with doom for humanity: "No matter what monsters have defiled or terrified the surface of the globe, we bear them within us. . . . We nourish all their types; they are only awaiting an opportunity to escape from us, to reappear, to reconstitute themselves, to develop, and to plunge us once again into terror."[27]

Maeterlinck, whose work on insects was mostly derivative of other writers, was entirely in line with contemporary scientific perceptions of the insect female, particularly the social insect female. Almost invariably the queen ant was described as turning into an "egg-laying machine" or a "mere egg-laying machine" after her "nuptial flight."[28] The description bears a curious similarity to Jung's description of hypertrophy of the maternal element, one possible form of his "mother-complex." The only goal of such a woman was childbirth, and her husband became "first and foremost the instrument of procreation," otherwise only "an object to be looked after

The "appalling idol" of maternity, the queen termite, surrounded by her hapless consorts. From William Morton Wheeler, *Foibles of Insects and Men* (New York: Alfred A. Knopf, 1928), 208.

along with children . . . and household furniture."²⁹ "Women of this type,"
continued Jung, "though continually 'living for others,' are, as a matter of
fact, unable to make any real sacrifice. Driven by ruthless will to power and
a fanatical insistence on their own maternal rights, they often succeed in
annihilating not only their own personality but also the personal lives of
[their] children."

Here was a woman whose instincts had become unduly prominent in
her psyche. Yet given the instinctual nature of the female, perhaps this was
to be expected. Victor Pelevin, a contemporary Russian author, has recently
explored the mother/ant as hapless victim of her instincts in his novel *The
Life of Insects* (1995). Like the Čapek brothers' *Insect Play* (1921), Pelevin's
novel is a modern bestiary; the human characters metamorphose into
insects and back again. An American businessman and his racketeering
associates are, at times, bloodsucking mosquitoes, while dropouts Maxim
and Nikita end their paranoid marijuana-smoking session by turning into
the "hemp-bugs" they have discovered in their stash, and dying a fiery
death in someone else's joint. The two main females in his book, however,
are an ant and her daughter. The ant, Marina, is a savage study in female
ambition and humanity. Like many of her insectan contemporaries, she
has little insight into her instinctual urges but blindly follows the mechanized patterns of six-legged life. In her particular case, she is programmed
to become a mother at all costs, mechanically adopting banal notions of
love from romantic films, and of maternal satisfaction from some interior
design. So strong are these mechanistic programs that, having emptied
her body of its physical resources in the production of eggs, this instinctual mother resorts to some surprising tactics (tactics also observed among
real ants):

> Days went by, until one morning she woke feeling hungry in a way she had
> never felt before. This was no longer the hunger of the skinny girl she had
> once been; it was the hunger of a huge mass of living cells, every one of which
> was squealing shrilly about how hungry it was. Marina . . . reached out to
> the clutch of eggs, picked out one in which a sexless worker was maturing,
> and before she had time to change her mind, she sunk her mandibles into the
> semi-transparent covering with a crunch. The egg tasted good and it was very
> filling, and before Marina came to her senses and regained her self-control,
> she had eaten another three.³⁰

This mother is a procreative machine: a robot of reproduction. As such, she is the incarnation of instinct. But why should her imago have bothered the mostly male entomologists of the early twentieth century? My claim is that the mechanical nature of the mother linked her to the industrialized, mechanized nature of modernity: mass society itself was perceived as feminized. Maeterlinck certainly linked the two themes—femininity and sociality—textually. He was both delighted and horrified by the image presented by the all-female social insects: their perfect social organization at inconceivable cost.[31] As he remarked, it was communism taken to the extent of castration and coprophagy (the most flagrant reversal of inside and out). Fabre, who was by contrast merely delighted by female reproductive behavior, was not inclined to draw any parallels with human society. In fact, a key difference between Maeterlinck's and Fabre's work was that all of Maeterlinck's insect writing concerned social varieties, while Fabre worked almost exclusively on solitary kinds.[32]

I have described elsewhere some typical early-twentieth-century texts that figure insects as disturbing because of their mechanized nature, and hence their connection to broader modernist concerns.[33] One interesting thing about them is that many figure a female character who pins together the twin concerns of modernity and feminization in the imago of the insect. *Metropolis* (1926), for instance, centers on the beautiful Maria, a queenlike individual with almost hypnotic—one might say instinctual—power over the workers. The film's evil scientist tries to create a simulacrum of Maria so that he can gain her power instead; it would be a perfect way to run his mechanized society.

More striking still is E. M. Forster's story "The Machine Stops" (1909), set in the hexagonal yet formicary-like catacombs of the future. Each individual is isolated in his or her cell, communicating only through the "Machine" that satisfies all their needs. The main communication in which the protagonist engages—via the Machine—is with his mother; on a phenomenal level, she is indistinguishable from the great, sinister mother of the story: the Machine itself. Perhaps his "mother" is just an invention of the Machine itself—which would explain her agitation when her son attempts to see her in person.

In such sources, the central presence of a female, ant-queen-like figure reveals how the mechanization or antification of society was viewed as a process of feminization. Correlatively, the all-female ant society was seen as the image of everything that Western males feared about modernity. Total war (the ants' all-too-human activity, lamented by the Čapeks in *The Insect Play*) had robbed men of their individuality and compromised their masculinity by making them weak, vulnerable, and afraid. Even after the Great War, modern society threatened to continue this process by making the working man take his place in the giant machine of industrial society, whether this took the form of a capitalist or centralized economy.

Once modern society was defined by its passive, deindividualized citizens, then it was forever restricted within its feminine mold, because it was in the nature of the female to reproduce, rather than to innovate. Indeed, that situation was already coming about, according to the myrmecologist W. M. Wheeler. The majority of men were not properly male, that is, antisocial; they lived "in collaboration with the women" and merely propped up the structure of society. There was only a "very small class" of "less social individuals" available to uphold the "great cultural values" (sciences, arts, technologies)." Wheeler thought that Russia was probably headed down the same evolutionary cul-de-sac as the termites, because it had so effectively socialized all its males. Like all such societies, it would be "peaceful and harmonious, but also stationary and incapable of further social evolution."[34] If a society had no antisocial males, it had no creative members; "the matriarchal clans of primitive man advanced towards civilization only after they had become patriarchal."[35]

Work on insect reproductive biology entered a new phase in the 1970s. As human gender categories came under pressure, so scientists once again found food for thought in the bizarre physiology and evolutionary-strategic behaviors of the six-legged.[36] In the early twentieth century, however, scientific and artistic autonomy were threatened by the new mass, feminized culture. Its imago was a mother-machine.

Conclusion

I have argued in this essay that the early-twentieth-century insect had, through its emblematization of instinct, two imagoes: the child (which was desirable) and the mother-machine (which was not). Both, however, must be interpreted in light of the representation in this period of insect and human as essentially creatures of the mass. It was the crowd (described by Gustave Le Bon in his seminal book of 1895) that encouraged the most primitive human instincts to come to the surface, just as it was the insect crowd—social insects—that displayed instinct at its most complex and sophisticated. Fabre's solitary insects were passing out of scientific fashion as ants, bees, wasps, and termites came to the fore.

Jung's archetypes, moreover, had to be located in a *collective* memory; similarly Freud posited that the consulting-room phenomenon of transference was a trace of the direct psychic communication employed by ants.[37] This understanding, the instinctual imago as a member of the mass, enables us also to supplement the gendered reading of Kafka employed here with its more usual Marxist interpretation. According to this version, the bourgeois ordering of society has Gregor as a spineless, brainless "creature" of the boss even before the metamorphosis begins.[38] By reframing that social order as feminized, the two historically plausible readings are rendered complementary.

Two imagoes, then, understood as members of the mass, were present in early-twentieth-century entomology. Writers at various points on the disgust-desire continuum have gone on to shape Western reactions to the insect to this very day. Each extreme of reaction invokes its opposite, and their overlap is titillation. Ugh! Show it to me again, only this time ten times life size!

NOTES

1. Leland O. Howard, *The Insect Book: A Popular Account of the Bees, Wasps, Ants, Grasshoppers, Flies and Other North American Insects* (London: Hutchison, 1902).

2. See especially *Nature-Study Review* 6 (September 1910). By contrast, children were encouraged to keep the ant equivalent of dollhouses, since these "Marthas" would teach them the values of cleanliness, housekeeping, mutual aid, bravery, and devotion to the young. Naomi Rogers gives an excellent account of the fly campaigns and their propagandistic imagery in "Germs with Legs: Flies, Disease, and the New Public Health," *Bulletin for the History of Medicine* 63 (1989): 599–617.

3. Paulo Palladino, *Entomology, Ecology, and Agriculture: The Making of Scientific Careers in North America, 1885–1985* (Amsterdam: Harwood Academic Publishers, 1996). The origin of this trend in North America and its slow dissemination elsewhere explain why Europeans like Bartok could remain kindly disposed toward insects for some time later.

4. Kafka's friend was Gustav Janouch; the book was David Garnett, *Lady into Fox* (London: Chatto and Windus, 1922). Quoted in Franz Kafka, *The Metamorphosis*, trans. and ed. Stanley Corngold (New York: Norton, 1996), 75; originally

from Corngold, *Conversations with Kafka*, trans. Goronwy Rees (New York: New Directions, 1971), 22.

5. For the influence of Haeckel on Kafka, see Mark M. Anderson, "Sliding down the Evolutionary Ladder? Aesthetic Autonomy in *The Metamorphosis*," in Kafka, *The Metamorphosis*, 154–72.

6. Fabre, *Social Life in the Insect World*, trans. Bernard Miall (London: T. Fisher Unwin, 1912), 150–78; the tale originally appeared in Fabre, *Souvenirs entomologiques: Etudes sur l'instinct et les moeurs des insectes*, 10 vols. (Paris: Delagrave, 1879–1907), 1:67–79. See also *Souvenirs entomologiques*, 1:207–20 and 2:14–37.

7. Jung, "On the Nature of the Psyche," in *Collected Works*, ed. Herbert Read, Michael Fordham, and Gerhard Adler, vol. 8 (London: Routledge and Kegan Paul, 1960), sec. 398. The essay was originally published in 1954.

8. Compare with Jack London's description of primal memories resurfacing in *The Call of the Wild*; see *Call of the Wild and White Fang* (Ware, Hertfordshire: Wordsworth, 1992), 31–32.

9. Jung, "Basic Postulates of Analytical Psychology," in *Collected Works*, vol. 8, sec. 673. The essay was originally published in 1934.

10. Jung, "On the Nature of the Psyche," sec. 438.

11. Poe, "The Gold Bug," in *Tales of Mystery and Imagination* (Ware, Hertfordshire: Wordsworth, 1993), 1–30.

12. Kevin Sweeney discovers both materialist and dualist accounts of behavior in Kafka's tale; it is only a small step further to interpret these as animal (unreflective instinctual impulses) and "human" (instinct tempered with the insight and check of rationality). Sweeney, "Competing Theories of Identity in Kafka's *The Metamorphosis*," in Kafka, *The Metamorphosis*, 140–54.

13. Some examples of Fabre's involvement of children are *Souvenirs entomologiques*, 2:144–45, 6:4–6, 8:3–4, and 9:94.

14. See, for example, Mrs. Rodolph Stawell, *Fabre's Book of Insects* (London and Edinburgh: Thomas Nelson, 1925); and Eleanor Doorly, *The Insect Man* (Harmondsworth, Middlesex: Penguin, 1936).

15. See *Nature-Study Review* 1 (January, May, September, and November 1905); ibid., 6 (September 1910).

16. In *Nature-Study Review* 3 (November 1907), Maurice A. Bigelow discussed whether children were naturally naturalists (236–39). Letters and followup articles in subsequent issues of the *Review* continued the debate.

17. Peckham and Peckham, *On the Instincts and Habits of the Solitary Wasps* (Madison, Wis.: published by the state, 1898), 58; and *Wasps Social and Solitary* (Boston and New York: Houghton, Mifflin, 1905), 119.

18. Wheeler, *Demons of the Dust: A Study in Insect Behaviour* (London: Kegan Paul, Trench, Trubner, 1931), ix.

19. Notes found in Wheeler's desk after his death. Wheeler papers, Pusey Library, Harvard University.

20. See, for example, Auguste Forel, *The Social World of the Ants Compared with*

That of Man, trans. C. K. Ogden, 2 vols. (London: G. P. Putnam's Sons, 1928), 2:xxxiii–xxxv; and *Out of My Life and Work,* trans. Bernard Miall (London: George Allen and Unwin, 1937), 30–36; Howard Evans and Mary Evans, *William Morton Wheeler, Biologist* (Cambridge: Harvard University Press, 1970), 20–21. Wheeler remarks on the importance of the early influence of entomologists in *Demons of the Dust,* 22, giving some examples from the lives of early entomologists. L. O. Howard's introduction in his *The Insect Book* is a marvelous autobiographical account of the country boy as "natural naturalist." See also Edwin Teale, *Dune Boy: The Early Years of a Naturalist* (London: Robert Hale, 1949). Some more recent versions of this phenomenon are Margaret Hutchinson, *Childhood in Edwardian Sussex: The Making of a Naturalist* (Hindhead, Surrey: Saiga Publishing, n.d.); Ronald Lockley, *Myself When Young: The Making of a Naturalist* (London: André Deutsch, 1979); and Edward O. Wilson, *Naturalist* (Harmondsworth, Middlesex: Penguin, 1995), 47–61.

21. Letters from Fairchild to Wheeler; quotations from letters dated July 7, 1927, and May 26, 1927, Wheeler papers, Pusey Library, Harvard University.

22. The undesirable face of the untrained unconscious was shown by the "savage." If North Americans acquired antipathy toward instinct through the labor of professional entomologists, the Europeans' feelings in the same period were largely shaped by dramatic encounters with insects in the colonies, as I have argued elsewhere. In their innumerable hordes, their mutual indistinguishability, and their psychological otherness, insects were almost irresistibly mapped onto the human "others" of Africa and India. See Sleigh, "Empire of the Ants: H. G. Wells and Tropical Entomology," *Science as Culture* 10 (2001): 33–71.

23. Straus, "Transforming Franz Kafka's *Metamorphosis,*" in Kafka, *The Metamorphosis,* 126–40.

24. Fabre, *Social Life in the Insect World,* 79–85. See Frederick Prete and M. Melissa Wolfe, "Religious Supplicant, Seductive Cannibal, or Reflex Machine? In Search of the Praying Mantis," *Journal of the History of Biology* 25 (1992): 91–136.

25. C. V. Legros, *Fabre, Poet of Science,* trans. Bernard Miall (London: T. Fisher Unwin, 1913); Abbé Augustin Fabre, *The Life of Jean Henri Fabre the Entomologist,* trans. Bernard Miall (London: Hodder and Stoughton, 1921). More recent treatments of Fabre include Marion Thomas, "Rethinking the History of Ethology: French Animal Behaviour Studies in the Third Republic (1870–1940)," Ph.D. thesis, University of Manchester, 2003. For the context of educational secularism, see Nicole Hulin, *Les femmes et l'enseignement scientifique* (Paris: PUF, 2002).

26. Maeterlinck, *Life of the White Ant,* trans. Alfred Sutro (London: Allen and Unwin, 1927), 99–101.

27. Maeterlinck, in *Hearst's Magazine,* March 1920.

28. See, for example, Wheeler, *Ants: Their Structure, Development, and Behavior* (New York: Columbia University Press, 1910), 185; and "The Queen Ant as a Psychological Study," *Popular Science Monthly* 68 (1906): 291–99; O. E. Plath, "Insect Societies," in *A Handbook of Social Psychology,* ed. Carl Murchison (Worcester,

Mass.: Clark University Press, 1935), 83–141, 127–29; William Mann, "Stalking Ants, Savage and Civilized," *National Geographic Magazine* 66 (1934): 171–92, 172–73.

29. Jung, *Four Archetypes* (London: Routledge and Kegan Paul, 1972), sec. 167.

30. Pelevin, *The Life of Insects*, trans. Andrew Bromfield (London: Faber, 1996), 154.

31. See particularly Maeterlinck, *Life of the White Ant*, 16–19.

32. The "Fabre" of social insects was perhaps the Boer Eugène Marais, who made a number of studies of termites, published in South Africa and Belgium in 1925. See Marais, *The Soul of the White Ant*, trans. Winifred de Kok (1937; reprint, Harmondsworth, Middlesex: Penguin, 1973). Marais allegedly committed suicide in 1936 upon discovering his work had been plagiarized by Maeterlinck (3).

33. Sleigh, *Ant* (London: Reaktion, 2003), 148–52.

34. On the basis of the heckling that interrupted Wheeler's lecture, the *Brooklyn Eagle* ran the headline "Women Resent Charge They Would Stagnate the World." Lena Philips, the president of the National Council of Women, merely remarked tartly, "Why, the first curious person in the world was Mother Eve. Adam was contented enough." Evans and Evans, *William Morton Wheeler*, 268–69.

35. Wheeler's words here echo the writing of Friedrich Engels in *The Origin of the Family, Private Property, and the State in the Light of the Researches of Lewis H. Morgan*, trans. Alick West (1884; London: Lawrence and Wishart, 1940). Engels covers previous theories of maternal-based societal evolution and advances his own, in a striking parallel to the queen-dominated evolution of the formicary.

36. See Olivia Judson, *Dr Tatiana's Sex Advice to All Creation: The Definitive Guide to the Evolutionary Biology of Sex* (London: Chatto and Windus, 2002).

37. For Jung, extrasensory perception and other instances of supernatural psychic phenomena were also relics of the intuitive communications that existed among social insects. He read with interest recent research establishing that bees danced to show their nest mates the exact location of good food sources. Rejecting the notion that the bees' was a conscious communication, Jung concluded that they used instead some kind of parallel, dispersed nervous system to achieve the same effect as humans can using the cortex of the brain. He wondered whether similar communications operated in humans via the sympathetic nervous system, which, unlike consciousness and the cortex, did not sleep. Carl Jung, "Synchronicity, an Acausal Connecting Principle," in *Collected Works*, vol. 8, sec. 955–57. The essay was originally published in 1952.

38. See note on the translation of this phrase in Kafka, *The Metamorphosis*, 5.

15

Portraits of the Nonhuman

Visualizations of the Malevolent Insect

NICKY COUTTS

> The insect does not belong to our world. . . . [It brings] something
> that does not seem to belong to the customs, the morale, the
> psychology of our globe. One would say that it comes from another
> planet, more monstrous, more dynamic, more insensate, more
> atrocious, more infernal than ours. . . . [There is a] profound
> inquietude inspired by these creatures so incomparably better armed,
> better equipped than ourselves, these compressions of energy and
> activity which are our most mysterious enemies, our rivals in these
> latter hours and perhaps our successors.
> [Insects] are never so widely separated from us as when they appear
> to resemble us the most.
>
> —E. L. BOUVIER, *The Psychic Life of Insects* (1918)

The entomologist Jean-Henri Fabre, a contemporary of Bouvier, noted that the praying mantis is alone among insects in its ability to articulate its head and so direct its gaze. Because the mantis shares with humans, and most mammals, the ability or the appearance of inspecting and examining, Fabre noted with fascination that it "almost has a physiognomy."[1] Indeed, the head or face of the mantis also bears an uncanny resemblance to generic representations of extraterrestrials, broadly adopted in science fiction films and described by those who believe they have witnessed a nonhuman visitation. For instance, the mantis and the alien share a triangular-shaped head with large eyes set widely apart, tapering down to neat mouth parts and chin. Both can appear to stand upright with long, thin, dexterous arms. In short, the mantis characterizes the paradox described by Bouvier: on the one hand, it more closely resembles human

298

form than most other insects; on the other, it is precisely because of this familiarity, blended disconcertingly with the unfamiliar, that it appears so overwhelmingly strange and "otherworldly" to us. As Bouvier intimates, we may fear or aspire to many of the qualities that insects possess, but like the Red Queen in Lewis Carroll's *Through the Looking Glass,* who must be approached by walking in the opposite direction, the more we move toward insects and subject them to our anthropomorphic gaze, curiously the more difficult they are to "meet" or grasp, and the further away from us they seem.

To analyze the anxieties posed by Bouvier, I examine visual works from the medieval period to the beginning of the twentieth century. The chapter's first section focuses on insects during the medieval plagues, arguing that their unnerving proximity to the human cadaver during this period led to an enduring association with evil and fragmentation. Early tempter statues and transi tombs, fifteenth-century works by Matthias Grünewald and Hieronymus Bosch, and an installation by the contemporary artist Damien Hirst are analyzed to unravel insects' characterization as a malevolent intruder, an enemy force, threatening to undermine confidence and belief in the integrity of social and religious structures. Further alterations to how we perceive insects arose during the period that saw the invention and development of the microscope, when intimate details of insects' appearance were revealed for the first time. The effects of size, scale, camouflage, and mimicry are explored through an examination of works by William Blake, the surrealist Georges Caillois, and the contemporary artists Mark Fairnington and John Stezaker. Finally, the predatory and alien qualities possessed by insects, reflecting fears that they might outlive and surpass us, are considered in the work of the artists Caroline Chalmers and Liz Arnold.

The Unholy Insect

At the core of Catholic teaching during the Middle Ages was a desire to preserve heaven and hell as separate realms. The anthropologist Mary Douglas cites Peter 1:16, which states, "Be ye holy for I am holy," meaning little more than "be ye separate."[2] "Holiness" derives literally from "wholeness" and is exemplified by completeness, purity, and definition. The scriptures of Leviticus 11:2–42 and Deuteronomy 14:3–20 similarly sought to preserve these separations through the prescription of classification, ceremony, and ritual.

For instance, the Old Testament instructs that species of cows should not be interbred, fields should not be sown with two kinds of seed, and garments should not be made from more than one type of cloth. All who confused or ignored these prohibitions or came into contact with hybridity would be regarded as unclean and contagious, facing both punishment from God and rejection from society. However, this doctrine was challenged by the dramatic influence the great plagues of Europe had on an individual's experience of witnessing decay during the Middle Ages. Notably a gradual erosion of the unquestioned belief in the teachings of the church, which dominated the medieval world, was accompanied by a proliferation of insect imagery.

From the thirteenth to the sixteenth century, representations of the insect were prevalent in memento mori imagery, appearing, for example, on the backs of statues such as *Frau Welt,* a version of whom was sited at the Cathedral of Worms in southwest Germany circa 1300, and *The World Tempter* or *Prince of the World* at Strasbourg circa 1280–85 and Nurnberg circa 1310. The tempter statues reflect the medieval preoccupation with the conflict between good and evil, and with the temptations of the world that lead away from the church and pious obedience to God. *The World Tempter* was depicted as a handsome prince, usually crowned, holding an apple or a flower that symbolized the transient joys of the living world. His association with the devil is only apparent when viewed from behind; his back is riddled with stylized and generic insects, worms, frogs, and snakes. *Frau Welt* similarly symbolizes the deception of the world. Again she is beautiful from the front but is found to be infested with devouring creatures when viewed from behind. A twelfth-century preacher warned, "'Weltdienst ist Teufelsdienst'—whoever serves the world will receive as payment her daughter who is eternal death, damnation."[3]

The tempter figures conflate insects with the devil, deceit, and worldly desire, characterizing the threat to the wholeness of the body posed by sin. Although the church asserted that the body would revert to pure diabolical matter if the individual concerned behaved immorally, evidence to the eye during the plagues suggested that to decay and be eaten by insects and worms was the fate of all cadavers, whether the living had behaved morally or otherwise.[4] Insects therefore embodied evidence that both refuted the church's insistence on the possibility of staying whole after death, and suggested the distressing possibility that no moral act could protect the body from disintegration. Insect imagery accompanied cracks in the belief system in a climate of growing fear and doubt.

Contributing to the insect's association with malevolence during this period is their positioning on the tempter statues. They disturb because they are placed furtively on the shadowed side, active literally behind the backs of the faithful, hidden initially from view. The fair face of the statues is seen against the backdrop of the church as the "holy" sanctuary is approached, while the insects on their backs are seen only when leaving the building with the temptations of the world as background. Holiness, as prescribed by the Old Testament, denoting clear divisions between the worlds of the living and the dead, is also distorted by the symbolic presence of insects represented where they do not belong. As an invading force preying on the flesh while it is still living, separations between what can be deemed alive or inert become molten. Keeping death "alive" through blurring distinctions between the body and the corpse, insects represent the act of breaking the body down, stealing and remolding the flesh, causing the desired unity and wholeness of the body to fragment, erode, and threaten ultimately to disappear completely. Literally two-faced, the statues use the deceptive, corruptive association of insects to warn viewers of their potential fate.

From the mid-fourteenth century to the seventeenth, the fair and diabolic appearances of the corpse, previously conjoined in the tempter statues, were represented separately. Transi tombs usually comprised a depiction of the cadaver just after death with, positioned directly beneath it, a secondary representation of the same body after it had been buried for some time and had been partially devoured by insects and worms.[5] When the first transi tombs were made, the Black Death had already ravaged much of Europe, and the familiar sight of mass death and decay would have given most people firsthand experience of seeing insects on corpses, inciting anxieties concerning the very idea of an afterlife.[6] Reflecting this uncertainty, insects on tombs represented a scurrying army of evil, worldly soldiers blocking the path to salvation. They were believed to be spontaneously generated, a process closely associated with the devil—both from and of the earth. The church continued to place responsibility for the presence of these devouring insects on the individual, asserting that insects hatch in the cadaver from pockets of sin.[7] In a similar way to the tempter statues, transi tombs advocated piety and obedience to God in order to avoid the worldly temptations, which, it was believed, would lead to the erosion of the body after death. However, their central role was to highlight the dangers of passage from the physical world to the afterlife. The word "transi" derives from the Latin verb *transire*, from *ire*, "to go," indicating unresolved passage, or purgatory, focusing not on destination or arrival but on the indefinable state, place, or act of transition. The physical void incorporated into the structure of the transi tombs, between the two representations of the cadaver, was unmapped and anxious. The historian Simon Schama reflects this doubt when he describes cracks appearing in the belief system during the Black Death. He cites a monk's reminiscences, alluding to a frustration of categories on which he feels he can no longer depend. Emphasizing the breakdown of cause and effect, the fragility of passage between one dependable state and another, the monk writes: "There was in those days death without sorrow, marriage without affection, want without poverty, flight without escape." [8] Schama adds, "Everything that had been taken for granted became suddenly questionable."[9] The form of the transi tomb questioned how the decay and disintegration of the body after death could be reconciled with the idea of eternal life and salvation, requiring as it did the continued wholeness of the body. Transi tombs functioned not so much as a timely warning, as did the tempter statues, but as a plea for the safe passage of the deceased through to the afterlife, harnessing the harsh dualities and contradictions of its time into a clear yet confrontational form. Onlookers were witness to a lament for preservation during this intermediate, intangible state, willing mind to still prevail over diabolic matter. Protection was sought from the insect parasites that threatened to bar the way to heaven, consuming all symbolic vestiges of wholeness and reducing them to fragments.

By the late fifteenth century, further uncomfortable visualizations of the insects' threat to undermine clear distinctions between the worlds of the living and the dead were emerging in the work of Matthias Grünewald and Hieronymus Bosch. For example, *Dead Lovers* (c. 1470, controversially attributed to Grünewald) is a disturbing image of a couple who appear to convulse in a *danse macabre,* tormented by the insects and reptiles portrayed devouring them.[10]

The painting was made after the artist witnessed firsthand, while carrying out the superior's commission, the advanced effects of the plague, physical decay, and disease at the monastery of Isenheim, a hospital during the artist's lifetime. The graphic depiction, in minute detail, of flies, snakes,

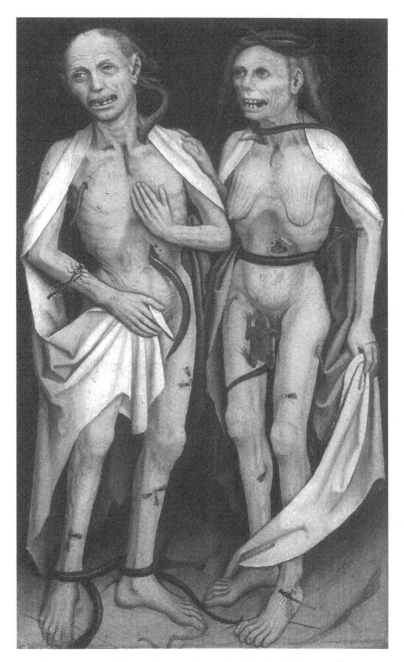

Matthias Grünewald, *Dead Lovers* (c. 1480). Musée de l'oeuvre Notre Dame de Strasbourg. Photograph by A. Plisson.

frogs, and beetles feeding on the bodies of the seemingly "undead" lovers demonstrates Grünewald's complex vision of nightmare and euphoria. This aspect of his work was later to be of great influence to the surrealists, feeding into imagery produced by artists such as Salvador Dalí and Luis Buñuel. Grünewald's portrayal of insects suggests that he perceived them as both real horrors—living monsters of the physical world—and messengers, symbolic of the devil's designs, indicating the agonies and the ecstasies of sinful liaisons. In Grünewald's image, the dead are consumed by life in the form of insects, mirroring perversely the touch of death from the point of view of the living.

With the church, its prohibitions, and its segregations still prominent in Europe, Grünewald's representation of an impure melding of categories could be interpreted as an expression of what the medieval scholar and theorist Georges Bataille terms "the sacred." In *Visions of Excess,* Bataille, who admired the work of Grünewald, describes "the sacred" in the following terms:

> Christianity has made the sacred "substantial," but the nature of the sacred, in which today we recognize the burning existence of religion, is perhaps the most ungraspable thing that has been produced between men: the sacred is only a privileged moment of communal unity, a moment of the convulsive communication of what is ordinarily stifled.[11]

For Emile Durkheim (1858–1917), cited in Mary Douglas's *Purity and Danger: An Analysis of Pollution and Taboo,* "the sacred is the object of community worship. It can be recognized by rules expressing its essentially contagious character"; Douglas adds that "the sacred is essentially fluid and needs to be hedged in by prohibition. . . . It must be treated as contagious."[12] In *Dead Lovers* the viewer is aware of seeing what should not be seen. Heaven and hell are represented in a state of overlap and infection, their contagion of each other indicated by the presence of devouring, seething insects and reptiles. Danger is implicit in the hidden moment of undead union between the two lovers. Defined partially by the prohibitions that ensure its elusivity, the sacred in *Dead Lovers* also relies on the viewer's desire to unmask intangible qualities in the image. Grünewald's insects could be identified as contagious agents at the heart of "holiness," necessary simultaneously to define it and indicate its potential disintegration.

Bosch similarly visualized the insect as both messenger from the devil and insidious earthly invader. As an inversion of heaven's white-winged angel, the messenger insect is, for him, similarly winged yet dark, segmented, and crawling; a monster figure with a predatory and parasitic relationship to humans. *Haywain* (1485–90) demonstrates Bosch's perception of the fragile divide between angels and insects, emphasizing their potential for disturbing similarities and symmetries. In the left panel of the triptych, Bosch describes angels falling from heaven as the crime scene unfolds in the Garden of Eden. Eve accepts forbidden fruit from the serpent as the angel figures transform into insects and rain down behind her. In the central and right-hand sections of *The Last Judgment* (1504) and *The Temptation of St. Anthony* (c. 1500), Bosch describes the insect form when it has landed on earth and descended further to hell. His dark, crowded, clamoring scenes suggest concealed, stifled worlds where grotesque misfits are caught in the process of metamorphosis, uncomfortably exposed between their human status and inhuman destiny, captured on their journey toward formlessness. Veined wings and carapaces are described welded onto human body parts. Moths, beetles, and ladybirds are hideously distorted through ambiguous marriages to unrelated forms. For the cultural historian Marina Warner, it is the insect's essentially inarticulate appearance that has provoked such negative associations with the devil and the underworld. She observes, "Insect metamorphosis offered a special menacing connection with the aberrational processes of hell, where . . . forms lose their integrity."[13] Bosch's depictions of insects evoke the real and imagined fear of disintegration after death, which, for him, the plagues may recently have made a reality. Rejecting the terms of holiness, Bosch uses anomalous and ambiguous forms to convey the anxieties and horrors facing all the living. Borrowing from secular image sources, Bosch's hybrids are evolved from a history of fearsome shape-shifters from folklore and myth. As for the tempter statues, his representations of insects indicate matter out of place. Plucked from the visual, physical, and mythical worlds and introduced to a relatively alien theological scene, insect hybrids roam incongruously.

The contemporary artist Damien Hirst reworks many of the themes evoked in Bosch's works, sharing his characteristically medieval preoccupation with anxieties surrounding dying, death, and the fate of the cadaver. In *A Thousand Years* (1990), Hirst alludes to these concerns, perversely, through the removal or absence of the human body. Insects as symbolic agents of disease, decay, and disappearance are literally framed alone in Hirst's work. It is as though the most uncomfortable aspect of Bosch's depictions of hell has been isolated and now confronts the viewer. *A Thousand Years* consists of a large glass construction containing a rotting cow's head, an insectocutor, and a multitude of flies. The insects breed in the cow's head; the maggots pupate and emerge as flies and then risk being zapped and killed by the electrocutor as they fly around inside the sealed construction. A pile of dead flies builds up on the floor as the cycle continues, appearing to create more slime for the flies to feed on. *A Thousand Years* draws attention to the insect's malevolent associations in a number of ways. First, the piece is presented as some sort of crazed experiment, an insect holocaust; the glass cabinet containing the flies appears to be made for the abject voyeur, the deranged scientist at large. Second, the horror of what should be a life cycle is presented instead as the circuitry of death. The dead appear to be breeding life in order to feed death, as opposed to, for example, Christian ideals that focused on life followed by an afterlife. This negative inversion, compounded by the proximity of flies to flesh, the sight of maggots breeding profusely, and the inevitable stench, accumulates in an image of apocalyptic atrocity. The parasitic behavior of the flies, segregated from external referents, illuminates the horror of irritant marginal creatures and their activities unnaturally concentrated in one place at one time. Reminiscent of insects witnessed feeding on corpses during the plagues of Europe, Hirst's mass of flies is repellent because time has been condensed and the eye is forced to accommodate what it has come to fear, agents of fragmentation outnumbering, overwhelming, and preying on a vestige of wholeness. Third, *A Thousand Years* exposes the uncomfortable spectacle of the insect's prolific reproductive powers. Historically, both the Virgin Mary and the devil have been associated with fertility. However, in the Middle Ages, whereas the identity of the Virgin with a single child is complicit with wholeness and singularity, the devil, through spontaneous generation, was thought to be mocking this concept by filling the world with his many insect descendants. With spontaneous generation still believed to be the devil's tool, insects that seemed to be created from the substance of rotting flesh were found to embody an uncomfortable parallel to the spontaneous realization of the Christ child within the Virgin Mary's womb. As infernal counterparts to purity, segregation, and singularity, Hirst's insects appear to thrive in a malnourished environment. Appearing impervious to their toxic surroundings, the insects of *A Thousand Years* are victors in conditions where humans would perish. They are survivors of the apocalypse.

Apparition and Enlargement

As the plagues began to die down in Europe and the sight of funereal insects devouring the body became less familiar, the next historic event to transform, and go on to deeply influence, contemporary perceptions of insects was the invention and development of the microscope in the late sixteenth century and the early seventeenth. During the early sixteenth century, little was known not only of how insects propagate or what and how they eat but also of their respiratory systems and longevity. Centuries of belief in the fantastic had saturated perceptions of the insect to such an extent that it is no wonder that information gleaned through the microscope initially had little immediate effect on preconceptions. As a result, some descriptions of what was seen through early microscopes directly equated insects with creatures of the imaginative or mythic worlds. This is demonstrated in a description of what a group of early scientists believed they witnessed through the lens of a microscope during the Great Plague of London in 1665. Dr. Harvey, the king's physician to the Tower of London, recalls their observation of "living creatures of strange, monstrous and frightful shapes, like dragons, snakes, serpents."[14] Rather than broadening the divide between perceptions of the real and the imaginary, Harvey suggests that the interpretation of images gleaned through the early microscope sometimes gave rise to the reverse. Malevolent monsters were believed to reside in diminutive insect forms, revealed through the process of magnification.

Although enlarged descriptive images of insects were developed in the mid-seventeenth century, notably by Jan Swammerdam and Robert Hooke, the first significant example of a magnified insect-human hybrid was not produced until the early nineteenth century when William Blake painted *The Ghost of a Flea* (1812). Allegedly created from sketches made in the company of a ghost, half man and half insect, that appeared to the artist, the image captures the atmosphere of hallucination described by Blake in related texts. The parasitic flea in this enlarged and morbid characterization carries a bowl for the collection of human blood. It is depicted thirsty and prowling, with its tongue drooling and clawed fingers curled. It paces along

William Blake, *The Ghost of a Flea* (1812).

a window ledge, dimly lit against the night sky, with the freakish incident of a falling comet depicted in the background. Blake recounted that the monster spoke to him during its visitation, explaining its stature, disclosing that an enlarged flea, such as itself, is a creature to be truly feared, as it is capable of unimaginable devastation. In *The Compleat Flea,* Brendan Lehane cites the flea's words to Blake:

> As the rebels among angels were cast down with Lucifer, so the most destructive of men—this flea would have us believe—are consigned to fleas' frames to keep them from overmuch mischief. All fleas, it confided to Blake, were inhabited by the souls of such men as were by nature bloodthirsty to excess, and were therefore providentially confined to the size and form of insects; otherwise, were he himself for instance the size and form of a horse, he would depopulate a great portion of the country.[15]

Blake's "flea" shares with Bosch's depictions of the inhabitants of hell a melding of insect characteristics with other larger forms to create uniquely disorientating imagery. The outcome of this incongruous marriage of size favors the larger human form over the natural diminutive size of the flea. This results in the flea being enlarged in the imagination to match the size of the human whose form it shares. In so doing, the alien details of the flea's makeup become amplified. The magnification of the insect in this way produces an atmosphere of deceitful apparition, as though the rare and secretive event unfolding may just as suddenly disappear. The appearance of the insect becomes inseparable from the event of viewing it momentarily. Mirroring insects' mutable status during metamorphosis and mimesis in the physical world, our perception of them as ominous shape-shifters, impossible to visually resolve, is strengthened through hybridity.

Named after Blake's apparitional image, a series of collages titled *The Ghost of a Fly* (1994–97) by John Stezaker similarly conveys an atmosphere of deceit and illusion. Stezaker uses found photographs of flowers in vases and mirrors them on a vertical axis. However, not all of each original image is revealed in the works. Lost in the center of the symmetries are areas of overlap where, for example, the "bodies" of the vases might be. These vanished sections lend the images an emaciated quality while simultaneously invigorating the created forms with life. In all the images, an ambiguous head or face can be discerned. In most, it is overwhelmingly insectlike as

John Stezaker, two images from the series *The Ghost of a Fly* (1994–97).

the heads and stalks of the flowers become multiple legs and quivering antennae, and the shrunken vases become a fleshy abdomen and thorax. In many, the "insect" revealed appears to have its legs outstretched, as though convulsing or dancing. The viewer encounters a frozen, hallucinogenic moment—a trick of vision. The images hover irresolvably between animacy and inanimacy, appearance and disappearance. Through mirroring a familiar form and incorporating into a single image an imperfect copy, a phantom is created, a ghostly impression of the inscrutable insect world.

In the series of paintings *Mantidae* (1999–2001), Mark Fairnington uses observational and descriptive techniques to simulate not only the apparitional appearance of the insect in Blake's and Stezaker's works but also many of the attributes previously discussed that contribute to perceptions of insects as malevolent and as harbingers of misfortune.[16] The series relies on an unsettling use of scale, mimesis, and ambiguous association with the domains of the living and the dead to elicit disquiet. Fairnington's paintings depict preserved specimens of mantises complete with mounting pin and evidence of their deterioration after death. The artist uses a greatly enlarged scale to transport the appearance of the insect from the familiar domain of the small and relatively insignificant to the monstrous and alien.

Specimen 4, for example, is over two meters high and almost two meters wide. The mantis depicted becomes a mirage to the senses, a fancy-dress character playing at scaring; a macabre description of the living dead. The anthropomorphic pose each insect adopts in the series, usually pictured upright on its hind legs, elicits an appearance of dancing, apparently mocking the viewer, reminding him or her of life from the point of view of death. The true-to-life detail turns out, more accurately, to be true-to-death, and the desiccated mantis corpse appears to mock the viewer silently as the details of its ghoulish makeup become apparent. Slowly the decayed, blackened joints, the incomplete legs, and the shriveled abdomen become apparent to the viewer. Its four-eyed stare adds to our discomfort. Bulbous eyes continue to glint from a curiously delicate head. These are amplified by the ocelli, the eye-shaped markings on the underside of the insect's wings. In *No Go the Bogeyman*, Warner refers to Lacan when she observes that the ocelli on insect wings "represent acutely the distinction he makes between the eye that sees and the gaze that is sensed but does not see, 'the underside of consciousness.'"[17] In Fairnington's image the fake, blind "eyes" of the mantis reflect the potential fear of the observer. They are incomprehensible in themselves. Posing as the eyes of a larger predator, the mystery of the ocelli is that they evolved long before mammals existed. It cannot, therefore, be the eyes of mammals—our eyes—that are imitated, unless by prophecy. Older eyes, perhaps from the giant monstrous reptilian era of the dinosaur, lie beyond a form that we are capable of recognizing. In *Specimen 4* they appear to stare back at us from dusty wings. Both pairs of dead and unsee-ing eyes suggest the loss of a clear center of identity. Instead we are con-fronted by a transfixing image, an unidentifiable imprint evoking infinite formlessness behind a sightless image.

Mark Fairnington, *Specimen 4*, from the series *Mantidae* (1999–2001).

PREYING AND OTHER VISUAL DECEITS

In *Purity and Danger*, Mary Douglas speculates on the relationship between ambiguous or anomalous appearance, cultural and social status, and its association with malevolence. She compares perceptions of insects to those of witches, considering both to be analogous to people living in the interstices of power structures who can be considered a threat to those whose status is more defined.

> Witchcraft, then, is found in the non structure. Witches are social equivalents of beetles and spiders who live in the cracks of the walls and wainscoting. They attract the fears and dislikes which other ambiguities and contradictions attract in other thought structures, and the kind of powers attributed to them symbolise their ambiguous, inarticulate status.[18]

In Douglas's view, the insect, like the witch, cannot be posited entirely outside society or find permanent solace within it. Instead it can be seen weaving intricately from one subsystem to another, operating alternatively as a legitimate and then illegitimate intruder. Like the witch, the insect lurks between the visible act and what humans assert as the invisible thought. Threat of harm does not depend on the insect's actions; its ambiguous status alone makes it dangerous intrinsically.

Freud's writings on extreme phobias in *Totem and Taboo* parallel Douglas's assertion that fear of insects can have little to do with specific causal associations. A true phobic, as opposed to a patient suffering from obsessional neurosis, will not associate his or her phobic subject with a past anxious experience. Freud comments on how "strikingly often [phobic triggers are] very small animals like bugs and butterflies."[19] For the increasing number of patients suffering from insect phobias, the insect is terrifying for no logical reason. It is simply dangerous in itself.

The natural capacity for the insect, in particular the praying mantis, to be perceived as dangerous, to disorient and deceive the eye, became a preoccupation for the surrealists Georges Caillois and André Masson.[20] Observing the mantis's capacity for mimesis led Caillois to consider the wider implications of the insect's ability to shape-shift. In *Le mante religieuse*, a study of the mantis based on an eclectic range of myths, tales, and observations, Caillois cites a story from the folklore of the bush people of South

Africa, where the mantis is established as a central mythological figure.[21] The story reflects the impact that the mantis's natural ability to assume disguises appears to have had on the bush people's confidence in the accuracy and primacy of human vision. The story begins with the central character, grandfather mantis, assuming the form of a dead hartebeest. Local children find the animal and cut it up for food. They attempt to carry it home in pieces, but the severed parts begin to move, and the head speaks to them. The terrified children drop the different sections of the hartebeest as it reforms into a whole. Resuming his insect shape, the mantis then chases the children to their escape. The adult bush people explain to their children that the mantis played dead to disappoint them. Through mimicking food, which the children desire, and then revealing that their eyes deceived them, the mantis tricks the hunters into a transformation of their own, from being hunters to becoming hunted. Making fools of humans for "believing their eyes," the story exploits human vulnerabilities when faced with mutable forms. It demonstrates how an elusive appearance can make a predator all the more fearsome and daunting in the imagination.

Caillois considered the mantis the ultimate mimetic creature. He describes as "insectoid psychosis" its inability to sustain the distinction between itself and its immediate environment, comparing the experience of viewing the insect to a feeling of dissolving into "similarity" suffered by many schizophrenics. Mark Fairnington evokes just this sensation in the painting *Still Life (Praying Mantis)* (1997). Appropriated from a photograph taken with narrow depth of field, *Still Life (Praying Mantis)* is a painting of a mantis that appears to conspire disconcertingly with its surroundings, sinking into the putrid yellows and greens of its background, melting into similitude. Implicit in *Still Life (Praying Mantis)* is the mantis's voracious predatory appetite. Similar to the grandfather mantis in the Hottentot bush tale, it looms ambiguously, poised on the cusp of disappearance. With little distinction made between the mantis and its background, it is as though nature itself is threatening to devour and consume.[22]

Caroline Chalmers explores the relationship between disguise, visual ambiguity and predation in the series of photographs entitled *Foodchain* (2000).[23] The series is based on the activities of some captive mantises reared in the artist's New York loft. Mantises are pitched against each other and against larger predators that they would not normally encounter in the wild. Chalmers meticulously documents their battles for survival, demonstrating the mantises' guile even when faced with low odds for success. Notable in her photographs are the mantises' sophisticated, and sometimes comic, attempts to trick, fool, and mesmerize their prey. The insects appear to stop at nothing in their lust for supremacy, even attacking a fully grown tarantula. Their predictable, almost mechanical desire to attack and consume, whatever the odds for survival, indicates why the surrealists considered the mantis the closest living creature to the automaton.

ENDNOTE

The painter Liz Arnold demonstrates a final attribute of the insect's ability to unsettle and disturb in a series of anthropomorphic images that include *Mythic Heaven* (1995) and *Uncovered* (1995). Both question the longevity of human dominance over the environment and explore the possibility, as feared by Bouvier, that insects will survive and succeed us. In *Mythic Heaven,* a lovesick ladybird smokes a cigarette with its back partially turned to the viewer, blowing perfect rings into an improbably blue sky. The insect

Mark Fairnington, *Still Life (Praying Mantis)* (1997).

here has become human, replacing us, adopting our world and assimilating it seamlessly into its own. *Uncovered* is similarly both sinister and comic. Wearing underpants and bra, an insect stands upright, posturing confidently with two pairs of folded legs in place of human arms. Her eyes glow demonically, similar in color to the molten sunset behind her. In the background is the postapocalyptic, darkened silhouette of a ruined city, while gleaming white in the foreground are the spoils of her supremacy, discarded mammalian bones. For Arnold, insects appear to have the last word, mocking humans and their evident limitations, deposing us with style. In Arnold's paintings, nature has indeed consumed, and the human race in its entirety has been reduced to fragments and obsolete symbols. These representations of insects at home in our world, adopting the trappings of the modern cityscape, seem to warn or remind us that among human remains there will always be insects.

NOTES

1. Fabre, *The Social Life of Insects* (London: T. Fischer Unwin, 1912), 69.

2. Douglas, *Purity and Danger: An Analysis of Pollution and Taboo* (New York: Routledge, 1966), 51. The Bible, New Revised Standard version, Anglicized edition.

3. Quoted in Kathleen Cohen, *Metamorphosis of a Death Symbol: The Transi Tomb in the Late Middle Ages and the Renaissance* (Berkeley and Los Angeles: University of California Press, 1973), 81. See also A. F. Schönback, *Alt Deutsche Predigten* (Graz, 1886–91), 1:52, which shows another representation of *Frau Welt* as a beautiful woman whose lifted skirt shows her withered legs ringed with snakes.

4. Beginning in the eleventh century in France and Italy, then spreading to western Germany and England, the heretical sect of Neo-Manichaeans, the Cathares, spread the belief that evil was not simply the absence of God as held by the Christians but instead active and threatening. The Cathares believed that all matter was created by the powers of evil and was itself evil. "Corruptibilia" was a word used by the Cathares to designate the entirety of nature, indicating its association with despair and confusion (Cohen, *Metamorphosis,* 82).

5. The word *gisant* is sometimes used in place of *transi,* meaning any recumbent sepulchral figure, living or dead. "Transi" specifically refers to a tiered structure with one representation placed on top of another; with the whole body above and the fragmented corpse below.

6. Cohen cites Johannes Nohl's *Chronicle of the Plague Compiled from Contemporary Sources,* which charts the devastating effects of the plague on people's everyday lives. One chronicler describes eleven huge trenches dug in Erfut in 1350, which were covered only after twelve thousand corpses had been thrown into them. The

sight of decaying corpses together with the inevitable mass of insects as an intrinsic part of their erosion was therefore not an unfamiliar sight to most.

7. For Cohen, the carving of insects on tombs illustrated a belief in spontaneous generation and might also reflect the belief of Pliny that living creatures hatch directly from parts of the human body; for example, after death the spinal marrow was thought to transform into a snake. (See Pliny, *Natural History,* 10:66, quoted in Cohen, *Metamorphosis,* 79.) The writer of Ecclesiasticus (10:11) also associated the corpse with the sudden appearance of insects: "For when a man is dead, he shall inherit creeping things." Cohen further cites a thirteenth-century monk from Heilsbronn who called the body *madensack,* or sack of maggots (80). See also W. Stammler, *Frau Welt, Eine Mittelalterliche Allegorie* (Freiburg, 1959), 32. The appearance of insects in the human cadaver resulting from their sins while living is intimated in Grünewald's *Dead Lovers.* Cohen observes that death, in its uncomfortable and distressing appearance, seems to have come about as the result of the couple's love, and the devouring creatures that plague them in death, with the incongruous addition of a dragonfly, are palpable symbols of their sin (82). Hope for the prevention of insects devouring the flesh after death sometimes took the form of building tombs even before the owner had died. Bishop Schonberg (d. 1516) in Naumberg is one such example. Intended as an object of contemplation in his lifetime, the inscription on his tomb read: "Deeds alone make men survive after death. / Deeds make a man die before the day of his death. / Hence I am urged by the stone to spend life well, and before death / I have prepared for myself the gifts of death that I may not die before death" (quoted in Cohen, *Metamorphosis,* 87).

8. S. Schama, *A History of Britain, at the Edge of the World? 3000 BC–AD 1603* (London: BBC World-Wide, 2000), 230.

9. Ibid.

10. There is debate among scholars surrounding both who painted *Dead Lovers* and when it was painted. I am citing René Passeron, *The Concise Encyclopedia of Surrealism* (London: Omega Books, 1974), 100. It is proposed here that Grünewald lived from around 1455 to 1528. However, there is dispute over these dates, and some believe Grünewald lived from around 1475 to 1528. With *Dead Lovers* dated circa 1470–80, this would make it unlikely that Grünewald was the painter. With no accurate dates remaining and attribution uncertain, I am citing Grünewald as the artist. However, with the date of the painting and knowledge of where it was painted more certain than the details of its author, it remains true that following the Black Death in the fourteenth century, outbreaks remained frequent, and sudden disease and death followed visibly by decay were a familiar occurrence. *Dead Lovers,* or *Les amants trépassés,* kept at Musée de l'oeurve Notre Dame de Strasbourg, is attributed to "a Swabian Master." Swabia is a historic region in southwest Germany, centering on the Black Forest.

11. Bataille, "The Sacred," in *Visions of Excess: Selected Writings, 1927–1939* (Manchester: Manchester University Press, 1985), 242.

12. Douglas, *Purity and Danger,* 21, 22.

13. Warner, *No Go the Bogeyman: Scaring, Lulling, and Making Mock* (London: Chatto and Windus, 1998), 173.

14. Harvey, in vol. 1 of *The City Remembrancer, Narratives of the Plague 1665, Fire 1666, and Great Storm 1703* (1769).

15. Lehane, *The Compleat Flea* (London: John Murray, 1969), 20.

16. See Fairnington, *Dead or Alive: Natural History Painting* (London: Black Dog, 2002).

17. Warner, *No Go the Bogeyman*, 181.

18. Douglas, *Purity and Danger*, 104.

19. Sigmund Freud, *Totem and Taboo: Resemblances between the Psychic Lives of Savages and Neurotics* (New York: Moffat, Yard, 1918), 210. The increase in patients suffering from insect phobias has risen dramatically since Freud's observations. The psychiatrist Phillip Weinstein asserts that insect-related syndromes "are far more common than is indicated by the literature: almost every dermatologist knows of a couple of cases, as do most entomologists and pest control officers." See Weinstein, "Entomophobia," *Cultural Entomology Digest* 2 (1994).

20. See also W. L. Pressly, "The Praying Mantis in Surrealist Art," *Art Bulletin* 55 (1973): 600–615.

21. *La mante religieuse: Recherché sur la nature et la signification du mythe* (Paris: Aux Amis des Livres, 1937).

22. In many cultures, the mantis is thought to possess the "evil eye." For example, the Romans believed that if someone fell sick, "the mantis has you in his eye" (Caillois, *La mante religieuese*, 1). Caillois further writes that "the appearance of the mantis announces the famine, it daubs with disaster and misfortune all the animals it sees" (1). Its gaze is widely perceived as a mirror of fear, signifying the approach of emptiness, the consumption of all it beholds. Caillois goes on to equate the menstrual blood of women in many primitive cultures with the evil eye of the mantis. These women are thought to be as dangerous to their men as the female mantis is to her mate. Whereas in many societies the glance of a menstruating woman has also been associated with turning men into statues, the eye of the mantis is believed to fix and then consume her mate, removing him from representation. This fear is reflected in the folklore of the Hottentot and bush people of South Africa. Both are matriarchal societies for whom the mantis is the most prominent mythic character. For an overview of bush tales featuring the mantis, see W. Bleek, *A Brief Account of Bushmen Folk-Lore and Other Texts* (London: Trubner, 1875), and W. Bleek, *Reynard the Fox in South Africa, or Hottentot Fables and Tales* (London: Trubner, 1864).

23. Chalmers, *Foodchain: Encounters between Mates, Predators, and Prey* (New York: Aperture, 2000).

16

Si**z**e **M**atters

Big Bugs on the Big Screen

RICHARD J. LESKOSKY

The ubiquity of insects and related arthropods in everyday life and their pervasive influence on humans make it unsurprising that they should appear in motion pictures, the most popular and populist art form of this and the previous century.[1] What is unexpected, though, is that they should appear as frequently as they do in highly magnified, unnatural forms in the so-called big bug films. This particular subgenre of science fiction film (and horror film) enjoyed an efflorescence in the 1950s when various radiation-induced monstrosities stalked the cinematic landscape and UFOs whirled across movie screens. After some relatively fallow decades, the big bug film is now enjoying a renascence both on the big screen and in direct-to-video releases in the first decade of the new century. Obviously, more than the whims of filmmakers is at work in the continued popularity of this offbeat genre. But the question also arises as to why such films might be popular with audiences, given the widespread aversion to normal-size insects and spiders. Surely magnifying the object of fear or revulsion should correspondingly magnify the viewer's aversion to the sight before him or her and so make the film less appealing.

Popular film genres, however, often present viewers with, to say the least, unappealing sights or concepts—undead horrors such as vampires and zombies, for example, or the dismembered victims of insane killers.[2] The appeal, as with big bug films, is that of immersing oneself in a particular fear while remaining completely safe from the real-world circumstances and effects of that fear. In the case of big bug films, however, viewers face not only their fears of creepy crawlers but also other more deeply seated anxieties

319

such as loss of life, stature, and identity. The viewer similarly confronts in these movies anxieties over various other real-world phenomena such as threats posed by radiation, pollution, and the unintended consequences of scientific experimentation. Big bug films thus allow the viewer to face in perfect safety a whole range of fears; the fact that the films center around a basic incongruence between the depicted creatures and the viewer's real-life experience of them only serves to make the depicted horrors easier to deal with.

Before discussing big bug films and their appeal to audiences, however, it is necessary to stipulate or clarify a few points. The term "big bug films" derives from the popular perception of the creatures involved and not from the classifications of entomologists. It constitutes perhaps the most recognized subcategory of "insect fear films" (which also include films about normal-size swarming insects and about the inappropriate or at least ill-advised scientific use of various aspects of insect biology). In fact, though, nothing an entomologist would classify as a true bug (order Hemiptera) has ever appeared in a big bug film.[3] The designation "big bug" in this case also refers to creatures that are not insects (class Insecta) but the uneducated observer might include in that category—specifically, members of the class Arachnida such as spiders and scorpions. Conversely, other members of the phylum Arthropoda (most notably members of the class Crustacea such as crabs) are not included even though they may be related more closely to insects than are, say, spiders.

It should also be noted that "big" is a relative term in at least two ways. First, the bug must be big in relation to a human being in the same film. That relationship may arise, however, not from the bug being any greater than its normal size in the real world; instead, the human being may have been shrunk to subinsect size. This is the case obtaining most notably in *The Incredible Shrinking Man* (dir. Jack Arnold, 1957), *Honey, I Shrunk the Kids!* (dir. Joe Johnston, 1989), and *Antibody* (dir. Christian McIntire, 2002), but in each case the "big bug" aspect of the film is restricted to one or two episodes rather than serving as the main story element. In the shrunken-human variation of the big bug film, the bug represents only one of many new threats to the protagonist—posed usually by things ordinarily innocuous to full-size individuals. The problem for the humans is not so much the relative bulk of their insect opponents but rather their own intrinsic yet unaccustomed smallness. The whole world has become hostile, the humans have literally been cast down from their high perch at the top of creation, and the presence of the bug acts as a final seal on the humans' debased status, the conclusive affirmation that the natural order has been reversed.

Second, there are different degrees of "bigness" to be considered. The largest insects or arachnids in the real world can easily (for the daring, nonentomophobic person so inclined) be held in the hand. For various reasons, they cannot get larger than that, and certainly not large enough to pick up Volkswagens. The surface area–volume ratio would work against them as their size increased, rendering them virtually immobile as they achieved giant stature. Then, too, they have exoskeletons, which cannot grow with the animal but must be shed periodically, leaving them temporarily unprotected against predators and the persistent demands of gravity. And their respiratory system, depending on a system of tubes (tracheae terminating in tracheoles) to deliver oxygen from the environment to the cellular level, simply could not function effectively in a creature much larger than current living insects.[4]

The natural order reversed! Entomologist Patricia Medford (Joan Weldon) is about to discover that humans may no longer be the dominant species on earth in *Them!* (1954).

The laws of physics and biology prove to be no impediment for the determined filmmaker, however, and movie bugs may grow to varying degrees of enormity. Roughly, they come in three levels: behemoth size, human size, and poodle size. (This last level is not as frivolously named as it might appear at first: just as poodles come in various sizes, so do oversize insects that nonetheless still remain smaller than humans, and a wasp the size of a toy poodle is something to be just as wary of as a mosquito the size of a standard poodle.) Even at the lower end of the poodle-size range there must be some form of puppetry or some manipulation of the image to create the illusion of a larger-than-normal specimen, and characters in the film will react to the creatures as though they were unique and freakish.

Usually the number of bugs in a big bug film is inversely proportional to the size of the bug. In the poodle-size range, the threat posed by the bug and the difficulty of coping with it are always multiplied by greater numbers of actual creatures, and there is some overlap at this point with the sort of insect fear film that relies on swarms of normal-size insects for its menace. At the human-size level, the number of creatures often drops to one for reasons that I will discuss later. In any case, the big bugs of this size are usually not manifest in great numbers. Once behemoth size is achieved, the number usually drops to one (most likely for budget considerations more than anything else), although there are significant exceptions, and the use of computer-generated imagery in such films is now making multiple giant arthropods more of a regular feature.[5]

OTHER OUTSIZE ANIMAL FILMS

It is worth noting a corollary phenomenon at this point—namely, that there are about half as many films featuring giant creatures that are not terrestrial arthropods as there are big bug films.[6] What makes this curious is that various mammals (lions, tigers, and bears, say) are known to prey on humans given the right circumstances, that others (for example, elephants, rhinos, hippos, bulls, boars) have caused human deaths in other situations, and that still others (wolves, most notably) have a reputation (albeit largely mythical) for attacking humans. Furthermore, perhaps because of the preceding facts, humans have historically hunted these creatures—as well as others possessed of varying degrees of aggressiveness when hunted. Yet there is only a tiny number of films in which giant versions of such creatures stalk the screen; and even in these cases, the enlarged creatures are not that much larger than the largest normal members of their species. In *Grizzly* (dir. William Girdler, 1976), the title bear is variously reported to be fifteen or eighteen feet tall and is played by a real bear measuring eleven feet. *Hulk* (dir. Ang Lee, 2003) at one point has the protagonist battling three gamma-ray-enhanced dogs (including one poodle and two more obviously attack-dog types) about the size of Shetland ponies. The Australian *Razorback* (dir. Russell Mulcahy, 1984) probably features the normally threatening mammal scaled up proportionately the most, since its monster hog appears to be about as large as a pickup truck.[7]

One can hypothesize that such wild mammals are perceived as sufficiently dangerous at their normal sizes so that presenting audiences with a lion the size of a trailer, say, would not elicit enough added terror to make the effort or expense worthwhile. Audiences are also sufficiently familiar with such creatures from zoos, nature documentaries, other fiction films, and other sources of information, and therefore grossly magnified versions might be less likely to support a willing suspension of disbelief.[8] Most audience members would also be aware of how relatively easy it is to dispatch even very fierce normal mammals with firearms, further mitigating the threat posed by enlarged versions.

Mammoth mammals (to continue the alliterative nomenclature) in films tend to be either apes or rodents. King Kong and his descendants, imitations, and reincarnations account for a significant percentage of giant mammal films but also have different symbolic mechanisms at work. The giant-ape movies—including *King Kong* (dir. Merian C. Cooper and Ernest B. Schoedsack, 1933), *The Son of Kong* (dir. Ernest B. Schoedsack, 1933), and *Mighty Joe Young* (dir. Ernest B. Schoedsack, 1949), all with animated apes by Willis O'Brien, but also in their remakes done by other artists—universally present their sizable simians in a sympathetic light, most often doomed or at least seriously endangered by their ill-fated attachment to a human female. They might rampage through our cities or chew on the slower natives, but they possess sufficiently intelligible emotions to evoke some sense of empathy on the part of the audience.[9]

The mammals with the greatest proportional gains in size in monster films (even though they do not reach the behemoth level of a Kong) tend to be those that share some features with insects—that is, they are relatively small compared to humans, they are numerous, and they are generally considered to be pests. Rats are the most popular of these—see, for example, *Food of the Gods* (dir. Bert I. Gordon, 1976), *Deadly Eyes* (dir. Robert Clouse, 1982), *Food of the Gods II* (dir. Damian Lee, 1989), and *Rodentz* (dir. Miles Feldman, 2001).[10] But shrews and rabbits have also popped up as oversize menaces in films memorable chiefly for their lack of production values—*The Killer Shrews* (dir. Ray Kellogg, 1959) and *Night of the Lepus* (dir. William F. Claxton, 1972), respectively.

Outside the order Mammalia and aside from *The Giant Gila Monster* (dir. Ray Kellogg, 1959) and *The Giant Claw* (dir. Fred F. Sears, 1957), which features a huge albeit alien bird, most nonbug giant monster films feature aquatic animals. Preceding most such films was the giant squid that put in a memorable appearance in the Walt Disney Jules Verne adaptation, *20,000 Leagues under the Sea* (dir. Richard Fleischer, 1954). Octopuses have come in for their fair share of monstrous rampaging in *It Came from Beneath the Sea* (dir. Robert Gordon, 1955), *Octopus* (dir. John Eyres, 2000), and *Octopus 2: River of Fear* (dir. Yossi Wein, 2001), as have alligators in *Alligator* (dir. Lewis Teague, 1980), *Alligator II: The Mutation* (dir. Jon Hess, 1991), and *Lake Placid* (dir. Steve Miner, 1999) and leeches in *Attack of the Giant Leeches* (dir. Bernard F. Kowalski, 1959) and *Leeches!* (Dir. David LeCoteau, 2003). Colossal crabs show up in the title role in *Attack of the Crab Monsters* (dir. Roger Corman, 1957) and in one adventure in *Mysterious Island* (dir. Cy Endfield, 1961), and even giant crayfish show up in the Republic Serial *Panther Girl of the Kongo* (dir. Franklin Adreon, 1955).

Apparently, aquatic creatures are sufficiently alien and unknown in their own right to viewers while having a (justified) reputation for attacking humans that filmmakers perceive them as ready means of inducing fear in an audience. The practical consideration that a creature that would naturally be mostly submerged and thus out of sight during most of the action and therefore cheaper to film may also play a significant role in the decision to embark on such a project.

EARLY BIG BUG FILMS

Very soon after the birth of the cinema, filmmakers began presenting audiences with fantastic images of the improbable and the impossible. Fantasy film pioneer Georges Méliès and other erstwhile magicians filmed their stage acts and then went on to create tricks and illusions possible only through the manipulation of the cinematic apparatus.[11] After 1910 Winsor McCay amazed vaudeville audiences with his animated drawings, and Willis O'Brien brought dinosaurs to life on the screen with stop-motion animation. From the beginnings of these forays into the fantastic, filmmakers used oversize arthropods as images to amaze and affright their viewers.

In 1901 Georges Méliès produced *Le brahmane et le papillon* (more alliteratively in English, *The Brahmin and the Butterfly*)—arguably the first big bug film. The film typically stars Méliès himself as a magician (in this case, the Brahmin); in a forest he summons a giant caterpillar, which he proceeds to place into a large cocoon and then turns into a butterfly (equally typically, a chorus girl in costume). The butterfly he then changes into an Oriental princess, but when he bends to kiss her foot, she changes him into a caterpillar. This first big bug film, interestingly enough, demonstrates a recurring aspect of many later such films featuring human-size bugs— namely, a confusion or conflation of human and insect. Here the beautiful butterfly is engagingly transformed into a beautiful woman, but the Brahmin is also disturbingly transmogrified into a caterpillar, which then crawls offscreen after the woman.

Although big bug films may have had their flowering in the science fiction cinema of the 1950s, instances of big bugs as immediate threats to a human actually began with some of the earliest animated cartoons. In 1912 Winsor McCay, pioneering American animator and creator of *Little Nemo in Slumberland, Dreams of a Rarebit Fiend,* and other newspaper cartoon series, made his second animated cartoon, *How a Mosquito Operates* (based on one of his *Rarebit Fiend* strips), which featured a mosquito, wearing a top hat and tails, who when first seen is roughly human-size. When he actually settles down to drawing blood from his victim, though, he is the size of a toy poodle.[12] The initial large size of this insect derives from contemporary popular cultural references to Jersey skeeters, especially large and aggressive mosquitoes from the marshes of New Jersey, and the disparity in the size of the mosquito in the two sequences of the film (lurking outside the victim's door and attacking the victim in his bed) demonstrates an early aesthetic tension between the symbolic and the practical in terms of representation. In 1921 McCay returned to oversize insects in *Bug Carnival,* one in an animated *Rarebit Fiend* series: a tramp settles down for a nap in a woodland setting after eating a cheesy Welsh rarebit and dreams of human-size insects performing various circus acts; when at last a correspondingly large spider swings out over him on a strand of silk and lands on him, he awakens in panic.[13]

Additionally, one of the most famous examples of lost film footage is an early big bug episode. A scene in *King Kong* that showed injured crewmen in Kong's jungle being set upon by giant spiders was edited out of the feature soon after its initial release because of the scene's violent and horrific nature, and the footage was subsequently lost.

The lineage of big bug films in part thus recapitulates in broad terms the history of film animation. *How a Mosquito Operates* was drawn entirely by McCay himself on sheets of paper, with each frame of film representing a completely different drawing. By the time of *Bug Carnival,* McCay was using cels and assistant animators to reduce the number of drawings and the workload on the chief animator—a system that represented the industry standard for the next several decades. The stop-motion animation of *King Kong* by Willis O'Brien, a pioneer in this area who also animated

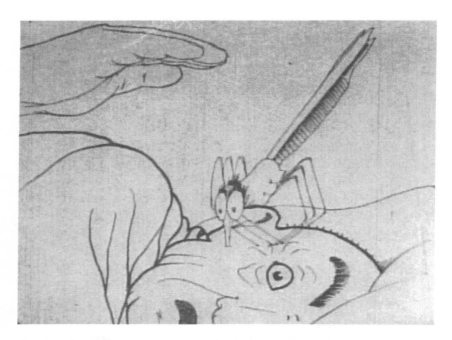

Terror in the night! An oversize mosquito feeds on a distraught sleeper in Winsor McCay's *How a Mosquito Operates* (1912), the first animated cartoon to depict an outsize insect.

the monsters in *The Black Scorpion* (dir. Edward Ludwig, 1957), represented the most sophisticated method for bringing big bugs to the screen until the use of computer animation in *Starship Troopers* (dir. Paul Verhoeven, 1997) to present various and numerous alien bugs.

BIG BUGS IN THE 1950S

As noted earlier, though, the 1950s marked the first great flowering of big bug films, with at least a dozen movies featuring big bugs as the main story device or as the menace in a significant episode, and several other films featuring them in minor episodes (often, it seems, using the same large spider puppet in different films). During that period, the average American was beset with various fears stemming from the Cold War—fear of invasion, fear of conformity, fear of nuclear war or nuclear contamination, and a general fear of otherness. These fears found simultaneous expression and exploitation in the popular cinema of the time, and especially in film noir, horror films, and science fiction films. Big bug films played on a number of these fears.

Generally, invasion fears were embodied in science fiction films about literal invasions by extraterrestrials, but they are also manifest in most of the more prominent big bug films of the time.[14] The bugs are characterized as an invading force, and they are met with the might of the United States military (the Mexican army in the case of *The Black Scorpion*), although usually not with initial success on the part of the military. In *Them!* (Dir. Gordon Douglas, 1954), one of the archetypal big bug films, myrmecologist Dr. Harold Medford (Edmund Gwenn) describes the ants in a presentation to a group of military leaders thus: "Ants are the only creatures on earth, other than man, who make war. They campaign, they are chronic aggressors, and they make slave laborers of the captives they don't kill. . . . Even the most minute of them have an instinct and talent for industry, social organization, and savagery that makes man look feeble by comparison." He concludes by noting that unless this problem is dealt with, "Man as the dominant species of life on earth will probably be extinct within a year." This declaration of all-out war between humanity and the giant arthropods echoes his assertion in the preceding scene, back in New Mexico where the ants originated and where initial attempts at exterminating the entire colony failed to kill two young queen ants before they flew off to form other

A lurid lobby card for *Them!*. One of the first and still one of the best of the big bug films, *Them!* was nominated for an Oscar for special effects.

colonies, that "we haven't seen the last of them. We've only seen the beginning of what may be the end of us."[15]

The authoritative recitation of the natural powers and attributes of insects or arachnids and the threat they pose to humanity because of their great size (and therefore similarly increased abilities) is a standard element of big bug films, just as is the failure of the military to defeat the menace on its first try. Typically it is delivered by a professor or scientist surrounded by various emblems of knowledge and expertise (such as a microscope or other laboratory equipment, shelves of books, diagrams of insect anatomy, and so on). In the twenty-first-century version, this recitation (and other bits of pertinent information) can also be delivered by a bookish teenager.

The fear of invasion is further evoked in 1950s big bug films by having the bug move from its initial sighting in some wilderness area into a major city to attack humans in their homes and streets and other places generally thought safe at the time. In *Them!* the ants go from the New Mexico desert to the storm drains of Los Angeles. The giant grasshoppers in *Beginning of the End* advance from rural east central Illinois (not a wilderness, but sparsely populated) into Chicago. The title creature in *The Deadly Mantis* (dir. Nathan Juran, 1957) migrates from the Arctic Circle, where it was frozen in ice for millions of years, to New York City, where it is finally brought down in the confines of a traffic tunnel. In this last case, the mantis must fly through the distant early warning line of radar stations and at least two other lines of U.S. radar defense to reach New York.

The film actually begins with a lengthy documentary section on the DEW line, its construction, and its function to prevent or at least warn of a sneak attack coming over the North Pole from an unmentioned Soviet Union. By penetrating all our radar defenses and evading our jet fighters, the giant mantis calls into question the ability of those lines of defense to provide the United States with valid protection against an invading human force and the atomic bombs it would likely be delivering.

With all the talk of nuclear war, atom and hydrogen bombs, radioactive fallout, nuclear energy and its benefits and dangers as well as the images of the results of the bombings of Hiroshima and Nagasaki that would still be fresh in the minds of Americans, an abiding concern with atomic bombs and atomic radiation seems only natural for the period. People built bomb shelters in their backyards, schoolchildren were taught to "duck and cover" in the event of an atomic bomb being detonated, and pictures of nuclear test explosions were relatively common images in magazines and television of the period. Big bug films similarly displayed a fascination with radioactivity and its effects on living organisms.

In *Them!* the ants grow to their immense size as a result of residual radiation from the first atom bomb tests. In *Beginning of the End* the grasshoppers feed on produce, the growth of which has been accelerated and increased by radiation. A nutrient activated by a radioactive isotope is the culprit in *Tarantula* (dir. Jack Arnold, 1955). And in *The Incredible Shrinking Man* (dir. Jack Arnold, 1957), a radioactive cloud contaminates the protagonist, starting his title process and thereby leading him eventually to battle a proportionately much larger tarantula. Radiation has nothing to do with the creature's size in *The Deadly Mantis,* but its ability to penetrate America's defenses carries with it the implication that the country is vulnerable to nuclear attack.

How big was it? Col. Joe Parkman (Craig Stevens) demonstrates the relative sizes of the giant mantis and the C-47 plane it destroyed in *The Deadly Mantis* (1957).

Big Bugs in the Twenty-First Century

By the twenty-first century, radiation seems to have gone well past its half-life in the popular imagination—at least as reflected in big bug films. Of the sixteen big bug films produced since 2000, only *Monster Island* (dir. Jack Perez, 2002) has its creatures caused by radiation (residual from A-bomb tests on the island decades earlier).[16] Magic actually accounts for more—for example, the giant spiders in *Harry Potter and the Chamber of Secrets* (dir. Chris Columbus, 2002) and *The Lord of the Rings: The Return of the King* (dir. Peter Jackson, 2003). Six, however, depend on genetic engineering of one sort or another for their monsters: *Spiders* (dir. Gary Jones, 2000), *Tail Sting* (dir. Paul Wynne, 2001), *Mimic 2* (dir. Jean de Segonzac, 2001), *Spiders 2: Breeding Ground* (dir. Sam Firstenberg, 2001), *Mimic Sentinel* (dir. J. T. Petty, 2003), and *Bite Me!* (dir. Brett Piper, 2004). This would seem to suggest that DNA research and genetic engineering are of greater popular concern than nuclear war or radiation contamination in the new century.[17]

Worry over unintended consequences of genetic engineering first found expression in big bug films in *Mimic* (dir. Guillermo del Toro, 1997).[18] The premise here originates in a viral plague striking children in New York City that is spread by cockroaches. To combat the virus, scientists decide to eliminate all cockroaches in the city, and to do this they engineer a new insect with DNA from termites and mantids, among others, to spread an equally engineered plague that targets roaches. Once that is accomplished, the so-called Judas breed is supposed to die off itself, since only sterile females have been released. Of course, things do not work out that way, and three years later the Judas breed has mutated into a human-size form with external markings that make it look vaguely human in the dark, since this large form has a tendency to stand upright. It now also has lungs, eats people, and is multiplying in the subway tunnels. The only way to combat this menace is for the scientist (Mira Sorvino) who developed the Judas breed to go into the subway tunnels herself in a sort of personal expiation and fight the creatures mano a mano (in very loose terms) while her husband (Jeremy Northam), a CDC official, tries to blow them up en masse, equally undergoing a personal purgatory for his part in the original scheme.

The relative popularity and critical cachet of *Mimic* certainly guaranteed imitators, and there have even been two sequels of increasingly inferior quality and decreasing numbers of insects. It should perhaps be noted that in addition to a certain currency of concern surrounding genetic research, referencing it visually in a film can be far less costly than mocking up plausible radiation sources.

THE WORLD OUT OF PROPORTION

Apart from different topical fears (radiation, genetic engineering gone wrong) varying over the decades, other psychological factors at work in big bug films have remained fairly constant. Some variation correlates with the relative size of the bugs, but some fear factors remain constant across all three levels. Insects and arachnids are as foreign to human experience as any familiar creature could possibly be. We encounter them every day, often in our own homes, sometimes on our own bodies, yet they are inalienably different from us. They have a multiplicity of legs and possibly even wings, they are orders of magnitude smaller than us, they have hard shells. Their faces are not like any mammal's: no nose, too many or differently structured eyes, no ears, antennae, radically different sorts of mouths. Add to that the fact that they ignore us totally except when they feed on us. One can look at animals in the zoo and see them looking back not only through the bars but across the millions of years of evolution separating them from us. There is a deep kinship we sense with other mammals. One can even find one's pet fish getting excited and acknowledging one's approach at feeding time. But the only recognition one can hope for from a pet insect or arachnid is that it will not bite, having become accustomed to being handled.

There is no emotional connection between the human world and the insect world even though our existence arguably depends on theirs. They are the ultimate alien creatures and become only more so when they prey on us—the mosquitoes, lice, and fleas that suck our blood when we are alive, and the flies and beetles that consume us when we are dead and not immediately tended to.[19]

Filmmakers thus have an immediately recognizable source of unease in confronting the Other, the alien, when they make a big bug film.[20] The marked increase in production of such films in the first years of this century indicates that filmmakers working in a wide range of budgets and formats have recognized this, and that for low-budget filmmakers in particular, this is a comfortable shorthand method for generating horror and fear in audiences.

At the poodle size level, the operating mechanism is similar to that posed by normal-size swarming insects. The protagonist humans face a threat that would not necessarily be overwhelming if only a single individual creature were involved. Unfortunately, that is not the case in the film. Instead there are large numbers of the creatures, and being significantly larger than normal, they pose a heightened individual threat in addition to the collective menace, a situation that increases the horror of the situation exponentially. The wasps in *Food of the Gods,* for instance, and even the steroid-enhanced creatures in *Ticks* (dir. Tony Randel, 1993) are formidable but not overpowering one at a time, but in numbers they present a serious threat. Since the creatures at this level of magnitude are large enough that individual features can be made out (as opposed to the relative obscurity of all but gross body parts in the case of most normal-size arthropods), any natural revulsion the viewer may have over them is heightened. At this size, it is the general appearance of the creature, now uncommonly visible in greater detail than heretofore, which affects the viewer, whereas at the other end of the scale, the sheer size of the beast captures one's attention first.

At the human size level, strange things happen in big bug films. It is at this size that one can actually imagine one-on-one combat with the Other, except that in the fictional world of the film (as opposed to the real world, where the laws of physics apply), the creature often still retains most or all of its proportional strength and speed and all of its unconcern for its human foe. Beyond this aspect, however, there is a strange conflation of the human and the insect at this size, as noted earlier with respect to the Méliès film. It is at this level that one encounters were-insects, as it were—creatures that were once human but have become insects in whole or in part or the reverse of this, the insect that has become the simulacrum of a human.

Among the former, we have *The Fly* (dir. Kurt Neumann, 1958) and *The Return of the Fly* (dir. Edward Bernds, 1959), *The Wasp Woman* (dir. Roger Corman, 1959) and its 1995 remake, and the 2001 version of *Earth versus the Spider* (dir. Scott Ziehl), which bears no relation to the 1958 film of the same title.[21] In all of these, a human takes on the appearance of an insect or spider, always with fatal consequences to himself or herself and usually to others as well. These are all characters who have been careless or foolish in their employment of experimental technologies and pay a horrible price. The spirit of Franz Kafka's Gregor Samsa from *Die Verwandlung* hangs heavy over these films, though none of them come near the psychological

depths of that work, and Gregor's metamorphosis lacks the cinematic motivation of the films (that is, he did nothing obvious to cause his change).
Unlike Gregor, the humans who become part insect or spider in these films
take positive and ill-advised actions that lead directly to their horrific conditions and usually to their deaths as well.

The latter, insect-to-human transformers include the vampiric death's-
head moth in *The Blood Beast Terror* (dir. Vernon Sewell, 1968) and the
South American beetles in the 1989 satire *Meet the Applegates* (dir. Michael
Lehmann). In both cases, the erstwhile insects have intentions that hold dire
consequences for humans (the moth plans to breed a race of giant vampire
moths, and the beetles plan to blow up a nuclear power plant in retribution
for the destruction of their Amazon jungle home). One of the weirdest
(and worst) of the big bug films, *Mesa of Lost Women* (dir. Ron Ormond
and Herbert Tevos, 1952), has the mad scientist Dr. Arana (Jackie Coogan)
switching growth hormones between humans and spiders. He winds up
with one intelligent human-size spider, several tall sexy women with long
fingernails, and a number of melancholy male dwarfs.

Finally there are *Mimic* and its sequels, where the human-size insects
develop camouflaging that makes them appear human from a distance in
the dark. Though not rational like the creatures in the previous paragraph,
they do intend to propagate their own species, which would have deadly
consequences for humans. The human-to-insect transformations capital-
ize on fears of losing one's identity, of becoming something alien to one's
traditional self, of losing control, of becoming less than human or nonhuman. The insect-to-human shape-shifters play on our fears about dealing with others—that others may be deceiving us about their intentions
and their attitudes toward us, that underneath an attractive exterior may
lurk something alien.

What is truly odd about big bug films in the human-size range is that
the mingling of human and insect also introduces a sometimes bizarre sexual element. The fly-headed scientist in *The Fly* is married, and it is his
wife's horrified reaction to the sight of him that contributes to his decision
to commit suicide. The cosmetic company executive in *The Wasp Woman*
hopes to renew her youthful looks and sexual allure through the use of an
untested wasp enzyme serum. The were-spider in the made-for-TV *Curse
of the Black Widow* (dir. Dan Curtis, 1977) is moved to violent murder by
sexual jealousy, among other motives. Things become more explicit (if

ultimately inexplicable) in *The Blood Beast Terror*, where the were-moth seduces young men in her pretty-girl form and then reverts in midembrace to a murderous insect horror. *Meet the Applegates* sees human society corrupting the naive beetles with sex, drugs, alcohol, and shopping. *Mesa of Lost Women*, in a category by itself, abounds with material supportive of a wide variety of fetishes (mute yet powerful women with long, dangerous fingernails and weak, subservient males, for example, provide a highly masochistic subtext for this film).

Oddly enough, the most erotic of the big bug films is probably Méliès's 1901 *Le brahmane et le papillon* with its mutual transformations of insect to human and human to insect. Although as innocent a conjuring act as the rest of Méliès's work, the film stands out in that it is rare that the Méliès main character is changed into something else by another character—and by a woman at that. Méliès was generally obviously in control both in front of and behind the camera; it was he who made beautiful women appear, disappear, and metamorphose into other beings. The masochistic elements in the film are therefore relatively anomalous in his work, and proportionate to the two-minute length of the film, they certainly must qualify it as the most sexually charged big bug film. His character bends to kiss the foot of the princess, formerly the butterfly, and during this gesture of abjection and subservience, she transforms him into a caterpillar—an insect of the sort she had once been, an immature version at that, and phallic in shape.[22]

The behemoth category films present the perfect confrontation with the Other, with the completely alien. When insects tower over humans, the natural order has been overturned. Mankind is no longer at the top of the food chain, the dominant form of life on the planet.[23] Nor in the more classical literary and religious formulation is the human race even in the middle of the great chain of being between the angels and the beasts. Instead, mankind has been relegated to the bottom, at the mercy of what had formerly been held to be the lowest of creatures. This is more than a denial of identity; it is a denial of worth, a denial of a place within the natural order, a denial of a future ("the beginning of the end"). It is how the apocalypse would have gone if the writer of Revelation had been not John but an entomologist.

Among the largest of the big bugs, we find a preponderance of natural predators, with only a few exceptions. Parasites show up in only a couple of instances. An extra-large tick pops up (or more literally out—of a character) at the finale of *Ticks*. A skin mite threatens the crew of a miniaturized

experimental vehicle injected into the bloodstream of a terrorist to deacti-
vate the microscopic remote-control detonator wired to his heart in *Antibody* (2002). Grasshoppers, generally herbivorous, develop a fondness for
snacking on humans in *Beginning of the End*. In this context it is interesting to note that the film's title has explicitly apocalyptic connotations, as
opposed to the more traditional big bug films' titles, which merely identify the particular film's monster (*Tarantula, The Black Scorpion, Spiders*)
or both identify the creature and emphasize its menacing nature (*Earth
versus the Spider, The Deadly Mantis, The Giant Spider Invasion*).[24]

Of course, the Japanese *Mothra* (1961) and its sequels feature a giant
moth and often its caterpillar stage of development as well. Neither moth
nor caterpillar form consumes humans, however; Mothra merely knocks
down buildings, either by the direct application of force or by the blast of
air generated by its wings flapping. In many ways, Mothra is a very different sort of big bug. First, it is the only big bug with a name. Second, its films
include a (quasi-)religious element in that the giant moth is worshipped
by the human natives of its home island. Third, its rampages usually have
benign motives—namely, at least in the original film, to protect two tiny
singing humanoids from its home island who act as its priestesses. Fourth,
the creature undoubtedly has more significance to its Japanese audience,
given the importance of moth-produced silk in the Japanese economy and
culture, than any American big bug has for its home audience.

But for these exceptions, the largest big bugs are all recognized predators—ants, spiders, mantids, scorpions. In fact, though, they are predomi-
nantly not insects at all, with various sorts of spiders dominating at this
level. Spiders make particularly effective big bugs, since they already occupy
a significant place in the panoply of human fears (which has warranted
a clinical name, arachnophobia). The largest real spiders have sufficiently
intimidating appearances that they have long been used as normal-size
threats in many films. Of course, all spiders have an even greater number of
legs than insects and too many eyes for the comfort of the human observer
(if one is willing to get close enough to discern such detail). The larger
species appear hairy, which only serves to heighten human revulsion, since
hirsuteness seems to blur the lines between arthropod and mammal. Spiders
also have no qualms about setting up webs where humans can easily observe
them catching and devouring their prey, so humans have a keener sense of
what spiders are capable of than they do with fierce insect predators such

as dragonfly nymphs. Spiders wrap their prey in silk and consume them alive. Female spiders even have a tendency to consume their mates. Venomous spiders do pose real dangers to humans and cause a generally small but usually well-publicized amount of pain and death each year. In short, it is not surprising that audiences have a general predisposition to regard spiders negatively, and filmmakers are not above capitalizing on this.

There are also practical considerations for using a spider as a monster. The larger species are sizable enough to function as live actors in front of the camera, either for the initial normal-size stages of a monster's development or with a modest amount of optical tinkering once behemoth size has been reached. This obviates the need for more-expensive model animation, animatronics, or computer imaging and so is a staple for filmmakers with low budgets. In films with giant spiders, humans do not merely wind up at the bottom of the food chain but are also symbolically dehumanized by being reduced to the status of a fly, the common food of spiders in popular culture (in sayings and in animated cartoons, for example). They face the imminent threat of having their very essence sucked out and being left mere dry husks. Probably the most horrific scene in any big bug film is the penultimate shot of *The Fly* (1958), when the human-headed fly, caught in the web of a proportionately huge spider, screams at the approach of the arachnid, "Help me! Help me!" The natural order is subverted in so many ways in this shot that it overwhelms any objections the logical mind might have to the scene.

Conclusion

Big bug films have a venerable history going back to the earliest days of the cinema (albeit with large gaps in the time line) and have enjoyed peaks of production in the 1950s and the first decade of the twenty-first century. They play on a multiplicity of fears and desires within their audience, and they answer various practical needs of their creators. As movie technology has advanced, big bug films have employed the latest developments in animatronics and computer imaging but also continue to take advantage of low-tech potentials in low-budget projects.[25] As audience concerns have changed over the decades (from the dangers of radiation and Soviet invasion in the 1950s to genetic engineering and its unintended consequences in the present century), big bug films have adapted to feed on and into those fears. They benefit, moreover, from being able to allow their audiences to confront a range of anxieties beyond mere insect fear, so that the viewer's pleasure in being able to face these terrors in safety operates on multiple levels. The big bug films seem to be as hardy, then, and to have as assured a future as the arthropods that star in them.

NOTES

1. For an overview of insects in the cinema, see May R. Berenbaum and Richard J. Leskosky, "Insects in Movies," in *Encyclopedia of Insects,* ed. Vincent H. Resh and Ring T. Carde (San Diego: Academic Press, 2003); James Mertins, "Arthropods on the Screen," *Bulletin of the Entomological Society of America* 32 (1986): 85–90; and Stacy Alaimo, "Discomforting Creatures: Monstrous Natures in Recent Films," in *Beyond Nature Writings: Expanding the Boundaries of Ecocriticism,* ed. Karla Armbruster and Kathleen R. Wallace (Charlottesville: University Press of Virginia, 2001), 279–96.

2. For a study of vampire and zombie films that sees such encounters with the undead as providing the viewer with a reaffirmation of life and survival, see Gregory A. Waller, *The Living and the Undead: From Stoker's "Dracula" to Romero's "Dawn of the Dead"* (Urbana: University of Illinois Press, 1986). For a Freudian-based feminist interpretation of slasher films that sees them as appealing to masochistic fears and desires in the audience, see Carol J. Clover, *Men, Women, and Chainsaws: Gender in the Modern Horror Film* (Princeton, N.J.: Princeton University Press, 1992). See Walter Kendrick, *The Thrill of Fear: 250 Years of Scary Entertainment* (New York: Grove Press, 1991), for a discussion of how horror in popular entertainment helps audiences cope with the fear of death.

3. The Jackie Chan action film *The Tuxedo* (dir. Kevin Donovan, 2002) deals with a plot to contaminate the world's supply of freshwater by means of (normal size) water striders, but this is the only instance of true bugs being used in any sort of insect fear film.

4. For a more detailed discussion of why truly large insects are not physically possible, see May Berenbaum, *Bugs in the System: Insects and Their Impact on Human Affairs* (Reading, Mass.: Addison Wesley, 1995).

5. For a discussion of why having a single such invader is not a good strategy— at least for the invading organism—see Berenbaum and Leskosky, "Life History Strategies and Population Biology in Science Fiction Films," *Bulletin of the Ecological Society of America* 73 (1992): 236–40.

6. Of course, dinosaurs tromp through quite a few films, but they are generally presumed to be the normal size for dinosaurs and so do not qualify as giant monsters as construed here—that is, creatures that have become monstrous by virtue of having their size significantly increased. Dinosaurs are therefore not included here.

7. Even fantastical hybrids from mythology such as griffins and folkloric creatures such as werewolves (neither of which will be considered further here) remain fairly true to the scale of their components.

8. A rare feline predator—a "giant" house cat—does appear briefly in *The Incredible Shrinking Man* (1957). This is, of course, a normal cat who presents a threat to the protagonist only when he shrinks to the approximate size of a mouse. Here no question of implausibility resides in the cat itself, since it is the human who has changed size in the story.

9. Not counted here are giant-human films such *The Amazing Colossal Man* (dir. Bert I. Gordon, 1957), its sequel, *War of the Colossal Beast* (dir. Bert I. Gordon, 1958), and *Attack of the 50 Ft. Woman* (dir. Nathan Juran, 1958), which similarly present their outsize lead characters sympathetically even when they are on a rampage. Furthermore, films and videos featuring giant women, mostly made by amateurs, are more plentiful than one would suspect from checking mainstream film guides. They cater to a very specific sexual fixation among their viewers and makers.

10. The reader will find the works of producer-director Bert I. Gordon cited numerous times throughout this text, since he built his career on films about giant animals and humans. He is still known in the film industry as "Mr. Big" because of this penchant—and because of his fortuitous initials.

11. Chiefly, though many other tricks were used, this consisted of having the performers freeze in position, stopping the camera, adding, removing, or replacing an object (or an actor) in the scene, and then resuming the cranking of the camera, with the effect being produced of the object having suddenly appeared from nowhere, disappeared from the set, or transformed into something else. For further discussion of Méliès, see John Frazer, *Artificially Arranged Scenes: The Films of Georges Méliès* (Boston: G. K. Hall, 1975).

12. Based on attire and general anthropomorphized facial characteristics, the mosquito here is clearly a male. In reality, only female mosquitoes bite humans. McCay depicted giant mosquitoes in at least three of his numerous comic strips, and the film mentioned here began its life as part of McCay's lightning sketch vaudeville act. For more information on Winsor McCay and his animated films, see John Canemaker, *Winsor McCay: His Life and Art* (New York: Abbeville Press, 1987).

13. The pattern established in McCay's original comic strip was somewhat different from that of the films. The strip would invariably begin in the sleeper's dream, become more threatening or surreal in its imagery, and end with the dreamer (always a different individual in each strip) awakening with a vow never again to eat rarebit before going to sleep. McCay undoubtedly figured that the animated films would last too long for the always abrupt awakening to work for the audience without an initial indication that a dream might be about to commence.

14. In fact, *Killers from Space* (dir. W. Lee Wilder, 1954) has alien invaders planning to use giant insects as part of their program of conquest. They are, however, foiled before they can get to that stage. For an extensive discussion of alien invasion films of the 1950s, see Patrick Luciano, *Them or Us: Archetypal Interpretations*

of Fifties Alien Invasion Films (Bloomington: Indiana University Press, 1987). For a broader discussion of 1950s horror and science fiction films, see Mark Jancovich, *Rational Fears: American Horror in the 1950s* (New York: Manchester University Press, 1996).

15. This line may perhaps have inspired the title of the 1957 *Beginning of the End* as much as the plot of *Them!* informed its script, with grasshoppers standing in for ants.

16. *Monster Island* is a deliberately nostalgic evocation of 1950s big bug films for the MTV generation. The filmmakers purposely used stop-motion rather than the currently more popular CGI for aesthetic as well as economic reasons and tossed in other elements (a mad scientist, a campy tribe of natives) in an effort to evoke and spoof the older films.

17. Concerns over toxic waste (that is, chemical or biological rather than nuclear) also find expression in big bug films, though not to any great degree. Deliberate criminal dumping of such waste causes mosquitoes to reach poodle size in *Skeeter* (dir. Clark Brandon, 1993), and accidental release of hazardous materials causes dramatic size increases in spiders in *Eight-Legged Freaks* (dir. Ellory Elkayem, 2002) and in cockroaches in *Bugged* (dir. Ronald K. Armstrong, 1997).

18. See also Susan A. George, "Not Exactly 'of Woman Born': Procreation and Creation in Recent Science Fiction Films," *Journal of Popular Film and Television* 28, no. 4 (Winter 2001): 176–83.

19. Nonetheless, of the parasites that feed on humans, two of the most common, fleas and lice, have never shown up as big bugs.

20. In fact, *Alien* (dir. Ridley Scott, 1979) and its sequels could reasonably be considered big bug films, since the alien creatures owe much of their biological development to terrestrial parasitoids and other insects. I have not done that here, since the alien creatures are generally not referred to in the films as bugs, as opposed to the more superficially insectoid creatures in *Starship Troopers* (dir. Paul Verhoeven, 1997) and its direct-to-video sequel, *Starship Troopers 2: Hero of the Federation* (dir. Phil Tippett, 2004).

21. The third film in the *Fly* series, *The Curse of the Fly* (dir. Don Sharp, 1965), does not qualify as a big bug film, since there is no fly-scientist hybrid in the film. Instead, descendants of the original scientist continue his experiments with equally disastrous, albeit not entomologically influenced, results. I also do not include David Cronenberg's 1986 remake of *The Fly,* since the main character never achieves a sufficiently flylike appearance. In Chris Walas's 1989 sequel, *The Fly 2,* he does come close enough to qualify. I would also not include films where only some insect traits are transferred to a human without any sort of alteration of the general human features. An example of this would be *She Devil* (dir. Kurt Neumann, 1957), wherein a woman is treated with a serum derived from fruit flies and acquires their ability to mutate quickly; she uses this ability mainly to change her hair color. *Invasion of the Bee Girls* (dir. Denis Sanders, 1973) similarly leaves its transformed females looking human (except for an oddness about the eyes) but

inclined to murderous nymphomania. *Spider-Man* (2002) and *Spider-Man 2* (2004) would also not fit the were-insect category, since the main character still appears human.

22. Coincidentally, some current amateur filmmakers specialize in a fetishistic genre called "crush films," which record young women, either shod or barefoot, stepping on insects, worms, and other small creatures. They even have their own private publication, the *American Journal of the Crush-Freaks.*

23. Arguably that would be insects in any case, based on parameters such as number of individuals, total biomass, length of inhabiting the planet, geographic distribution, and so on.

24. It should also be noted that when a big bug is deemed to be perceived as normally not that threatening in its own right, the title will obscure its identity (*Them!, The Blood Beast Terror, Meet the Applegates, Monster Island*). *Empire of the Ants* (Bert I. Gordon, 1977) does identify its insect menace, but in the context of a more dramatic phrase; in any case, this title actually derives from an H. G. Wells short story (the film is also known as *H. G. Wells' Empire of the Ants*), although the plot has been altered beyond recognition.

25. At least two other relatively low-budget methods have been employed in big bug films and have not been touched on here and so are perhaps worth mentioning at this point. *Tail Sting* uses a man in a giant scorpion suit for its largest creatures, and *The Giant Spider Invasion* (dir. Bill Rebane, 1975) relies on a Volkswagen in a spider suit for its largest arachnid invader.

17

Entomophagy

Representations of Insect Eating in Literature and Mass Media

SARAH GORDON

"Waiter, there's a fly in my soup!" is the familiar comical exclamation of a culture long terrified and disgusted by accidental insect ingestion. Another image reflecting the same fear is the Old Woman Who Swallowed a Fly, a marginal character of folktale and folk song.[1] The second line of the rhyme, "I don't know why she swallowed a fly," expresses the confusion and morbidity surrounding entomophagy, or insect eating, in popular culture. Likewise the recognizable tune of "Fly in the Buttermilk, Shoo Fly, Shoo" belies Western cultural biases against insects and the perceived dangers of insects in the culinary milieu.[2] Negative human perceptions of the insect world—as we have seen in the present volume—are historically and culturally associated with pests, plagues, disease, and squalor.[3] Many insects have long been considered dirty or repulsive and associated with a richly derogatory and utterly unappetizing semantic field: creepy-crawly, squirmy, slimy, bugs, vermin, infestation, critters, cooties, parasites, germs, writhing, swarming, teeming, biting, stinging, et cetera. They have been condemned as the carriers of the bubonic plague, malaria, the dengue, and most recently the West Nile virus. Insect phobias and arachnophobia remain common today. A significant number of anti-insect articles in modern medical journals address the prevention of entomophagy, reinforcing derogatory insect images. Nevertheless the late twentieth century and the early twenty-first have witnessed the transformation of the image of the insect in contemporary Western culture. The transformation from monstrous taboo to popular spectacle in the representation of insects as human food has occurred in a wide range of literary genres and popular media. At the intersection of an exploration of gastronomy, entomology, and spectacle, this chapter explores perceptions of entomophagy as both an acceptable and transgressive practice in literature and popular culture from the theoretical point of view of cinematic spectacle, investigating the manner in which texts and images portray and sensationalize the consumption of insects. Images and representations of entomophagy entail transgression, play, and spectacle. Audiences and spectators also engage in voyeurism and play in looking at entomophagy as exotic and other.

The distinction between insect eating for survival and insect eating for entertainment is essential. At least two primary functions of entomophage foodways are discernible in any genre: survival tactics and spectacle. The two functions may be combined, as for instance in Aztec culture, where insect eating was not anathema.[4] When food is scarce it becomes an object of desire. When food is plentiful or less scarce it becomes an even riper object, but an object of spectacle. As we have seen in previous chapters, insects may take on a variety of roles, meanings, and associations. Alimentary practices involving insects are present in some cultures where insects play an important role in diet, nutrition, and ritual. Survival-secured populations may turn to insect-eating foodways for diversion—exotic tastes and unusual novelty entertainment. Entomophagy is therefore both a spectacular and gustatory experience. In the culinary domain, insects and invertebrates may be visible as a dietary resource, a delicacy, a curiosity, or at times, as in the folk references earlier, an unintentional and unwelcome ingredient.[5] If we regard such phenomena through the lens of cinematic theory, it will become evident that entomophagy is not only a gustatory but also a spectacular act. Entomophagy may involve nutrition or exist simply to horrify or please spectators. An extensive ethno-entomological study is beyond the scope of this essay, which chooses to focus on entomophage discourse and practice in Western literary production and visual mass media. This cross-genre exploration of entomophagy addresses the importance of communication and audience. The experience of insect consumption is rich in varied representations and a wide range of cultural production: poetry and prose, television (the genres of food and reality television and news reports), film, cookbooks, children's books, and edible popular material culture. In addition, considering consumers and spectators, we will see how culture puts an extraordinary emphasis on images of insects, whether good or bad, taboo pests or needed sustenance.

Insects, whether pests or menu items, carry meaning. The examples explored here show the range of culturally relative attitudes surrounding entomophagy.[6] The consumption of insects, as does the consumption of many foodstuffs, involves communication and convention, rhetoric and ritual. The discourse of consumption is therefore rich in signs and codes. Entomophagy, more so than other forms of consumption, can embody other appetites, sins, transgressions, tensions, and desires. It is portrayed with fear or appreciation of insects, or the need to control. The implicit message may vary as established cultural orientations and conventions regarding food come into play. Insect-eating practices are seen as acceptable in many cultures for diverse reasons of survival, taste, and tradition. Cultural influences dictate audience reactions to depictions of entomophagy in text or on-screen. Whereas in many cultures entomophagy is an accepted and frequent dietary necessity or ritual, in some Western cultures, as in much of North America, these practices may often be viewed as—and are portrayed in mass media and popular culture as—unacceptable, taboo, or at best exotic.[7]

We are not only what we eat physically; "we are what we eat socially and politically . . . symbolically and spiritually."[8] Historical-cultural differences and markers dictate perceptions of entomophagy. For example, consumption of insects (nonanimal flesh) is condoned by the Bible. In contrast, the uncleanliness and unseemliness of insects are emphasized in the Bible. Certain insects, several types of locusts, are suggested as edible fare in the Bible. The Koran also mentions edible locusts. The central insect-related section of the Bible, Leviticus 11:1–47, treats dietary laws, and entomophagy is addressed. The Bible provides practical images of edible and nonedible insects, without the senses of spectacle and play we have today. All flying insects that walk on four legs are forbidden. All insects with knees that hop are edible, including every kind of large, long-headed, green, and desert locust. John the Baptist's diet includes locusts and wild honey in Mark 1:6.[9] In addition, insects have been linked to "Manna from Heaven."[10] The biblical landscape is swarming with locusts, flies, maggots, hoppers, scorpions, moths, and ants (and is sweetened with honey). Humans are warned that all creatures that "teem on the ground or have many legs you shall not eat because they are vermin that contaminate" (Leviticus 11). Though many types are edible, the overwhelming number of references in the Bible to locusts and insects shows them as harbingers of doom and destruction. In the Bible, it is considered unclean to eat species of insects that are not

condoned, or even to touch them; one who touches their dead bodies is unclean until evening. Though Leviticus suggests rules for eating locusts, this
may be contrasted with the vegetarian diet and renewable edible resources
of green plants and fruit trees offered in Genesis 1:29–30. Meat eating
(without blood) is authorized in the anthropocentric Genesis 9:1–4, placing humans above mammals, birds, and insects in the hierarchy of living
things; in the suggestion of dominion over the animals, these creatures are
to be dominated, feared, or controlled by humans.

Across generic, temporal, and geographic borders, entomophagic signs
represent an opportunity for entertainment within the discourse of consumption. Human entomophagy is often portrayed as perverse or playful
in text and image and linked to animal insectivore behavior. It is often used
as transgressive spectacle, meant to call into question convention and contemporary conceptions of the body. The juxtaposition of food and insects
challenges cultural conventions in many genres of artistic production. In
literature, entomophagy is inextricably tied to identity; images of it are historically and culturally defined in writing from the Bible to contemporary
poetry. Television and film provide a glimpse of otherwise taboo or unfamiliar practices. Reality TV appropriates and transforms rituals from different global cultural practices, rendering them sensational, repugnant, or
exotic. These spectacular diversions provide the audience with an opportunity for vicarious culinary transgression.

Spectacle, Sensation, and Subsistence: Insects as the "Other" Food

The theoretical vocabulary of spectacle is useful for addressing representations of entomophagy. In considering modern visual and textual representations through cultural, cinematic, and spectacle theory, we may
apply theory from Darley, Debord, Polan, Baudrillard, and others. Some of
Debord's notions of spectacle, substitutive visual mediation, illusion, and
diversion inform my investigation.[11] Some aspects of Darley's theoretical
framework are useful in the exploration of visual representations of entomophagy in film and television. Darley's poetics of visual culture address
spectator experience and consumption and explain the spectator's stimu-
lation in relation to realistic and illusionistic elements of visual culture,
particularly in the digital realm of cinema and video games. Darley sees the

spectator's relation to visual culture as sensual, and he shows how spectators may become greatly affected by, if not "intoxicated" with, visual stimuli. He suggests "that the spectator of the [digital visual] forms under consideration is more of a sensualist than a 'reader' or 'interpreter.'"[12] The texts and media investigated here play to audience sensations in showing insect consumption. Spectacle relates to the power of the image and audience interpretation, where viewer response is visual or visceral. Postmodern aesthetics, especially in today's reality TV, sometimes privilege spectacle over meaning.[13] Dana Polan's definition of spectacle is applicable to this context, "an imagistic surface of the world as a strategy of containment against any depth of involvement with that world."[14] Thus on one level, images of insect eating remain mere images in representational media; in the role of spectators, we are not generally involved in actual entomophage foodways.

Audiences thus take part in passive viewing and the vicarious pleasure of spectacle. Aimed at provoking emotional response in spectators, sensationalized portrayals of entomophagy engage curiosity, fear, anxiety, and even phobias surrounding the insect kingdom. The audience may experience forms of visual pleasure and desire or visual disgust at the food insects that become the objects of their curious gaze. Sensationalism is the stimulating and provocative interaction between the spectator and the producer of the images. Recently Pauline Adema has explored the current vogue of cooking shows and the visual pleasures of watching others prepare and eat food on television. I suggest that some of her observations could be extended to other sorts of vicarious reactions to food on television. We also experience vicarious thrills and excitement in watching the spectacle of entomophagy on the small screen, since "television offers safe and economical ways to experience familiar and exotic pleasures."[15] In television and cinema, the prying eye of the camera heightens our curious gaze on unusual actions. Audiences of literary portrayals of insect eating and viewers of analogous images may both experience pleasure or squeamishness in a vicarious manner.[16]

On the one hand, in instances where insect eating is attached to survival, we have what philosophers have termed the idea of "food as fuel."[17] Edible insects are known globally by those who depend on them for subsistence. A protein-rich lifesaving resource for soldiers in the *U.S. Army Survival Guide,* insects provide vital nutrients in survival situations.[18] Bug eating is also related to the survival and self-reliance of the prisoners in the film *Papillon* (where prisoners in French Guyana face starvation and the horrors of incarceration), the title of which is evocative of the paradoxical freedom and fragility of the insect world through the image of the butterfly.[19] Many insects have a low level of toxicity and are useful in alleviating hunger. Conversely, the objectification of food is part of human existence and involves heightened voyeuristic pleasure when portrayed on-screen. Culinary objectification may occur at the dinner table or on-screen. Curtin and Heldke explain: "The substance project for personhood, which stresses autonomy and independence, must understand our relation to food as *objectified; food is understood as 'other.'*"[20] Thus food (and especially unusual food), as an object, is constructed as "other," either to fulfill bodily needs, or to satisfy the desire for pleasure, or both. The otherness of entomophagy is explored in the novel and in poetry, often focusing on relations to other cultural practices or on the manner in which human relations to nature are constituted. A few examples will suffice here.

POETRY AND PROSE

Difference and exoticism attract audience voyeurism to representations of entomophagy in the modern novel. Though the presence of insects in literature may indicate squalor—as, for instance, the cockroaches and vermin that plague the protagonist's kitchen in Upton Sinclair's *The Jungle*[21]— many novelists portray insects as something more than signifiers of poverty. Burroughs's *Naked Lunch* is a striking example of insects transformed.[22] Gabriel García Márquez treats the wonder of explorers colonizing the New World and seeing entomophagy for the first time. García Márquez's novel *The General in His Labyrinth* alludes to Simón Bolívar, who, while visiting a Mexico City market in 1799, remarks on the number of strange insects and animals being sold for food: "They eat everything that walks!"[23] Here entomophagy, as a survival tactic and tradition for the indigenous people but a mysterious practice for the Spanish in colonial times, is the exotic spectacle of the other, fascinating because it is unfamiliar to the reader as well as to the surprised narrator, who exclaims in wonder that he has witnessed foreign entomophage practices.[24] For the observer, these practices are part of the exotic setting, the otherness of the land. Thus the García Márquez novel differs from depictions such as those found in *Dracula* in its portrayal of entomophagy, losing its abnormal, deviant, and disgusting associations. For those practicing insect eating in *The General in His Labyrinth*, it is merely a form of subsistence, not deviating from societal gastronomic norms.

Turning to poetry in this cross-genre survey, we discover the importance of entomophagy in environmental and ecological poetic discourse, in which subsistence and transgression are combined. Entomophagy is a manifestation of the human relation to nature as one of consumption. Here I confine my study to one example of how human-insect relations are explored through consumption. The idea of the ecological self is at the heart of this poem that considers bees and bee eating. The poetry of Mary Oliver has an ecological theme.[25] She underlines the inspiration for her work in one interview: "In order to want to save the world, we must learn to love it—and in order to love it we must become familiar with it again. That is where my work begins." Her poetry shows many forms of human to animal transformation, part of her exploration of the other. In her poem "The Honey Tree," the ingestion of honey is a sign of joy, and the eating of bees—whether intentional or not—is part of her ecstatic consumption of nature, blurring the borders between nature and the conventional human construction of identity that occurs with appetite:

And so at last I climbed
the honey tree, ate
chunks of pure light, ate
the bodies of bees that could not
get out of my way, ate
the dark hair of the leaves,
the rippling bark,
the heartwood. Such
frenzy! But joy does that,
I'm told, in the beginning.
later, maybe,
I'll come here only
sometimes and with a
middling hunger. But now
I climb like a snake
I clamber like a bear to

the nuzzling place, to the light
salvaged by the thighs of bees and racked up
in the body of the tree.

. . . .

and singing in the
heaven of appetite.[26]

In her appetite for the insect product of honey and the bees in the honey-
comb, Mary Oliver allies herself with the natural world and distances herself
from humanity. She transforms seemingly grotesque and normally inedible
objects into a thing of natural beauty and wonder through the association
with honey.

In the environmental discourse of "The Honey Tree," Mary Oliver expresses human appetites and relationship to nature, using a strong entomophage image. The human body, the tree's anthropomorphic body, and
bees' bodies are highlighted in this portrait of unbridled appetite. Through
consumption, a transformation takes place. The repetition of eating terms
amplifies the ecstatic transgression and urgency of the act. She likens herself
to other entomophage species, especially the honey-loving bear. Furthermore, without hesitation, she eats the bees unable to flee her feeding frenzy.
Boundaries between human self and animal or insect other are blurred as
she becomes in a sense what she eats. Here we see the same dichotomy of
familiar and unfamiliar as in other genres as the narrator relates to nature
by eating insects, the honey, and the natural insect habitat.

Bees and bee products have played a role in human culinary culture,
though the Oliver poem is one of the rare instances in which they are
ingested together. Honey and bees were sacred in ancient Egypt, with honey
prized in ancient, medieval, and early modern kitchens. Medieval tavern
owners and doctors prized honey for its positive qualities and its usefulness
in mead. In medieval England, bees and bee products were so valued that
a prayer was recorded to coax passing bees to remain on one's land:

Sit down, sit down, bee!
St. Mary commanded thee!
Thou shalt not have leave,
Thou shalt not fly to the wood.
Thou shalt not escape me.

Nor go away from me.
Sit very still,
Wait God's will.[27]

This pro-insect discourse, reminiscent of the Ten Commandments, shows insects valued as a food source and a cherished part of nature. This is for the sake of survival, rather than spectacle. Even today royal jelly, beeswax, various types of honey, and many other bee products are prized as nutritional supplements or exotic delicacies.[28]

The "Fear Factor" in Entomophagy: Reality and Documentary Television

Moving from delicacy to delightful disgust, we see that appetite and consumption are portrayed in a different way on television. Entomophagy is at its most spectacular in its reflection in mass-media productions such as documentaries of "extreme" insect cuisine by the Food Network Channel and reality TV game shows such as *Fear Factor* and *Survivor,* where contestants squeamishly devour whole insects to win games or eat insect-infested food to sate their hunger. The genre of reality survival and adventure challenge TV is flourishing.[29] Indeed, entomophagy has become nearly a commonplace in "docu-stunt" and "docu-real" television.[30] Such shows often involve eating spectacles and play on recent popular (especially American and Asian) fads of eating contests and transgressive eating. Here bees and other insects are transformed into harmful and scary creatures by the discourse of fear and context of exoticism that frame these spectacular shows. Bee swarms, scorpion pits, pizza with grub worms and coagulated blood, cockroaches passed between couples' mouths, clear plastic coffins full of giant Madagascar hissing cockroaches, live dragonflies, roach blender drinks, worm wine and worm sausage, and a cricket-eating contest have all appeared, much to the disgust and titillation of the American spectator conditioned to seeing playful and transgressive eating in reality and culinary television.

NBC's *Fear Factor* challenges are shockingly sensational with their revolting menus.[31] A roulette game that required participants to eat African cave-dwelling spiders, which the host deems "uglier than regular spiders," was featured in a *Fear Factor* Las Vegas special that emphasized spectacle and play as live spectators looked on during filming.[32] This was one of the stunts that had no losers and drew a big crowd who cheered when asked, "Do you want her to eat it?" This type of on-screen active audience participation reflects the voyeurism and vicarious excitement of the spectators in their own homes. The host encourages a reluctant female contestant: "This is nothing. These are just little bugs. If you were starving, you would eat it. It's not that bad . . . throw it down, bite it, chew it, do it . . . just chew it and swallow." The verbal cues in this episode clearly portrayed the sensations of disgust and amazement targeted in the audience. The reference to survival entomophagy is merely a gesture in the playfulness of the game. Furthermore, the *Fear Factor* prime-time "reality" game show is a self-proclaimed spectacle intended to provoke fear, disgust, thrills, and awe. The Las Vegas setting of the show adds to the contrived spectacle of consumption. The stunt coordinator alludes to the spectacle and illusion of fear and danger in his three main criteria for choosing stunts: "'It must attack your fears, it must be a challenge as opposed to a thrill ride and it has to be a game.' Over the years, Perry's become sort of a fear expert. . . . 'The most challenging part of my job is to make it look dangerous and to be as safe as I can.'"[33] Thus *Fear Factor*'s goals in portraying entomophagy are illusion and diversion, as Debord suggests more generally of spectacle in our society. Debilitating fear or regurgitation of the stunt insects disqualifies contestants. The scare tactics of *Fear Factor* are for the audience's benefit perhaps more than contestant psychology.

Occasionally, entomophage spectacles go too far. In the United Kingdom, entomophage reality TV is soon to be censored, as evidenced by the following newspaper report:

> JUNGLE reality show *I'm A Celebrity Get Me Out Of Here* could face the axe. Telly watchdogs have banned bosses from feeding creepy-crawlies to contestants. The main highlights on this year's ITV show consisted of John Fashanu and eventual winner Phil Tufnell trying to stomach a menu of exotic grubs, flies and worms. But that part of the show will now have to be shelved.
>
> The Broadcasting Standards Commission rapped similar show *Fear Factor* on Sky One after viewers complained when it showed contestants eating as many insects as they could in a set time limit. A spokesman for the BSC said the programme had gone beyond what was normally acceptable, adding: "The panel considered that the graphic and extended footage of the consumption and treatment of the insects, purely for entertainment, had exceeded

acceptable boundaries. . . ." *Fear Factor* will now have to edit its content and drastically reduce the number of insect games it uses—or face punishment from telly watchdogs. And ITV bosses now have to decide whether they can go forward with *I'm A Celebrity* without such a major element of the programme. A TV insider said: "Everyone remembers Fash and those bugs." "Then Tuffers went on and bit the heads off some huge bugs. It was great TV. They'll need some exciting new challenges otherwise the show is finished."[34]

This article on the banning of insect-eating television competitions demonstrates that such activities form the basis for the spectacle of reality TV. Moreover, in a criticism of "exceeding acceptable boundaries," it shows a discourse with a negative bias toward transgressive entomophagy, even if the insects ingested by contestants are indeed edible and elements of normal foodways around the globe. Clearly, some spectators continue to see edible insects as bad taste and bad TV.

The spectacle of entomophagy does not leave the observer distant or undetached. The shock value of CBS's multiseason *Survivor* provides an exotic spectacle for viewers. In *Survivor* both survival entomophagy and spectacular entomophagy are present in a fictional, controlled environment. *Survivor* is framed within a multifaceted environment of exoticism and voyeurism in carnivalesque ambience of play. In one season, contestants ate bug-ridden grains to sate their hunger during their grueling sojourn in the Amazon rain forest. Here spectators caught a skewed glimpse of survival entomophagy, still portrayed in a sensationalized manner and in the contrived setting of game and play. Also in nonsubsistence-related aspects of the same game, they test their palates on the foreign delicacies, vertebrate and invertebrate, on remote insect-infested desert islands and in exotic jungle locations.

Not only televised game shows or so-called reality programming features the spectacle of entomophagy; television and online news reports also sensationalize insect eating and focus on the nontraditional aspects of consumption. In a cursory review of the CNN news network's sensationalist treatment of the subject, one notices a marked interest in insect eating, with reporting on everything from entomophagy opportunities for travelers in Southeast Asia, to insects that were once survival fare during the Chinese Cultural Revolution now returning to Beijing restaurants as delicacies (scorpions, cicadas, locusts, grasshoppers, bean worms, and silkworms), and from firefly chemicals and insect potion equivalents of Viagra, to Purdue University's annual experimental entomology fair called Bug Bowl. In an August 26, 2003, CNN report on a new cricket-spitting contest at Rutgers, the sensational, eye-grabbing television screen scroll read, "P-tui: Cricket Spitting Contest," reassuring the audience with "crickets frozen, not squirmy." All these reports are accompanied by a playful discourse—full of puns and sensational images and lacking in scientific or dietary information—that presupposes an anti-entomophagy audience. *CNN Headline News* on September 24, 2003, featured the unusual screen scroll "Cuban insect eating: He's not pretty." Concerning such news stories, as the journalistic adage goes, it is only news when man bites dog, or in this case, when man bites insects. Such unexpected stories attract and hold audience interest. The CNN headlines capture the curious spectator's attention, disgust, or desire with unfamiliar images of edible creatures meant to thrill, shock, and please. The compelling or dramatic stories arouse audience concerns by appealing to the negative images surrounding insects. Moreover, sensational headlines judge practices and reinforce audience taboos, preconceptions, and fantasies surrounding entomophagy.

Though not as sensationalized, the National Geographic Channel plays on audience fear and ignorance surrounding insects and insect eating. The titles of the nature episodes alone suggest the sensationalized perception offered to fascinate spectators: *National Geographic Nature's Nightmares: Pests and Parasites, Nature's Nightmares: Infested!, Dr. Cockroach,* and *National Geographic Showcase: Superfly.*[35] These titles show insects as somehow supernatural, echoing the playfulness of media, game, and reality television. In the first, entomologists offered reassuring advice for audiences who may have been shocked or amazed by the statistical information given on the number of insects present in their food. The show emphasizes that accidentally ingesting bread beetles or "weevily pasta" is not dangerous and, as a historical anecdote, that it was a common practice for sailors. It also claims that men would be more likely to eat insects in their food than women. Finally, the program noted that "eating insects should not cause concern" and that, if anything, insects are an "additional source of protein." This attempt to render the perception of unintentional entomophagy benign also added to the documentary spectacle. Many visual representations of insects and entomophagy play on human taboo, our "fear factor." *Giants: Spiders,* produced by the Discovery Channel, includes lurid images of barbequed tarantulas the size of dinner plates cooked in bamboo.[36] Insects, edible or not, are seen as other, or even otherworldly, playing on awe, ignorance, and fear. National Geographic's *Alien Empire* insect documentary shocked and titillated spectators with the probability that insects are Earth's dominant life-form; with their evolutionary history, the show warns in a grave conclusion, they will surely outlast humans.[37]

Our fears of insects are further allayed and culinary desires awakened by cooking shows, as on the Food Network Channel's *Extreme Cuisine*, the Japanese import *Iron Chef*, and others. Off-screen, a similar phenomenon is manifest in entomophage cookbooks, discussed later. Again, these voyeuristic shows use unfamiliar images and ingredients in a gourmet context to heighten our visual pleasure. Edible insects are shown to be unusual delicacies. These out-of-the-ordinary shows test the limits of the TV cooking show genre, exoticizing food and attracting visual desire through spectacle. Cooking shows provide spectacle of a dual nature, in vicarious entertainment that is both playful and instructive. Beyond gourmet are the fanciful novelty recipes including images of insects that were prepared with children and parties in mind by Gale Gand and the celebrity chef Sara Moulton in a special "creature feature" episode of *Sweet Dreams*. So-called Bug Juice, Ladybug Cupcakes, Spider Cupcakes, and Butterfly Pizza were deemed more appetizing and festive desserts because their decorations represented familiar images of child-friendly creepy-crawlies.[38] Involving what Debord would call the phenomena of diversion and illusion, the visual effect of simulated entomophagy was essential to the success of these recipes. Similarly, the recipe for Morton Bay Bug Salad with Mango-Ginger Dressing was featured on the Food Network's *Keith Famie's Adventures,* and was touted as an "easy" yet exotic recipe for viewers to reproduce. Bug dishes thereby do more than provide a conversation piece at the table; they play an important role in the exoticism and global consumption culture portrayed in food television and elsewhere in cookbooks and culinary texts.

MARKETING ENTOMOPHAGY: COOKBOOKS, POPULAR MATERIAL CULTURE, AND CHILDREN'S LITERATURE

Entomophagy is a growing spectacle for curious consumers of popular culture. That cockroaches are no longer unwelcome in every cook's kitchen is evinced by the recent vogue of insect recipe books. Though most Europeans and Americans continue to find entomophagy distasteful, in recent years insects at the dinner table are becoming a common theme in cookbooks. As novelties, many insect cookbooks are often more sensational spectacles than they are practical guides. Such books often focus on cultural aspects of entomophagy and do not necessarily intend for readers to reproduce the bug dishes, though a vicarious experience is possible. Some cookbooks demystify, while others mystify. Insects even enter the domain of gourmet dining, as in numerous Japanese cookbooks or the elegant recipe book *Insectes à croquer* (Insects to Munch), produced by the Montreal Insectarium. A similar French culinary guide is *Cuisine des insectes: A la découverte de l'entomophagie,* by Gabriel Martinez, offering serious instruction.[39] Many other ingredients are included to render insects more palatable in these two gourmet guides. In others, such as the humorous *The Eat-a-Bug-Cookbook,* familiar American recipes such as pancakes, pizza, and alphabet soup are defamiliarized with the addition of edible invertebrates. Many entomophage recipes combine well-known elements with exotic insect main ingredients, resulting in such unexpected creations and puns as *The Eat-a-Bug-Cookbook's* appetite-whetting and evocative dishes: "Cockroach à la King," "Pest-o," "Three Bee Salad," or "Fried Green Tomato Hornworms." Continuing in this humorous discourse of entomophagy, the science-writer author of *The Eat-a-Bug-Cookbook* and *The Compleat Cockroach,* in a 1998 online interview with CNN Interactive, expresses this notion of entomophagy as confronting culinary convention: "What counts as good food in our culture is what we're raised on. Some people won't touch okra. It's a subjective thing. I think part of the fun of the book is challenging people's food beliefs."[40] Interest in food insects is not waning. Peter Menzel and Faith D'Aluisio offer a photo-essay volume, *Man Eating Bugs: The Art and Science of Eating Insects,* including diverse entomophage scenes and dishes from around the globe.[41] Several volumes of entomophage cookbooks have been published by Ten Speed Press in Berkeley, California. The *Food Insects Newsletter* is another source of recipes and scientific research on entomophagy.[42] Moreover, public curiosity in entomophagy appears to be growing. There are many entomophage events in popular culture; the San Francisco Insect Zoo, the Cincinnati Zoo, college Bug Bowls, the Montreal Insectarium, and other diverse public venues offer patrons occasions to participate in insectivore activities and to dispel myths surrounding the insect kingdom, promoting edible insects.

Akin to such exotic entomophage cookbooks, picture books, and events, other representations of insect eating in material culture play on dispelling fear and culturally familiar negative stereotypes of bugs. If we consider food items in popular culture, we find that recently the exotic discourse of entomophagy has been realized in candy and other manufactured food items. Honey and bee by-products are an accepted favorite of consumers worldwide. Countries across Asia have long sold insect products for human consumption. Chocolate-covered crickets or ants and so-called jumping beans are favorite souvenirs of tourists to Mexico. Thai water bugs tempt visitors to Bangkok markets. In some countries, certain insects are sold at a higher price than caviar.

In addition to nutrition, food insects have other reputed qualities. The Mexican mescal worm has long been the subject of lore, with its reputedly hallucinogenic or intoxicating properties when eaten from the bottom of a tequila bottle. Similarly, mysterious aphrodisiac qualities have long been attributed to so-called Spanish fly potions. Medicinal entomophagy figures heavily in the history of medicine and pharmaceuticals.[43] Whether commercial prophylactic or home remedy with curative or hallucinogenic properties, insects play an important role in medicine. William Burroughs drew on the association between cockroaches and drug consumption in *The Exterminator* and *Naked Lunch* (becoming cinematic spectacle in David Cronenberg's 1992 entomophilic film *Naked Lunch*).[44] Berenbaum's *Bugs in the System* provides a historical survey of insects in pharmacopoeias from early modern times to the present day.[45]

In a spectacle for consumers, Western companies use insects in their food products for their novelty quality. Many brands of gummy worms, gummy spiders, and bug-shaped confections are available, especially for the Halloween sales season. Food festivals and entomological events feature insect fare across the country. Cricket ice cream is available in Utah, and there is an unusual yet trendy insect-themed Insect-Café in New York City. Countless Halloween candies mimic insect forms. Moreover, many candy brands propose candies that are only sugary, colorful representations of insects.

Approaching fears and fascinations surrounding insects with play, insect candy is a growing form of entomophagy (real or simulated). While most candy only resembles insects in its form or packaging, the Hotlix company of Pismo Beach, California, is remarkable because it offers a line of *real* insect "Insect-n-side" candies.[46] Hotlix is a pioneer in the industry and sells original flavorful novelty candies from chocolate-covered ants to spicy barbeque worms to colorful bug lollipops. This innovative and successful product line includes clear sugar-free tequila suckers with real worms, flavorful "Worm-in-Apple Suckers," and mint-flavored candy with crickets, called "Cricket Lick-Its," as novelty flavorings in their amberlike edible lollipops. Puns and wordplay are common in branding, as in television titles. Several companies in the United States, Mexico, and Asia sell real insect candies and chocolates. These are exotic, if not appetizing, products with tremendous visual marketing appeal. One Asian foods Web site even offers canned Thai water bugs, with the packaging decorated with images of the insect inside.[47]

Also a feat of marketing, images of insect eating abound in the field of modern children's literature, marked by curiosity, mischief, and, in particular, disgust.[48] *Insect Soup: Bug Poems* by Barry Louis Polisar, *Chocolate-Covered Ants* by Stephen Manes, *Guts* by Gary Paulsen, and *How to Eat Fried Worms* by Thomas Rockwell all cater to childhood fears, fascinations, and fantasies of insects.[49] In the docu-real *Guts,* characters eat insects to survive in Paulsen's guide to wilderness nutrition. The jacket of *Chocolate-Covered Ants,* targeting preteens, is more spectacular and less subsistence based, promising a tale of humor and transgressive eating:

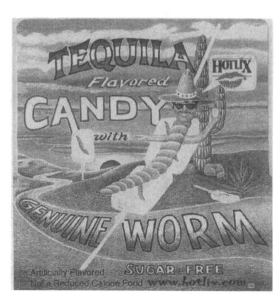

Introduced in 1991, Hotlix's "Tequila Flavored Worm Sucker" here strikes a relaxed (and bibulous) pose. Note the artificiality of the flavoring but the genuineness of the worm. Courtesy of Hotlix Candies.

In a humorous tale of sibling rivalry, Max and his brother learn more than they will ever want to know about eating ants. What begins as a joke, in which Max threatens to turn Adam's ants into chocolate-covered treats, turns into all-out guerrilla warfare. Max's impulsive bet that people actually eat ants backfires when he cannot find any in the stores and must try to create his own home microwaved version. Max tricks Adam into eating his concoction, at which point Mother puts an end to ant-eating, making bets, and practical jokes.

The children's culinary fantasy *How to Eat Fried Worms* depicts similar experimentation with entomophage recipes, also depicting characters' initial disgust turned to appreciation of this unusual diet. In these children's books, all forms of transgressive or bizarre eating lead to fascination, humor, or humorous disgust. This phenomenon and attraction to that which is "other" shares some similarities with the popularity of video games featuring fanciful insects as exaggerated, grotesque, and visually exiting foes, often with exotic alien or robotlike qualities.

Conclusion

The global phenomenon of entomophagy has always existed and is fast becoming a popular subject of diversion and curiosity in literature and mass culture. Though space does not allow a comprehensive review of entomophagic representations, we have witnessed significant examples in which entomophagy is perceived as transgressive consumption or used as spectacle. Such spectacle recalls taboos, awakens visual desire, and provokes a strong reaction among spectators, be they readers, television audiences, consumers, or cinema audiences. Exhibition and spectacle form the basis of entomological entertainment. Entomophagy may leave spectators on the edge of their seats or give them the proverbial butterflies in the stomach. It may provide voyeuristic pleasure or visual disgust. Entomophagy in film, television, and text appeals to the fear of the other, the horror of the strange. We have observed how different images of entomophagy feed audience appetites for the scary and repulsive, or the unusual and exotic. The taboo of bug eating escapes repression through cinematic and textual spectacle. The camera constructs meaning for spectators fascinated by the horror and difference of sensational insect eating. Finally, even as the medium changes, images of entomophagy not only constitute consumers' identities but may also (re)construct spectators' identities and question their perceptions of insects and of themselves as consumers.

NOTES

1. Another folk reference is the nursery rhyme "Little Miss Muffett," which refers to Dr. Thomas Mouffet, the seventeenth-century naturalist who purportedly fed his daughter spiders to see what would happen.

2. These lyrics are from the folk song entitled "Skip to My Lou." Many American folk songs include human-insect interaction, for instance, the song "Boll Weevil."

3. Randy Malamud, in "How People and Animals Coexist," *Chronicle of Higher Education,* January 24, 2003, B6–10, provides a new perspective on anthrozoology, reminding us that "our culture manifests a tremendous consciousness for animals, for good and for bad" (B6). He cites an art project that uses an electric "Insect-O-Cutor," and suggests that "a crucial task for anthrozoology must be to decenter the human perspective and discover the animals' authentic reality—certainly a complex concept, but one that may be more easily understood by antithesis to cultural constructions of animals" (B8). In the texts and media considered in the present chapter, we rarely escape such anthropocentric constructions of insect identity for these creatures at the bottom of the food chain that become objects of food and play.

4. Gene Kritsky and Ron Cherry, in *Insect Mythology* (New York: Writers Club Press, 2000), offer an overview of insect signs and mythology in Aztec culture, as well as Native American and Asian cultures.

5. See May R. Berenbaum, *Bugs in the System: Insects and Their Impact on Human Affairs* (New York: Addison Wesley, 1995), 165–76, for a concise scientific and ethnographic survey of intentional and unintentional insect-eating practices, including FDA regulations and nutritional comparisons between insects and other food sources (177–86). After reviewing the numbers, she concludes with some level of encouragement: "Basically, there's nothing inedible about insects from the human perspective. A quick examination of the composition of insects reveals that they're not so different from beef, pork, or fish. The chitinous exoskeleton is by and large indigestible, but then again, so is apple skin. . . . Insects are even rich in vitamins and minerals (so maybe it's the worm a day and not the apple it's eating that keeps the doctor away). Not only are insects nutritionally suitable as a food source, they're economically feasible as well" (178). As David George Gordon reports, FDA regulations allow as many as 56 insect parts in every peanut butter and jelly sandwich, up to 60 aphids in 31½ ounces of frozen broccoli, and two or three fruit-fly maggots per 200 grams of tomato juice. See *The Eat-a-Bug Cookbook: 33 Ways to Cook Grasshoppers, Ants, Water Bugs, Spiders, Centipedes, and Their Kin* (Berkeley: Ten Speed Press, 1998). One type of cheese made near the Puy-de-Dôme, France, is traditionally made with maggots. Jean-Louis Thémis's recipe book *Des insectes à*

croquer: Guide de découvertes (Montreal: Les Editions de L'Homme, 1997), published under the auspices of the Montreal Insectarium, provides additional statistical dietary information.

    6. Entomophagy was first studied in detail and advocated in Western culture by Vincent M. Holt as early as 1885 in *Why Not Eat Insects?*, briefly anthologized in Erich Hoyt and Ted Schultz, *Insect Lives: Stories of Mystery and Romance from a Hidden World* (Cambridge: Harvard University Press, 1999), 40–41.

    7. On entomophage practices and recipes in different cultures, see Calvin W. Schwabe, *Unmentionable Cuisine* (Charlottesville: University of Virginia Press, 1979), 364–83.

    8. Deane W. Curtin and Lisa M. Heldke, *Cooking, Eating, Thinking: Transformative Philosophies of Food* (Bloomington and Indianapolis: Indiana University Press, 1992), 11–12.

    9. The reader is referred to *Honey: A Comprehensive Survey,* ed. Eva Crane (New York: Heinemann and Crane, Russak, 1975), which provides an in-depth cultural and scientific history of honey.

    10. Hoyt and Schultz, *Insect Lives,* 31.

    11. Guy Debord, *The Society of the Spectacle* (New York: Zone, 1994).

    12. Andrew Darley, *Visual Digital Culture: Surface Play and Spectacle in New Media Genre* (London: Routledge, 2000), 169.

    13. For an appraisal of reality TV and credibility in the digital age of visual culture, see Arild Fetveit, "Reality TV in the Digital Era: A Paradox in Visual Culture?" in *Reality Squared: Televisual Discourse on the Real,* ed. James Friedman (New Brunswick, N.J.: Rutgers University Press, 2002), 119–37. He explains the reality show phenomenon thus: "In a deeper psychological sense, the proliferation of reality TV could be understood as a euphoric effort to reclaim what seems to be lost after digitalization" (130).

    14. Polan, "'Above All Else to Make You See': Cinema and the Ideology of Spectacle," in *Postmodernism and Politics,* ed. Jonathan Arac (Minneapolis: University of Minnesota Press, 1986), 63.

    15. Adema, "Vicarious Consumption: Food, Television, and the Ambiguity of Modernity," *Journal of American Culture* 23, no. 3 (2000): 119.

    16. The landmark study by Laura Mulvey, *Visual and Other Pleasures (Theories of Representation and Difference)* (Bloomington: Indiana University Press, 1989), refines the notion of visual pleasure and the cinematic gaze.

    17. Curtin and Heldke, *Cooking, Eating, Thinking,* 12–13.

    18. *U.S. Army Survival Manual: FM 21-76* (New York: Apple Pie Publishers, 1992).

    19. *Papillon,* dir. Franklin J. Schaffner (Warner Studios, 1973).

    20. Curtin and Heldke, *Cooking, Eating, Thinking,* 11.

    21. In Ben Jonson's *Volpone* (1606), though parasites are seen in a pejorative light, consumption is used as a less transgressive motif.

    22. See William S. Burroughs, *Naked Lunch: The Restored Text,* ed. James Grauerholz and Barry Miles (New York: Grove Press, 2003).

23. García Márquez, *The General in His Labyrinth* (New York: Random House, 1995).

24. See Steven Starker, "Fear of Fiction: The Novel," *Book Research Quarterly* 6, no. 2 (1990): 44–60, on the origins of sensationalism in the genre of the novel.

25. Douglas Burton-Christie, in "Nature, Spirit, and Imagination in the Poetry of Mary Oliver," *Cross Currents: The Journal of the Association for Religion and Intellectual Life* 46, no. 1 (1996): 77–87, reveals the attachment to nature in Oliver's poetry.

26. Mary Oliver, "The Honey Tree," in *Literature and the Environment,* ed. Lorraine Anderson, Scott Slovic, and John P. O'Grady (New York: Addison Wesley, 1999).

27. See Robert Lacey and Danny Danziger, *The Year 1000: What Life Was Like at the Turn of the First Millennium* (Boston: Little, Brown, 1999).

28. Bees have long had an association with human food and bounty, as in the 1935 M. M. Cole folk song "That Big Rock Candy Mountain," in which one hears "the buzzing of the bees in lollipop / cigarette trees near the soda water fountain." Today the cosmetic company Burt's Bees features several bee products with packaging featuring bees and bee honeycombs. Sue Monk Kidd's southern gothic novel *The Secret Life of Bees* (New York: Penguin USA, 2003), in which a young woman is raised by a group of African American beekeeping sisters after the apparent accidental death of her mother, uses insects (and honey) as a powerful message in an exploration of sisterhood, mothering, and identity; each chapter includes a pertinent citation on bees and their behavior.

29. MTV's shock stunt show *Jackass* and the reality game show *Road Rules* both rely on occasional insect eating for spectacle and ratings, for instance, a stunt where the performer inhales an earthworm through his nose and regurgitates it out through his mouth, aired in September 2003. In the reality game genre, television shows such as *Survivor, Fear Factor,* and the Nickelodeon Channel's game shows for children incorporate the element of play into their spectacles, with challenges and contests.

30. In discussing "docu-real fictions," John Caldwell, in "Prime-Time Fiction Theorizes the Docu-Real," in *Reality Squared,* 259–92, also coined these terms, referring to television programs that, among other things, show "documentary looks and imaging as part of their *mise-en-scène,*" and noting that "the genre, then, invokes marketing and programming strategies as well as aesthetic forms" (259).

31. Details and images of *Fear Factor* episodes and stunts may be found at http://www.nbc.com/Fear_Factor/stunts. Transgressive eating is growing in popularity in many genres of television, not limited to documentaries or game shows.

32. Aired September 2003.

33. For more insight from this reality show's host, see http://www.nbc.com/Fear_Factor/interview_perry.shtml.

34. Mark Jefferies, "Insect Eating to Be Banned: You've Had Your Phil of TV Bugs," *Daily Star,* September 30, 2003.

35. Aired August 2003.

36. Aired October 2003.

37. Aired January 1996.

38. Aired October 2002.

39. Martinez, *Cuisine des insectes: A la découverte de l'entomophagie* (Paris: J.-P. Rocher, 2000).

40. Jamie Allen, "Writer Offers 33 Ways to Eat Bugs," interview with George David Gordon, July 30, 1998, CNN, http://www.cnn.com/books/news/9807/30/eat. a.bug. See also Gordon's *The Compleat Cockroach: A Comprehensive Guide to the Most Despised (and Least Understood) Creature on Earth* (Berkeley: Ten Speed Press, 1996).

41. Peter Menzel and Faith D'Aluisio, *Man Eating Bugs: The Art and Science of Eating Insects* (Berkeley: Ten Speed Press, 1998).

42. *Food Insects Newsletter,* ed. Florence V. Dunkel, Department of Entomology, Montana State University, *www.hollowtop.com.*

43. Representations of medicinal insects abound; for instance, in the film *Greystoke: The Legend of Tarzan* (dir. Hugh Hudson, 1984), the hero feeds a wounded colonial soldier with grubs to cure him of a wound and help him regain his strength with the insects' protein.

44. On different forms of consumption in *Naked Lunch,* see Jonathan Paul Eburne, "Trafficking in the Void: Burroughs, Kerouac, and the Consumption of Otherness," *Modern Fiction Studies* 43, no. 1 (1997): 53–92.

45. Berenbaum, *Bugs in the System,* 165–76.

46. Hotlix Candy, http://www.hotlix.com/bugfun.htm.

47. These products, mostly Thai in origin, can be found, for example, at http://www.dcothai.com/food/insects.htm.

48. The phenomenon of disgust has received recent critical attention in Winfried Menninghaus, Howard Eiland, and Joel Golb, *Disgust: The Theory and History of a Strong Sensation* (Albany: State University of New York Press, 2003). See also the volume of essays *Bad: Infamy, Darkness, Evil, and Slime on Screen,* ed. Murray Pomerance (Albany: State University of New York Press, 2003), for more on the pleasure that spectators derive from scary, negative, or disgusting cinematic images.

49. Polisar, *Insect Soup: Bug Poems* (Silver Spring, Md.: Rainbow Morning Music, 1999); Manes, *Chocolate-Covered Ants* (New York: Apple, 1993); Paulsen, *Guts: The True Stories behind the Hatchet* (New York: Laurel Leaf, 2002); Rockwell, *How to Eat Fried Worms* (New York: Yearling, 1953).

Publication History

An early version of chapter 5 appeared as "Cassandra's Worms: Unravelling the Threads of Virginia Woolf's Lepidoptera Imagery," *Hungarian Journal of English and American Studies* 9, no. 1 (2003): 101–17. Reprinted with permission.

The French version of chapter 9 by Bertrand Gervais appeared as a chapter in his essay *Lecture littéraire et explorations en littérature américaine* (Montreal: XYZ Éditeur, 1998), 147–69.

"r-p-o-p-h-e-s-s-a-g-r," copyright 1935, 1963, 1991 by the Trustees for the E. E. Cummings Trust. Copyright 1978 by George James Firmage, from *Complete Poems: 1904–1962*, by E. E. Cummings, edited by George J. Firmage. Reprinted by permission of Liveright Publishing Corporation.

Archy and Mehitabel, by Don Marquis, copyright 1927 by Doubleday, a division of Random House, Inc. Reprinted by permission of Doubleday, a division of Random House, Inc.

Four lines from poem 620, "It makes no difference abroad," reprinted by permission of the publishers and the Trustees of Amherst College from *The Poems of Emily Dickinson*, edited by Thomas H. Johnson (Cambridge, Mass.: Belknap Press of Harvard University Press). Copyright 1951, 1955, 1979, 1983 by the President and Fellows of Harvard College.

Contributors

May Berenbaum is a member of the faculty of the Department of Entomology at the University of Illinois at Urbana-Champaign. Her research interests are in the area of insect chemical ecology, but she is devoted to fostering scientific literacy and has written numerous magazine articles, as well as four books, about insects for the general public, including *Bugs in the System: Insects and Their Impact on Human Affairs* and *Buzzwords: A Scientist Muses on Bugs, Sex, and Rock 'n' Roll*. She has gained some measure of fame as the organizer of the Insect Fear Film Festival at the University of Illinois, an annual celebration of Hollywood's entomological excesses now in its twenty-first year.

Eric C. Brown holds a B.A. in zoology and a Ph.D. in English. He is assistant professor of English at the University of Maine at Farmington. He has written on insects and colonization in the New World, and on insects and eschatology in Edmund Spenser's *Muiopotmos*, and is completing a book-length study of entomology and the arts in the early modern period.

Yves Cambefort is research scientist at the French National Institute for Scientific Research (CNRS) and the University of Paris–VII. He has published a small series of books on taxonomy, ecology, and the mythology of beetles, including *Dung Beetle Ecology* (coedited with Ilkka Hanski), two books on cultural entomology (*Le scarabée et les dieux* and *Voyage en coléoptère*), and three books on Jean-Henri Fabre's biography, works, and correspondence.

Marion W. Copeland, professor emeritus of English at Holyoke Community College in Massachusetts, now devotes herself to her interest in animals in literature. She lectures and tutors at the Center for Animal and Human Relations at the Tufts Veterinary School and is a member of the boards of NILAS (Nature in Legend and Story) and the Dakin Animal Shelter. She has written many book reviews and essays, as well as two books, *Charles Alexander Eastman (Ohiyesa)* and *Cockroach.*

Nicky Coutts is a fine art fellow at Middlesex University, London, and lecturer in critical and historical studies at the Royal College of Art. She has worked as commissioning editor of *Make: Magazine of Women's Art* and as associate editor of *Coil: Journal of the Moving Image.* Her interest in the high incidence of insects in contemporary imagery was first explored in two papers published in *Coil.* She writes for contemporary art magazines and journals and commissions artists' books as director of a small publishing company, Mantis.

Bertrand Gervais is professor in literary studies at Université of Québec in Montreal. He is the director of Figura, the Research Center on Textuality and the Imaginary. He teaches American literature and literary theories, specializing in theories of reading and interpretation. He has published essays on literary reading and twentieth-century American literature, and his current work focuses on the apocalyptic imagination, on the labyrinth in contemporary literature, and on hypermedia and new forms of texts. He is also a novelist.

Sarah Gordon is assistant professor of French at Utah State University. Her research explores the intersection of material culture and literature, and her book *Culinary Comedy* is forthcoming. She was a former restaurant reviewer in France.

Cristopher Hollingsworth is assistant professor of English at the University of South Alabama. The author of *Poetics of the Hive: The Insect Metaphor in Literature,* he is currently editing a scholarly collection on Lewis Carroll's Wonderland and cultural space.

Heather Johnson teaches literature at Dublin City University and the Dun Laoghaire Institute of Art and Design in Ireland. She has published articles on embodied subjectivity in the work of Angela Carter, and her research interests include the gothic genre, twentieth-century British literature, and the female surrealists.

Richard J. Leskosky is the associate director of the Unit for Cinema Studies at the University of Illinois at Urbana-Champaign. He is a former president of the Society for Animation Studies and conducts research on precinematic illusory movement devices. He has collaborated with May Berenbaum on a number of projects relating insects and cinema.

Tony McGowan is assistant professor at the United States Military Academy at West Point, where he teaches American literature, criticism, and composition. His interests include nineteenth-century American literature and visual culture. He recently wrote an afterword to a new facsimile edition of Edgar Allan Poe's *Poems, 1831*.

Erika Mae Olbricht is assistant professor of English at Pepperdine University, where she teaches early modern literature, drama, and theater. She is writing a cultural history of early modern British beekeeping.

Marc Olivier is assistant professor in the Department of French and Italian at Brigham Young University, where he teaches French literature and civilization. His publications focus on literature, science, and technology, including studies of microscopy and literature, Rousseau and botany, and the popular dissemination of natural history. He was a guest curator at Brigham Young University's Museum of Art for "Nostalgia and Technology," an exhibition on the socialization of domestic technology from the seventeenth century to present.

Roy Rosenstein is professor of comparative literature at The American University of Paris. His many publications include *The Poetry of Cercamon and Jaufre Rudel* and *Etienne Durand: Poésies complètes*.

Rachel Sarsfield recently completed her doctorate on Virginia Woolf and insect imagery. She is looking forward to a future in academia that has a few less creepy-crawlies in it than at present.

Charlotte Sleigh is senior lecturer in history of science at the Centre for History and Cultural Studies of Science, University of Kent. She is interested in the recent history of natural history and biology, and in the relationship between science and literature. Her research has focused on the cultural and scientific representation of insects—especially ants—in the nineteenth and twentieth centuries. Her publications include *Ant* and *Six Legs Better: A Cultural History of Myrmecology*.

Andre Stipanovic teaches Latin and philosophy at the Hockaday School in Dallas, Texas. His recent work centers on the poetry of Vergil, Catullus, and Horace.

Index